W9-BLO-464

CONTEMPORARY MUSICIANS

ISSN 1044-2197

CONTEMPORARY MUSICIANS

PROFILES OF THE PEOPLE IN MUSIC

LUANN BRENNAN, Editor

VOLUME 23
Includes Cumulative Indexes

GALE

DETROIT · LONDON

Contents

Introduction ix

Cumulative Subject Index 241

Cumulative Musicians Index 269

Introduction

Fills the Information Gap on Today's Musicians

Contemporary Musicians profiles the colorful personalities in the music industry who create or influence the music we hear today. Prior to *Contemporary Musicians,* no quality reference series provided comprehensive information on such a wide range of artists despite keen and ongoing public interest. To find biographical and critical coverage, an information seeker had little choice but to wade through the offerings of the popular press, scan television "infotainment" programs, and search for the occasional published biography or exposé. *Contemporary Musicians* is designed to serve that information seeker, providing in one ongoing source in-depth coverage of the important names on the modern music scene in a format that is both informative and entertaining. Students, researchers, and casual browsers alike can use *Contemporary Musicians* to meet their needs for personal information about music figures; find a selected discography of a musician's recordings; and uncover an insightful essay offering biographical and critical information.

Provides Broad Coverage

Single-volume biographical sources on musicians are limited in scope, often focusing on a handful of performers from a specific musical genre or era. In contrast, *Contemporary Musicians* offers researchers and music devotees a comprehensive, informative, and entertaining alternative. *Contemporary Musicians* is published three times per year, with each volume providing information on almost 80 musical artists and record-industry luminaries from all the genres that form the broad spectrum of contemporary music—pop, rock, jazz, blues, country, New Age, folk, rhythm and blues, gospel, bluegrass, rap, and reggae, to name a few—as well as selected classical artists who have achieved "crossover" success with the general public. *Contemporary Musicians* will also occasionally include profiles of influential nonperforming members of the music community, including producers, promoters, and record company executives. Additionally, beginning with *Contemporary Musicians 11,* each volume features new profiles of a selection of previous *Contemporary Musicians* listees who remain of interest to today's readers and who have been active enough to require completely revised entries.

Includes Popular Features

In *Contemporary Musicians* you'll find popular features that users value:

- **Easy-to-locate data sections:** Vital personal statistics, chronological career summaries, listings of major awards, and mailing addresses, when available, are prominently displayed in a clearly marked box on the second page of each entry.

- **Biographical/critical essays:** Colorful and informative essays trace each subject's personal and professional life, offer representative examples of critical response to the artist's work, and provide entertaining personal sidelights.

- **Selected discographies:** Each entry provides a comprehensive listing of the artist's major recorded works.

- **Photographs:** Most entries include portraits of the subject profiled.

- **Sources for additional information:** This invaluable feature directs the user to selected books, magazines, and newspapers where more information can be obtained.

Helpful Indexes Make It Easy to Find the Information You Need

Each volume of *Contemporary Musicians* features a cumulative Musicians Index, listing names of individual performers and musical groups, and a cumulative Subject Index, which provides the user with a breakdown by primary musical instruments played and by musical genre.

Available in Electronic Formats

Diskette/Magnetic Tape. *Contemporary Musicians* is available for licensing on magnetic tape or diskette in a fielded format. The database is available for internal data processing and nonpublishing purposes only. For more information, call (800) 877-GALE.

Online. *Contemporary Musicians* is available online as part of the Gale Biographies (GALBIO) database accessible through LEXIS-NEXIS, P.O. Box 933, Daton, OH 454012-0933; phone: (513)865-6800, toll-free:800-543-6862.

We Welcome Your Suggestions

The editors welcome your comments and suggestions for enhancing and improving *Contemporary Musicians*. If you would like to suggest subjects for inclusion, please submit these names to the editors. Mail comments or suggestions to:

The Editor
Contemporary Musicians
The Gale Group
27500 Drake Rd.
Farmington Hills, MI 48334-3535

Or call toll free: (800) 347-GALE

Yolanda Adams

Singer, songwriter

Yolanda Adams is the exuberant songstress with the trademark appearance: a definitive preference for haute couture. But Adams is more than a singer and her unpredictable gospel music is not confined by traditional styles. She sings jazz, rhythm and blues, and pop along with modern and traditional gospel. Her single motivation in singing, she maintains, is to spread the gospel. In her songs she appeals to people of all ages and lifestyles and especially to those who might miss the traditional message. Adams is not only a musical evangelist, but an associate minister of God in her own right.

Yolanda Adams was born in Houston, Texas, where she was raised in a close and loving family. Adams's father was an industrious man, stable and honest. He instilled in his family a strong faith and encouraged his children to dream and set their goals accordingly. Adams was not yet in high school when her father passed away but the inspiration he passed to her and to her five siblings never died. Adams, the eldest of the six children, recalled a household filled with music. Her mother studied music in college and Adams attests to growing up amidst a continuous background of symphonies, jazz, and rhythm and blues, along with modern gospel. Adams, who was born in the 1960s, developed a particular affinity for the sounds of Stevie Wonder and Nancy Wilson.

Adams grew tall and willowy and, when surpassed six feet in height, she developed an interest in modeling.

She explored that career briefly, but ultimately elected to dedicate herself to elementary education. She taught elementary school in Houston and sang in her spare time. She was privileged to sing with the Southeast Inspirational Choir under the directorship of the late Thomas Whitfield. Adams advanced to lead singer of the choir, and eventually Whitfield, a noted singer and producer, encouraged her to record some songs. A recording session was scheduled during her summer vacation in 1987 and the resulting album, *Just as I Am,* was released by Sound of Gospel Records that same year.

Tribute Records was impressed by the album and offered Adams a contract in 1990. Adams opted to embark on what she called a faith walk—She resigned from her teaching position of seven years and signed with Tribute Records. Later she confided to Sandy Fulk of the *Richmond Times-Dispatch,* "Everything I've done has been a faith walk." Her faith walking proved steady and sure, as her second album, *Through the Storm,* which appeared in 1993, collected a trio of awards: the Gospel Music Association's Dove Award, an Excellence Award, and the Stellar Award for Best Female Contemporary Artist. The album also earned a Grammy Award nomination for Best Contemporary Soul Gospel Album.

In 1993, Adams recorded *Save the World* and collaborated with other artists on *Bring It to Jesus* and *March On. Save the World* added three new Stellar awards to Adams's collection: Album of the Year, Song of the Year, and Best Solo by a Female Performer. The hit album received a Grammy Award nomination as well, and Adams's faith walking picked up speed. In 1994, she performed at the AZUZ evangelical conference in Tulsa, and later that year she released *At Her Very Best* with the Southeast Inspirational Choir. The following year Adams recorded *More than a Melody.*

A Special Year

The year 1996 was very special for Adams. She spent a very merry Christmas that year performing at A White House Family Christmas Celebration. Her experience at the White House was both an honor and a thrill for Adams, who received a standing ovation. Her album *Live in Washington* was nominated for a Grammy Award for Best Contemporary Soul Gospel Album. Earlier that year she accepted an invitation to Cornell University in Ithaca, New York to headline the 20th Annual Festival of Black Gospel, in part a celebration of Black History Month. Adams won her fifth Stellar Award in 1996 for Female Vocalist of the year. That was also

For the Record . . .

Born in Houston, TX, in the early 1960s, the eldest of six siblings; married Timothy Crawford, Jr., a stockbroker and former NFL football player, in the summer of 1997.

Modeled briefly during the 1970's; elementary school teacher during the 1980s; debut album, *Just As I Am,* 1987, Sound of Gospel Records signed with Tribute Records, 1990; released *Through the Storm, 1990; Save the World,* 1993; *More Than a Melody,* 1995; *Live in Washington D.C.,* 1996; toured with Kirk Franklin's "Tour of Life" in 1996-97.

Awards: Stellar Award for Best Female Contemporary Artist, 1991; GMA Dove Award, 1991; Excellence Award, 1991; Stellar Awards for Song of the Year, Album of the Year, and Best Female Solo Performance, 1993; Stellar Award for Female Vocalist of the Year, 1996.

Addresses: *Manager*—Shiba Freeman-Haley, 12201 Pleasant Prospect, Mitchellville, MD 20721; *Record company*—Tribute Records, 3310 W. End Ave., #200, Nashville, TN 37203, (615) 385-0079; fax (615) 383-2947.

the year that Adams joined Kirk Franklin and the Family, Fred Hammond, Sister Cantaloupe, and others in the "Tour of Life", a gospel stage review that premiered in Tulsa, Oklahoma at the end of October. By April of 1997 the ambitious cast had traveled to over 50 cities.

Highlights of 1997 included two Grammy Award nominations, a live concert in Montreal, Canada, and a guest appearance on "Celebrate the Gospel," a talk show on Black Entertainment Television (BET). Adams was the show's first guest ever—BET visited her at home, and the taped interview aired for the program premier. During Christmas season that year it was standing room only at the "Christmas Glory" concert in Chicago, where Adams appeared with Andrae Crouch.

The Martin Luther King Jr. holiday in 1998 kept Adams busier than ever. She undertook a whirlwind weekend of commitments, back and forth between Texas and Virginia. On Thursday, Friday, and Saturday, January 15 through January 17, Adams held auditions and commenced practice with the Fort Worth Choir under her direction for the Martin Luther King Jr. Day concert celebration. On Sunday, January 18, she was in Richmond, Virginia for a featured appearance at the Freedom Classic Festival, a traditional rivalry basketball game between Virginia State University and Virginia Union University. The annual Freedom Classic Festival is also held in honor of Martin Luther King Jr.'s Birthday, and Adams was scheduled to perform in concert with the Imani Singers, a gospel choir from Richmond's First Baptist Church. Following her performance, Adams returned to Fort Worth for the Monday evening performance of the Fort Worth Choir.

Behind the Scenes

Adams is particular in her likes and dislikes. She loves children, distrusts politicians, and shuns the sensational aspects of modern media. She ignores critics who disprove her digressions from traditional gospel styles, declaring that her music is, according to Deborah Gregory of *Essence,* "Contemporary, jazzy and fun." Indeed Adams is quick to emphasize the need for innovative modern music styles, such as hers, to reach out to youth and in particular to provide an alternative to gangsta rap. Adams not only sings, but she writes and produces songs. She also served as an active representative of FILA, the popular athletic wear manufacturer. As a member of the company's community outreach program, Operation Rebound, Adams traveled to schools and talked openly with young people about the dangers of drug abuse and alcoholism.

In the summer of 1997 Adams married Timothy Crawford, Jr., a stockbroker for Meryll Lynch. Crawford was a former professional football player and played with the New York Jets and the Indianapolis Colts. The couple lived in Houston, Texas.

Selected discography

Just as I Am, Sound of Gospel Records, 1987.
Through the Storm, Tribute Records, 1991.
Save the World, Tribute Records, 1993.
More Than a Melody, Tribute Records, 1995.
Live in Washington, D.C., Tribute Records, 1996.

With Others

Bring It to Jesus, 1993.
March On, 1993.
(with Southeast Inspirational Choir), Paula Records, 1994.
Shakin' the House: Live in L.A., 1996.

Sources

Periodicals

Tennessee Tribune, October 23, 1996, p. 4.
Richmond (Virginia) Times-Dispatch,(Weekender Sectio),
    January 15, 1998,
Essence, February 1996, p. 64.

Online

Metroactive Music, "'Melody' Maker," <http://
    www.metroactive.com/metro/03.21.96/adams-9612.htm>
    (from March 21-26, 1996 issue of Metro.)
"Yolanda Adams," Back to Gospel, <http://199.212.60.93/
    IS234101/Serina/YOLANDA.HTM>.

—Gloria Cooksey

Alien Sex Fiend

Rock band

From the band's moniker alone it is apparent that Alien Sex Fiend have every intention of raising eyebrows, if not shocking completely. However, there is much more to their story than that. Since the early 1980s, the London, England, based outfit have released a slew of records which exceed the status of gimmickry. Like contemporaries the Cramps, Alien Sex Fiend have relied upon a tongue in cheek style of horror film-inspired imagery, setting them apart from a host of gothic rock bands who offer similar theatrics without a glimmer of irony. Unlike the Cramps' blend of comic-book rockabilly, Alien Sex Fiend base their musical style on a blend of boisterous punk rock and synthesizer driven dance music, looking forward towards change rather than back. As Greg Fasolino wrote in an online article, "Darwin would have been proud of Alien Sex Fiend, a highly successful musical organism that has resisted over a dozen years worth of attempts at pigeonholing and ... have yet to stand still in any zone of space and time."

Alien Sex Fiend's roots are firmly entrenched in the North London club scene that thrived in the wake of punk rock in the late 1970s. The band's Nik Fiend circulated among several bands during 1976 and 1977, including the short lived groups Demon and Demon Preacher, both of which left behind few recorded artifacts. Fiend's penchant for the macabre antics of rock

singer Alice Cooper, famous for loading his stage with snakes, guillotines, and other ghastly props, set him apart from many of his punk contemporaries, and after finding a like-minded set of cohorts, Alien Sex Fiend formed to help forge the new genre of gothic rock. Joined by his synth-playing wife Chrissie, who adopted the stage name Mrs. Fiend, Fiend rounded out the original Alien Sex Fiend lineup with apartment-mate David James/Yaxi Highriser on guitar and drummer John Freshwater/Johnny Ha-Ha.

After producing a demo-tape that received good reviews in underground papers, the band was invited by Ollie Wisdom of the group Specimen to play their first live show at London's Batcave club in December of 1982. It quickly became apparent that stage performance was as vital to Alien Sex Fiend as recording music, and their display of smoke machines and zombie-like makeup played a part in the burgeoning gothic subculture. However, unlike a number of gothic acts that emerged from the same period such as Christian Death or Specimen, Alien Sex Fiend injected a campy self-awareness into their seemingly morbid proceedings, and listeners outside of the gothic lifestyle grew to appreciate the band's flair. While becoming in-house cult favorites at the Batcave, the group was soon invited to play larger venues, adding to their busy schedule. "The only lows were attempting to hold down day jobs and having to go to work pretending you'd had a normal evening," Nik Fiend recalled to Mick Mercer in an online article, "when in reality you've been up all night recording in Trident studios or doing a gig."

Beginning a twelve year relationship with the Anagram label, the Fiends released their debut single, "Ignore the Machine" and album, *Who's Been Sleeping in My Brain?,* in 1983. A landmark of gothic rock, the album offers a unique array of vaguely psychedelic guitar and pulsing rhythm, topped off by the trademark vocals of Nik Fiend, who alternates between a deadpan drone and a wailing tremolo. With such highlights as "Wish I Woz a Dog" and "Wild Women," *Who's Been Sleeping in My Brain?* created a landscape of B-movie imagery and hallucinogenic references that usually avoided outright profanity, but was nevertheless sure to shock the conservative listener. The prolific group continued to issue a number of singles that scored high marks within clubs and on independent charts, including "R.I.P.," "Dead and Buried," and "E.S.T. (Trip to the Moon)," all released in 1984. As evidenced on that year's *Acid Bath* album, the Fiends had begun to move away from privileging the guitar as the hub of their music, and increasingly leaned on Mrs. Fiend's synthesizer and tape loops to provide spooky, yet danceable, electronic tracks. However, the departure of drummer

For the Record . . .

Members include **Rat Fink, Jr.,** (joined band, 1985),guitars; **John Freshwater** (Johnny Ha-Ha), drums; **David James** (Yaxi Highriser), guitar; **Doctor Milton,** (joined band, 1987), keyboards; **Chrissie Wade** (Mrs. Fiend), synthesizers and tape programming; **Nik Wade** (Nik Fiend), vocals.

Band formed in North London, England, 1982; debuted at cult hub the Batcave, December 1982; released debut album *Who's Been Sleeping in My Brain?* for Anagram, 1983; created the memorable *"It" the Album* which landed the band a spot of Alice Cooper's "The Nightmare Returns" tour, 1986; released the breakthrough dance record *Another Planet*, 1988; enjoyed mainstream visibility when the video "Now I'm Feeling Zombified" was played on MTV's *Beavis and Butthead* program, 1990; created the first CD Rom soundtrack album, *Inferno—the Odyssey Continues*, 1994; released ambient-techno album, *Nocturnal Emissions,* 1996.

Addresses: *Email address*—asf@asf-13thmoon.demon.co.uk

Ha-Ha became a temporary setback in the band's creative trajectory. The 1985 album, *Maximum Security,* utilized an often monotonous sequencer in lieu of a drummer, and on the whole the record lacked the kinetic edge that fueled earlier releases.The following year saw the band's pioneering sound of dance-oriented gothic rock reach maturity with the single "I Walk the Line" and the soon to follow *"It" the Album.*

End of the Gothic Era

"It" the Album represented both the end of the group's initial phase and its most creative undertaking yet. Moving in directions beyond the scope of goth subculture, songs such as "Manic Depression" and "Get Into It" retained the Fiends' vision of ghastly kitsch, but delved into realms of extreme psychedelia and techno. While the band had by no means become mainstream, the band had expanded their appeal so much that Nik Fiend's idol, Alice Cooper, offered Alien Sex Fiend the opening slot on his "Nightmare Returns" tour. Working with a bigger budget and several years of experience

under their belts, the Fiends' all-important onstage theatrics could then rival Cooper's. As Fasolino wrote of the tour, the band's live show had evolved into "a creature-feature cabaret with Munsterian magician Nik as ringleader, armed with his array of lethal props, and surrounded by utterly gonzo self-designed stage sets."

Provoked by mounting tensions within the band, Yaxi Highriser left Alien Sex Fiend in 1987, leaving Nik and Mrs. Fiend alone at the helm. This hiatus quickly ended with the induction of new members Rat Fink, Jr., and Doctor Milton in 1988, who collectively took up the duties of keyboards, guitar, and drums. By this point in their career, the band had largely shed its gothic musical style, as well as its pancake makeup and mascara, and had become more in step with industrial and electronica–music often dominated by aggressive beats and experimental use of new technology. While the 1988 album *Another Planet* made use of electronically sampled sounds on tracks like "Nightmare Zone" and the crudely punned "Sample My Sausage," the Fiends pushed the envelope even farther by setting a cut-up medley of their material to beats inspired by American techno music on the single "Haunted House," released in 1989.

Band Embraced Electronic Age

Throughout the 1990s, Alien Sex Fiend continued to break out on new fronts, grafting their dance sensibilities onto the terrain of computers and cyberspace. In 1994, the group again demonstrated their cutting-edge thinking by releasing the first ever soundtrack for a CD Rom computer game called *Inferno–The Odyssey Continues.* The cool, spaced-out flavor of the soundtrack prefaced the dramatic new direction Alien Sex Fiend's music took after the formation of their own label, 13th Moon Records, in 1995. Bearing almost no resemblance to the band's formative efforts save for its aesthetics of shock, the notable 1997 release *Nocturnal Emissions* was, in Fasolino's words, "a cybernetic jamboree, opening with 1996's groundbreaking single "Evolution," a dancefloor juggernaut full of otherworldly blips, bleeps, and bastard beats ... *Nocturnal Emissions* will take you on a journey farther out than any previous trek in the band's fabled, frenetic career."

In spite of the Fiends' embracing of all things electronic, Nik Fiend has continued to produce work in a much more time-honored medium–oil painting. The self-taught Fiend applied the same irreverence in his painting as in Alien Sex Fiend's music and his work has been used consistently for the group's album covers and stage backdrops. In 1996, Fiend's horrific works, dating back to 1982, were given their own exhibition at the Sussex Art Club in Brighton, England, but the singer showed no sign of conceding to art gallery decorum. "I like to challenge whatever is acceptable," Fiend told Chryste Hall in an online interview. "When I started to work with oils, the first thing I read in an art book was "do not use black," so of course I ran out and got a load of black paint!" Fiend has truly established himself as a multimedia trouble maker, and despite the release of a 1998 retrospective of Alien Sex Fiend's career to date, his journey into the bizarre seems far from over.

Selected discography

Who's Been Sleeping in My Brain?, Anagram/Relativity, 1983.
Acid Bath, Anagram/Epitaph, 1988.
Maximum Security, Anagram, 1985.
"It" the Album, Plague/Anagram, 1986.
Here Cum Germs, PVC/Anagram, 1987.
All Our Yesterdays, Plague/Anagram, 1988.
Another Planet, Caroline/Anagram, 1988.
Too Much Acid?, Plague/Anagram, 1989.
The Singles 1983-1995, Anagram, 1995.
Nocturnal Emissions, 13th Moon, 1996.
The Legendary Batcave Masters, Cleopatra/13th Moon, 1998.

Sources

http://www.asf-13thmoon.demon.co.uk.biog.html
http://www.asf-13thmoon.demon.co.uk/biog/maggot.html
http://www.asf-13thmoon.demon.co.uk/gallery/index.html

—Sean Frentner

Anonymous 4

Vocal quartet

Anonymous 4, a vocal ensemble of four women, contributed as much as any other individual or group to the emergence of medieval vocal music as a popular musical style during the 1980s. However, during a decade that saw the aggressive marketing of chant recorded by the Benedictine monks of Santo Domingo de Silos and the rather outrageous Mediaeval Baebes—12 women who have been compared to the Spice Girls—Anonymous 4 hopes to prove that its worth is based on the members' skills as performers and music historians. The group sings sacred medieval chant and polyphony, most often performing their carefully researched a cappella works in churches. Their recordings have often topped the *Billboard* classical music charts, beginning with the 1993 compact disc *An English Ladymass*.

Mark Swed commented on the group's surprise hit status in the *Los Angeles Times*: "The quartet is successful beyond the wildest dreams of these former New York free-lancers who used to eke out a living singing in various early-music groups around the city." Swed laughed at a *Chamber Music Magazine* comparison of Anonymous 4 and the Beatles because of their quick jump onto the music charts, but conceded "there actually is something just a little bit Beatles-esque about the quartet. The closeness of range of the three sopranos and one alto voice has some of the same sweetness of the Beatles' falsetto close harmonies. And there is even a hint of the Beatles' puckish humor in the women's give-and-take among themselves."

Formed as a trio in 1986, the ensemble evolved into a quartet in 1988, when Ruth Cunningham joined founding members Marsha Genensky, Susan Hellauer, and Johanna Maria Rose. The quartet's name often requires explanation: the word "Anonymous" is traditionally used when a composers name is unknown and "Anonymous 4" is a reference to an unknown thirteenth-century composer who was given the designation by nineteenth-century musicologist Charles-Edmond-Henri de Coussemaker. The name has taken on further resonance because of the popular joke among female historians that "Anonymous" was a woman.

Influenced in Early Music and Folklore

The members of Anonymous 4 have all received degrees in music and have extensive experience in instrumental and vocal performance. Ruth Cunningham attended the New England Conservatory of Music, where she earned a Bachelor of Music (B.M.) degree in Performance of Early Music. She began her career as a Baroque flute and recorder player and later studied voice. In addition to performing with Anonymous 4, she teaches and plays recorder and flute. Marsha Genensky has a bachelors degree (B.A.) in Music and folklore from Scripps College and a masters degree (M.A.) in Folklore and Folklife from the University of Pennsylvania. She first performed as a traditional folk singer, but went on to master other vocal techniques. With a background in Jewish sacred music, Anglo-American folksongs, shape note songs, and harmonic singing, Genensky writes and adapts readings for the quartet. Susan Hellauer received her B.A. in trumpet from Queens College. Her interest in music from the Middle Ages and Renaissance prompted her to begin taking voice lessons and to study medieval musicology at Queens College and Columbia University. Hellauer does music research for the quartet. Johanna Maria Rose holds a B.M. in voice from the Manhattan School of Music and a M.A. in Early Music Performance (voice and recorder) from Sarah Lawrence College. She also does literary research and adapts readings for the group.

The group's 1992 debut album, *An English Ladymass,* gave listeners their first taste of English polyphony as performed by Anonymous 4. The recording was comprised of music from thirteenth and early fourteenth centuries, which Anonymous 4 collected to form a composite of the kinds of music that would have been heard during masses honoring the Virgin Mary. Such compositions dominated English polyphony during that

For the Record . . .

Members include **Ruth Cunningham**, *Education:* New England Conservatory of Music; **Marsha Genensky**, *Education:* Scripps College, University of Pennsylvanis; **Susan Hellauer**, *Education:* Queens College and Columbia University; **Johanna Maria Rose**, *Education:* Manhattan School of Music, Sarah Lawrence College.

Began as a trio in 1986 and evolved into a quartet in 1988, when Cunningham joined Genensky, Hellauer, and Rose; recorded first album, *An English Ladymass*, 1993; perform regularly across the United States and Europe; have made several recordings for Harmonia Mundi; contributed to the 1996 soundtrack *Voices of Light* that accompanied the silent film *The Passion of Joan of Arc*.

Addresses: *Management*—Herbert Barrett Management, 1776 Broadway, New York, NY 10019. *Record Company*—harmonia mundi usa, 3364 Robertson Blvd., Los Angeles, CA 90034.

time, judging from the fragments of musical documents that have been preserved. The richness of this theme was mined again for *The Lily and the Lamb* in 1995 and the motets and carols of *On Yoolis Night* in 1993.

Anonymous 4's 1994 album, *Love's Illusion,* sampled French motets based on texts from the Montpellier Codex on the theme of courtly love. These various motets probably have secular and religious origins. In 1997 the quartet released *Hildegard Von Bingen: 11,000 Virgins,* a collection of works by a German abbess that were written to celebrate the feast day of St. Ursula. The 11,000 virgins named in the title were said to have been martyred with Ursula when she refused to marry a pagan Hun chieftain. This music is exceptional among the works recorded by Anonymous 4 because it was probably intended to be sung by women, not men or boys. The greatest departure for the group, however, was its participation on the recording of a opera-oratorio by Richard Einhorn titled *Voices of Light,* which was a soundtrack inspired by the silent film *The Passion of Joan of Arc.*

The singer/researchers of Anonymous 4 have explained that it takes a special approach to prepare and perform medieval compositions, because of gaps in contemporary knowledge of such music. Hellauer noted in *Time,* "From the beginning we let go of all theories not explicitly described in medieval documents and with time and work let the music and our own intuition teach us what to do." Hellauer elaborated in a *New York Times* interview, saying, "you have to realize ... this music was not written for posterity ... So people didn't waste time indicating whether it was loud, soft, slow or fast, because they were there giving those instructions. As for vocal tone, there are descriptions in treatises. But when you read something that says, for instance, 'you should not beat your throat together,' how are you supposed to know what that means in terms of sound?" With such concerns in mind, the group has adopted a vocal technique that differs from that of operatic tradition; *New York Times* reviewer Allan Kozinn described it as "a pure tone, virtually without vibrato and easily blended."

Performed Most Often in Churches

For their live performances, Anonymous 4 most often appears in churches. These concerts combine music, poetry, and narrative, with the group working to provide a satisfying, unified program. Again, the fragmented nature of medieval music makes this difficult, as Rose explained in the *New York Times:* "We try to make our programs more than just a collection of our favorite pieces.... We spend a lot of time digging through material that nobody else sings. And because the pieces tend to be very short, we try to come up with ways to present them cohesively, so that our programs are not just strings of one-minute pieces."

The live and recorded performances of Anonymous 4 have earned them warm praise from audiences and critics. Susan Larson commended the ensemble in the *Boston Globe* as "a quartet of pure-voiced women with a scholarly and literary bent ... [and an] abstruse repertoire that nobody but musicologists used to care about ... they are marvelous musicians, meticulous researchers, and they never dumb down or glitz up their material." Writing for the *Christian Science Monitor,* M. S. Mason exclaimed, "They transport the listener back hundreds of years to another world. Most, though not all of their music is sacred, offering an island of serenity in a sea of twentieth-century noise—a respite from contemporary stress. The more one listens, the purer the sound seems." Similarly, composer/reviewer Russell Platt wrote in the *Minneapolis Star Tribune,* "I cannot imagine purer vocal tone. The chants were unison in the highest sense: not simply a matter of breathing together, but of handling the flow and curvature of the line to produce the impression of a single heavenly instrument." He went on to compare their polyphony to the sound of four oboes, "their tone deliciously reedy and blurred."

Anonymous 4 has performed throughout the United States and Europe and they have been heard on National Public Radio's "Performance Today," "A Prairie Home Companion," and "Weekend Edition." They have also been featured on WETA-FM's "Millennium of Music" and WNYC-FM's "Around New York."

Selected discography

An English Ladymass, Harmonia Mundi, 1992.
On Yoolis Night, Harmonia Mundi, 1993.
Love's Illusion, Harmonia Mundi, 1994.
The Lily and the Lamb, Harmonia Mundi, 1995.
Noel Collection, Harmonia Mundi, 1996.
A Star in the East, Harmonia Mundi, 1996.
(Contributor) *Voices of Light* (soundtrack), Sony Classical, 1996
Hildegard Von Bingen: 11,000 Virgins, Harmonia Mundi, 1997.

Sources

Periodicals

Billboard, August 30, 1997.
Boston Globe, June 20, 1995, p. 62; April 28, 1998, p. C8.
Christian Science Monitor, April 17, 1998, p. B4.
Los Angeles Times, February 3, 1995, p. F1.
New York Times, May 4, 1990, p. C24; May 22, 1997, p. C22.
Minneapolis Star Tribune, March 18, 1997, p. 4.

Online

The University of Chicago, Howard Mayer Brown International Early Music Series, http://tuna.uchicago.edu/humanities/concerts/early, 1995.
www.allmusic.com, All-Music Guide, 1998.
www.harmoniamundi.com, harmonia mundi u.s.a., 1998.

—Paula Pyzik Scott

Aqua Velvets

Surf band

Noted for their atmospheric and hypnotic surf music, the Aqua Velvets surfaced as part of an instrumental rock movement that drew sounds from the 1950s and 1960s and embraces a "less is more" aesthetic. *Guitar Player*'s Chuck Crisafulli described the sound of the Aqua Velvets as, "more akin to (Link) Wray than Return to Forever or Rising Force.... The Aqua Velvets revive the venerable sound of Southern California surf-rock."

The band consists of guitarist Miles Corbin, bassist Michael Lindner, drummer Don Spindt, guitarist Hank Manninger, and keyboardist Spencer Chan. Although the band's music undeniably inspires dancing—as witnessed at all of their live shows—their free-flowing instrumental style effortlessly lends itself to soundtracks and television scores. Their music has been featured in numerous various independent films, and television shows such as MTV's "House of Style," "Singled Out," and CBS' "Nash Bridges." They've also had tracks in dozens of specials on the Discovery Channel, ESPN's "Maxout", ABC, and Fox, and were featured in three neo-surf anthologies—including Rhino's *Cowabunga! The Surf Box*. A.T. at *Pipeline* magazine described their music as, "scene-setting, private eye, smoky nightclub, foggy backstreet mode ... soundtrack for a nineties film noir, all moody atmosphere plus melody ... file under tasty modern guitar instrumentals." A staff writer for the *Los Angeles Daily News* wrote, "(The band) doesn't slavishly imitate others or attempt to duplicate the past. All songs on the aptly titled *Guitar Noir* are originals and many are quite good."

In spite of success with television, films, music reviewers, and concert audiences, the Aqua Velvets are a specific niche band whose members feel ardently about the unusual music they create. All of the band members still held part-time jobs after the release of their fourth album, *Guitar Noir;* Corbin, who was raised in Fairfax, VA, worked as part-time manager of the snack bar underneath the lifeguard tower at Stinson Beach, just north of San Francisco, which was dubbed "Surfer's Grill". Lindner, from San Francisco, worked as a Porsche mechanic and part-time middle-school music teacher. Chan, from Dublin in Ireland, worked as a piano teacher. Manninger, from Berkeley, CA, raised Jack Russell terriers, and Spindt, from El Cerrito, worked as an internet consultant. Corbin told the *San Francisco Examiner-Chronicle,* "We play locally (in San Francisco) to stay in form, but record companies don't give tour support anymore. So rather than quit our day jobs and come home broke, we stay here and work the music out of our own office, placing tunes on TV commercials and soundtracks and doing our own A&R and legal work."

Band members cite a wide array of musical mentors as early influences, encompassing rock, jazz, surf music, movie music, and alternative rock; the list includes the Beach Boys, the Ventures, the Shadows, the Beatles, the Rolling Stones, Ennio Morricone, Angelo Badalamenti, Elvis Costello, U2, Chris Isaak, Dick Dale, the Doors, the Grateful Dead, Jimi Hendrix, Miles Davis, the Grateful Dead, and the Talking Heads. The band incorporates a Latin beat into many of their songs, particularly on *Guitar Noir*'s "Casbah Club," "Mysterious Mambo," and "Argentina". Corbin concentrates on the details of pick-and-whammy in order to create a distinctive surf effect rather than utilizing special effects. He usually accents the end of a musical phrase with a little tremolo, just as a vocalist might use vibrato for added effect.

Corbin described his band's sound to Crisafulli as, "neo-surf spaghetti western," and said he approaches composing as if the music is going to be the soundtrack to a movie that will never exist. He is often inspired by a visual image rather than a lyrical one. The first two songs the Aqua Velvets recorded were studio experiments in film scoring, and Lindner and Corbin enjoyed the music so thoroughly that they decided to form a band around it. The Aqua Velvets debut, *The Aqua Velvets* was released in 1992 and featured neo-surf sounds with a garage band/grunge sensibility. For their debut release, the AquaVelvets meshed Ennio Morricone-style movie music with the atmospheric sound of Angelo Bandalamenti, the razor-sharp twangs of Link

For the Record . . .

Members include **Spencer Chan**, keyboard; **Miles Corbin**, guitar; **Michael Lindner**, bass; **Hank Manninger**, guitar; **Don Spindt**, drums.

Music featured in numerous various independentfilms and television shows such as MTV's "House of Style," "Singled Out," and CBS' "Nash Bridges"; tracks in dozens of specials on the Discovery Channel, ESPN's "Maxout", ABC, and Fox; featured in three neo-surf anthologies, including Rhino's *Cowabunga! The Surf Box*; debut release *The Aqua Velvets,* 1992; released *Surfmania,* 1995; *Nomad,* 1996; *Guitar Noir,* in 1997.

Address: *Record company*—Milan Records, 1540 Broadway, 28th floor, New York, NY 10036; phone, (212) 782-1261. Website: http://www.milanrecords.com

Wray, and the freewheeling surf rock of the Ventures. The album took nearly four years to make, and was recorded in their basement studio at home until neighbors complained about the noise. They eventually completed the album at the garage where bassist Lindner worked as a mechanic. The album's guitar overdubs were recorded in the back of a Volkswagon van.

Surfmania was released three years later in 1995 and featured quirky singles like "Mexican Rooftop Afternoon," "Martini Time," Surf Samba," and "Cabana Del Gringo". Of all the material the Aqua Velvets released from 1992 -97, the 12 cuts on *Surfmania* were most reminiscent of Dick Dale, the Surfaris, and the Ventures. *Nomad,* released in 1996, was a surf rock compilation, with an emphasis on the surf portion of "surf-rock". The Aqua Velvets released *Guitar Noir* near the end of 1997, featuring songs such as "Mysterious Mambo," "Mermaids After Midnight," and "Twilight of the Hep Cats". Candace Murphy of the *San Jose Mercury News* wrote, "As for *Guitar Noir,* all that"s missing is the fog." The staff music writer for *Music Reviews Quarterly* wrote, "This recording has a dark lightness to its tone which results from the inherent brightness of the guitar tones contrasted with minor-keyed melody lines. That has all

been planned and executed with surprising consistency and skill on *Guitar Noir*."

The Aqua Velvets appreciate the surf rock pioneers that came before them; Corbin told Crisafulli, "People sometimes think of the Ventures as this odd, isolated phenomenon at the beginning of rock and roll, but there's really just a short gap between what the Ventures and Dick Dale were doing and what John Cipollina, Jerry Garcia and Robby Krieger started doing a couple of years later. From 1963-67 it was the surf instrumental guys who really pushed the rock guitar envelope." The Aqua Velvets infuse the traditionally happy surf sound of days of yore with a darker edge, experimenting with the strange and bizarre sounds of atmospheric surf music and creating their own multi-layered style.The staff reviewer for Baltimore's *Music Monthly* wrote, "*Nomad* was met with widespread national acclaim, which helped to establish the Aqua Velvets as one of today's hottest instrumental combos. *Guitar Noir* is destined to take the band onto an entirely new level."

Selected discography

The Aqua Velvets, Riptide Records, 1992.
Surfmania, Mesa Records, 1995.
Nomad, Mesa Records, 1996.
Guitar Noir, Milan Records, 1997.

Sources

Periodicals

Billboard, December 6, 1997.
Chicago Heights Star, January 8, 1998.
Guitar Magazine, December 1997.
Guitar Player, February 1996.
Los Angeles Daily News, January 2, 1998.
Marin Independent Journal, February 12, 1998.
Music Monthly (Baltimore, MD), December 1997.
Music Reviews Quarterly, Winter 1997-1998.
Pipeline, December, 1997.
San Francisco Examiner-Chronicle, November 9, 1997.
San Jose Mercury News, October 26, 1997.

Online

http://205.186.189.2/cg/amg.exe; AMG (All-Music Guide)

—*B. Kimberly Taylor*

Art Ensemble of Chicago

Jautz Group

Called "the premier avant garde free improvisational ensemble of the day" by the New York Times' John Rockwell, the Art Ensemble of Chicago (AEC) has been a major force in experimental music since the middle 1960s. The group's music combines elements of traditional and avant garde jazz, African music, modern classical music, and popular forms such as blues, rock and reggae, with other art forms like performance art and theater. All AEC members play more than one instruments, including percussion, and they switch instruments frequently during performances. Bird calls, bicycle horns, kazoos and thousands of other "little instruments" also make up part of their sonic arsenal and have helped erase many traditional jazz boundaries and introduce another element of fluidity into their work. Finally, the Art Ensemble has provided a model for cooperative musical endeavors, first within the Association for the Advancement of Creative Musicians (AACM), and second as a performing unit that, despite fluctuating finances and the diverse interests and far-flung personal projects of its members, has remained intact for more than thirty years.

The Art Ensemble's roots lie in the turbulent jazz world of Chicago of the mid-1960s. At a time when the nightclub jazz scene was dying, a group of young musicians organized by pianist Muhal Richard Abrams, started playing informal weekly sessions together. The group, which became known as the Experimental Band, attracted promising, young Chicago musicians like Jack DeJonette, Anthony Braxton, and Henry Threadgill, as well as three students from Wilson Junior College, Roscoe Mitchell, Joseph Jarman, and Malachi Favors.

The Experimental Band's music was heavily influenced by the "free" playing of players on the forward-most fringes of jazz: Ornette Coleman, John Coltrane, Albert Ayler, Eric Dolphy, and Cecil Taylor. Playing avant garde jazz in Chicago, practically guaranteed the Experimental Band would not find any paid gigs. But it also meant that they could play whatever and however they wanted in their weekly rehearsal sessions. The group soon became tightly knit musically; it would have a lasting impression on the artistic lives of its young musicians. "In having the chance to work in the Experimental Band with Richard and the other musicians there, I found the first something with meaning/reason for doing," Art Ensemble member Joseph Jarman told Sam Ottenhoff, "That band and the people there was the most important thing that ever happened to me."

In May 1965, the group, again led by Abrams, founded a nonprofit musicians' cooperative, the Association for the Advancement of Creative Musicians. The organization's purpose was to organize opportunities for public performance of members' music and to help ensure that member musicians worked. AACM groups began playing theaters, coffeehouses, churches, bars and universities around Chicago.

Bassist Malachi Favors and sax players Joseph Jarman and Roscoe Mitchell, of the Art Institute, met in the AACM scene. Favors, whose playing was heavily influenced by Chicago bassists Israel Crosby and Wlibur Ware Jarman, was an early participant in the Experimental band sessions. Jarman's interests ranged over many art forms; he wrote poetry, studied the theater, played a variety of reed instruments, and he incorporated them all in his concerts. Mitchell began playing sax and clarinet as a teenager. In the early 1960s, he met Albert Ayler playing in the Army band. He heard his first Ornette Coleman records around that time as well, but by his own admission neither Coleman nor Ayler struck a particularly strong chord at first. "I didn't quite understand, because I was caught up in Art Blakey, the Jazz Messengers, things like that," he told Downbeat's John Corbett. " Some of what [Ayler] was playing I didn't understand until a blues got played; when he played the first couple of choruses relatively straight, that started to make a connection to me."

Delmark Records producer Chuck Nessa heard Mitchell play a concert in 1966. The next day Mitchell had a Delmark contract. The record he made, Sound, had, in

For the Record . . .

Members include **Lester Bowie**, (born 1941, Frederick, MD, raised St Louis, MO), trumpet, cornet, percussion, "little instruments," divorced, remarried, four children; **Joseph Jarman,** (born Sept. 14, 1937, Pine Bluff, AR), raised Chicago, IL, saxophones, percussion, "little instruments," *Education:* Wilson Junior College, Chicago, IL, School of the Art Institute, Chicago, IL **Malachi Favors Maghostut,** (born August 22, 1937, Chicago IL,) acoustic bass, electric bass, percussion, "little instruments,") *Education:* Wilson Junior College, Chicago,IL. **Roscoe Mitchell,** (born August 3, 1940, Chicago, IL), saxophones, percussion, "little instruments," *Education:* Wilson Junior College **Famoudou Don Moye,** (born 1946, Rochester NY), drums, percussion, "little instruments," *Education:* Wayne State University, Detroit, MI

Career: Mitchell, Jarman, Favors, and Bowie meet as members of the Association for the Advancement of Creative Musicians in the middle 1960s; form the Art Ensemble c. 1968; moved to Paris name is changed to Art Ensemble of Chicago, 1978; Moye joins group in Paris the same year.

Addresses: *Home* Lester Bowie, Joseph Jarman, Brooklyn, NY; Malachi Favors Magostut, Famoudou Don Moye, Chicago, IL; Roscoe Mitchell, Madison, WI; *Management and Record Company*—Art Ensemble of Chicago Operations, A.E.C.O. Productions, PO Box 53429, Chicago, IL 60653

critic John Litweiler's words, "a monumental impact." It turned its back on the "energy music"—"all out blowing," in Chuck Nessa's words to Sam Ottenhoff—being played by Coltrane and Ayler. Silence was as important to Mitchell's music as sound. *Sound* and his Mitchell's second album *Congliptious* seemed to point to a new path for jazz, at a time when the prevailing free jazz was being increasingly seen as a dead end.

The group on those two groundbreaking LPs consisted of Roscoe Mitchell on reeds, Malachi Favors on bass, Robert Crowder on drums, and a young trumpet player from St. Louis, Lester Bowie. Bowie had played with a number of R&B artists, including Little Milton, Ike Turner; Oliver Sain and the soul singer Fontella Bass, who was also Bowie's wife. In 1965, he moved to Chicago where he was doing session work at Chess Records and playing advertising jingles, when a Chess employee took Bowie to one of the Experimental Band's rehearsals. The Art Ensemble of Chicago's thirtieth anniversary booklet quoted Bowie: "I never in my life met so many insane people in one room!" But within a few days he and Roscoe Mitchell were playing together. After *Sound* was completed, Bowie had his own record session and made *Number 1/Number 2* accompanied by Mitchell, Favors, and Jarman.

A short time later the four men formed the Art Ensemble—the group on *Congliptious* was called Roscoe Mitchell's Art Ensemble. For about two years they played gigs under that name, they first became known as the Art Ensemble of Chicago in Paris. They played coffeehouses and university venues, primarily in and around Chicago. Many things about the group were unheard of at the time. They were a jazz quarter without a drummer; the members took turns playing percussion. They fused aspects of traditional jazz with cutting edge experiments. At the same time, however, they incorporated a heady amount of humor in their music, with the so-called "little instruments" introduced by Joseph Jarman: toy musical instruments, bicycle horns, bird calls, rattles, kazoos and other diverse noise-makers. The Art Ensemble made avant garde music that you could have fun listening to.

Jarman brought theater to Art Ensemble performances. They might parade around the hall before or during a concert. Once they booked one site and performed at a completely different one. Another time, as the audience entered, they were given paper bags to wear over their heads. Jarman and Favors took to wearing traditional African clothing and painted faces during performances. At the height of the civil rights movement the gesture was highly confrontational and together with the Art Ensemble's revolutionary music, helped identify them with radical black politics. "Guerrilla jazz," is what critic Gary Giddins called their music. And that political element was highlighted by the motto they adopted: Great Black Music: Ancient to the Future.

Expatriate Musicians

Lester Bowie explained to L. "Chicago Beau" Beauchamp what led the Art Ensemble to move to Paris in 1969. "We wanted to be professional musicians playing jazz. We found that we had a unique style ... a unique way of playing together, and we wanted to do that exclusively for our whole living. We felt the only way we could do that would be to pick up as a unit and start developing out concepts together, somewhere else.

Since some people had expressed interest in us in France, and we had records out over there, and they were pretty popular, France was the natural choice." In June 1969, the group told their last concert audience "America is in your hands now," packed up, and sailed for Europe. They were a sensation from the time they arrived in Paris. In two years there, they recorded eleven albums, including *A Jackson In Your House* and *Message To Our Folks*, did three film scores, made countless radio and television appearances, and had a constant schedule of concerts, many sponsored by the French government.

Once in France they found a drummer, Don Moye. Moye had come to Europe in May 1968 with the Detroit Free Jazz Band, had studied native drumming in North Africa and played in Paris with Steve Lacy, Pharoah Sanders and Sonny Sharrock. His arrival changed the direction of the Art Ensemble's music and brought mixed responses from the group's fans. Some lamented that Moye's often furious drumming eliminated the large role silence had come to play in Art Ensemble music; others appreciated Moye's unifying presence, especially during the Art Ensemble's more abstract moments.

The group returned to the United States in April 1971, determined to work together on large scale productions and to pursue their individual projects. With the high praise they had won from jazz critics while in Paris, they also decided to start demanding performance fees in line with their new reputation. Bowie told Downbeat's Larry Birnbaum "We damn near died." They were able to find a meager two to three gigs a year. Most of their time was spent rehearsing and working on their own projects. They played their homecoming concert at the University of Chicago in 1972, a performance Delmark Records released as *Live at Mandel Hall*. Much of the group's income came from government grants—an NEA grant supported the production of *Fanfare for the Warriors* (Atlantic), for example—and university workshops they offered. Their fortunes finally picked up after a long-term engagement at the Five Spot in New York and a well received west coast tour.

Group Projects, Individual Projects

In 1978, the Art Ensemble formed their own label, AECO. The idea for the label was not a new one Don Moye told *Downbeat's* Birnbaum at the time. "The label has been in existence for about six years, at least on paper. We've been compiling and cataloging our music ever since we've been together, but it's only now that we've been able to pull together all the necessary factors, the economic factor, the time element, etc."

AECO's first release—and its only Art Ensemble recording—was a performance at the Montreux Festival in 1974. Since then it has released solo work by Jarman, Favors and Moye.

Blending group and individual work is an important part of the Art Ensemble's basic philosophy. "We've got our basic structure to the point where it continues on and people still have time to develop their own individual careers and realize some of their personal projects," Moye told *Downbeat's* Birnbaum. "That's one of the necessary elements of a functional cooperative, to allow everyone room for personal development and expansion." Lester Bowie agreed. "All the members of the Art Ensemble have special areas of expertise—so between us we can operate over a wide range of music. We have five different people with five different lives and sets of experiences which are brought in to make up the music," he told Mike Hennessey on the occasion of the Art Ensemble's thirtieth anniversary. "This isn't a band where a leader dictates the way everything should be done."

In the late seventies the Art Ensemble also signed a recording contract with the label ECM. The deal that was considered a minor controversy in some quarters. Why was a group whose music and persona was so intimately bound up with black music and experience, who often explicitly rejected ties to the white classical musical heritage, on a label comprised mainly of white European artists? Such questions were put to rest when the Art Ensemble released some of their most acclaimed work on ECM, including, *Full Force* and *Urban Bushmen*.

New Directions

In the middle 1980s, the group signed with the Japanese label DIW, where they have recorded ever since. Their recordings with DIW have taken the group into hitherto unexplored territory. On *Ancient to the Future: Dreaming of the Masters Vol. 1* the Art Ensemble interpreted the work of other composers for the first time, music by Otis Redding, Bob Marley, Jimi Hendrix, Fela Anikulapo Kuti, and Duke Ellington. It was followed up with two other *Dreaming of the Masters* albums, one dedicated to John Coltrane and one to Thelonious Monk. The latter was a landmark collaboration with another master, Cecil Taylor. It was only the second time the Art Ensemble had recorded with a piano player. Their 1990 release, *Art Ensemble of Chicago Soweto*, was another collaboration, this one with the Amabutho Zulu Male Chorus.

In the 1990s, the members of the Art Ensemble have devoted more and more of their time to personal projects:

Roscoe Mitchell's Sound Ensemble and Note Factory, Lester Bowie's Brass Fantasy and the Leaders, Malachi Favors Maghostut's Projections, and Famoudou Don Moye and Sun Percussion Summit. Joseph Jarman retired from the group completely in the mid-nineties. But after thirty years and more than forty albums—not counting bootlegs—the Art Ensemble has not given up the ghost—it continues to perform occasionally as a quartet, in the United States and Europe.

While realizing the Art Ensemble will never achieve mass popularity, Malachi Favors believes there is a potential for greater interest in their music. In America, Favors told *Downbeat*'s John Litweiler, "we have different music for different purposes, but it just so happens that the sex part of music—the rock or rhythm & blues—is overdone. Travelling in the States, the response in the colleges and the different places where we play has been tremendous. People are waiting to hear what the artist has to say, and eventually they come around to hearing what's going on in the music .... if people could hear our music, they would respond."

Selected discography

Albums

Bap-Tizum, Atlantic, 1972
Live At Mandel Hall, Delmark, 1972
Fanfare for the Warrior, Atlantic, 1973
Nice Guys, ECM 1978
Full Force, ECM 1980
Urban Bushmen, ECM, 1980
Ancient to the Future, DIW, 1987
Dreaming of the Masters, DIW, 1990
Art Ensemble of Chicago Soweto, (w/Amabutho Zulu Male Chorus), DIW, 1990
Dreaming of the Masters: Thelonious Sphere Monk, (w/Cecil Taylor) DIW, 1990

Malachi Favors Moghostut, *Natural and the Spiritual*, AECO, 1974
Lester Bowie, *Numbers 1 & 2*, Nessa, 1967
Lester Bowie, *Rope-a-Dope*, Muse, 1976
Lester Bowie's Brass Fantasy, *Serious Fun*, DIW, 1989
Roscoe Mitchell Sextet, *Sound*, Delmark, 1966
Roscoe Mitchell Art Ensemble, *Conglipitous*, Nessa, 1968
Roscoe Mitchell, *Nonaah*, Nessa, 1978
Roscoe Mitchell and the Sound and Space Ensembles, Black Saint, 1983
Roscoe Mitchell, *Hey Donald*, Delmark, 1995
Famoudou Don Moye, *Sun Percussion Solo, Vol. 1*, AECO, 1975
Famoudou Don Moye, *Jam For Your Life*, AECO, 1991.

Sources

Books

Beauchamp, L. "Chicago Beau." "Interview with Lester Bowie," *30 Years Art Ensemble of Chicago*, AECO, undated
Hennessey, Mike. "The Art Ensemble of Chicago," *30 Years Art Ensemble of Chicago*, AECO, undated
Litweiler, John. *The Freedom Principle*,

Periodicals

Downbeat, May 3, 1979; April 1997; June 1992.

Online

Ottenhoff, Sam. "The Sixties, Chicago, and the AACM," Available at http://www.kenyon.edu/projects/AACM/
Chuck Nessa Interview, Available at http://www.kenyon.edu/projects/AACM/

Additional material provided by the Association for the Advancement of Creative Musicians and AECO

—*Gerald Brennan*

Artifacts

Hip hop trio

The hip-hop trio Artifacts, comprised of MCs El da Sensai (William Elliot Williams), DJ Kaos (Virgshawn Perry), and Tame One (Rahem Brown), were described by *Vibe*'s Christian Ex as, "decidedly geared toward the elusive chimera that is Hip-Hop Purist." Based in Newark, NJ, the trio is noted for verbal stamina, memorable rhymes, and eschewing traditional gangsta rap. *The Source*'s Durwin Chow described the group's music as, "antagonistic freestyle barrages centered around infectiously simple yet assuaging choruses." In an interview with Rigoberto Morales of *The Source,* El da Sensai described why the band was content being labeled "underground" in the realm of hip-hop. He said, "If it wasn't for groups like us, Beatnuts, Common, Organized, or the Roots ... There wouldn't be any underground, nothing secondary to run to ... where else would you go? It's also a place where you start, and start over."

El da Sensai and Tame One earned a reputation as outstanding graffiti artists in the 1980s by "bombing," which is replacing blighted walls with smooth graffiti murals. Starting in 1980, they "bombed" walls throughout Essex County, which encompasses Newark, Irvington, and East Orange, NJ. They called themselves the Boom Skwad, and later Da Bomb Squad, and attracted an avid group of graffiti-loving fans. Both El da Sensai and Tame One were raised in Newark, where Tame One's cousin, Redman, also enjoyed acclaim as a rap artist. They attended Arts High in Newark, and often spent weekend days there honing their artistic skills, playing sports, enjoying field trips, and learning to emcee, deejay, and to break-dance.

Tame One told *The Newark Star-Ledger*'s Steven T. Walker that he and his partners were perceived as artists by their neighbors since wall art is frequently the only the only type of art that inner-city children see. Youngsters in the area would reproduce Tame One's graffiti tag after seeing it on a wall because they liked the way it looked. Tame One added, "I guess I could be seen as kind of an art teacher." Walker maintained that graffiti is as tied in with hip-hop culture and music as breakdancing and twin turntables, and that the Artifacts are an outgrowth of the early pioneers of rap. Walker said, "The group takes pride in its reputation as graffiti artists as well as rappers, almost damning current trends that make superstars out of emcees who seem content in imitating or blatantly covering R&B songs from the past two decades." El da Sensai told *Hip Hop Connection,* "I think rhyming is like painting a piece....As you go along, you just write different styles of rhymes. When you paint a piece, you use all different styles and you got a different style for every piece." The Artifacts are one of the few hip-hop/rap groups who pay tribute to the mostly bygone era of graffiti art, along with rappers

For the Record . . .

Members include **Rahem Brown** (Tame One), **Virgshawn Perry** (DJ Kaos), and **William Elliot Williams** (El da Sensai); based and raised in Newark, NJ.

El da Sensai and Tame One earned a reputation as outstanding graffiti artists in the 1980s, calling themselves the Boom Skwad and later Da Bomb Squad; one of the few hip-hop/rap groups who pay tribute to the mostly bygone era of graffiti art; released debut album *Between a Rock and a Hard Place* in 1994; the album's first single, "The Ultimate," was featured on the gold-selling High School High soundtrack; released *That's Them* in 1997.

Addresses: *Record company*—Big Beat Records Inc/ Atlantic., 1290 Avenue of the Americas, New York, NY 10104; (212) 707-2531; fax (212) 405-5650.

Masta Ace, Rakim, and KRS-One. Their debut album, *Between a Rock and a Hard Place,* was released in 1994 and featured numerous references to graffiti, particularly in the singles "Wrong Side of Da Tracks" and "Come On Wit Da Git Down". DJ Kaos joined the Artifacts shortly before the release of the band's second album.

The Artifacts typify the thoughtful, party-style hip-hop which was prevalent in the early 1990s, evoking the type of music found among groups like Brand Nubian, Pete Rock & C.L., Main Source, and Organized Confusion, *Thrasher* magazine's Chris Nieratko wrote, "*Between A Rock and a Hard Place* broke all boundaries by delivering honest, accessible lyrics." Although the Artifacts didn't break into mainstream success with a radio-friendly hit, their debut release was generally considered by critics to be substantial,and woefully overlooked. The album's first single, "The Ultimate," was featured on the gold-selling High School High soundtrack. *The Source* called *Between A Rock and a Hard Place,* "the purest hip-hop album this year ... the Artifacts are a refreshing blast of the lifeblood of hip-hop...." *Between A Rock and a Hard Place* fared well enough to allow the Artifacts to create their own sound and retain their artistic freedom, and when label mate Lil' Kim reached gold status, the Artifacts were roundly encouraged to release more material.

Before releasing their sophomore album, *That's Them,* in 1997 the band toured the country and spent a lot of time in the studio. *That's Them* took a year to complete, and was infused with their trademark witty lyrics and with a more intense rap sound. The title of the album stemmed from the fact that kids used to shout, "That's them!," when they saw the duo on the street. Mr. Walt from Da Beatminerz contributed to "Gettin' Hot" on That's Them, and V.I.C. of the Beatnuts contributed to "The Interview" and "This is The Way". "Collaboration of Mics" was produced by and feature sLord Finesse, as well as Lord Jamar of the Brand Nubians. Lord Jamar helped the group record the original demo for "Wrong Side of Da Tracks" and is viewed by the group's members as a mentor and an older brother. Adam Keane Stern of *Seconds* magazine wrote, "That's Them isn't flashy and transcendent,but neither is Newark. Tame and El are just looking out for health, wealth and self. Like they say on "The Ultimate": 'I'm not in it for the gimmicks or satisfying critics/I just want my own like the Hassidics'."

Adam Kush of Austin's *Daily Texan* wrote, "The duo has managed to keep a street perspective, while being far more relaxed and positive than many ... This ability to straddle two often divergent styles of rap is impressive, and should allow the Artifacts to continue to make classic, underground, albums,regardless of how few people take notice." This assessment is correct, but the Artifacts have been noticed and appreciated by their east coast hip-hop artist peers, which renders them the "hip-hop musician's musicians," so it's likely that the group won't retain their underground status for long noted Kush. *Urban Network Magazine* summed up the Artifacts with, "Though best appreciated by those who live and die for hip-hop, this is a powerful East Coast representation of where hip hop lives."

Selected discography

Between A Rock and a Hard Place, Big Beat/Atlantic, 1994.
That's Them, Big beat/Atlantic, 1997.

Sources

Periodicals

BRE, March 14, 1997.
CMJ, April 7, 1997.
Daily Pennsylvanian, April 24, 1997.
Daily Texan, April 24, 1997.
Hip Hop Connection, July 1997.
Mixmag, July 1997

MR, May 1997.
Newark Star Ledger, June 12, 1997.
On the Go Magazine, May 1997.
Queen's College Quad, May 12, 1997.
Seconds, June/July 1997.
The Source, May 1997; April 1997.
Tafrija, April 1997.
Thrasher, September 1997.
Urban Network Magazine, April 11, 1997.
Vibe, April 1997.

Online

http://www.cdnow.com/cgi-bin/mserv...gename=/RP/CDN/
   FIND/popsearch.html

—B. Kimberly Taylor

Teodross Avery

Saxophone

Saxophonist Teodross Avery recorded two major-label albums before graduating from the Berklee School of Music at the age of 22. His youthful output was hailed by reviewers as original, eclectic, and distinguished. Geoffrey Himes of the Washington Post wrote, "Unlike so many young Marsalis acolytes with an academic background ... Avery isn't tied to a conservative vision of jazz history.... He joins James Carter and Joshua Redman as the most promising saxophonists of their generation." Avery combines elements of funk, fusion, hip-hop, and free-jazz to define and explore his sound, and his aptly-titled second release, *My Generation,* reflected his borderless approach to jazz most favorably. Himes wrote, "This modern eclecticism wouldn't matter a bit if Avery weren't able to incorporate these ingredients into swinging, bluesy solos or if he weren't able to project such a gutsy, distinctive voice on his tenor and soprano saxes."

Avery's early musical influences were the sounds of hip-hop, rap, reggae, and funk music. *Fly!* magazine's Damian Rafferty reported that Avery claimed he only wanted a degree in music from Berkeley to please his mother, yet he made the most of his time at Berklee's College of Music. During an interview with *Contemporary Musicians,* he described his father as, "a closet musician". Avery told Rafferty, "I was coming to Berkelee to learn some things I particularly wanted to learn,

I just had to learn how to do them. Plus, I have an open mind about learning. I don't have the conservatory mentality even though I did go to college." Avery made a conscious decision upon entering school not to let teachers stifle his creativity, retaining his vision and focus while maintaining his desire to learn and grow as a musician.

After recording on Carl Allen's *The Pursuer* while still in college, Avery was approached during his third year by the GRP record label. Avery told Rafferty, "At first I was very hesitant... I was thinking I'd really like to get some more experience playing with other jazz musicians—and get more status—but then I started looking around and seeing how many really good players I knew who weren't getting any work.... I decided to go ahead and work hard and make the best record I could and continue to practice and write music...." Rafferty wrote that Avery "sees paths where others see walls" due to his wide range of early musical influences and, as a result of this broad range, his jazz compositions are mature and broad. Avery released his debut album, *In Other Words,* in October of 1994. He stayed closer to the mainstream in his first release than in his second, and he displayed exceptional skill in both composing and playing. Avery told Rafferty that he purposely didn't want to be pegged as a particular type of jazz musician, since fans would expect him to remain in that niche and it would be difficult to branch out and experiment. He felt that if he began his career as a broad-based, musically unpredictable jazz musician, he could follow any musical path he chose in the future. He explained to Rafferty, "I don't really like to put labels on the music I play because I don't want to be prohibited. I just call it music.

After *In Other Words* was released, Rafferty wrote, "Here (is) someone who really does have the bite of Giant Steps Coltrane, the lyricism of Joe Henderson...." What set *In Other Words* apart from numerous other new jazz releases at the time was Teodross' attitude. He told Rafferty that he didn't want to imitate the 1950s or 1960s for the duration of his career. He said, "There is a certain amount of history to learn but you have to move forward and try new things." He acknowledged that musical experiments might hit or miss, but the important thing is to try. He added, "Not everybody likes to take chances, but I think I'm the kind of person that wants to put other styles of music into my music—but still have jazz roots at the same time."

Avery's debut release was comprised primarily of his own compositions. His sophomore album, *My Generation,* was released in February of 1996. He worked with a rhythm section whose chordal center shifted with

Born July 2, 1973 in Oakland, CA,; one of five children; *Education:* Berklee School of Music.

Combines elements of funk, fusion, hip-hop, and free-jazz; recorded on Carl Allen's *The Pursuer* while still in college; approached during his third year in college by the GRP record label; released debut album, *In Other Words,* October 1994; sophomore album, *My Generation,* released February of 1996.

Addresses: *Record company*—GRP Records Inc., 555 W. 57th Street, 10th floor, New York, NY 10019, (212) 424-1007

up-from-the-swamp exaltations.... On the whole, this is a fine sophomore effort."

Avery displays musical sophistication that portends a successful, innovative future. He creates delightful jazz tension by sometimes playing against the beat and the melody rather than within them, and he approaches romantic instrumental ballads in a style reminiscent of Miles Davis. Himes wrote, "Avery transforms Janet Jackson's 'Anytime, Anyplace'... the same way that Miles Davis once handled Frank Sinatra's 'My Funny Valentine'." Avery also presents fusion numbers that generate musical invention around a funk groove, demonstrates an ability to create a unique, expressive sax solo within a mainstream context, and skillfully uses dissonance and Eastern music drones in the style of Pharoah Sanders. Himes summed Avery up when he wrote, "In any setting, Avery displays a remarkable discipline for one so young, preferring to play the few notes that matter rather than show off his speed."

almost every track and included pianist Charles Craig on three tracks, guest guitarist John Scofield on three tracks, Mark Whitfield on three tracks, and Peter Bernstein on one track. Since each musician contributed a different, unique feel, the resulting album was lively and unpredictable. Bassist Rodney Whitaker and drummer Greg Hutchinson also contributed to *My Generation.* The single "Addis Ababa" celebrated the Ethiopian part of Avery's lineage; Willard Jenkins of Jazztimes wrote, "He exhibits a ripening tenor tone and, though no stranger to prodigious velocity, Avery concentrates more energy on trying to get inside the muse rather than overrunning it." Jenkins continued, "'Lover Man' is Whitfield's entry point, Avery playing off his lovely textures in a duet intro. It is with this reading that one is deeply impressed by Avery's onrushing maturation." The album also features a playful attempt at hip-hop with a rap by Black Thought of Roots and a hip-hop rhythm modified for an elastic, syncopated feel—but the inclusion is merely a lighthearted nod to hip-hop rather than a serious endeavor. Avery also included a musical tribute to his father with "Mode For My Father" and a tribute to his mother with "Salome." Jenkins wrote, "Donald Brown's 'Theme for Malcolm,' with its gentle taste of reggae, is a distinctive line and Sco's wicked solo is yet another in his long line of deeply grooved,

Selected discography

In Other Words, GRP Records, 1994.
My Generation, Impulse, 1996.

Sources

Periodicals

Fly!, September 23, 1995.
Jazztimes, March 1996.
Washington Post, March 15, 1996.

Online

www.cdnow.com/cgi/bin/mserv...AVERY*TEODROSS/
    ddcn=SD-11107+181+2 (6/2/98)
www.impulserecords.com

Additional source material was obtained through a phone interview with Avery on 8/2/98.

—B. Kimberly Taylor

Badfinger

Rock group

Badfinger were masters of the pop song, from soulful ballads to country-style bouncers to out-and-out rockers. So adept were they that they were touted as the successors to the Beatles when they first appeared on the scene in the late 1960s. Indeed they had much in common with the Fab Four. They recorded their most popular albums for the Beatles label, Apple. At one time or another, the band worked on projects with all four individual Beatles. And like the Beatles, Badfinger's career ended in a flurry of financial mismanagement, greed, and personal recriminations that last to this day.

Badfinger got its start in 1964 when apprentice electrician and guitarist Pete Ham formed the Iveys in Swansea, Wales. The line-up consisted of Ham, drummer Mike Gibbins, bassist Ron Griffiths, and guitarist Dai Jenkins. Bill Collins, a band manager from Liverpool, heard the Iveys playing the bar circuit around Wales. With the promise of a gig backing-up a popular singer, Collins persuaded the band to pack up and move to London. There they shared a house in Golders Green with Collins' other band, the Mojos. When Jenkins left the band, Collins replaced him with a guitarist from Liverpool, Tom Evans.

In London, The Iveys struggled. They were perennially short of money and Collins kept them on a short leash. They were backing up singer David Garrick who would have been a one hit wonder except his single "Dear Mrs. Applebee" was never really a hit. But Ham, Evans and Griffiths had all begun to write for the band. Their sound and songs awoke interest in Swingin' London. Ray Davies of the Kinks expressed interest in working with them. Collins, unfortunately, tended to interpret such interest as a threat to his power over the group and most offers came to naught.

One offer Collins could hardly refuse came from Mal Evans. Evans, an old Liverpool buddy of the Beatles, took to the Iveys from the first and decided to make them his pet project at Apple, the label the Beatles had just founded. In 1968, he played an Iveys tape for Paul McCartney who was so impressed he asked to hear more. On July 23, 1968, the Iveys signed with Apple. "The ultimate goal was to get was to get a recording contract," Ron Griffiths recalled in *Mojo*. "But to get one from Apple was really exciting. Yet we were still living at Galders Green, getting eight pounds a week each."

The Iveys' first single was a bright pop ditty by Tom Evans entitled "Maybe Tomorrow." An LP of the same name followed. But for reasons never explained, it was never released in Britain or the United States. As they prepared to start their second album, Apple decided they needed a new name, one that wasn't so old-fashioned and corny. The Beatles bounced a few around but Neil Aspinal, another Liverpool crony, suggested Badfinger, from "Badfinger Boogie," which had been John Lennon's original working title for "With a Little Help From My Friends."

Cracked the Top Ten

By 1969, the Beatles were being torn apart by personal tensions while Apple was self-destructing from bad—or nonexistent—management. After the *Maybe Tomorrow* fiasco, everyone seemed to lose interest in Badfinger—at least until Ron Griffiths complained about the Beatles apathy in a British music magazine. Shortly afterwards, Paul McCartney visited Golders Green and brought Badfinger a song. He had written "Come And Get It" for the film, *The Magic Christian,* that featured Peter Sellers and Ringo Starr. McCartney offered the song to Badfinger. One proviso was that Badfinger record the song

exactly as McCartney had arranged it on his demo. "This is the hit sound. Do it like this and we're all right, we've got a hit," McCartney is quoted in Dan Matovina's *Without You: The Tragic Story of Badfinger.* Matovina also relates how McCartney produced the single and persuaded the producers to use two additional Badfinger songs in the film. Badfinger's single—virtually a note for note copy of McCartney's version included on the Beatles *Anthology 3*—eventually cracked the Top Ten in both the United States and Britain.

Badfinger was suddenly world famous. But for bassist Ron Griffith the fame was short lived. His marriage to his pregnant girlfriend had created conflict at Golders Green. On the eve of the band's first great success, Griffith was out. To simplify the search for a replacement Tom Evans agreed to switch to bass. Collins brought in another Liverpool guitarist, Joey Molland, smoothing out the switch..

Magic Christian Music, released at the beginning of 1970, was a potpourri of different styles, from driving rock to doleful ballads to melodramatic music hall tunes. Griffiths played bass on the record but his name did not appear on the record jacket; Molland's name was listed although, as Matovina. Some songs had been recycled from *Maybe Tomorrow,* others were new Badfinger. The band's second album, *No Dice,* was released in November 1970. A bracing mix of rock, pop, country and ballads, the record reached number 28 on the Billboard charts and its single, "No Matter What," hit number 8.

But it was another song on *No Dice* that made the biggest impact. While Badfinger was recording their third album, Harry Nilsson invited them down to the studio where he was working and played the version of Ham and Evans "Without You" he had just finished. Badfinger's version was a bare bones guitar-organ-bass-drums arrangement, Nilsson's had a lush string arrangement and top-of-the-line production values. "They were stunned!" Nilsson later told Dan Matovina. According to Matovina, Pete Ham said afterwards "As soon as we heard it, we knew that was the way we wanted to do it, but never had the nerve." Nilsson's version reached number one in 1972 and became one of the most successful singles of all times. Mariah Carey, relying heavily on Nilsson's arrangement, took the song to the top of the charts again in 1994.

Missed the Wave

Bill Collins, meanwhile, had brought in an American, Stan Polley, who before long had gained complete control of Badfinger's finances. Under Polley, the band began touring the States incessantly, an attempt to get Badfinger better established there and finally seize the big success that was eluding the band although it seemed constantly to be within their grasp. They had two top ten hits after all, and written a number one hit; they had played on John Lennon's *Imagine*, on George Harrison's *All Things Must Pass*, and on Ringo Starr's single "It Don't Come Easy." But tastes were changing. The two-minute pop songs on AM radio had evolved into longer FM-oriented styles like heavy metal and progressive rock. Badfinger's crisp, well-crafted music was passé. They missed the wave that crested in the middle sixties and were too early for the next pop wave, typified by bands like the Cars and Squeeze, that hit in the late seventies.

The band recorded their third Apple LP in the midst of their grueling tour schedule only to have the record, produced by Geoff Emerick, rejected by the label. It looked like the project was going to die on the vine until Beatle George Harrison stepped in spring 1971 and offered to produce the album from scratch. During the sessions Harrison asked the band if he could play the lead guitar part on the song "Day After Day." To get the sound Harrison wanted he and Ham played the part in unison, live in the studio. The song went on to be Badfinger's third Top Ten single, reaching number four in the USA.

Halfway through the second attempt, sessions were interrupted when Harrison left to organize the concert for Bangla Desh. Badfinger was one of the groups that played the concert on August 1, 1971; Pete Ham accompanied Harrison on "Here Comes the Sun." Afterwards Harrison was busy producing the album *Concert for Bangla Desh* and had to bow out of any further work with Badfinger. A third producer, Todd Rundgren, was brought in to finish up the work. Opinion on Rundgren was mixed. One unnamed band member, quoted in *Mojo*, called Rundgren "very domineering, very egotistical," Mike Gibbins told Dennis Dalcin of *Audities* "I think Todd was the best producer." The album Rundgren-produced, *Straight Up*—with four tracks credited to Harrison—was one of Badfinger's finest LPs. It included classics like "Day After Day," "Baby Blue," "Suitcase," and "Name of the Game." The record also went one to be a sought-after collector's item. In the mid-1980s, the record collector's magazine, *Goldmine* polled its readers on which LPs they would most like to see released on CD and *Straight Up* topped the list, beating out even *Sgt Pepper* which had not yet been released on compact disk.

Despite their growing popularity, Badfinger were not living the easy life of the stereotypical rock star. Stan

Polley had them touring constantly. All band income went through his accounts and group members had to settle for a meager salary. "They had two hits on the charts and 'Baby Blue' on the way," Joey Molland's wife Kathie told Parke Puterbugh of *Rolling Stone*, "and we were living on packaged soup." Tom Evans admitted in *Mojo* "We were treated like kids when it came to money." Adding to the dissatisfaction was the unreliable old equipment Polley refused to let them replace. When Polley started looking for a more lucrative deal and started getting nibbles from Warner Brothers, Badfinger's days with Apple were numbered. They recorded one last Apple album, the critically-underrated *Ass*, that included later concert favorites like "Blind Owl" and "Timeless." The record was the last Apple recording by an artist other than one of the Beatles.

Signed with Warner Bros.

Polley meanwhile had signed the band with Warners, a contract that required the band crank out albums at the backbreaking pace of two albums a year for three years. It was the beginning of two years of grinding touring and recording. Their first Warners release, *Badfinger*, was released to the sound of resounding critical and popular silence. At the same time internal personal and financial disagreements—many of the same sort that helped destroy the Beatles—began tearing away at the band. same dissatisfaction was simmering in the band over Polley's handling of finances. Mike Gibbins walked out for a short time. Pete Ham left only to return when Warners said they would drop Badfinger if he were not in the band. And after the completion of *Wish You Were Here*, considered the band's masterpiece, Joey Molland quit and was replaced with keyboard player, Bob Jackson.

Wish You Were Here was released in 1974 to good reviews and was selling 25,000 copies a week when matters took an abrupt turn for the worse. Charging Polley's company, Badfinger Enterprises, with improper use of some hundreds of thousands of dollars in advance money, Warners pulled all copies of the record from stores. The label also rejected another nearly completed LP, tentatively entitled *Head First*. It has acquired the reputation of the great lost Badfinger album. Selections appeared for the first time on Rhino's 1992 *Best of Badfinger Vol. II*.

By 1975 the band was in dire straits. They were broke. No money was coming from Polley; Apple, nervous at the likelihood of getting pulled into the legal maelstrom, started paying the band's royalties into an escrow account. All but Pete Ham had grown increasingly mistrustful of Polley and wanted to get rid of him. Pete Ham felt himself in an untenable position: his band-mates resented him for his trust toward Stan Polley, his band's career was completely stalled, he was £2000 in debt, he had a mortgage to pay off, and his girlfriend was seven-months pregnant. On April 23rd, after a night of drinking with Tom Evans, he scribbled out a brief suicide note blaming everything on Stan Polley, and hanged himself in his garage.

The road seemed to be at an end for Badfinger. Polley and Warners eventually came to an agreement, but the band was left out in the cold. The remaining members went their separate ways. Gibbins returned to Wales, eventually playing drums on Bonnie Tyler's megahit "It's a Heartache.". Molland and Evans were back where they had started in the sixties, working day jobs as carpet layers or pipe insulators and playing music when they could. Molland formed a group called Natural Gas in Los Angeles; Evans joined The Dodgers in England. In 1978, Molland and Evans reformed Badfinger. They asked Gibbins to play with them, but the producer of their first LP refused to work with him. Evans and Molland recorded two albums together, *Airwaves* on Elektra in 1978 and their final original Badfinger LP, the aptly-titled *Say No More* on Radio Records in 1981. Both labels dropped the band unceremoniously. Molland toured as Badfinger for a short time, then Evans and Gibbins put together their own touring Badfinger which was well received but plagued by lack of money, crooked managers and bad planning. On November 18, 1983, lightening struck for the second time. Estranged from Molland and Gibbins by disputes over "Without You" royalties, and beset by his own money problems and ongoing depression over Pete Ham's death, Tom Evans hanged himself.

Interest in Badfinger continued through the 1980s despite the fact that their albums were only available in cut-out bins or second-hand. In 1989, *Rolling Stone* estimated that the group had sold some 14 million records worldwide. The 1990s saw a resurgence in fandom, stimulated by the release of a couple of greatest hits packages and most of the Apple catalog on CD. Molland continues to perform with a trio called Joey Molland's Badfinger. He occasionally releases an album under his own name. Chances of a Molland-Gibbins Badfinger reunion are slim. They toured together in the late 1980s but as a result of disputes over money and the band's recording legacy, the two have not spoken in nearly a decade. Each promotes his own view of the band's history. Gibbins cooperated with Dan Matovina in the writing of *Without You: The Tragic Story of Badfinger*, an encyclopedic history of the band. Molland has denounced the book and cooperated instead with Greg Katz' in the making of *Badfinger: The Documentary*. Both Gibbins and Molland are said to be writing their own histories of the group.

Selected discography

Albums

Magic Christian Music, Apple, December 16, 1970, reissued 1991.
No Dice, Apple, November 9, 1970, reissued 1992.
Straight Up, Apple, December 13, 1971, reissued 1993.
Ass, Apple, November 26, 1973, reissued 1996 (Great Britian).
Badfinger, Warner Brothers, February 1974, reissued 1991 (Germany/Japan).
Wish You Were Here, Warner Brothers, October 1974, reissued 1991 (Germany/Japan).
Airwaves, Elektra Records, March 1979.
Say No More, Radio Records, 1981.
The Best Of Badfinger, Vol II, Rhino Records, 1990.
The Best Of Badfinger, Apple/Capitol, May 1995.
After The Pearl (Joey Molland), Earthtone Records, 1983.
7 Park Avenue (Pete Ham), Rykodisc, 1997 .
A Place In Time (Mike Gibbins), Forbidden Records, 1998 .

Singles

"Come And Get It," Apple, 1970.
"No Matter What," Apple, 1971.
"Day After Day," Apple, 1972.

Sources

Books

Matovina, Dan, *Without You: The Tragic Story of Badfinger*, San Mateo, CA: Frances Glover Books, 1994 (available from 7 West 41st. Ave. #229, San Mateo, CA 94403-5105, USA. Phone and Fax: 650-508-9585.

Periodicals

Rolling Stone, August 10, 1989.
Mojo, April 1998.

Online

Dennis Dalcin, "Mike Gibbins Interview, ailable at http://audities/mag/interview/int_mgib.htm.
"Day After Day," available at http://www.scuzz.com/stardust/badfinger.html.
http://www.znet.com/~nutopia/discography.html.
http://members.aol.com/BADFINGER3/.

Album Notes

Straight Up, Capital, CDP 7 81403 2.
Day After Day, Rykodisc 10189.
Badfinger BBC In Concert, Strange Fruit SFRSCD 031.
Best of Badfinger, Capital.

Additional materials provided by Capital Records and Entertainment Services International.

—Gerald E. Brennan

Arthur Baker

Producer

Producer, remixer, and occasional musician Arthur Baker is probably known best to many as the person who put the remix artist to the fore but his influence upon modern popular music extends far beyond that. After creating the pioneering hip-hop single "Planet Rock" with rapper Afrika Bambaataa in the early 1980s, Baker continued to bring new dance artists to light, as well as remixing many already established acts. While behind the scenes work has always remained his forte, Baker orchestrated several albums under several names (Backbeat Disciples, Criminal Element Orchestra) which provide a fair overview of Baker's wide-reaching style. "I'd like to be known as one you can't categorize," Baker told High Fidelity's Crispin Cioe in 1985. "At first they pegged me as hip-hop, then they pegged me as the king of remixers. If I can bring my sound to a diversity of artists without changing theirs, I'll escape being pigeonholed. Then people will say, "He's different; he's a renegade.""

Born and raised in Boston, Massachusetts, Baker was a disc jockey in the 1970s, giving him his first taste of dance music, as well as an interest in production. Admiring the studio techniques of Thom Bell and Kenny Gamble-Leon Huff, two producers who helped create the Philadelphia (or "Philly") soul sound, Baker enrolled in several sound engineering courses in college. Baker soon adapted Gamble & Huff's innovations to his own liking, and produced a minor hit for the Boston act TJM.

However, Baker's wife Tina had a sudden career change in 1980, and the two moved to New York City, where Baker's own work would skyrocket.

Unable to sustain a living as a DJ in New York, Baker floundered for a brief period sweeping floors for a record distributor to make ends meet. However, the lively culture of New York nightclubs, most notably the Funhouse in Manhattan, offered Baker a myriad of ideas as well as connections with like-minded fans of dance music. As Baker told Cioe of the Funhouse, "[t]he energy there and at the Roxy [Theater] was so intense that you could predict the future just by showing up on a hot night." Indeed, many future dance stars would emerge from the Funhouse, including pop divas Madonna and Lisa Lisa, as well as Baker's protege John "Jellybean" Benitez. Along with Benitez, it was in this setting that Baker met Tom Silverman, president of the cutting-edge dance label Tommy Boy, who in turn introduced him to vocalist and DJ Afrika Bambaataa.

Baker, Bambaataa, and Silverman were all keenly aware of the currents of culturally diverse forms of dance music that melded together in the streets and parties of New York, and were anxious to commit such a marriage of sounds to record, resulting in the outfit Soulsonic Force. Starting with majestic synthesizer lines borrowed from the song "Trans-Europe Express" by the experimental German band Kraftwerk, and then overlaying them with the beats and rap vocals found in urban American dance music, Baker and Bambaataa in 1982 created "Planet Rock," generally acknowledged as a milestone in dance music which put Baker on the map. Although Baker had already released the single "Jazzy Sensation" with Bambaataa, it was "Planet Rock" that hooked the public at large and helped break the race barrier in hip-hop. "I think the important thing about all of this," Baker told Rolling Stone's Debby Miller in regard to the explosion of hip-hop, "is that this is the first meeting of black and white music in a long time that is really making any sense and meaning anything."

Baker followed up the critical and commercial success of the Soulsonic Force singles with a string of other hits, such as "Looking For The Perfect Beat" by Afrika Bambaataa and "Play At Your Own Risk" by Planet Patrol. Initially, Baker's work in what he called urban dance rhythms fared best in the U.K. and on U.S. dance charts, due to what Baker saw as pervasive racism in the American record business. However, by the end of 1983 Baker had become something of a celebrity within dance culture, with his portly, long-maned personage even appearing in the video for "Confusion" by the British synth act New Order, a cut that Baker produced and co-wrote. Word of Baker's talent for making dance

For the Record . . .

Born April 22, 1955, in Boston, MA; married to recording artist Tina B. *Education*— attended Hampshire College, in MA.

Started as a disc jockey in Boston during the 1970s; relocated to New York City in 1980, where he became a regular at the influential Funhouse nightclub; recorded "Planet Rock" with Soulsonic Force, 1982; launched Streetwise Records and Shakedown Studios, 1982; cowrote, produced, and appeared in the video for New Order's "Confusion," 1983; produced "Candy Girl" for New Edition," 1983; remixed Cyndi Lauper's "Girls Just Want To Have Fun," 1984; organized benefit outfit Artists United Against Apartheid with "Little Steven" Van Zandt, 1985; started Criminal Records label, 1986; released *Merge*, the first album with the Backbeat Disciples, 1988; released second Backbeat Disciples record, *Give In To The Rhythm*, 1992; continued with side project Criminal Element Orchestra, 1996.

Addresses: *Record company*—RCA, 1133 Avenue of the Americas, New York, NY 10036.

records spread, and he was tapped by high profile artists like singer Diana Ross to collaborate. Along with engineer and synth player John Robie, who had played on many of Baker's early pieces, the producer launched the independent dance label Streetwise, and found himself steadily at work in his own Shakedown Studios.

As Baker's credibility grew throughout the mid-1980s, so did the range of artists that invited him to produce or remix their music. Dance rhythms remained at the helm of his ongoing project as a technical innovator, but his resume of associates began to include artists from numerous backgrounds, including classic rockers like Bruce Springsteen and Jeff Beck, pop singers such as the New Wave inspired Cyndi Lauper, and the reggae group Black Uhuru. In addition, Baker continued to cultivate groups taking their first steps, such as the youthful R&B act New Edition and the group Freeeze, with whom Baker had the hits "Candy Girl" and "IOU," respectively. Whatever the status of the artists at hand, Baker and Robie were known for a high level of spontaneity, imagination, and personal involvement in the recording process. "I hate mixing records," Baker quipped to Miller in regard to his emotional ties with studio work. "I hate finishing a record. It's like watching your kid grow and then sending it out in the world."

In 1985, Baker went out on a professional limb by inaugurating a project to fight the kind of racism within the music industry that he had castigated all along. With the aid of "Little Steven" Van Zandt, an ex-member of Bruce Springsteen's E Street Band, Baker organized a virtual army of musicians under the banner Artists United Against Apartheid to attack the policy of racial segregation then endorsed by the white South African government. Specifically, Baker and Van Zandt called for musicians to boycott Sun City, a posh South African resort town that catered to rich white audiences. The resulting effort was the benefit single and album *Sun City,* delivered by many singers who had declined to play in South Africa, many of them already cohorts of Baker such as Bambaataa, Springsteen, the soul-tinged pop duo Hall and Oates, and singer Will Downing. Baker's intention of including a list of those who had repeatedly played Sun City in the single incited flak from record companies, and like many benefit projects, the release failed to sell to as many people as hoped for. Nevertheless, he saw it as a worthy effort. "We didn't do it to raise dollars," Baker told *Billboard* in August of 1985. "We were working to raise consciousness and as far as that goes, we were successful. The whole Sun City operation was exposed for the world to see."

For a brief period after *Sun City,* Baker kept a lower profile, due to the controversy of the Artists United project, as well as to other legal and personal problems Baker's label, Streetwise, had been subjected to a number of lawsuits over rights to the band New Edition, and the label was crushed as a result. In addition, Baker had only just recovered from a heavy drug habit that had compromised his creativity. "I was 100 pounds overweight, taking cocaine every night and a really heavy drinker," Baker told *Melody Maker*'s Alf Billingham several years later. "My experience is that if someone's high on cocaine than everything they say is gonna be a lie. It's either euphoria or depression, that's the truth." After relocating to the more receptive British shores, Baker was ready to re-establish himself.

In 1986, Baker was firmly back on his feet, and set up his new label Criminal Records. In addition, Baker returned to soundtrack production for the first time since the 1984 breakdancing film Beat Street with the successful Pretty in Pink and Something Wild albums. Mixing and production were of course still part of Baker's musical diet, including several hit records with longtime associates New Order, but he began to take seriously an offer extended to him by Epic Records, that of creating an album under his own name. Baker's strong interaction with most of his productions made such a prospect less than a debut in the strictest sense, but a tempting opportunity nonetheless.

It was not until 1989 that Baker's own record, *Merge,* was realized, after Epic scrapped his initial demo tape and was replaced by A&M as the label of distribution. Hardly a "solo" record, *Merge* featured a pot pourri of talent collected as the Backbeat Disciples, including 1970s soul legend Al Green, vocalist Martin Fry of the group ABC, and singer Jimmy Sommerville of Bronski Beat and the Communards. With Baker co-writing, producing, and even contributing drum beats to *Merge's* twelve cuts, he maintained a balance that impressed critics and dance fans alike. "Despite the horribly modern graphics and our natural aversion towards superstar collusions, *Merge* works brilliantly," raved Paul Lester, one of *Melody Maker's* most visible critics, "a portable compendium of potential monster hits that eschews the stylistic monomania of most dance albums while never succumbing to indecisive eclecticism." As usual, Baker's biggest audience was found in the U.K. and in clubs, and the album did not take off in American pop charts.

Despite the commercial floundering of *Merge,* the album's kaleidoscopic appetite helped a wide range of acts to continue to solicit Baker's recording mastery in the 1990s. As Baker told *Billboard's* David Nathan, "I didn't want to make a gimmicky album. It would have been easy just to do a house oriented album but I wanted to stay true to myself. Although a lot of industry people have seen me as being simply dance oriented, I've always had more diverse tastes." Nevertheless, dance mixes remained to be seen as Baker's specialty and veterans like ex-Blondie chanteuse Debby Harry and chameleonic singer David Bowie were among the many who put Baker at the helm of their club-oriented releases.

By the time Baker assembled a new incarnation of the Backbeat Disciples in 1992, dance music had begun to grasp a toe-hold in the American mainstream market, partially helped by the barrier-breaking trend of the so-called "alternative" market, and few could deny Baker's influence in the growth of such popularity. However, upon the release of *Give In To The Rhythm,* the second Disciples album, some critics felt that Baker had fallen behind, and lacked the freshness offered by his younger dance contemporaries. "It would be unremarkable and inoffensive if it wasn't so presumptuous," *Melody*

Maker's David Bennun wrote of the album in February of 1992. "The clubs where you're likely to hear this kind of glossed-over neo-house all night exist only in TV dramas about divorcees made by clueless directors who once heard a [1970s disco singer] Donna Summer record."

Despite such biting criticism, Baker was forgiven in most quarters, although the lack of hits on both Backbeat Disciples records created the general impression that Baker was at his height interpreting the music of others. By the mid-1990s, the legacy of Baker's contributions to hip hop and dance music over the previous decade began to surface on a slew of compilation albums such as the series Club Classics and Old School Jams. In the meantime, Baker continued to sponsor unknown acts such as Nation of Abel and Brooklyn Funk Essentials, as well as dabbling with his own side project Criminal Element Orchestra, proving that he was still willing to take chances in the creation of vital new music. "Of course, it would be nice to sit on a perch and enjoy all of the riches in life," Baker mused to *Billboard's* Larry Flick in 1994. "But so many people in the business have a short memory. You've got to keep on pushing and hustling. It can be a real drag sometimes, but if you really love what you're doing, it's worth the work. And at this point, I still really love what I do."

Selected discography

As producer or remixer:

(Soulsonic Force), "Planet Rock," Streetwise, 1982.
(Afrika Bambaataa), "Looking For The Perfect Beat," Streetwise, 1983.
(Planet Patrol), "Play At Your Own Risk," Streetwise, 1983.
(New Edition), "Candy Girl," Streetwise (original release), 1983.
(New Order), "Confusion," Factory/Qwest, 1983.
(Cyndi Lauper), "Girls Just Want To Have Fun," Portrait, 1984.
(Bruce Springsteen), "Dancin In The Dark," Columbia, 1985.
(Artists United Against Apartheid), "Sun City," Manhattan, 1985.
(Black Uhuru), "Brutal," 1986.
(New Order), "Blue Monday 1988," Factory/Qwest, 1988.
(David Bowie), "Fame 90," RCA, 1990.
(Pet Shop Boys), "Paninaro '95," EMI, 1995.
(Criminal Element Orchestra), "Go Around," Fourth & Broadway, 1996.
(Secret Knowledge), "Kris Needs Must!," 1997.

Arthur Baker and The Backbeat Disciples:

Merge, A&M, 1989.
Give In To The Rhythm, RCA, 1992.

Sources

Billboard, July 27, 1985;August 24, 1985; August 16, 1986; November 18, 1989; March 27, 1993; July 9, 1994.
High Fidelity, April 1985.
Melody Maker, March 26, 1988; August 5, 1989; August 26, 1989; February 29, 1992; March 7, 1992; October 19, 1996.
Musician, May 1985.
Rolling Stone, October 13, 1983.
Village Voice, January 25, 1983; January 1, 1985.

—Sean Frentner

Roosevelt Barnes

Blues guitarist, harmonica player

© Jack Vartoogian. Reproduced by permission.

The fact that the last show Roosevelt "Booba" Barnes played before his death in 1994 was at the Rock and Roll Hall of Fame in Cleveland probably suited him just fine. A Delta bluesman through and through, Barnes' guitar and vocal style has been likened to that of his musical idol, Howlin' Wolf. His on-stage acrobatic antics garnered him notoriety—he was known for leaping and duckwalking about the stage and playing his guitar between his legs, behind his head and with his teeth. He spent most of his life in the blues clubs of Mississippi and Chicago but toured the United States and Europe to great reviews. The critical reviews of his one and only full-length release, *The Heartbroken Man*, indicated Barnes had the makings of a full-blown blues star but a reputation for being a money wangler, and his open, bitter criticism of fellow blues workers earned him a good number of important enemies. His somewhat extravagant lifestyle—he sported flashy clothes, yet drove a ratty, old van—drained whatever financial successes he happened upon as a blues player. His musicianship didn't suffer any from his private affairs, though, and he continued to wow audiences in this country and abroad until shortly before he died.

Roosevelt Melvin Barnes was born September 25, 1936, in Longwood, Mississippi. He had visions of stardom the first time he slid his lips across a toy harmonica at age seven. Barnes received gifts of harmonicas from his brother Frank and, while learning to play the instrument, began performing for plantation owners and fellow sharecroppers. Considering the on-stage shenanigans, singular musical skills and showmanship he became known for, he must have been a spectacle even then. He mimicked what he heard on local radio station KKFA's King Biscuit show—which exposed him to the likes of Sonny Boy Williamson (Rice Miller)—and from locals like harp player Houston Boines and slide guitarist Boyd Gilmore. He quickly mastered them enough to earn street tips in nearby Greenville, Mississippi. Over the years, he picked up the nickname "Booba" from a brother who'd worked with booby traps in the Army. Barnes himself dropped the "y" for an "a."

Still in his early teens, Barnes was earning money by hustling on Nelson Street—a Greenville pass known for its rough trade and blues activity—and catching and selling fish, when he wasn't collecting 78 rpm records of blues legend Howlin' Wolf. Barnes idolized Wolf. He was ecstatic when Wolf made a stop in a local club in 1951 and invited Barnes not only to load in the band's gear, but to sit in on the set, as well. Barnes continued throughout his career to emulate Wolf in many ways. From his gravely voice to his sexually suggestive use of the microphone on-stage, Barnes possibly proved to be Wolf's greatest disciple. Barnes knew it and was proud.

Born Roosevelt Melvin Barnes September 25, 1936, Longwood, MS; died April 3, 1996, Chicago, IL; ten children.

Started playing harmonica for fellow sharecroppers and plantation owners at age 7; joined Jones Brothers at age 17; learned guitar, 1960; formed his own band the Playboys, 1957-58; moved to Chicago, 1963; returned to Greenville, MS, 1971; opened Barnes' Playboy Club in Mississippi, 1982; appeared on soundtrack *Mississippi Blues,* 1982; released his only record, *The Heartbroken Man,* 1990, Rooster Blues ; relocated to Chicago in 1990; recorded for soundtrack *Deep Blues,* 1992; continued touring almost until his death of lung cancer in 1996.

As he boasted to *Guitar Player* in a 1994 interview, "They say I sound more like Wolf than Wolf did." And Howlin' Wolf became fond of young Barnes, too, calling him "Little Wolf." Barnes also was mentored by another of his idols, harmonica player Charley Booker, and often went to Greenville gigs with him.

Barnes—who was already a popular juke joint harp player at age 17— joined his brother-in-law Little Jerry Jones' band, the Jones Brothers. The band ended up being the house band for five years at Leroy Grayson's gritty "shack in the woods," which all the blues giants of the time—Earl Hooker, Elmore James, Junior Parker, and Guitar Slim, among others—flocked to. Barnes reminisced about Grayson's place in the liner notes for *The Heartbroken Man.* "Drinkin' that corn whiskey and gamblin'," he remembers. "A lot of people from Arkansas come there and wouldn't leave. They'd come on Friday and stay till Sunday morning." Being in an established band also got him performing around more of Mississippi and Arkansas. In 1957-58, Barnes formed his own three-piece with drummer John Parker and guitarist Essie B. Cooper, and made the rounds in the Greenville clubs. He didn't start playing guitar until he was in his mid-twenties, in 1960.

Chicago vs. Home Sweet Mississippi

Howlin' Wolf's success weighed so heavily on Barnes' vision of blues greatness that, in 1958, he left Mississippi for the big city blues tradition of Chicago, Illinois.

Over the next decades, Barnes flitted between the stardom he was searching for in the Windy City and homesickness for his Mississippi Delta. In 1971, he made a long-term move back to Greenville. Chicago wasn't as good to Barnes as it had been to Wolf, who'd ruled the Chicago blues scene. In a profile written after his death by the man who may have tolerated and believed in Barnes most, Rooster Blues' Jim O'Neal, "He never attained top-drawer status…. Had he stayed in Mississippi he probably could have remained king of the Delta juke joints," he wrote for *Living Blues* in the March/April 1997 issue. O'Neal goes on to note that blues fans search Mississippi for the Playboy Club, and though he'd been a subject of great interest to several documentarians down south, they had no desire to follow him to Chicago.

Back in Greenville, Barnes did reign over Nelson Street again. He played with all of the street bluesfolk—one at a time or all in the same band—including John Price, T-Model Ford, Frank Frost, and Otis Taylor. He was a regular at all the Greenville haunts, but it was a bartending musician job he had at the Flowing Fountain that inspired him to do his own thing. As quoted on his liner notes, "If I can do it for him, I can do it for myself," he decided. So in 1982, in an old furniture store at 928 Nelson Street, Barnes' Playboy Club was born.

If Barnes was king of Nelson Street, the Playboy Club was his throne. He owned the club every day, but he ruled Friday and Saturday nights there. He also lived—with his family—in the back of the club. French documentarian, Bertrand Tavernier and his film crew tracked Barnes down for a live performance in 1982, and three tracks were released on the film's soundtrack, *Mississippi Blues.* The French crew was just the first of a slew of media who came in search of the Delta great, but their enthusiasm for his way of life couldn't keep his attention—he needed to go back to Chicago. He felt this time would be different, that he would be treated as his fame accorded up north, and that he'd be all right because he'd be doing what he loved. So after the release in 1990 of his first and only full-length record, *The Heartbroken Man,* on Rooster Blues, Barnes closed the Playboy Club and left Greenville for Chicago again. As cited in O'Neal's '97 story, Barnes told Joe Atkins of the Jackson *Clarion-Ledger* that this time, Chicago would receive him "as the person I am. A star. That's what I am."

Bad Attitude

Having just released his big record, Barnes was at a crest. He toured heavily to all the major American blues festivals—the Mississippi Valley Blues Festival, the Ann Arbor Blues Festival and New Orleans JazzFest. He performed outrageously in B.B. King's in Memphis, Buddy Guy's Legends in Chicago, and Manny's Car Wash in New York City. He toured Europe and received nothing but praise. One tired British journalist for *R&B Juke Blues,* in London, wrote that, once Barnes got on stage, "he proceeds to bounce off the walls! … I am totally exhausted, and he's only played one number. We are treated to an hour of this … and then he reappears in a white suit for another hour's worth." His wild look, with his frizzy hair, iridescent suits and sequins, did the trick. His penchant for extreme showmanship endeared him to crowds, even if his sales of his autograph put them off a bit.

He tested his star power back in Chicago, though, and it didn't turn out in his favor. After a number of on-stage snubs to long-time friends and fellow musicians, sneaky deals with promoters and producers, and stories of his armed solution to arguments, his old buddy, Delta veteran T-Model Ford worked the word on the street— Booba'd gone to Chicago and lost his mind. Barnes' notoriety finally got the best of his band, who'd backed him all the way, and they left Chicago for Greenville in the early 1990s. The Playboys' departure left Barnes without a band that shared his down-home passion for the gritty Delta blues.

Booba Called It Quits

The second time around, *The Heartbroken Man* defied any boundaries imposed on it by genre. Re-issued in 1995, the record garnered more widespread approval, with reviews reaching beyond the blues community. Of course all the blues publications gave it resounding approval, but it even earned notice in *Option,* a hip, lifestyle magazine targeted at club and dj culture. The critique in the November-December 1995 issue began, "Some blues can be so boring." The writer continued, "… this disc gets me jumping and shouting…. This band kicks music out with no apologies and plenty of grit. Nothing fancy, just mean, physical blues." Out of the mouths of young blues fans, and Booba Barnes has a new generation of fans.

After being diagnosed with lung cancer, Barnes still continued to perform live. His last live show was in February of 1996 at the Rock 'n' Roll Hall of Fame for an educational program about the blues and rock's black roots. Roosevelt Melvin "Booba" Barnes died Wednesday, April 3, 1996 at a Chicago nursing home. He told a reporter from the *Philadelphia Inquirer,* a few months before his death, "You think of somethin' and put it in there, I'm a bad man, it'll be true." Although he spent his life pleasing crowds, his funeral was sparsely attended by members of the blues community.

Selected discography

"How Many Years Must This Go On" b/w "Going Back Home," Rooster Blues, 1987.
Deep Blues (soundtrack), Anxious/Atlantic Records, 1992.
The Heartbroken Man, Rooster Blues/Rounder Records, 1990, reissued, 1995
Mississippi Blues (soundtrack), Milan Records, 1982.

Sources

Periodicals

Guitar Player, July 1994, p.24;August 1996, p. 24.
Living Blues, March-April 1994, p. 72.
New York Times, 1994.
Option, November-December 1995.
Philadelphia Inquirer, January 5, 1996.
R&B Juke Blues Magazine, 1994.
South Blues Rag, June 1996.

Online

www.rounder.com
rockhall.com
www.bluespeak.com
www.jp.jazzcentralstation.com

Additional information for this profile was taken from liner notes by Jim O'Neal, *The Heartbroken Man*, and from Rooster Records publicity materials, 1998.

—Brenna Sanchez

Beat Farmers

Rock band

From their beginnings in San Diego 1983 until the untimely death of founder Country Dick Montana in 1995, the band would pack local Sand Diego watering holes with punkers, bikers, country fans, and rock and rollers. They became a cultural phenomanon with a huge following even though their albums never got any air play or support from the record companies. Formed tightly around the abilities and antics of front man Country Dick Montana, the band had a reputation for being serious party animals. Punk music was just waiting to grab hold on society and country music was also experiencing a rebirth. The Beat Farmers were able to appease both audiences melding all these different sounds, sometimes referred to as cow-punk.

The Beat Framers began when front man Montana, or as known in high school as Dan McLain, took a break from the band The Penetrators. Always getting into problems in high school, Montana was just as well-known for his musical talents as his loud mouth. Voted San Diego's top band, The Penetrators had a glorious following there. During time off between recording, McLain formed Country Dick and the Snugglebunnies.

The stage show, which hadn't changed much from the beginning, usually consisted of Montana taking regular swigs of beer while pounding out a crowd pumping song on his drums. Occasionally, he would emerge from behind his drums and entertain the audience with his accordion, or his deep voice. According to Kevin Ranson in the *Detroit News,* Country Dick had a talent for "scatological lyrics, cheerful vulgarity and booming bullfrog vocals." He loved to entertain, pull practical jokes and put on a show. Some say he formed the band just to be able to throw a party every night. According to Howard Owens at the Country Dick Montana memorial web site, "A Beat Farmers show was a party and the party always started early for Country Dick. He showed up at gigs before the sound check, arriving with the road crew. While the rest of the band lounged at the motel, Country did was drinking and joking around with fans. He signed autographs, posed for pictures, remembered birthdays and faces. He drank and laughed and hugged old acquaintances."

But it wasn't just his stage presence that brought people to see the show. The Beat Farmers had talent. They took turns playing different instruments throughout the show. They also took a lead from Country Dick and took on pseudonyms. Joey Harris became Dick Everly and played guitar, wrote lyrics and sang; Jerry Raney, became Shameful Dick, who also sang and played the drums and guitar. Other members included Paul Kamanski as Everly Dick and Buddy Blue, a slide guitarist. Blue eventually left the Beat Farmers and had some solo success. The musicians were inspired by bands like the Kinks, the Byrds, the Sex Pistols, the Clash and the Ramones. Montana was so influenced by the Kinks that early in his music career, he became president of the Kinks Preservation Society. As the Beat Farmers began listening to performers like Elvis Presley, Hank Williams, and Randy Newman, they began to blend country rock and rockabilly into their songs.

In 1984, the Beat Farmers officially became San Diego's favorite band, as decided in a Battle of the Bands. The Beat Farmers began playing larger and larger clubs. Their original haunt, Spring Valley Inn, in el Centro, California, was just too small to fit their growing number of fans. They opened for Los Lobos and began talking with Rhino Records about a recording contract. With the album *Tales of the New West* released in 1985, the band was ready for an extended tour. After releasing two albums with Rhino Records, the band moved to Curb Records and recorded four more albums, including a live album and a greatest hits collection. Their first album with Curb was *Van Go,* and according to a review in *Melody Maker,* "The unusual thing about the Beat Farmers is that they sound as if they actually did have a damned good time in the studio making this album." While the singles never received much air play and sold poorly, the albums were considered a critical success, along the lines of Frank Zappa. All the while, the Beat Farmers constantly packed larger and larger bar clubs.

For the Record . . .

Members include **Buddy Blue**, guitar; **Joey Harris**, (Dick Everly), guitar and vocals; **Paul Kamanski**, (Everly Dick); **Rollie Love**, bass; **Country Dick Montana** (1955-1995), drum, vocals; **Jerry Raney**, (Shameful Dick), guitar, drum, vocals.

Group formed in 1983. Released debut album *Tales of the New West*, 1985; *Glad N' Greasy*, 1985, (originally released as EP on Demon Records in the U.K.); *Van Go*, 1986; *The Pursuit of Happiness*, 1987; *Poor and Famous*, 1989; *Loud and Plowed and ... Live*, 1990, *Greatest Hits*, 1995; and *Viking Lullaby*, 1994.

Address:*Record company*— Curb Records 3907 West Alameda, Burbank, CA. 91505. *Fan Club*—D PO Box 2128 El Cajon, CA 92021.

"The Beat Farmers could pack any bar in the world, but he couldn't crack *Billboard*'s Hot 100," mentioned a website dedicated to the Beat Farmers.

The band toured England in 1985 and recorded the EP *Glad and Greasy* for the British label Demon. In 1986, the Beat Farmers found themselves opening for Elvis Costello in Belgium. A year later, they released *The Pursuit of Happiness* on Curb. The album included the song "Make It Last," which nearly received country readio airplay, but upon hearing the rest of the album, radio station executives decided it really didn't fit in with a country format. The Beat Farmers decided to retour Europe, where they had enjoyed good support. The end of the tour almost came in 1990 when Montana was diagnosed with thyroid cancer. While undergoing surgery and treatments for the disease, the Beat Farmers continued to amuse audiences, even though people warned Montana to take it easy. But he was a musician that couldn't rest. Montana began playing and recording with cow-punk prankster, Mojo Nixon, and anyone else who wanted to play. He also continued his heavy drinking.

It was soon after the surgery that the Beat Farmers received a high compliment from then King of Late Night David Letterman. One night he told Paul Schaefer he wanted to quit the *Late Show* so he could go on the road with the Beat Farmers. In 1994, the band signed to a new record company, Sector 2 Sector. They had not been in a recording studio for almost 10 years and the result, *Viking Lullabys,* according to a website, "was critically acclaimed but failed to sell." The last album the band recorded together was *Manifold,* and it was released just before the Canadian tour that took Montana's life. Country Dick Montana died on stage, playing his drums. At the age of 40, he left behind many fans, followers, some albums to be proud of and numerous unpaid beer tabs across the world. The people that saw a live show were changed forever. While never experiencing true pop stardom, the Beat Farmers rarely had to worry about having fun.

Selected discography

Tales of the New West, Rhino, 1985.
Glad N' Greasy, Rhino, 1985.
Van Go, Curb, 1986.
The Pursuit of Happiness, Curb, 1987.
Poor and Famous, Curb, 1989.
Loud and Plowed and ... Live, Curb, 1990.
Viking Lullabys, Sector 2 Sector, 1994.
Greatest Hits, Curb, 1995.

Sources

Periodicals

Detroit News, September 27, 1991.
Melody Maker, July 20, 1985; July 19, 1986.
Rolling Stone, May 23, 1985.

Online

http://www.bblink.com/usr/lib/X11/Mosaic/farmhand.html.
hhtp://www.hbo3.com/dick/.
http://www.sdam.com/artists/bt.

—*Gretchen Monette*

Bevis Frond

Rock group

The Bevis Frond have been playing their own distinctive style of rock music for over a decade. Its leader, Nick Saloman, began performing thirty years ago as a guitarist in cover bands during the mid-1960s in Swingin' London. In 1980, Saloman released a ninety minute cassette to a few friends of himself playing original material under the alias The Bevis Frond. The Frond's music is at times blisteringly psychedelic, other times pastoral and folk-influenced. His Woronzow label has become a cottage industry of independently produced rock, releasing albums appreciated by an expanding following.

Nick Saloman recalls his musical influences, "My earliest musical memories begin with my Mum playing the piano to me-she is a fine pianist.... I got into The Shadows and started playing guitar when I was seven. [The first concert I saw] was Frankie Vaughan in 1958-my Mum also took me to see The Beatles for my tenth Christmas present! Then as I got into my teens I started getting really interested in the psychedelic rock scene. I started going to small clubs in 1968 and more or less saw all the bands of that time onwards. I got my first band together at this time and called it The Bevis Frond Museum, playing covers of Jimi Hendrix, Cream, and Country Joe and The Fish."

For the next decade, Saloman was a member of numerous commercially unsuccessful bands. By 1980, fed up with the lack of support his band's, The Von Trap Family, demo received, Saloman founded the Woronzow label to release a single. Two years later, a motorcycle accident almost crippled one of his arms; Nick purchased a home recording studio with the resulting insurance settlement money.

While working as a record dealer, Saloman became close friends with writer Phil McMullen; the two frequently exchanged tapes of favorite obscurities. McMullen recalled in *Magnet,* "One of the tapes had this mystery track at the end, I couldn't guess who it was, and he said, 'Oh, that's me.'" McMullen and other friends who heard his demos urged Saloman to release an album. The resulting *Miasma,* released in 1987 under the resurrected name Bevis Frond, quickly sold out a pressing of 500; it was followed by *Inner Marshland, Triptych,* and a collection of out takes entitled *Bevis Through the Looking Glass.*

Nick Saloman came upon the Bevis Frond's sound by accident. He explained to *The Boston Phoenix,* "When you're [as old as I was at the time] and you've never gotten anywhere, you kind of think that you've had it. So I just started doing self-indulgent stuff on my own without worrying about things like getting a record deal. I honestly didn't think anyone would care. But lo and behold, people were interested, and it changed my life."

After several albums of extended, spacey jams, Bevis Frond's 1989 album *Any Gas Faster* featured more concise songs and fewer guitar solos. "I've done a lot of albums with 20-minute guitar solos, so I don't have anything to prove there.... I became interested in the idea that bands like The Stones, The Who, and The Move could be both chart and head bands, writing hit singles and good music," he told *Option* about The Bevis Frond's new direction.

In 1989, Saloman and Phil McMullen founded a music magazine, *The Ptolemaic Terrascope.* Its focus was simple, according to Saloman in *Magnet,* "Most magazines seemed one-dimensional. It didn't matter if the people we wrote about were up-and-coming or past it. We just decided to write about what we liked."

The Bevis Frond released a watershed double album in 1991, *New River Head.* The album covered Bevis's musical terrain brilliantly, from the jazzy freakout "White Sun," to the folky "Waving." Other highlights include the straight ahead pop-rock of the title track, the garage-rock raveup "Undertaker," and the rollicking "Wild Jack Hammer," based loosely on Mick Jagger. By the mid

For the Record . . .

Members include **Cyke Bancroft** (band member c. 1986-91), saxophone; **Dominic Colletti** (band member c. 1987-90), bass; **Martin Crowley** (band member c. 1986-1991), drums; **Graham Cumming** (band member c. 1987), organ; **Ric Gunther** (band member c. 1990-94); **Nick Saloman** (born March 11, 1953, London, founder), son of Joanna (a teacher and author) and Walter Saloman (a banker and enlistee in the Royal Air Force), married Janet Saloman, has a daughter, Debbie; guitars, keyboards, vocals; **Adrian Shaw** (joined band c. 1990), bass, vocals; **Andy Ward** (born September 28, 1952, London; band member c. 1994-98), drums; **Bari Watts** (bandmember c. 1990-94), guitar.

Formed c. 1985 in London, England; released debut album *Miasma* on own Woronzow label, 1987; signed American distribution deal with Reckless Records, 1988; headlined Terrastock Festival, Providence, RI, 1997; appeared on Mary Lou Lord, *Got No Shadow*, Work/Sony Records, 1997; headlined Terrastock West Festival, San Francisco, 1998.

Addresses: *Record company*—Flydaddy Records, P. O. Box 545, Newport, RI 02840. *Website*—www.terrascope.org.

1990s, The Bevis Frond became too popular to remain a studio-only band, and a touring line-up solidified with former Hawkwind bassist Adrian Shaw and ex-Camel drummer Andy Ward.

In 1997, *The Ptolemaic Terrascope* announced that it was in financial trouble. Dozens of artists, including The Bevis Frond, created two benefit CD collections, *Succour* and *Alms*. Several bands then offered the proceeds of a concert in Providence, Rhode Island, to support the publication. According to McMullen, "It seemed like a good opportunity to bring The Bevis Frond over for an American debut and perhaps turn the gig into more of an 'event.'" The Terrastock Festival featured an eclectic lineup, from 1960s heroes to current cutting edge bands. The festival was such a success that another was held in San Francisco in 1998. Between Terrastock events, The Bevis Frond released two excellent albums, *Son of Walter* and *North Circular,* and

Saloman collaborated with Mary Lou Lord on her *Got No Shadow* album.

Saloman recently commented about his involvement with various rock music since the 1960s, "The major difference between [the psychedelic] scene and now is that music has become ... compartmentalized. In 1969 you could see Black Sabbath supported by [folk rockers] Fairport Convention and [psychedelic jazz band] The Soft Machine ... and it seemed really natural." He continues, "I think the [1970s] progressive era was basically psychedelic musicians making lots of money and getting all the drugs and equipment they could ... [and] show how brilliantly they could play.... Punk was a very welcome and necessary reaction to that, but ... I was dismayed that it became really unfashionable to play an instrument properly. I'm afraid that attitude prevails in England to this day."

With The Bevis Frond, Nick Saloman entertains fans worldwide while retaining full control of his music. He proudly asserts, "I will never sign a major label deal unless they give me huge amounts of money ... everyone's a hypocrite if the price is right!"

Selected discography

Miasma, Woronzow, 1987.
Inner Marshland, Woronzow, 1987.
Bevis Through The Looking Glass, Woronzow, 1987.
Tryptych, Woronzow, 1988.
The Auntie Winnie Album, Reckless, 1988.
New River Head, Woronzow, 1991.
A Gathering of Fronds, Reckless, 1991.
London Stone, Woronzow, 1992.
Sprawl, Woronzow, 1994.
Superseeder, Woronzow, 1995.
Son of Walter, Flydaddy, 1996.

Sources

Boston Phoenix, April 18, 1997.
Bucketfull of Brains, May/June, 1989; Winter, 1990.
Guitar Player, February, 1997.
Magnet, February/March, 1997.
Option, January/February, 1990.
Ptolemaic Terrascope Terrastock Special Edition, December, 1997.

Additional information was obtained from an interview with Nick Saloman.

—*Jim Powers*

Big Mountain

Reggae band

Archive Photos, Inc. Reproduced by permission.

In the 1990s, Big Mountain had two self-imposed challenges. Philosophically, they wanted to spread their positive messages of "One World/One People" peace and harmony throughout the world. Musically, they sought a balance between commercial success and their reggae roots. Their 1994 hit "Baby, I Love Your Way" garnered international success, but also resulted in some criticism among reggae fans and critics. After the wave of popularity began to recede, Big Mountain focused on more of a balance in their career. "The bottom line is we all see a real serious voice in the way people deal with each other socially," singer Quino told Lee O'Neill in *Reggae Report.* "Reggae people are conscious people. I see reggae as being a rallying cry for this new time."

Growning up in San Diego, California, Quino was exposed to the various Latin American musical styles. At the age of 13, he saw reggae legend Bob Marley on the television news program *60 Minutes,* and his love for reggae was born. In 1986, Quino joined a reggae band called Shiloh, who would release their debut album three years later. By 1992, the members had changed their name to Big Mountain, which was inspired by a mountain peak on a Navajo reservation in Arizona.

During that same year, they released their first album *Wake Up* on Quality Records. Their single, "Touch My Light," reached 46 on *Billboard*'s pop charts, an unusual accomplishment for an unknown reggae band. From the beginning, Big Mountain was plagued by several line-up changes. At one point the group went through four guitarists in one month before settling on Jamaican guitarist Tony Chin. Chin's reggae roots were unquestioned, as he was a founding member of one of reggae's most sought after backing bands, Soul Syndicate. He also had stints with the Peter Tosh band, as well.

With the new line-up in place, Big Mountain performed on the 1993 Reggae Sunsplash USA tour. Quino told *Reggae Report* that the tour was like "jumping off a cliff and hoping to fly." Big Mountain jumped right back in the studio the following year, but encountered some difficulties. Having ran out of money before the record was complete, their crew decided to pack up and go home. Their savior came in the form of Ron Fair, executive producer for the movie *Reality Bites.* Fair asked the band if they would be interested in recording a reggae version of Peter Frampton's hit "Baby I Love Your Way" for the film. Sensing that the knock on the door was indeed opportunity, the band recruited saxophonist Warren Hill to contribute, and launched an international number one hit. The success of "Baby I Love Your Way" allowed them to finish their next album, *Unity,* and release it on Warner Bros. Records before the

Members include **Kevin Batchelor**, horns; **Tony Chin**, guitar; **Santa Davis**, drums; **Michael Hyde**, keyboards; **Jerry Johnson**, horns; **James McWhinney**, percussion/vocals; **Joaquin McWhinney** ("Quino") vocals; **William Shively**, bass; **Billy "Bones" Stoll**, keyboards.

Band formed as Shiloh, 1986; changed their name to Big Mountain and released their debut *Wake Up* on Quality Records, 1992; released hit single "Baby I Love Your Way" on the *Reality Bites* soundtrack, 1994; signed to Warner Bros. Records, 1994; released *Resistance*, 1996; released *Free Up* on Giant Records, 1997.

Addresses: *Record company*—Giant Records, 729 Seventh Ave, 12th Floor, New York, NY 10019.

end of the year. With new found notoriety, Big Mountain was able to tour the world in support of the album with stints in Europe, Japan, South America, and Jamaica, where they played the original incarnation of the Reggae Sunsplash.

By 1995, Big Mountain had reached a crossroads in their career. "There wasn't enough straight-ahead roots (on *Unity*), and it's important to let people know we're a reggae band," Quino told *Reggae Report*. They decided to let go of the demands of success and popularity and stick with their deep reggae influences and the core reggae audience. "We're still balancing how much we're willing to sacrifice to gain exposure," Quino told Peter Cronin in *Billboard,* "but everyone involved has been respectful of the fact that we are a reggae band."

Later that year, veteran drummer Santa Davis joined the band. Davis grew up in Kingston, Jamaica, where he developed his talent in a youth Drum Corp. He began performing as a professional drummer in the mid-1960s, and went on to play with such reggae legends such as Wailing Souls, Soul Syndicate, Bob Marley, Jimmy Cliff, Andrew Tosh, and Peter Tosh. Davis confessed to O'Neill in *Reggae Report* how joining Big Mountain infused his playing with fresh inspiration. "This is the best thing that's happened to me in a while," said Davis. "They're young and open to new ideas it's like working on a whole new level."

Davis was the perfect catalyst for the band's redefined focus on their next release, *Resistance*. The album opens with the track "Hooligans," a song about the violence among inner city youth. Big Mountain's 1996 world tour included stops in Brazil, where reggae was gaining popularity. "We went to Brazil three times in 1996," Quino said in the band's record company bio. "It's like a gold rush, sooner or later every reggae band finds out about it. Not every nation is on the same cycle with reggae. Sometimes it's big in one place and not in another, but it's always burning hot somewhere."
Big Mountain recruited two new members in 1997, keyboardist Michael Hyde and bass player William Shively. As the band returned to the studio, they sought to continue the momentum they started on *Resistance*. "We wanted to put together a record that would establish us as a driving force behind reggae music in America," Quino said in the band's bio. They achieved their goal of balance with their next release *Free Up*. They continued their revolutionary philosophy, but also added a love song and two cover tunes to the mix—Al Green's "Let's Stay Together" and Gary Wright's "Dream Weaver."

With Big Mountain standing firmly on the reggae high road, Quino told O'Neill in *Reggae Report* that the band never regretted the path they had chosen. "Looking back, when you have a worldwide hit, people think, This is easy," said Quino. "You're riding high and feeling [good]. Then, you release three singles that basically flop. It's a trip the way you learn your business. Things had to happen the way they did."

Selected discography

Wake Up, Quality Records, 1992.
(Contributor) *Reality Bites* (soundtrack), BMG/RCA, 1994.
Unity, Warner Bros. Records, 1994.
Resistance, Warner Bros. Records, 1996.
Free Up, Warner Bros. Records, 1997.

Sources

Periodicals

Billboard, April 16, 1994.
Entertainment Weekly, July 29, 1994.
Reggae Report, Volume 14, Number 5.

Online

"Big Mountain, New Album, New Lineup, New Tour," *Reggae Report,* http://www.bigmountain-onelove.com.

Additional information was provided by Giant/Warner Bros. publicity materials, 1997.

—*Sonya Shelton*

Blackstreet

R&B group

Before launching his own project, Blackstreet's Teddy "Street" Riley had already established himself as a producer for some of the biggest names in R&B and rap, such as Kool Moe Dee and Bobby Brown. In 1993, Riley and Chauncey "Black" Hannibal formed the quartet Blackstreet, melding the elements of hip hop and classic R&B crooning that Riley had handled with finesse in the studio control room. After the commercially successful debut *Blackstreet* was released in 1994, half of the group departed. Unflustered, Riley and Hannibal drafted two replacement members and cut their follow-up album *Another Level* in 1996, which surpassed the strength of their debut.

New York City native Riley began his career as a teenager in 1984, working behind the scenes with a multitude of performers. In addition to producing and re-mixing, Riley often lent his vocal talents to acts such as the middle of the road balladeer Billy Ocean, ex-New Edition vocalist Bobby Brown, and the audacious rap outfit Wrecks-N-Effect. Riley's credibility stemmed from more than reliable craftsmanship, as his collective work, though diverse, belies a coherent style. By the end of the decade, Riley had become one of the principle founders of "New Jack Swing," a hybrid of R&B, hip hop, and rap noted for its smooth flavor and danceable grooves.

In 1988, Riley first tried his hand as a full-fledged performer as a backup vocalist in the group Guy, a trio that in turn became major players in the New Jack Swing school. With albums such as their self-titled debut and its 1990 sequel *Future,* Guy became a strong influence upon the next wave of R&B vocal acts like Boyz II Men and Jodeci. However, friction between lead vocalist Guy and Riley snowballed into a bitter breakup in 1992, although rumors of a reunion plagued Riley for years. Despite the band's commercial success, Riley later looked back on Guy with less than fond memories. "I feel now that Guy was there for the money, rather than the music, although I didn't know it at the time," Riley told Tony Farsides at *Dotmusic* online.

Along with bolstering Riley's resume, Guy's career also crossed the paths of Riley and writer/producer Chauncey Hannibal, a New Jersey born singer who had provided Guy with backing vocals. The like-minded twosome decided to pick up where Guy had left off, and after recruiting members David Hollister and Levi Little, Riley and Hannibal christened their new group Blackstreet in 1993. Riley's credits were by this time second to none—he had been handed the American Society of Composers, Authors, and Publishers (ASCAP) Songwriter of the Year Award in 1992—and Blackstreet's newest recruits also boasted impressive resumes. Hollister had written and produced for R&B acts such as Mary J. Blige and Patti Labelle, and Little had played guitar, bass, and keyboards for the group Image of Truth. As a whole, Blackstreet had experience in every area of studio recording, and their emergence caused many R&B enthusiasts to eagerly await their first steps on record.

In 1994, the foursome released *Blackstreet* on Interscope Records to the warm reception of R&B fans. The album itself sold over a million copies, and featured several hit singles, including "Booti Call" and "Joy." However, just as Blackstreet was establishing its identity as a group, members Little and Hollister quit the project. Riley's years as a producer had afforded him ample connections to young talent, and fortunately Blackstreet had no problem finding Eric Williams and Mark Middleton as able replacements. As Riley remembered to *Imusic* online, "[t]he departure of Levi and David was unexpected and a little unsettling at first, but we still wished them well. You see, Chauncey and I have always made Blackstreet's long term vision a priority. So when Mark and Eric stepped in we immediately realized the change was a blessing in disguise."

In Blackstreet's new enlistees, Riley had provided his group with two powerful lead vocalists. William—who had almost joined the quartet the first time around—had the rich experience of singing in a gospel choir, and the Brooklyn-born Middleton had a mastery of tenor and falsetto singing. If anything, Blackstreet had enabled

Members include **Chauncey "Black" Hannibal**, (born in Paterson, NJ), vocals; **Dave Hollister** (born in Chicago. IL, left group 1995), vocals; **Levi Little**, (born in Paterson, NJ, left group 1995), vocals; **Mark Middleton**, vocals (born in Brooklyn, joined group 1995); **Teddy "Street" Riley**, (born October 8, 1967, New York City), vocals, instruments, electronics; **Eric Williams**, (born in New Jersey, joined group 1995), vocals.

Band members Riley and Hannibal met working with Guy in the late 1980s; Blackstreet formed in 1993 after the downfall of Guy in the previous year; released self-titled debut album, 1994; released *Another Level,* 1996.

Addresses: *Record company*—Interscope, 10900 Wilshire Blvd., #1400, Los Angeles, CA, 90024; *Fan club*—Blackstreet Friends, P.O. Box 64737-525, Los Angeles, CA 90064.

itself to experiment in a wider spectrum of styles with its new lineup, and the new members were enthusiastic. "I've waited a long time for this opportunity," Middleton stated on the Blackstreet web page, "and God knows I couldn't be working with more talented, down-to-earth brothers than Teddy, Chauncy, and Eric. For us, it's all for one and all for Blackstreet."

The group soon took to the task of recording their second album, largely engineered at Riley's own studio, Future Recording, in his home town of Virginia Beach, Virginia. With a platinum debut under their belts, Blackstreet was met with the challenge of avoiding one of the most common pitfalls for new acts - the so-called "sophomore slump." However, when the foursome emerged from Future with the completed *Another Level* in 1996, fans, critics, and Blackstreet themselves all agreed that the sequel had in fact surpassed the original. "Our sound is stronger, tighter, and more diverse now," Hannibal beamed to *Imusic.* "And since Eric and Mark both sing incredible leads and harmony, me and Teddy have more vocal support than ever. It's a win-win situation any way you slice it."

The appeal of *Another Level's* nineteen cuts was indeed diverse, enticing listeners of differing musical tastes to buy the album. The first single "No Diggity," which is slang for "no doubt," was a catchy, hip-hop number that featured an intro by rap star Dr. Dre, and elsewhere the album featured a highly modified cover of "Can't Buy Me Love" by 1960's rock gods the Beatles, as well as the gospel-tinged finale "The Lord Is Real," a song based upon "Time Will Reveal" by the 1980s family group Debarge. At least one light jazz radio station put the smoother tracks "My Paradise" and "Let's Stay In Love" into its daily rotation. "Teddy Riley knows what he's doing," claimed Kevin Brown, a disc jockey for KBLX radio. "We are watching a master of the game, who deserves to be mentioned in the same breath as such composers as [Kenneth] Babyface [Edmonds] and [Kenny] Gamble & [Leon] Huff."

Some critics, such as *The New York Times'* Jon Pareles, praised Blackstreet for their positive attitude as well as for their musical abilities. In an era of obscenity-laden, violent, and often sexist genres like gangsta rap, groups like Blackstreet, who opted to draw upon the romantic balladeers of the past, were refreshing to many ears, lyrically and otherwise. "Blackstreet reduces 1970s soul to 1990s dimensions;" Pareles opined, "it pares down the melodies and replaces acoustic instruments with synthesizers and samples. But it retains the close harmonies of doo-wop, with all its overtones of constructive male bonding."

Blackstreet prepared to undertake their third album, but in the meantime Riley continued to be one of the busiest, most sought-after producers in the field. In addition to continued work with veteran R&B performers like Michael Jackson and Whitney Houston, Riley began to produce a material for a number of compilation and soundtrack records, including the *Soul Food* soundtrack, released in 1997, and the series *Maximum Club Classics.* By this point, Riley had amassed over thirty platinum records, and whatever the future of Blackstreet, he has surely helped shape the landscape of contemporary R&B music.

Selected discography

Blackstreet, Interscope, 1994.
Another Level, Interscope, 1996.

Sources

Periodicals

Billboard, May 16, 1992.
New York Times, November 24, 1996.

Online

http://www.blackstreet.com/

http://www.dotmusic.com/MWtalentblackstreet.html "Making Teddy Riley a star in the UK," *Blackstreet,* (June 2 1998).

http://www.interscoperecords.com

http://www.kblx.com/blackst.h

—Shaun Frentner

Judith Blegen

Operatic singer

As a leading soprano in the New York Metropolitan Opera, Judith Blegen earned a reputation as the singer whose appearance was as pretty as her voice. Blegen, the American beauty of the U.S. opera, made a name for herself in Nuremberg, Germany and in Vienna, Austria before conquering her homeland. Critics never cease to applaud her talent, and there is much to praise—from her light , "canary-like" tremolo, to her pleasing charm and dearth of ego bouts. Blegen, a surprisingly petite diva of Norwegian heritage, projects a sweetness equaled only by her musical talent and attractive appearance.

Blegen was one of five children born to Dr. Howard Martin Blegen and Dorothy Mae Anderson Blegen. Born in Lexington, Kentucky, she was raised in Missoula, Montana. Her father, a surgeon, and her mother, a violin teacher, reared their children in a musical environment. Several of the Blegen children were musically inclined; one of Blegen's sisters, an accomplished pianist, was naturally gifted with a sense of perfect pitch, which Blegen herself would develop over time as she learned to play the violin from her mother. Among Blegen's fondest childhood memories were of days spent around the house with the sounds of the New York Philharmonic Orchestra playing from the radio in the background.

Blegen's musical talent was enhanced by her dedication and energy, while her budding vocal talent was nurtured through voice lessons from the age of 14 and by singing soprano in her church choir. At 17, she weathered a hapless audition for the New York Metropolitan Opera during on-the-road tryouts held in Washington State but the experience left her undeterred and by her senior year at Missoula High School she was enrolled in music lessons at the University of Montana Missoula Campus. Blegen's childhood focused on music, to be sure, but by most standards she lived a very normal and typical life, active in her school life and congenial with her friends and peers.

After high school graduation in 1959 she enrolled at the Curtis Institute of Music in Philadelphia, where she chose to major in voice, although she continued her violin studies as well. At Curtis Institute, Blegen studied voice with Euphemia Gregory and advanced her violin skills under the instruction of Toshiya Eto and Oscar Shumsky. Blegen also worked with Martial Singher, formerly of the Metropolitan Opera, who coached her through her first operatic role of Susanna from the Marriage of Figaro as a project during a workshop at Curtis Institute. She spent her summers in enrichment programs, enhancing her skills in theater and opera through classes and apprenticeships in Santa Fe, New Mexico and Kansas City, Missouri and, again with

Singher, at the distinguished Music Academy of the West in Santa Barbara, California. In 1962 Blegen participated in, and won, the student auditions of the Philidelphia Orchestra, and in so doing, made her debut with the orchestra a year later.

European Career

In 1964, Blegen received her bachelor's degree from Curtis Institute and a Fulbright Scholarship which enabled her to travel to Rome to advance her voice studies under the guidance of Luigi Ricci. During her stay in Rome the fledgling soprano performed at the Festival of Two Worlds in nearby Spoleto. She sang at Spoleto from 1964-65, and again in 1966 when she performed as Mélisande in Debussy's Pelléas et Mélisande. Blegen also took advantage of her opportunity to learn to speak Italian, a skill she would find most useful in her future career.

Equipped with her formal education and special training in Rome, Blegen joined the Nuremberg Opera in 1965, where she became the lead soprano. In time Blegen, was offered a position with the illustrious Hamburg State Opera. She declined the offer, choosing to remain in Nuremberg until 1968 when she was offered a position at the Vienna State Opera. Unlike many operatic performers, Blegen was of the opinion that the crucial stepping stone to her success would be not in Milan at La Scala, but in Vienna which, in her estimation, was the music capital of the world.

From 1968 until 1970, Blegen performed in a variety of roles in Vienna, including Rosina in *Barber of Seville,* Norina in *Don Pasquale,* Zerbinetta in *Ariadne auf Naxos,* and Aennchen in *Der Freischütz.* At the Staatsoper in Austria, Blegen also sang the part of the comic heroine Adina in Gaetano Donizetti's *L'Elisir D'Amore,* one of her most popular roles, which she later performed at New York's Metropolitan Opera. In August of 1969 during a brief stay in the United States, Blegen performed with the Santa Fe Opera in a modern program by Menotti, *Help! Help! the Globolinks!* She ressurected the role in New York the following December, just prior to her debut with the Metropolitan Opera.

Metropolitan Opera

Blegen ultimately returned to the United States to become a leading soprano with the Metropolitan Opera Company, by far her longest affiliation with any opera house. She debuted at the Lincoln Center on January 19, 1970 as Papagena in Mozart's the *Magic Flute.* In December of that year, she sang as a stand-in in the more substantial role, of Marzelline in *Fidelio,* and by 1972 she played the lead role of Mélisande in *Pelléas et Mélisande.* Upon her return to the United States, Blegen also performed with the Opera Society of Washington, including a 1970 production of Gian-Carlo Menotti's macabre work, *The Medium,* which was released as a soundtrack by Columbia Records. Blegen's performance in the role of Monica was declared, "[S]pectacular ... most effective," by reviewer Justin Herman in *American Record Guide.*

Blegen established herself in a number of roles at the Metropolitan Opera, beginning with her Marzelline in *Fidelio.* She went on to perform as Sophie in *Werther,* and she added a new role to her repertoire, Sophie in *Der*

Rosenkavalier. In 1972, she revived her popular Susanna in *Marriage of Figaro* for a performance in San Francisco and again at the Edinburgh Festival in 1976. In 1973, she brought her Sophie (*Der Rosenkavalier*) to the Chicago Lyric Opera. Blegen also returned to Europe, to the Salzburg Festival in 1974 as Blondchen in Mozart's *Abduction from the Seraglio.* She performed her first recital in New York in 1974 and soloed with the New York Philharmonic that same year. She is further remembered for her Metropolitan Opera performances as Juliette in *Roméo et Juliette* and as Susanna in *Marriage of Figaro* in the late 1970s. Among her most memorable performances at the Metropolitan Opera was her 1981 portrayal of the fickle Adina, opposite the great tenor Luciano Pavarotti, in Donizetti's amusing bel canto comedy *L'Elisir D'Amore,* which was released on video tape.

Blegen characterizes herself as a coloratura (providing elaborate embellishment) soprano, but admits to her preference for the masters Mozart and Beethoven. She married Peter Singher, son of Martial Singher, in 1967 during her tenure at the Nuremberg Opera. Their son, Thomas Christopher was born on April 27, 1970 (Blegen's own birthday), just a few months after her Metropolitan Opera debut. The couple divorced in 1975. Blegen re-married in 1977 to Raymond Gniewek.

Selected discography

(with the Opera Society of Washington) *The Medium,* Columbia, 1970.

Selected videography

(with Leonard Bernstein) *Mahler, Symphony No. 8 in E flat major,* Polygram.

(with the Metropolitan Opera Company)*Un Ballo in Maschera,* 1980.

(with the Metropolitan Opera Company)*Hansel and Gretel,* Paramount, 1982.

(with the Metropolitan Opera Company)*L'Elisir d'Amore,* 1981.

Sources

American Record Guide, January-February 1997, p. 143(2); January-February 1998, p. 131(2).

Opera News, 18 March 1995, p. 10(5); 14 December 1996, p. 40(4); 28 December 1996, p. 28(4).

—Gloria Cooksey

David Bowie

Singer, songwriter

AP/Worldwide Photos, Reproduced by Permission

Few musicians have enjoyed the far-reaching success of David Bowie, a self-described "chameleon of pop" whose career has spanned three decades with little indication of slowing down or even becoming predictable. Bowie is noted for being one step ahead of the times, ushering in glitter or glam-rock, the androgynous look, transgender dressing, robotic rock, rock-funk fused with a futuristic sound, and the superstar rock musician as an actor, producer, painter, philanthropist, millionaire. *Rolling Stone*'s Seth Hinden wrote; "In 1997 Bowie broke new ground again with the Internet-only release of his single 'Telling Lies'....The electronic-themed release received positive reviews from critics, demonstrating that after more than 30 years in music, Bowie still has his pulse on the modern scene ... it looks like (he) won't be retiring anytime soon."

He was born David Robert Jones on January 8, 1947, in the working class section of London known as Brixton. His childhood was marked by difficulty. His publicist father and theater-ushermother married after his birth, which was a scandalous break from convention in 1947, and his brother was eventually confined to a psychiatric hospital. Bowie's teenage fighting in his rough neighborhood led to the paralysis of his left eye, the pupil of which was permanently dilated. He appreciated music from an early age and his parents provided him with recordings of American rock pioneers such as Fats Domino, Elvis Presley, and Little Richard, as well as introducing him to R&B and jazz. He also learned to play the guitar as a child, and took up the saxophone at the age of 12. He performed in a series of high school groups while studying commercial art at Bromley Technical High School in London, but he didn't take his career in music seriously until the early 1960s. He left technical school before earning a degree in order to work at an advertising agency, but soon discovered that he didn't enjoy the work he was doing and quit. He also studied with the Lindsay Kemp Mime Troupe for two and a half years, painted, and acted in small stage roles. At one time Bowie even considered entering a Buddhist monastery.

Bowie started his first serious group, Davie Jones and the King Bees in 1964, but their one single failed to generate much attention. Bowie then moved on to the Manish Boys, but the group didn't meet with much commercial success either. In 1965 Bowie discarded his real name, Davy Jones, in favor of the stage name David Bowie to avoid confusion with the London theater star Davy Jones, who later became well known for acting in televisions' "The Monkees". Freshly dubbed David Bowie, he joined a mod influenced band called The Lower Third which released one single and broke up. Bowie then joined a psychedelic band called The Buzz,

For the Record . . .

Born David Robert Hayward Jones, January 8, 1947, in London, England; son of Hayward (a publicist) and Margaret Mary Burns (a movie theater usher) ; one brother; married Angela Barnet 1970 (divorced 1980); married Iman, 1992; children: Joey Duncan Hayward Jones (name originally Zowie) from first marriage.

Worked in advertising and with the Lindsey Kemp Mime Troupe prior to musical career; performed with various bands throughout the 1960s, including David Jones and the Buzz, the Manish Boys, Davy Jones and the Lower Third, The Kon-rads, and George and the Dragons; solo performer from the late 1960s until 1989, when he formed the Tin Machine; solo performer between 1992 and 1998; motion pictures include *The Man Who Fell to Earth,* 1976; *Just a Gigolo, The Hunger, Merry Christmas, Mr. Lawrence,* 1983; *Labyrinth,* and *Absolute Beginners;* also appeared as the lead in the Broadway production of *The Elephant Man,* 1980; first musician to issue his own bonds, one of the first to release an Internet-only single.

Awards: Inducted into the Rock and Roll Hall of Fame, 1996.

Addresses: *Office*—641 Fifth Avenue, #22-Q, New York, NY, 10022; *Record company*—Virgin Records, 1790 Broadway, 20th Fl., New York, NY 10019, (212) 586-7700, fax (212) 765-0989; *E-mail*—atVirgin Records: www. virginrecords.com; www.davidbowie.com

which disbanded in 1966. His first real break came a year later in 1967 when he was offered a solo recording deal with Deram Records. Bowie released an eponymous solo album of folk-influenced pop music in late 1967 and garnered a lot of attention by opening for the popular band T-Rex.

Began with Space Oddity

Bowie enjoyed his first Top 10 hit in the United Kingdom in 1969 with the single "Space Oddity," which was the tale of a stranded astronaut influenced by the Stanley Kubrick's film "2001: A Space Oddessy". He also met his future wife, Angela Barnet, at this time and she convinced a friend at Mercury Records to listen to his music. Since the "Space Oddity" release coincided with the fervor of the American moon landing, Mercury records signed Bowie to rerecord "Space Oddity" for release in America—signaling the beginning of Bowie's music career in the U.S. Bowie released his first official solo album in 1970, titled *Man of Words, Man of Music,* with Tony Visconti on bass and Mick Ronson on guitar. The release had a psychedelic feel, and it's standout track was "Space Oddity". The album was rereleased in 1972 as *Space Oddity.*

Bowie married Barnet in 1970 and they had a son named Zowie Duncan Hayward Bowie in 1971. *The Man Who Sold the World* was released in 1971 as well, which featured Bowie in a dress and make-up on the cover. The album foreshadowed Bowie's glitter-rock persona and the advent of other glam-rock bands such as the New York Dolls and Slade, but it's over-the-top lyrics prompted Mercury to part ways with Bowie. RCA Records felt more confident of Bowie's musical potential and signed him, at the age of 24, for his next album. *Hunky Dory,* released later in 1971, combined his "glam," T-Rex-inspired sound with that of a 1960s pop style reminiscent of Bob Dylan and Anthony Newley. *Hunky Dory* included the single "Changes" and was described by John Mendelsohn in Rolling Stone as Bowie's "most easily accessible, and thus his most enjoyable work." Bowie had spent some time in New York City's wild underground art scene in the late 1960s and early 1970s, and had spent time with Andy Warhol, Lou Reed, and other cult figures. After the release of *Hunky Dory,* Bowie became a cult figure himself, noted for his outlandish cross-dressing, different colored eyes, and refreshing new sound. Bowie further sealed his fame with the release of *The Rise and Fall of Ziggy Stardust and the Spiders from Mars* in 1972, a sci-fi concept album about a band from outer space. The Spiders from Mars included Ronson, bassist Trevor Bolder, and drummer Woody Woodmansey. An ensuing international tour propelled Ziggy Stardust to the top of the charts, and Bowie capped off a productive year by producing Lou Reed's 1972 hit album *Transformer* and writing and producing Mott the Hoople's single "All The Young Dudes".

Explored Numerous Cutting-Edge Personas

Jay Cocks wrote in *Time* magazine, "Musically, Bowie always seems to know what time it is.... When he first hit the stage as Ziggy, decked out in make-up, dye job, and psychedelic costume, the rock world was ready. Too much karma, too much good vibes, too much hippy-dippy: audiences wanted decadence with a difference.

Bowie was there." Bowie, heralded as the king of glitter rock in the early 1970s, created a media sensation when he told an interviewer that he was bisexual. As the first rock star to come out in the open about this subject, he was the object of controversy. His sexual ambiguity fueled and occasionally eclipsed his celebrity. He later told Kurt Loder in *Rolling Stone,* "The biggest mistake I ever made ... was telling that ... writer that I was bisexual. Christ, I was so young then. I was experimenting."

Bowie was the first rock star to tantalize audiences with a wide array of "looks" or phases, foreshadowing Madonna by at least a decade. Bowie went from Ziggy Stardust to Aladdin Sane, an elfin man decorated with an electric blue lightening bolt drawn across his face and a painted-on teardrop. The album *Aladdin Sane* was released in 1973. At a London concert in July of 1973, Bowie shocked both his fans and his own band by announcing, "not only is this the last show of the tour, but it's the last show that we'll ever do," which marked the end of the Spiders from Mars. He released *Pin-Ups,* which was a collection of covers of British hits from the mid-1960s. Bowie mixed Iggy Pop's classic *Raw Power* album in 1973 and then, in 1974, set out to recruit a new band for the release of *Diamond Dogs* . *Diamond Dogs* was an eerily dark, futuristic-sounding release with a picture of Bowie on the cover as a half-man, half-dog. "Rebel Rebel" was the most popular single from the release and the album reached number five on the U.S. pop charts. In 1975, Bowie released *Young Americans* and was starting to morph into his "Thin White Duke" persona, slicking his hair back and donning white suits. The single "Fame" from the release was a disco hit recorded with the late ex-Beatle John Lennon. Soon after, quite appropriately, he starred in his first major film *The Man Who Fell To Earth.*

Station to Station was released in 1976, which generated the top ten single "Golden Years". Soon after, Bowie moved to Berlin and collaborated with producer/musician Brian Eno formerly of Roxy Music for the release of *Low* in 1977. Bowie then assisted Iggy Pop with his next two albums *The Idiot* and *Lust For Life* and toured as Pop's piano player before returning to Berlin, where he recorded 1978's *"Heroes"* with Eno and former King Crimson guitarist Robert Fripp. He moved to Switzerland later in 1978 and released *Lodger* in 1979. *Scary Monsters* was released the following year, featuring the singles "Fashion" and "Ashes to Ashes" which were also early MTV videos.

Major Changes in the Eighties

After a rather long breakup, Bowie and his wife Angela divorced in 1980. Turning to other creative outlets,

Bowie earned positive reviews as an actor for his lead role in the Broadway play *The Elephant Man* in 1980, and starred—along with Catherine Deneuve and Susan Sarandon—in the vampire thriller *The Hunger.* He then landed a supporting role in 1983's *Merry Christmas, Mr. Lawrence.* Director Nagisa Oshima told Kurt Loder that he chose Bowie for his film *Merry Christmas, Mr. Lawrence* after seeing him perform in The Elephant Man because Bowie projected "an inner spirit that is indestructible." The sentiment summed up Bowie's talent, intelligence, and ability to forge innovations as well. Bowie then recorded the hit single "Under Pressure" with Queen, which is famous for its bassline, used as the main sample in white bubblegum rapper Vanilla Ice's "Ice Ice Baby", and then announced he was foregoing drugs and homosexuality and leaving his longtime label RCA for EMI. He released his most commercially successful album to date in 1983, titled *Let's Dance.* The album featured the hit singles "Let's Dance," "Modern Love," and "China Girl,". Tonight was released in 1984, which included "Blue Jean" and the title track, a duet with Tina Turner. In 1986, Bowie appeared in the fantasy film Labyrinth and in Absolute Beginners. He also recorded Martha and the Vandellas' Motown hit "Dancing in the Streets" with Mick Jagger of The Rolling Stones in 1986.

Never Let Me Down was released in 1987, and the supporting tour for the album—the Glass Spider Tour—featured Peter Frampton as Bowie's backing guitarist. A "greatest hits" boxed set called *Sound and Vision* was released by the independent Rykodisc label in 1989 along with his entire back catalog up to *Scary Monsters* which had been long deleted by RCA. Bowie then formed a band called Tin Machine that released two eponymous albums, the first in 1989 and the second in 1991. The Tin Machine was not especially successful, and disbanded in 1992. Bowie married Somolian model Iman in 1992 and released *Black Tie, White Noise* in 1993. Bowie's first interactive CD-ROM project, *Jump,* was released at this time, followed by 1995's *Outside.* Bowie then toured the U.S. with Nine Inch Nails and Europe with Morrissey. In 1996 he appeared as his late friend Andy Warhol in the art-world feature film, *Basquiat.* Bowie was inducted into the Rock and Roll Hall of Fame in July of 1996.

Still Far Ahead of His Time

In 1997 Bowie released the Internet-only single "Telling Lies," followed by the release of the album Earthling. In 1998 he released a 40-minute remix from *Earthling* titled "I'm Afraid of Americans", which was remixed by Nine Inch Nails and Photek. In 1997 Bowie initiated a novel approach to getting richer by issuing his own bonds; it was an ideal way to land a giant lump sum of money—in Bowie's case, $55 million. People magazine wrote, "Backed by hit songs that should continue to earn for years, rockers can reap millions now and slowly pay back the bonds (which are really low-interest loans) with the old tunes' royalties." Bowie's prolific, original, and thoroughly memorable contribution to pop music has already stood the test of time—and passed with flying colors. He celebrated his 50th birthday in 1997 with an all-star concert at Madison Square Garden and the release of *Earthling*.

Selected discography

The Man Who Sold the World, Mercury, 1971.
Hunky Dory, RCA, 1971.
The Rise and Fall of Ziggy Stardust and the Spiders from Mars, RCA, 1972.
Aladdin Sane, RCA, 1973.
Pin Ups, RCA, 1973.
Diamond Dogs, RCA, 1974.
Young Americans, RCA, 1975.
Low, RCA, 1977.
Heroes, RCA, 1977.
Lodger, RCA, 1979.
Scary Monsters (and Super Creeps), RCA, 1980.
Let's Dance, EMI America, 1983.
Ziggy Stardust: The Motion Picture Soundtrack, RCA, 1983.
Tonight, EMI America, 1984.
Love You 'Til Tuesday, Deram/Polygram, 1984.
David Bowie: Man of Words/Man of Music, Mercury, 1969, later reissued as *Space Oddity*, RCA, 1984.
Never Let Me Down, EMI America, 1987.

Sound and Vision, Rykodisc, 1989.
Black Tie, White Noise, Virgin Records, 1993.
Santa Monica '72., Griffin Records, 1995.
Outside, Virgin Records, 1995.
Earthling, Virgin Records, 1997.

Sources

Books

Cann, Kevin, *David Bowie: A Chronology*, Simon & Schuster, 1984.
Edwards, Henry, and Tony Zanetta, *Stardust: The David Bowie Story*, McGraw-Hill, 1986.
Tremelett, George, *The David Bowie Story*, Warner Books, 1975.

Periodicals

Newsweek, July 18, 1983.
New York Times, May 20, 1976.
People, July 20, 1998.
Playboy, September 1976.
Raygun, February 1998.
Rolling Stone, January 6, 1972; October 4, 1979; May 12, 1983; October 25, 1984; April 23, 1987.
Time, July 18, 1983.

Online

"The Rolling Stone Network," *Biography*, www.rollingstone.com/biography/davidbowie
www.wallofsound.com/discography

—B. Kimberly Taylor

Alfred Brendel

Piano

AP/Wide World Photos. Reproduced by permission.

By the 1990s, Alfred Brendel was regarded as the foremost living classical pianist in the world. A name chiefly familiar to fans of classical music only, Brendel is far removed from the stereotype of the eccentric, flamboyant concert pianist in the vein of Arthur Rubinstein or David Helfgott. Furthermore, his performance repertoire is lacking in the more popular classics that are regarded as "crowd-pleasers," and onstage Brendel is quite restrained in demeanor. "Perhaps no other pianist of our time has so willfully avoided the ordinary channels to success and formulas for stardom and still arrived at the top of his profession," wrote Bernard Holland in a 1977 *New York Times* article. Scott Cantrell, writing for *High Fidelity* a decade later, concurred: "In an age supposedly devoted to the mediagenic, Brendel has broken all the rules."

Brendel is of Austrian heritage. He was born in 1931 in Wiesenberg, a locale in Moravia that now belongs to the Czech Republic but at the time of his birth was home to many German-speaking peoples. When he was three, his father abandoned his profession as an architect and took the family to the Adriatic coast of Yugoslavia; on a resort island called Krk, he ran a hotel. There, the young Brendel loved to entertain guests by operating the hotel's phonograph records; he sang along with the operas, which no doubt delighted the guests. Brendel also recalls being quite fond of German cabaret music of the era as a small child.

After a few years on Krk, the family moved to the city of Zagreb, where his father then ran a cinema. It was here that at the age of six Brendel began piano lessons, as most children of his middle-class background did at the time. By the time he was eleven, it became obvious that he possessed a great talent for the instrument. But World War II brought hardship, and in 1943 the family relocated once more to Graz, Austria. As a teenager, Brendel was recruited to dig ditches for the war effort, but suffered frostbite and managed to return to the safety of home as a result of his mother's efforts. He studied formally only till the age of sixteen, receiving a state diploma in music from the Graz Academy of Music in 1947. His studies were also rounded out with courses in composition and conducting, and like many other musical prodigies, he wrote his own works for the piano. One of these was performed in his debut recital in 1948 in Graz, an evening billed as "The Fugue in Piano Literature"; he also played selections from Bach, Liszt and Brahms.

Brendel's talents were not limited to music, however: at the time of his first recital, he was also enjoying a solo show of his watercolors in a Graz gallery just a few blocks away. His career as a pianist, however, began in

Born January 5, 1931, in Wiesenberg/North Moravia (now Czech Republic); son of Albert (an architectural engineer and later entrepreneur) and Ida (Wieltschnig) Brendel.; married Iris Heymann-Gonzala, 1960 (marriage ended, 1972); married Irene (Reni) Semler, 1975; children Doris (first marriage); son and daughter (second marriage). *Education:* Studied piano at the Graz (Austria) Academy of Music, graduated 1947.

Debuted as pianist, 1949, in Graz, Austria; made London debut in January of 1958; made North American debut in Montreal in 1961; first to record Beethoven's entire set of works for piano, Vox Label, 1962-65; New York City debut, 1964; signed to the Philips Classics label.

Awards: Brendel has achieved numerous Grammy awards over the course of his career, beginning in 1973, and has also won the Grand Prix of the Liszt Society, the Prix Mondial du Disque, the Edison Award, the Grand Prix des Disquaires, the Grand Prix de l'Académie Charles Cros, the Deutscher Schallplattenpreis, the Wiener Flötenuhr, the Japanese Record Academy Award, and the Gramophone Award. He is the recipient of honorary degrees from London University, 1978, Sussex University, 1981, Oxford University, 1983, and Yale University; knighted in 1989; made Honorary Bencher by the Middle Temple of the Inns of Court, London, England.

Addresses: *Agent*—Colbert Artists Management, Inc., 111 W. 57th St., New York, NY 10019-2211.

earnest in 1949 when he won a tough European competition for pianists called the *Concorso Busoni*, held in Bolzano, Italy. For the next few years, Brendel alternated intermittent master classes with renowned musicians of his day, such as Paul Baumgartner, Eduard Steuermann, and Edwin Fischer, with a great deal of self-study and practice. He would later term Fischer as perhaps the greatest impact on his style; he made several extended stays in Lucerne, Switzerland to study with him in 1949, 1950, and 1956.

But Brendel's virtuosity did not immediately pack concert halls, nor did his agents have an easy time booking engagements for him during these early years. Part of the blame perhaps lay in his playing style, once Brendel saw himself on television, and was surprised to see that his demeanor, in comparison to his playing style, was anything but restrained. He learned to tame his stage flailings and grimaces by practicing with a mirror.

And yet that same quiet, serious interpretation of the works of the great composers would also hinder Brendel's success. Audiences adore the flamboyant classical pianist, the David Helfgott, for instance, subject of the 1996 film *Shine,* or the Ignatius Paderewsky, a popular international figure in the interwar years who also headed the Polish government in exile, because they are entertaining to watch and were known to take great liberties in interpreting the classics. Brendel, however, was dedicated to performing the sonatas of Ludwig van Beethoven, or those of Franz Schubert or Johannes Brahms, with as much faithfulness to the composer's original intent as possible.

Renown for Mastery of Beethoven

Brendel, who eventually abandoned writing his own music, has said that he never really expected a career as a renowned pianist. He debuted in London in January of 1958, and in North America in Montreal in 1961; three years later, he played New York City for the first time at Hunter College. Over the next few years, he appeared in several dozen concert engagements per year, often with famed orchestras in Vienna, Berlin, London, and New York, among other top cities. During these years he became associated with the *Hammerklavier* sonata from Beethoven, a very difficult piece. But it was his recorded work for which Brendel first made a name for himself: he became the first pianist to record Beethoven's entire set of works for the piano. These sonatas appeared on the Vox label between 1962-65.

Brendel later re-recorded the complete cycle again in the 1970s for Philips, which has been his label for much of his career. He has also performed the entire body of sonatas on a few occasions. For Philips he has also recorded the works of Schubert and Mozart, and once more recorded the Beethoven works, making him possibly the only performer to ever do this three times in his career. This 10-CD set appeared on Philips in 1996. In some cases such works were re-recorded because of great advances in recording technology, a topic which Brendel addressed in a 1996 interview with Stephen Plaistow for the British journal *Gramophone.* "There are cases where I've found that the old tapes with their slightly dusty sound are more natural than the digitally recorded and all-too-clean sounds that were considered more realistic," Brendel said. "The walls of a good concert-hall have also a certain amount of patina, of dirt, which contributes to a pleasurable impression. But I do think things have now advanced, that the engineers now know how to use digital technique to better advantage, with warmer sound."

Demanding Schedule, Commercial Success

Mid-career, Brendel often performed extensively throughout the season, and regularly sold out venues such as New York's Carnegie Hall. During the 1982-83 performing calendar, he gave 77 recitals in eleven cities across two continents. His repertoire, in addition to the Beethoven sonatas, was generally confined to the brooding, nineteenth-century Central European composers. In light of this, one of Brendel's most notable achievements has been his efforts in reviving interest in the piano sonatas of Schubert, written in the 1820s and then largely ignored in the classical canon. Brendel included many of these works in his tour of the Soviet Union and Japan in 1988. The complex fugues of J. S. Bach have also been a favorite. The few times Brendel has ventured outside this repertoire have been in performing the more ebullient works of Franz Liszt and the twentieth-century compositions of a fellow Austrian, the modernist Arnold Schoenberg.

Brendel has been awarded a gold record, which he received when he passed the million-selling mark in 1978. Until 1972, he lived in Vienna, and occasionally conducted the master class both there and in visiting professor stints abroad. In 1972 he relocated to London, and concentrated his energies on music rather than teaching. He prefers to spend the majority of his time immersed in the study of scores, which is a requisite for both his concert recitals and hours in the recording studio. Poring over the scores helps him determine what the composer meant, and for this academic approach, for not injecting his own personality into the work, he has suffered criticism. As an essay on Brendel in *Notable Twentieth-Century Pianists* explained, "Disagreement rises concerning his sober, serious playing, a style that has attracted what amounts to a very large, devoted Brendel cult on one hand and, on the other, a vocal body of critics complaining that something is missing in his playing."

On the other hand, his peers are far more forgiving: "When I'm with Brendel, I know I'm in the presence of a man of genius," the renowned political scientist Sir Isaiah Berlin told A. Alvarez in a 1996 *New Yorker* profile

on the pianist. Alvarez termed Brendel's style an example of "selflessness.... He has a wonderful grasp of the structure of each piece, of the way it develops emotionally as well as intellectually, and this makes his playing strangely inward, as though he were following the composer's own train of thought and enabling the audience to share in the act of creation," the essayist wrote in the *New Yorker*.

A Jocular Polymath

Still an avid art-lover, in his spare time Brendel visits galleries and museums, and reads prodigiously. He lives in the Hampstead section of London and has a house in Dorset as well that boasts a swimming pool, which he uses to relieve his back problems, a common occupational hazard for pianists in later years, especially ones of above-average height such as Brendel. He collects art from around the world, and is especially fond of ethnographic works, but loves morbid cartoons as well, particularly the work of Edward Gorey and Gary Larson. He has published two collections of essays, *Musical Thoughts and After-Thoughts,* (1977) and *Music Sounded Out* (1990); he is an occasional contributor to the *New York Review of Books.*

Brendel is the recipient of numerous Grammy Awards for his records, and has been feted with several international prizes. He has received honorary degrees from London, Sussex, Oxford, and Yale universities, and was honored with the title of Knight of the British Empire in 1989. In London, he has also been made an Honorary Bencher of the Middle Temple of the Inns of Court, London, England, which very few outside the legal profession ever receive. In honor of Brendel's 65th birthday in 1996, his label issued a 25-CD deluxe limited edition, *The Art of Alfred Brendel,* which provided a comprehensive look at his career and included selections from the works of Beethoven, Brahms, Haydn, Liszt, Mozart, Schubert, and Schumann. "What particularly satisfies me about these achievements is that I owe my reputation not to the media or to the power of record companies but to my own playing," Brendel told Bernard Holland in the *New York Times.*

Selected discography

On Philips Classics (Netherlands) or Philips USA

The Art of Alfred Brendel (25-CD set), 1996.
Beethoven: The Five Concertos for Piano, 1996.
Alfred Brendal Recital.

Beethoven: Sonatas op. 31, no. 1 in G Major, no. 2 in D Minor, no. 3 in E-flat Major.
Beethoven: Sonata in C Major, op. 53; Sonata in F Major, op. 54; Sonata in A Major, op. 101.
Beethoven: 32 Sonatas (11-CD set).
Beethoven: Variations on a Theme by Diabelli, op. 120.
Brahms: Concerto No. 1 in D Minor, op. 15.
Haydn: Sonatas.
Liszt: Annees de Pelerinage.
Mozart Concertos.
Mozart: Sonatas in E-flat Major, K. 282; Sonata in F Major, K. 533/494; Fantasy in C Minor, K. 475; Rondo in A Minor, K. 511.
Schubert Impromptus D. 899 and D. 935.

Selected writings

Musical Thoughts and After-Thoughts, Princeton University Press, 1977.
Music Sounded Out, Robson Books, 1990.

Sources

Books

Gillespie, John and Anna Gillespie, *Notable Twentieth-Century Pianists,* Greenwood Press, 1995.
Stanley Sadie, editor, *New Grove Dictionary of Music and Musicians,* , Macmillan, 1980.

Periodicals

Gramophone, February 1996.
High Fidelity, May 1988.
New York Times, May 3, 1981, sec. II, p. 17.
New Yorker, April 1, 1996, pp. 49-55.

Online

http://www.geocities.com/Vienna/2192/brendel.html

—Carol Brennan

Lawrence Brown

Trombonist

AP/Wide World Photos. Reproduced by permission.

Lawrence Brown was virtually a "lifer" with the Duke Ellington Orchestra. In two stints, he spent nearly thirty years as an integral part of the most remarkable trombone section ever assembled and with the most honored musicians in the world of jazz. Along with other giants—saxophonists Johnny Hodges, Harry Carney and Ben Webster; trumpeters Cootie Williams, Bubber Miley and Rex Stewart; bassist Jimmy Blanton, drummer Sonny Greer and vocalist Ivie Anderson—it was Brown's specific sound that helped shape the Ellington musical persona. For it was Ellington's orchestra—that uncommon blend of unique timbres and personalities—that provided Duke's inspiration and gave voice to his genius. It is no accident that Brown's two arrivals in the band coincided with two spurts of creative energy and cohesiveness in the Ellington organization.

After moving, at age seven, from Kansas to Pasadena, California, Brown studied several instruments as a child: piano, violin, saxophone and tuba. He chose the trombone and quickly demonstrated unusual skills and dedication. For a while he harbored the idea of becoming a physician but the pull of music was too strong. It is said that his first professional job was playing for a Mother's Day service in Los Angeles for an audience of 6,000 at Aimee Semple McPherson's church. He began playing clubs such as the Los Angeles Cotton Club and the Club Alabam, in both Los Angeles and San Francisco with the bands of Curtis Moseby, Paul Howard and others. It was in this period that he served as a "strolling trombonist," playing with such control and delicacy that he visited tables to serenade the diners, much in the manner of the popular strolling violinists of the day.

In 1929 and 1930 he made his first recordings with Howard's Quality Serenaders. In 1930 he also appeared along with drummer/vibraphonist Lionel Hampton in the Les Hite orchestra. Under another name they backed the great Louis Armstrong in a group of sides that drew less than great comments from Gunther Schuller in his book *Early Jazz,* "These sides [are] listenable only when Louis is playing ... For the rest there is a wasteland ... Once in a while the elegant trombone of a Lawrence Brown ... penetrates the labyrinth of commercialism." Brown's developing style featured great facility and technique and a tonal quality reminiscent of a cello. As he told writer Stanley Dance in a 1965 interview: "It was my own idea, and I wasn't following anyone else. 'Why can't you play melody on the trombone just as sweet as on the cello?' I asked myself. Everybody was playing so loudly and raucously on trombone. I wanted a big, broad tone, not the raspy tone of tailgate, and if you think of the cello you can see how it influenced me."

This sound attracted the attention of maestro Ellington, who Brown joined in 1932. According to Bill Crow in his

Jazz Anecdotes, Brown had no written parts when he joined the Ellington band: "There were no third trombone parts, so I had to sort of compose my own parts. Then as the new numbers came out they started arranging for the third trombone. And Duke was superstitious as Brown related, "I didn't play with the band at first, because I was the thirteenth man. There was so much superstition. Oh, no, not thirteen men! I had to wait for the fourteenth man [altoist] Otto Hardwick, for about six weeks. And I didn't get paid until I played my first job." Brown had intended to stay for only a year but the Depression had hit the music industry hard and, since Ellington was able to survive, Brown's first tour with the band stretched over two decades.

A Voice Among Voices

Of Brown's 1932 addition to the Ellington band, Schuller wrote in *The Swing Era,* "Certainly the major new voice was Lawrence Brown, an extraordinarily versatile trombonist who brought a number of unique musical qualities to the orchestra and to Duke's sonoric palette. I believe the impact that Brown had on the so-called Ellington effect ... has never been fully appreciated. Not only did the Ellington band become the first to acquire a permanent trombone trio, but Brown was the first trombonist of any major black orchestra to develop a full-blown ballad and lyric style. This was some years before the emergence of players like Tommy Dorsey and Jack Jenney, still a time when the trombone was associated almost exclusively with 'hot' jazz, and hadn't quite lost its New Orleans 'tailgate' ancestry."

This unique trio of trombonists was completed by Joe "Tricky Sam" Nanton and Juan Tizol. Nanton, of West Indian heritage, specialized in the "jungle" sounds that characterized the early Ellington orchestras. He employed growls and a rubber plunger with a small mute in the horn to produce solos that expressed the gutsier side of Duke's creations. Tizol, from Puerto Rico, was classically trained and played the unusual valve trombone which gave him great flexibility and speed. Brown's smoothness and power, juxtaposed with his lyric qualities, made him a natural for playing lead. And despite their differences in personality and approach, these players could blend to produce an unmatched ensemble sound—or almost any effect the leader desired.

Classic Recordings

When, in May of 1932, Brown recorded his first solo with Ellington, it was on the almost impossible pop tune, "The Sheik of Araby." Schuller, whose technical analysis of jazz is always instructive, writes, "Brown's solo [is] jaunty, debonair, eloquent, topped by a graceful lip trill on a high B-flat, as effortless as if played on a flute ... in a style that combined lyricism, 'hot jazz,' swing and consummate technical command in a synthesis that no other trombonist at the time could muster." Indeed, those qualities were present on any number of recordings that Brown made with the band, causing some critics to question whether he belonged in the Ellington band, or whether Ellington was becoming too pretentious, having forsaken some of the raw sounds of the 1920s.

"Slippery Horn," "Ducky Wucky," "Bundle of Blues" and "Ain't Misbehavin'" are some of the early recorded vehicles for Brown solos. The orchestra made the first of many successful overseas tours in 1933, on which the Duke consorted with European royalty and the band solidified its growing reputation. Upon return, they became the first major black orchestra to tour theaters in Texas and Missouri. During the period from Brown's joining until 1940 this group recorded such memorable Ellingtonia as "Sophisticated Lady," "Solitude," "In A Sentimental Mood," "Reminiscing in Tempo," "Caravan," "I Let A Song Go Out of My Heart," "Ko-Ko," "Concerto for Cootie (Do Nothin' Till You Hear From Me)," "Cotton Tail," "Never No Lament (Don't Get Around Much Any More)" and "Transblucency," a vocal without words co-written by Brown for Kay Davis's unique voice. Brown also composed "The Golden Cress" and "On A Turquoise Cloud." "Yearning for Love (Lawrence's Concerto)" was a three-part composition written by

Ellington for Brown. "Black, Brown and Beige," Duke's lutionary 1943 excursion, also featured Brown's unique skills and, according to musician-critic Leonard Feather, saw "the elevation of jazz to an orchestral art."

Branching Out, Breaking Off

Beginning in 1938, the trombonist regularly recorded with a small group headed by bandmate Johnny Hodges, and made up exclusively of Ellington sidemen, including the pianist himself. Typically Hodges's group would include Brown, Cootie Williams, Harry Carney, Sonny Greer, the then-current bassist and the incomparable altoist as leader. These sessions were done against a backdrop of the full Ellington Orchestra's year-round travel and recording schedule. They were also a precursor to a major change in Brown's career and Ellington's Orchestra. Though the 1939 addition of the magical composer-arranger Billy Strayhorn, breakthrough bassist Jimmy Blanton and tenorman Ben Webster brought a fresh infusion of energy to the band, Brown and others were becoming restless. Two decades of grinding travel, the sameness of program night after night and the desire to showcase his own talents concluded in a move that shocked the music world and temporarily crippled the Ellington Orchestra.

Several Ellington stalwarts—Williams, clarinetist Barney Bigard, Webster, Tizol and Nanton among them—left the Duke at various times through the 1940s. But in 1951 Hodges, "permanent" drummer Greer and Brown defected, with Brown choosing to tour with a Hodges-led small group. Though Brown's own salary was at a peak at that time, the big band business was drying up for all but a few, and as he told Dance, "... the flexibility of the small band, the opportunity to spread out, make it interesting to the musician. And Johnny Hodges had a terrific little band." This tour lasted through about 1953, after which Brown free-lanced successfully in New York in the radio and recording studios, in 1957 securing "the best job in the business," a staff position with CBS. "But then came the cancellation of all the transcontinental radio programs, and everything started going into tape and they didn't need the same set-up or number of men." After working the New York clubs for a while, Brown answered a call from Duke and re-joined the big band in Las Vegas in 1960.

With the return of Brown, Hodges and Williams, the Ellington Orchestra of the 1960s, according to Schuller, "regained some if its earlier glory. With these exceptional voices back in place, many of the recordings of the sixties took on some of the orchestra's old luster and uniqueness." During this ten-year tour Brown was asked to take on an additional role, that of playing the growl and plunger solos originated by "Tricky Sam" Nanton. "I don't like the plunger," Brown told Dance, "but I imitate the tops—Tricky. That buzzing breaks your lip down and you have to wait a little while to get back to normal."

After ten more years with Duke, Brown retired from the music business in 1970. He engaged for some time in business consultancy and became politically active, helping with the Nixon re-election campaign. His last job was as an agent for the Los Angeles Local 47 of the American Federation of Musicians. Summing up his role with the Ellington Orchestra, Schuller wrote: "Brown, as leader of Ellington"s trombone section, was not only a great lyric player, but his solo style was so unique that it was virtually inimitable. At the same time he was no less of a 'hot' improviser ... Such versatility was unprecedented in the 1930s and is still relatively uncommon today." Brown is seen as an influence on such major players as Tommy Dorsey and Bill Harris.

Summing Up

Throughout his career Brown always demonstrated the highest standards of professional conduct. His was an independent spirit. In a business in which the use of alcohol and other substances was the norm, Brown never drank or smoked. Yet he was able to work, play and live with his differently disposed bandmates amicably.

His long-time leader wrote in *Music is my Mistress:* "As a soloist, his taste is impeccable, but his greatest role is that of an accompanist. The old-timers used to say, 'Soloists are made, but accompanists are born.' Lawrence Brown is the accompanist par excellence. During the many years he was with us, records prove that his solo performance had the widest range from classical standard up to, around, and above the jet-swept contour of the vision we almost hear."

Selected discography

Black, Brown & Beige (58 selections by Ellington and His Orchestra, recorded 1944-46); Bluebird, 1988.
Caravan (The Johnny Hodges All-Stars, Recorded 1947-51); Prestige, 1992.
Duke Ellington and His Orchestra, 1939-40; Forlane, 1992.
The Duke Ellington Carnegie Hall Concerts, 1943, 1944, 1946, 1947; Prestige, 1991.
Inspired Abandon; Impulse, 1965.
The Intimacy of the Blues (recorded 1967, 1970); Fantasy, 1991.

Sources

Books

Carr, Ian, Digby Fairweather, and Brian Priestley, *Jazz: the Rough Guide; The Rough Guides,* 1995.

Crow, Bill, *Jazz Anecdotes;* Oxford University Press, 1990.

Dance, Stanley, *The World of Duke Ellington;* Da Capo, 1970.

Ellington, Edward Kennedy, *Music is my Mistress;* Doubleday & Company, Inc., 1973.

Erlewine, Michael, et al, Eds., *All Music Guide to Jazz,* Miller Freeman Books, 1996.

Feather, Leonard, *The New Edition of the Encyclopedia of Jazz;* Bonanza Books, 1965.

Rust, Brian, *Jazz Records, 1897-1942*, Fifth Revised and Enlarged Edition, Volume 1; Storyville Publications, 1982.

Schuller, Gunther, *Early Jazz;* Oxford University Press, 1968.

Schuller, Gunther, *The Swing Era: The Development of Jazz, 1930-1945;* Oxford University Press, 1989.

Periodicals

Jet, October 3, 1988.

New York Times, September 9, 1988.

—*Robert Dupuis*

Paul Butterfield

Blues harp

Paul Butterfield lived a tortured life, wracked by drugs and alcohol. But before he died at the age of 44, he and his blues band had revolutionized blues. Besides simply proving that white boys could play the blues with feeling and versatility, he expanded the music by incorporating an unheard of variety of outside influences, from ragas to jazz, into the blues he played. He ushered, in psychedelic rock music, helped invent blues-rock and set a standard for jamming that few groups have been able to meet since.

Paul Butterfield was born on December 17, 1942 to a middle-class family in the Hyde Park neighborhood on Chicago's South Side. Butterfield grew up listening to blues and jazz on records that belonged to his brother and father, and on all-night blues shows on the radio. In high school, he was an all-state track star and a talented classical flutist. He was offered a scholarship to Brown University but turned it down to attend the University of Chicago in Hyde Park.

Part of the U of C's attraction lay in the fact that Hyde Park was surrounded on three sides by Chicago's black South Side. As a teenager, Butterfield was drawn to the blues clubs in the black belt where the greats of Chicago blues were still performing regularly: Muddy Waters, Howlin Wolf, Magic Sam, Otis Rush and others. He soon started playing blues guitar himself. While at U of C Butterfield met another young white blues fanatic, Elvin

Bishop. "We gravitated together real quick," Bishop recalled, "and started playing parties around the neighborhood, you know, just acoustic. He was playing more guitar than harp when I first met him. But in about six months, he became serious about the harp. And he seemed to become as good as he ever got in that six months."

Butterfield's main influences were Little Walter Jacobs, Muddy Waters and Otis Spann. He learned harp under fire, jamming in the clubs with his heroes. "I never practiced the harp in my life," Butterfield once told *Downbeat*, "Never. I would just blow it. Muddy knows that I used to come down to him and play some nothing stuff but nobody ever said 'Well, man, you're not playing too well.'" In the same interview, however, Muddy Waters pointed out that even then Butterfield had something unique in both his harp playing and his singing.

Eventually Butterfield dropped out of college to devote himself full-time to music. His first break came when Big John's, a Chicago blues bar, invited him and Bishop to play regularly. They accepted, and put together the Butterfield Blues Band, luring bass player Jerome Arnold and drummer Sam Lay away from Howlin Wolf's band with promise of more money. The band was one of the first racially mixed blues groups. In 1965, they brought Michael Bloomfield, who was also playing around Chicago at the time, in to play lead guitar. The group's energy stunned the Chicago blues scene and it wasn't long before they had a recording contract with Elektra Records. While they were making that first album, Mark Naftalin sat in on Hammond organ. His contribution—to eight of the album's eleven cuts—was so impressive that he stayed in the group after the sessions were finished. The band was renamed the Paul Butterfield Blues Band.

That first album, simply titled, *The Paul Butterfield Blues Band*, released in 1965, electrified the rock world. These songs were more than just covers of the old blues classics. They indicated a unique sensibility and pushed both blues and rock onto a new plain. Such was the impact of Butterfield's band that it was the first electric group ever invited to play the 1965 Newport Folk Festival. After they finished their well-received set, they took part in one of the legendary performances in rock history: they joined Bob Dylan onstage and accompanied him in his first performance with electric instruments. The set shocked the folk purists in the crowd, calling forth catcalls and boos. According to Butterfield, Pete Seeger even tried to cut the band's power cables backstage to force them to stop playing.

The second album by the Paul Butterfield Blues Band, 1966's *East-West*, explored uncharted territory. Called the first psychedelic album, it introduced an eclectic mix of new elements to the blues, including jazz, country and even Indian music. The 13-minute title track was one of the first extended jams on a rock album, setting a trend in rock that would eventually become *de rigueur* in hard rock.

The Butterfield band began to change in the latter half of the 1960s. *The Resurrection of Pigboy Crabshaw* was recorded without Mike Bloomfield, who had left to form the Electric Flay, and with a horn section (including the sax of David Sanborn). After the album's release, as it began to move toward a more rhythm & blues sound, Naftalin left the group. The group played the Woodstock Festival in 1969 and, that same year, Butterfield reunited with Bloomfield and Muddy Waters to make the record *Fathers and Sons.*

Not long afterwards, Butterfield moved to a house in Woodstock and a long period of decline began for the musician. He disbanded the band to form a new group, Paul Butterfield's Better Days, which recorded two relatively uninspired albums. For the rest of the 1970s, Butterfield performed only infrequently, mainly guesting on the records of other artists, making no records of his own. His appearance at the Band's Last Waltz concert was a high point in a period otherwise dominated to increasingly severe alcohol and drug problems.

In 1980, his health took a turn for the worse. He collapsed while recording and was found to have a perforated intestine. Over the next few years he was operated on four times for diverticulitis and peritonitis. Around 1983, a fan of Butterfield's, Ray Godfrey, heard about the bad shape Butterfield was in. An investment

banker, Godfrey set out to organize a limited partnership that would raise money to fund the regeneration of Butterfield's career. A manager was found, a band put together, and Butterfield returned to touring, often playing with as much intensity as he had ever showed onstage. In 1986 he recorded his last album, *The Legendary Paul Butterfield Blues Band Rides Again.* The high point of his rejuvenated career was said to be his appearance at a Rock and Roll Hall of Fame concert in 1987. He gave a moving speech to his old friend and mentor, Muddy Waters, who was being inducted into the Hall. He then led the assembled musicians in a spirited performance of "Dancin' in the Streets."

In late April, Butterfield's chronic stomach and liver problems flared up again and he had to be admitted to a hospital in Pittsburgh Pennsylvania. Days later, on May, 4, 1987, he was found dead in his home in Los Angeles. Shortly before his death, he had filmed a TV special with guitarist B.B. King. King later eulogized Butterfield saying "Paul was a great harmonica player, right up there with Sonny Boy Williamson, Rice Miller and Little Walter Jacobs." If Butterfield's music could be uneven, it always remained intensely personal and hearfelt. "I can't believe it when cats talk about music," he once told *Rolling Stone*, "and it has nothing to do with the basic concept: to make you feel good, to give something to you....The only thing I think about music is that it should be honest."

Selected Discography

Paul Butterfield Blues Band, Elektra, 1965.
East-West, Elektra, 1966.
The Ressurection of Pigboy Crabshaw, Elektra, 1967.
The Original Lost Elektra Sessions, Rhino, 1995.
East-West Live, Winner, 1996.

Sources

Books

Erlewene, Michael, Vladímir Bogdana, Chris Woodstra, and Cub Koda. *All Music Guide to the Blues*, San Francisco; Freeman Books, 1996.

Periodicals

Downbeat, August 1987; September 1989.
Esquire, October 1987.
Rolling Stone, June 18, 1987

—*Gerald Brennan*

Monserrat Caballe

Operatic singer

One of the greatest sopranos of her time, Montserrat Caballe made her professional debut in 1956. In 1990, she had released more than 80 recordings. By 1995, she had given around 3,800 performance of 88 different roles. She was especially known for her roles in operas by Mozart, Richard Strauss, and Wagner, and in Italian romantic operas. She filled her career with performances in a wide variety of operas from Bellini to Verdi and from Puccini to Wagner. As Stephen Willer wrote in the *International Dictionary of Opera*, "Montserrat Caballe is one of a handful of the greatest prima donnas of the twentieth century."

Montserrat Caballe was born during the Spanish Civil War in Barcelona, Spain. She grew up with parents who loved classical music and sang often. "Despite the Civil War and the difficult post-war period when you never knew where the next crust of bread was coming from, [my parents] were always happy and optimistic," Caballe told Serafin Garcia Ibanez in the *UNESCO Courier*. When she was a child, she would often listen to recordings of Miguel Fleta with her father. When she heard how Fleta could sing high notes extremely softly, she decided that she could learn to do it, too.

Caballe wanted to study music, but her parents could not afford to send her to school. They made an agreement with the Bertrands, a wealthy family in Barcelona, to help finance her studies. In return, Montserrat Caballe agreed to appear at the Barcelona opera house every season. She enrolled in the Conservatorio del Liceo at the age of 13. Her mother lied about her age, saying she was 15 (the minimum age for students) to get her in sooner. She studied breath control with Eugenia Kemeny, and learned her first operatic roles from the conservatory's musical director Napoleone Annovazi. Later, she studied Spanish song literature with Cochita Badia. Because of her strong training, she maintained a long career without much deterioration in her vocal quality.

In 1954, Montserrat Caballe received the Liceo Gold Medal for Singing, and decided to leave Spain to audition in Italy. She did not receive any roles there but did get cast in Basel, Switzerland. On November 17, 1956, Caballe made her debut singing Mimi in Puccini's *La Boheme*. She stayed in Basel for three more years, performing a variety of roles. She went on to sing in Germany, where she performed Violetta in *La Traviata*, Ariadne, Tatiana, Armida, and Rosina in *Il Barbiere di Siviglia*. During this time, Caballe would save her money to travel to other cities to see other opera singers perform. "I was sleeping in the trains," Caballe recalled to Robert Jacobson in *Opera News*. "It was a terrible time for the body, for the mind—but for the soul, it was something special."

In the late 1950s, she debuted in Vienna, Austria with her performance of Salome, her "very favorite" role. She won a prize from the Vienna Staatsoper for that production. From the late 1950s to the early 1960s, Caballe sang over 40 roles in seven years. She made her Teatro alla Scalla debut in 1960 as the First Flower Maiden in Wagner's *Parsifal*. The following year, she returned to Spain.

Her homecoming was realized in 1962 when she sang her first performance at the Teatro del Liceo in Barcelona. Not only was she able to perform in her hometown opera, it was then that she met her future husband, tenor Bernabe Marti. In 1965, Montserrat Caballe went on to gain worldwide recognition. She received an offer to fill in for the pregnant Marilyn Home in Donizetti's *Lucrezia Borgia* at New York's Carnegie Hall. On April 20, 1965, she sang on an American stage for the first time, and her career skyrocketed. She received overwhelming praise and recognition. Later that year, she made her debut at New York's famed Metropolitan Opera as Marguerite in Gounod's *Faust*.

Caballe continued to perform all over the world, and during that time, she married and had two children. When she received an offer from the Metropolitan Opera

For the Record . . .

Born Montserrat Caballe on April 12, 1933, in Barcelona, Spain; married: Bernabe Marti; two children. *Education:* Barcelona Conservatorio del Liceo, 1953.

Performed professional operatic debut as Mimi in Basel, Switzerland, 1956; received worldwide acclaim after New York's Carnegie Hall performance in *Lucrezia Borgia*, 1965; cancelled several performances due to operations and illness, 1974-83; performed in the debut of *Cristobal Colon* as Queen Isabella, 1986; sang at the Barcelona Olympics Opening Ceremonies, 1992; biography *Montserrat Caballe: Prima Donna*, 1995; career performances totaled approximately 3,800 in 88 different roles.

Addresses: *Record company*—BMG Classics, 1540 Broadway, New York, NY, 10036; (212) 930-4000.

for a 10-year contract in 1971, she turned it down because she would have to move her entire family, including her parents, to the United States.

Rumors Circulated of Career Demise

In the mid-1980s, Caballe began to develop a reputation as unreliable. She canceled several performances due to illness, and rumors circulated that she was not ill. "Caballe has become such a high-risk gamble that most major organizations are no longer willing to take a chance on her," Peter G. Davis reported in *New York*. Caballe responded to the criticism with the grace of a prima donna. "You never hear about the great success," she told Robert Jacobson in *Opera News*. "You always hear about my cancellations—because of big operations, on my knee in '69, for cancer in '74, my kidney operations in '76 and '82. I've had seven operations." In December of 1983, Caballe also had a minor heart attack. By January, she was back on her feet singing Herodiade and then Ariadne. In 1985, she had yet another surgery to remove a tumor.

In 1984, Caballe performed the title role in *La Gioconda* at the San Francisco Opera. Two years later, she debuted the role of Queen Isabella with Jose Carreras as Christopher Columbus in *Cristobal Colon*. Composer Leonardo Balada was commissioned by the Spanish government to write the opera about the explorer's voyage in recognition of its 500th anniversary. The cast performed the opera for five years as part of the celebration of the discovery of America.

In 1992, Hollywood Records released *Barcelona* an album of duets with Caballe and rock singer Freddie Mercury of Queen. Originally recorded in 1987, the album was not released until after Mercury's death. "All of the material (cowritten by Mercury) is penned in a style meant to snub rock in favor of "real opera" Jim Farber wrote in *Entertainment Weekly*, "but likable pop hooks keep peeping through." William Livingstone wrote in *Stereo Review*, "Uninhibited, almost campy combinations of rock and opera, the eight songs draw flat-out enthusiastic performances from both stars."

Olympic Performance Began Resurgence

That same year, Caballe appeared with five other Spanish singers at the Barcelona Olympic Games Opening Ceremony—including Placido Domingo, Jose Carreras, Giacomo Aragall, Teresa Berganza, and Juan Pons. The performance was so well received that the group went into the studio to record a commemorative album, *Domingo, Carreras, Caballe with Aragall, Berganza, Pons*, on RCA Records. William Livingstone wrote in *Stereo Review*, "Which champion gets the gold medal? Montserrat Caballe! Again, she demonstrates that she possesses one of the most beautiful voices ever to issue from a human throat."

The 1990s also brought a number of reissued recordings of Montserrat Caballe's many performances. Some of the later releases included: *Eternal Caballe: Arias, Scenes, Songs*, which featured her operatic performances and Spanish songs from 1965 to 1991; *Montserrat Caballe: Casta Diva*, with Caballe singing Schubert, Strauss, and Spanish songs by Falla and Mompou; and *Montserrat Caballe (Arias)*, a cross-section of the singer's career.

Her popularity surged again in 1995 with the publication of her biography, *Montserrat Caballe: Prima Donna*, written by Robert Pullen and Stephen Taylor. Stephanie Von Buchau wrote in *Opera News* that the authors' "critical acuity adds conviction to their conclusion that Montserrat Caballe may be the last authentic prima donna."

In 1996, Montserrat Caballe released a recording with her mother, Montserrat Marti. The RCA album, *Arias and Duets (Montserrat Caballe & Montserrat Marti)*, was the first recording for Montserrat Marti. It included solo recordings from both singers, as well as duets.

Another significant release came in 1997 with *Massenet: Manon* on VAI. Caballe had only performed *Manon* four times in her entire career. First, for two shows in New Orleans and one in Madrid in 1967, then in Bilbao in 1975. The CD included a composite of the two New Orleans performances, and became a treasure for collectors of her work. "Montserrat Caballe sings resplendently and gives the title role considerable sex appeal, with clear, idiomatic diction," wrote Bill Zakariasen in *Opera News*.

In looking back on her extensive career and many successes, Montserrat Caballe explained that soprano opera singers have a slight advantage. "A soprano's voice is a little like a mother's cry, which is why it attracts all human beings," Caballe told Serafin Garcia Ibanez in the *UNESCO Courier*. "The sound of a mother's voice expresses a feeling of intimacy, which has a truly magical effect on the listener." Caballe said the most grueling opera she'd ever sang was Bellini's *Il Pirata*. And one of her proudest moments came when she received the Paris Grand Prix for a recital of Spanish operetta known as zarzuela. "I've received many awards, but I'm most proud of the ones for my country's music," Caballe told Judy Cantor in *Harper's Bazaar*. "Those really filled me with joy."

Although her career in music provided great happiness in her life, Caballe never forgot her humble beginnings. She and her husband created a foundation that took in 500 to 600 orphans on a farm at the foot of the Pyrenees, as well as several other charitable actions. When she wasn't performing, she continued to live in Barcelona and performed there almost every year. She lived her life with grace and dedication, and proved herself in her glorious career as one of the greatest sopranos of the century.

Selected discography

Montserrat Caballe (with pianist Alexis Weissenberg), Angel, 1980.
Montserrat Caballe: Wagner, RCA Records, 1980.
Arie Antiche, London Records, 1980.
Montserrat Caballe Sings Wagner, CBS Records, 1983.
Montserrat Caballe, Giuseppe Di Stefano, Moss Music Group, 1985.
Montserrat Caballe Sings Romanzas de Zarzuelas, Moss Music Group, 1986.
Barcelona (with Freddie Mercury), Hollywood Records, 1992.

Montserrat Caballe, Shirley Verrett, RCA Records, 1992.
Jose Carreras, Montserrat Caballe: Souvenirs, Sony Music, 1992.
Montserrat Caballe: Rossini, Donizetti, Verdi Rarities, RCA Records, 1992.
Domingo, Carreras, Caballe, with Aragall, Berganza, Pons, RCA Records, 1992.
Montserrat Caballe (Carlo Felice Cillario), RCA Records, 1993.
Eternal Caballe: Arias, Scenes, Songs, RCA Records, 1994.
Montserrat Caballe: Casta Diva, RCA Records, 1995.
Montserrat Caballe (Arias), EMI Records, 1996.
Arias and Duets (Montserrat Caballe & Montserrat Marti), RCA Records, 1996.
Meyerbeer: L'Africane, Legato, 1997.
Puccini: Madama Butterfly, Legato, 1997.
Massenet: Manon, VAI, 1997.
Verdi: Luisa Miller, Myto, 1997.
Puccini: Turandot, Gala, 1997.

Sources

Books

LaRue, C. Steven, ed. *International Dictionary of Opera*, St. James Press, Detroit, 1993.

Periodicals

American Record Guide, May/June 1992, November/December 1992, July/August 1993, January/February 1994, March/April 1995, September/October 1995, January/February 1996, September/October 1997.
Consumer's Research, February 1986.
Entertainment Weekly, August 7, 1992.
Harper's Bazaar, August 1990.
High Fidelity, March 1984.
New York, January 31, 1983.
New Yorker, March 23, 1981.
Opera News, April 5, 1980; September 1980; August 1983; March 2, 1985; March 30, 1985; September 1987; December 10, 1994; July 1995; September 1996; January 25, 1997; March 8, 1997; September/October 1997; November 1997; December 6, 1997; January 17, 1998.
Stereo Review, February 1980, September 1980, May 1981, September 1992, December 1992.
UNESCO Courier, January 1995.
Wilson Library Bulletin, November 1993.

—Sonya Shelton

Sarah Elizabeth Campbell

Folk singer, songwriter

Contemporary folk singer Sarah Elizabeth Campbell was described by Mary Chapin Carpenter in the liner notes for *Running With You* as someone who "writes songs from her heart." Carpenter also added, "She sings them that way too." Campbell is distinguished by her hauntingly poignant voice, touching lyrics, straightforward vocal style, and depth of feeling. Her second release in 1994, *Running With You,* was nominated for a Best Folk Album of the Year NAIRD Award for independent musicians, and Campbell remains one of the most popular local musicians in her home town of Austin, Texas. Her unvarnished vocal quality sets her apart from many other folk singers, along with the strength and passion discernible at the core of her music. Campbell's music reflects her life. In an interview with Contemporary Musicians she said, "The songs I write are about things going on in my life. They're not songs or situations that I just dream up. I view it as a cheap form of therapy."

Campbell was born in Austin, Texas, in 1963; her mother sang and played piano—although not professionally—and her uncle was musically inclined as well. Campbell was one of three children. Her brother was also musical and became a guitarist for Delbert McClinton. Campbell recalls a childhood filled with music, but much of it was church music from the local Methodist church. She sang in church as a child and recalls "singing and eating a lot." She liked all types of music throughout her childhood and young adulthood, but was especially fond of Ella Fitzgerald, Etta James, Marcia Ball, Tracy Nelson, and Bonnie Raitt. She was also influenced by The Beatles, Elvis Presley, and Billie Holiday. Campbell began performing in public around the age of eleven or twelve and instinctively knew, beyond a shadow of a doubt, that she was meant to be a singer. There was never any other career option for her. She made her debut as the Virgin Mary in a church play.

Campbell considers herself a "wild child" when reflecting upon her youth. When she was sixteen and still in high school, all of her friends were in their 20s and 30s. Campbell said, "I flunked everything but art and music in high school." She began to pursue a singing career in earnest around the age of sixteen. Marcia Ball was her idol at the time and she used to hang out at the Split Rail in Austin in order to see Frieda and the Firedogs. She said, "I was a part of that crazy Austin music scene back in the early '70s, not as a performer, but as a sixteen year old in awe. Then I started singing and writing songs and pursuing my music career with much more seriousness.... Music has always been my passion." Campbell had little trouble performing before a crowd, and after five years or so in Austin's limelight, she decided to move on.

When Campbell was in her early twenties she left Austin for Boston, where she lived briefly before moving to northern California. Once she was firmly ensconced in her new home, she joined a group in northern California called Fiddlesticks that specialized in bluegrass and folk. She said, "It was an old-timey bluegrass band. There were four people in the band, and I was the singer, guitarist, and sometimes a banjo player." Campbell stayed with the band for twelve years before striking out on her own, and although Fiddlesticks never released an album, they did garner an avid following in northern California. Campbell became a regular on the folk festival circuit after leaving Fiddlesticks, and performed at the Strawberry Musical Festival in northern California, the Kerriville Music Festival in Texas, and folk music venues across the country. She was also invited to perform at Switzerland's Frutigen Singer/Songwriter Festival, where she left an enduring impression. Campbell generally spends half of each year on the road, usually touring between April and September.

Campbell's debut album, *A Little Tenderness,* was released in 1990 on the small, independent, California-based label Kaleidoscope. Kaleidoscope was noted primarily for the Kate Wolf catalog, and a woman in Wolf's band named Nina Gerber was Campbell's former guitar player. Gerber produced *A Little Tenderness,* and the album served to place Campbell in the national

For the Record . . .

Born May 13, 1963, in Austin, TX; one of three children.

Played with the folk/bluegrass band The Fiddlesticks for twelve years; released solo album *A Little Tenderness,* Kaleidoscope, 1990; released *Running With You,* DejaDisc 1994; contributed two songs to DejaDisc's *Pastures of Plenty: An Austin Celebration of Woody Gunthrie;* contributed "Sad Situation" to Threadgill's *Supper Session;* her original songs have been recorded or performed by Jim Messina, Rick Danko and Levon Helm (of The Band).

Addresses: *Record company*—DejaDisc, 537 Lindsey St., San Marcos, TX, 78666, (512)392-6610; fax (512) 754-6886; *Home*—3809 Red River, Austin, TX 78751.

spotlight. Her first release was well-received, and she was content with Kaleidoscope—but the label folded after the owner's wife suffered a major stroke. In 1994, Campbell released her second album, *Running With You,* on the Austin-based DejaDisc label. DejaDisc also bought Campbell's first album in order to rerelease it. Campbell was one of the top four finalists for the independent NAIRD music award for *Running With You;* it was in the running for the Best Folk Album of the Year NAIRD Award. In 1994, after DejaDisc moved its base to Nashville, Tennesee, Campbell left the label. She returned to her hometown of Austin and immediately reestablished herself as a premier local performer. She performed with her band and several guest artists each week at Austin's La Zona Rosa. She also hosted "Bummer Night" there, where one rule applied: sad songs only. As a result, the crowd moaned, cried, complained, and whined along with performers each week. Some of the guest artists at La Zona Rosa's "Bummer Night" have included Rosalie Sorrells, Peter Rowan, Tish Hinojosa, Odetta, Townes Van Zandt, Steve Young, Tom Russell, Kevin Welch, and Butch Hancock.

Campbell contributed tracks to two Austin music collections. She contributed two songs to DejaDisc's *Pastures of Plenty: An Austin Celebration of Woody Gunthrie,* which earned some of the highest praises for the album, and she contributed "Sad Situation" to Threadgill's *Supper Session.* Campbell recorded *Running With You* in Austin and used Bill Ginn—Leonard Cohen's keyboard player—as one of her producers; the other producer was Marvin Dykhuis, guitarist with Tish Hinojosa. Half of the album's twelve songs were written by Campbell, and in addition to her own material she included songs by John Prine, Karla Bonoff, Greg Trooper, Tom Russell, and Pierce Pettis. Campbell also included the first song Peggy Lee had a hit with, "Waiting For The Train (To Come In)" as well as the Boudleaux Bryant classic "Love Hurts". John Hagen from Lyle Lovett's Large Band contributed cello, Betty Elders contributed backing vocals, Paul Sweeney was featured on mandolin, along with Paul Pearcy on drums, Dave Heath on bass, and guitarists Brian Wood and Rich Brotherton.

Campbell's greatest forte is songwriting; her original songs have been recorded or performed by Jim Messina, Rick Danko and Levon Helm (of The Band). Campbell generally mixes her own original compositions with those of her favorite writers, and tends to favor material that soothes heartaches and eases dark, melancholic yearnings. "I am drawn to sad songs," Campbell admits, "I think my voice is built for it. That torchy stuff is easy for me to sing."

Selected discography

A Little Tenderness, Kaleidoscope, 1990; rereleased by DejaDisc in 1995.
Running With You, DejaDisc, 1994.

Sources

Online

"Sarah Elizabeth Campbell," www.allmusic.com/cg/amg.exe (June 3, 1998)
"Sarah Elizabeth Campbell," www.eden.com /~dejadisc/campbell.html (June 2, 1998)

Other

A Contemporary Musicians interview with Sarah Elizabeth Campbell on August 18, 1998.

—B. Kimberly Taylor

James Carr

Soul singer

In a span of five years, from 1965-69, James Carr went from singing in local gospel groups to become a 1960s soul sensation, then disappeared from the music scene after he developed a mental illness. Yet, his songs lived on through decades of cover versions by dozens of other artists. "Were it not for the extreme gravity of his psychological condition, he would have become one of the great soul singers, such was the strength and range of his voice," Hugh Gregory wrote in *Soul Music A-Z.* Carr returned to the recording studio in the early 1990s, receiving critical praise and proving that his talent had not waned after nearly 20 years away from the music industry.

Carr was born in Memphis, Tennessee, where he grew up singing with gospel choirs. "I learned everything in church," Carr told *Internotes.* "It's not different from singing pop music. The only difference is that instead of calling on God, you're calling on a woman." In the early 1960s, Carr worked with O.V. Wright in the Harmony Echoes, where he met his soon-to-be manager, Roosevelt Jamison. In 1963, Jamison led Carr to the head of Goldwax Records, Quinton Claunch. The meeting resulted in a record contract for Carr, and he released his first single, "The Word Is Out (You Don't Want Me)," the following year.

Carr continued to release singles over the next few years, and released the album *You'e Got My Mind Messed Up* in 1966. The title track, reminiscent of an Otis Redding ballad, became Carr' first hit single. During the same year, he released the single "Love Attack." In Colin Escott's description of the song in the liner notes of *The Essential James Carr*, he wrote, "you can hear the not-too-distant echoes of those gospel singers who would sometimes collapse and die right on stage."He followed that single up with "ouring Water on a Drowning Man, "which was later recorded by British rocker Elvis Costello.

In 1967, Carr released his biggest hit ever, "The Dark End of the Street." In *Esquire*, Kurt Loder described the song as "a tale of furtive love so frankly bereft of hope, it might send the most sanguine listener rooting around for a razor." "I like singing songs that are stories," Carr said in *Internotes.* "I sing songs that actually happened, so you could say I'm telling a story." The tune was later recorded and performed by numerous artists, including Aretha Franklin and Linda Ronstadt, and was used on the soundtrack for the film *The Commitments.* Despite his success, Carr continued his fevered musical pace. He released two more albums, *A Man Needs A Woman* and *Freedom Train,* in 1968. The following year, he released a cover version of the Bee Gees' "To Love Somebody" in his trademark soulful style. Not long after

For the Record . . .

Born June 13, 1942, in Memphis, TN.

Began singing in gospel choirs; signed to Goldwax Records, 1963; released debut single, "The Word Is Out (You Don"t Want Me), 1964; released debut album *You've Got My Mind Messed Up,* 1966; Goldwax folded, 1969; developed mental illness which kept him out of the music industry for over twenty years; released *Take Me to the Limit,* 1991; signed to Soul Trax and released *Soul Survivor,* 1994.

Addresses: *Record Company*—Razor & Tie Music Corp., 214 Sullivan St., #5A, New York, NY, 10012, (212) 473-9173, fax (212) 473-9174.

that single's release, though, everything began to change for Carr.

Carr soon found himself ill equipped to deal with the trappings of his newly acquired success. Feeling the mounting pressure of higher expectations from the music industry, as well as his fans, Carr retreated from reality. Carr's stress levels increased exponentially when Goldwax Records folded in 1969. The loss of his record company resulted in a total upheaval for Carr and his career, as he had already had a difficult time learning to cope with the price of fame. After Goldwax's demise, he began to rely more and more on drugs to help him get through the days, sometimes sitting in the studio, staring into space for hours at a time. Later, it was reported that he was suffering from a manic depressive illness.

"In five short years, James Carr cut some of the most majestic sides in Southern R&B history," wrote one reviewer in *Rolling Stone,* and his work had not gone unnoticed. When it became obvious that Carr would be unable to perform because of his illness, though, he returned to his native Tennessee to live with his relatives. Carr returned in 1977 with the single "Let Me Be Right," released on River City Records, only to return to his gospel music roots two years later. His early music continued its popularity with *At the Dark End of the Street,* a compilation of 14 of his greatest hits, released on Blue Side/Upside Records. *Stereo Review* urged readers to, "Imagine a cross between Otis Redding, Percy Sledge, and any number of gospel singers, and you'll begin to have an inkling of the power of his performances." Roy Greenberg wrote in his review of the LP in *Audio,* "One listen to *At the Dark End of the Street* will convince soul and blues fans that Carr must be counted among the best."

In 1991, former Goldwax President Quinton Claunch hooked up with Carr to resurrect his career. He arranged for recording sessions, which resulted in the album *Take Me to the Limit.* The album did not receive much attention, but Claunch and Carr didn't give up there. Three years later, Claunch formed a new label called Soul Trax Records, with Carr at the top of its roster. "I kept in real close contact with James Carr all these years," Claunch told Chris Morris in *Billboard.* "He had some problems a few years ago, but it's under control. He's back to being James Carr." Carr returned with a vengeance on his 1994 release *Soul Survivor,* an apt title after all he'd been through.

The album reflected Carr's trademark sound, updated for the 1990s. Chris Morris wrote in *Billboard,* "The abyss-voiced Carr sounds as assured and as vital as he did on his unforgettable '60s singles." Although he didn't receive the attention he had in the 1960s, with *Soul Survivor,* his strength, hope, and talent came through loud and clear.

Carr's comeback resulted in yet another hits compilation in 1995, *The Essential James Carr.* Released on Razor & Tie Music, it included many of his hits from the 1960s, once again proving the timelessness of those songs, and why so many artists continue to record their own versions of his work. After more than 30 years, Carr had yet to become a household name, but his music continued to live and inspire listeners across many musical genres.

Selected discography

You've Got My Mind Messed Up, Goldwax Records, 1966.
A Man Needs a Woman, Goldwax Records, 1968.
Freedom Train, Goldwax Records, 1968.
At the Dark End of the Street, Blue Side/Upside, 1987.
Take Me to the Limit, Ace Records, 1991.
Soul Survivor, Soul Trax Records, 1994.
The Essential James Carr, Razor & Tie Music, 1995.

Sources

Books

Gregory, Hugh, *Soul Music A-Z,* Da Capo Press, New York, 1995.

Periodicals

Audio, January 1988.
Billboard, June 18, 1994.
Esquire, April 1992.
Rolling Stone, July 2, 1987.
Stereo Review, September 1987, June 1995.

Online

http://webcom.com/~inotes/artist/c/james_carr.html http://
   www.retroactive.com/jan97/carr.html

—*Sonya Shelton*

Craig Chaquico

Guitarist, songwriter

Craig Chaquico gives credence to the oxymoron "rock and roll prodigy." Indeed Chaquico wrote his first song at age 12, played professionally in a popular San Francisco band at age 14, and joined in a professional studio session at age 16. Immediately upon graduation from high school, Chaquico joined the celebrated Jefferson Starship band and played with the group until 1990. He never missed a performance nor a recording session. After the demise of Starship, Chaquico embarked on a solo career in the musical genre of new age jazz, writing and performing uniquely poetic melodies for acoustical guitar.

Craig Chaquico (Cha-kee-so) was born in Sacramento, California on September 24, 1954 and was raised in a close-knit family environment with his parents who were particularly fond of music. His mother, a pianist and organist, played at church and his father played saxophone semi-professionally. Chaquico's admiration for his parents flourished over time. Although he idolized his first rock and roll heroes, "... Hendrix, Page, Clapton and Beck," Chaquico confided in retrospect to E.K. of

High Octave Music. Reproduced by permission.

For the Record . . .

Born September 26, 1954 in Sacramento, CA; raised in Sacramento, CA; married to Kimberly; one son, Kyle, born 1991;

Career: member of Steelwind from age 14; in 1971 played with Papa John Creech session with Jerry Garcia, David Crosby, and Graham Nash, including Jerry Garcia; first professional gig at age 16; lead guitar of Jefferson Starship, 1974-1990; first solo album *Acoustic Highway,* Higher Octave Music, 1994; released *Acoustic Planet,* 1994, *A Thousand Pictures,* 1996.

Awards: *Billboard Magazine* Top New Age Indie Album, for *Acoustic Highway,* 1994; Best Instrumental Guitarist of the Year, *Guitar Player Magazine;* BAMMY (Bay Area Music Awards) for *Acoustic Highway,* Outstanding Independent Album, 1994; Hearing Education and Awareness for Rockers (H.E.A.R.) artist of the month, May 1996.

Adresses: *Record company*—Higher Octave Music, 23852 Pacific Coast Highway, Suite 2C, Malibu, CA 90265

the *Rock N' Roll Reporter*, "Now that I have a family and am older, I realize my parents were my real heroes."

As a child, growing up on a farm in northern California, Chaquico imagined himself as a singing cowboy with a guitar on his knee. He first started to play acoustical guitar when he was in grade school, around ten years old. He loved the instrument and one day it became particularly precious to him. It was his guitar that kept his young life from falling apart after a serious auto accident when he was 12 years old. The Chaquico family, out in the family car, was struck by a drunk driver. The three were lucky to escape alive, although Chaquico himself suffered two broken wrists, a broken thumb, a triple fracture of one leg, and a cerebral hemorrhage which left him unconsciousness for three days immediately following the accident.

For some time afterward his life was a blur of wheel chairs, crutches, and corrective shoes. Unable to return to school for three months; Chaquico passed the time

playing the guitar. He didn't simply strum the guitar but played riffs and arpeggios all over the frets. His doctor, along with his parents, encouraged him to play as much as possible as a form of therapy to help recapture the dexterity in his wrists and thumb. All he could really use was one finger because of the casts that confined his hands and fingers. Chaquico's father promised to buy him a new guitar, an electric model, as an incentive to work hard and recuperate fully. Dauntlessly, Chaquico practiced, his fingers flew. He composed his first substantial melody during that painful convalescence, with his arms still wrapped in casts. The tune, "E-lizabeth's Song," was named for the doctor who brought him through that difficult time and for the E-string on the guitar, because that was all that he could reach with his fingers wrapped up in plaster. Although the entire song was composed for one string, high E, it is nonetheless lively, a busy song with an astonishing profusion of melodic riffs. In time, the creative 12-year-old healed, and he received the coveted electric guitar as a gift from his father. So dramatic was Chaquico's recovery in fact, that by the time he started high school he was truly a skilled guitarist, despite the debilitating accident.

Chaquico was only 14 when one of his teachers, Jack Traylor, invited him to join a band called Steel Wind, a popular combo in the San Francisco bay area. Chaquico was so young that he disguised his appearance with pasted-on whiskers in order to work in the clubs late at night. Steel Wind meanwhile caught the ear of Gracie Slick and Paul Kantner of the top-selling rock group the Jefferson Airplane. Slick and Kantner invited Chaquico to join in a recording session to back up Airplane violinist Papa John Creech for a solo album release called *Sunfighter* on Grunt Records—Slick and Kantner's own label. Chaquico, only 16 years old, was honored to play in the session with rock and roll greats David Crosby, Graham Nash, and the late Jerry Garcia.

Jefferson Starship and Starship

In 1974, after Chaquico finished high school he went straight to a world-class rock group, the Jefferson Starship, a reincarnation of the former Jefferson Airplane, under the direction of Slick and Kantner. Years of practice as a youngster, playing his old wooden guitar while healing from the auto accident, and jamming on his electric guitar as a teenager with Steel Wind paid off for Chaquico who stepped onto the stage and played lead guitar behind the world famous singer Gracie Slick. Chaquico's first performance with the Jefferson Starship was truly memorable because his high school band, Steel Wind, played the opener of Chaquico's debut concert with Jefferson Starship. Chaquico played with Steel Wind and then played with the Starship for the duration of that same concert.

After that first concert, Chaquico has played on every Jefferson Starship recording through 1984, at which time the group turned over and lost the rights to use the word Jefferson in their name. At that time the band was renamed to Starship, and Chaquico kept playing lead guitar. Eventually he held the distinction as the only member to play on every record and in every performance of Starship, including the band's time as Jefferson Starship. Chaquico stayed with Starship until 1990 when the group spontaneously dissolved. Starship earned a combined total of 13 gold and platinum albums during those years.

Solo Career

After Starship, Chaquico intended right away to assemble a new band and keep on performing. He first attempted to assemble a band called Big Bad Wolf. The failure of that group in part, combined with his wife's first pregnancy, led Chaquico to re-invent himself. Chaquico discovered very quickly that his pregnant wife Kimberly much preferred the soothing sounds of his old acoustic guitar to the brash electric instrument. In due time Chaquico was not merely playing his old guitar for his wife, he was singing to their unborn child, and writing songs for each of them. By the time son Kyle was born in 1991, Chaquico substantially had written the score of an entire CD release.

His first solo album, *Acoustic Highway,* was released in 1993 and was followed by a sequel, *Acoustic Planet* in 1994. Chaquico meanwhile worked with Washburn Guitar Company to design just the right acoustic guitar to suit his own ear and meet his professional needs. The collaboration resulted in the Craig Chaquico signature series guitar, a Washburn EA-20 model, with custom Chaquico features including wider frets, lower action, and steel strings. Chaquico, a die-hard environmentalist who lives by a redwood forest, negotiated with the Washburn company to "give something back," by planting a tree for every Chaquico guitar made. Overall the effect Chaquico achieved with his instrument design was that of an acoustic guitar that plays, feels, and sounds in many ways like an electric; and Chaquico plays the instrument as if it were electric, employing bends, stretches, hammer-ons, and other electric techniques. After taping *Acoustic Highway,* Chaquico gave his first live performance at the very same hospital where he had received treatment many years earlier as a 12-year-old auto crash victim.

His next album, *Acoustic Planet* toppled an album by new age conductor Yanni for the number one spot on the *Billboard* music chart in November of 1994. *Acoustic Planet* also received a Grammy nomination. Chaquico wrote a song for every memory of life it seems. He wrote the tongue-in-cheek "Sweet Talk" for his wife, after observing some men getting fresh with her as she sat in the audience one day while he performed on stage. Another song, "Autumn Blue," Chaquico wrote in a classic style for his father who passed away in 1995. Chaquico wrote "Kyle's World, like so many of his acoustic compositions, for his son. Chaquico's *Acoustic Highway* was inspired by the image of traveling along California's coastal Highway One, preferably by motorcycle. On a broader scale the album is about anything that "doesn't have to do with work or school." Chaquico, who loves to travel California's many highways on his Harley-Davidson motorcycle, promoted his first solo album by taking a series of guitar workshops on tour for Washburn Guitars. He took the tour around the United States on a Harley-Davidson motorcycle.

As new age act, Chaquico quickly assembled an assortment of popular jazzmen to fill out the sounds of his music. He collaborates almost exclusively with Ozzie Ahlers and generally tours and records with a band consisting of partner Ozzie Ahlers on keyboards, drummer Wade Olson, and bassist Jim Reitzel. Whenever possible, Chaquico employs the saxophone styles of John Klemmer. Chaquico also works frequently with flutist Douglas Spotted Eagle. Many of Chaquico's compositions were in fact based on stories of Native American legend related to Chaquico by Spotted Eagle. Chaquico's love affair with the earth and with nature is clearly displayed by the strong Native American influence in his work. In 1993, Chaquico joined Guitar, Saxes & More, a jazz tour with featured headliners Richard Elliot, Peter White, and Rick Braun. The tour has been all over the United States, from Oklahoma City to Pompano Beach, Florida, to Anchorage Alaska.

Chaquico the Man

Privately Chaquico is a husband and father. His son, Kyle, was born on July 11, 1991, at 7:11 a.m. during a solar eclipse, a real treat for Chaquico who is fascinated by astronomy. The family lives in Mill Valley, in California's majestic Marin County. Chaquico loves the whole outdoors. In July of 1998, he performed at the JVC Winter Park Jazz Festival in the Colorado Rocky Mountains, a festival where patrons are instructed to "take only pictures, leave only footprints." He is an avid long-distance runner, and he loves scuba diving, especially the feeling of weightlessness. As a youngster he thought that music would always be a great hobby, since he planned to study commercial art. Instead he finds that drawing and painting are now his hobbies and music his career. Chaquico also writes poetry, as published on the jacket of his *Thousand Pictures* album.

Chaquico's professional involvements extend far beyond concerts and recording sessions. It is him playing Gumby's guitar on the soundtrack of the Gumby movies! In May of 1996 Hearing Education and Awareness for Rockers (H.E.A.R.) named Chaquico as the artist of the month, citing in particular his social commitment. In the winter of 1997 he performed a benefit concert at Central California Women's Facility (CCWF) in Chowchilla for the Bread and Roses organization, a social consciousness group that brings live music to confined populations. Chaquico is especially committed to the National Association of Music Therapy (N.A.M.T.). His involvement with that organization is intensive. He works with pediatric, geriatric, and psychiatric patients in particular, averaging about one performance per week for patients. His work with N.A.M.T. included a concert he played for survivors of the 1995 bomb blast in Oklahoma City. When Chaquico plays at a hospital or medical facility, he regularly leaves behind at least one musical instrument, a Chaquico signature guitar from Washburn. In 1997, he was honored by the Mayor of his home town Sacramento, for his extensive work with N.A.M.T.

Chaquico, distinctive in his art, paints pictures without colors and writes poetry without words. His every song tells a story and proffers a piece of either his personal life or his views on living—from love relationships to the size and shape of the universe.... His songs are his poems. He is a man of extremes and extreme sensitivity.

Selected discography

(with Jefferson Starship) *Dragon Fly,* 1974.
Acoustic Highway, Higher Octave Music, 1993.
Acoustic Planet, Higher Octave Music, 1994.
A Thousand Pictures (includes "Kyle's World"), Higher Octave Music, 1996.
Once in a Blue Universe, Higher Octave Music, August 26, 1997.

Sources

Periodicals

Billboard, 5, June 1993.
Bread & Roses Newsletter, Winter 1997.
Jungle Beat Artists Interviews, July 1993, available at
Music Connection, 7 June 1993 to 20 June 1993.
Rock N' Roll Reporter, December 1995.
Washington Sunday Times, 25 February 1996.

Online

"Craig Chaquico," *Jungle Beat Artist Interviews,* http://www.simplesystems.com/beat/inter/jb-int2.htm (August 2, 1998).

—Gloria Cooksey

Clannad

Irish folk group

The history of popular music is rife with stories of grizzled, veteran acts with long, rich histories that are suddenly "discovered" through the most unlikely happenstance, and the Irish group Clannad is a perfect example. Formed in the late 1960s in the remote county of Donegal in Ireland, Clannad had been creating a unique blend of traditional folk songs, haunting vocals, and electronic innovations for two decades when in 1993, the inclusion of a song in a Volkswagen commercial made the group near-celebrities in America. The German car company found their phone lines buzzing with people interested not in buying a car, but in their commercial's enchanting music. Consequently, Clannad had an album enter *Billboard*'s charts for the first time, and were welcomed by a new and unexpected share of fans. Despite their new found popularity, the band continued unshakably on their quest into the mystical past of their country's heritage.

Clannad's story is very much a family saga, as its members are all blood relatives from the Northwest of Ireland who have built a deep working relationship over many years. In the late 1960s, the Brennan brothers, Pol and Ciaran, along with sister Maire focused a shared love of their Celtic musical heritage into the creation of a band. Although the siblings all boasted versatile musical abilities, the central lineup consisted of Pol playing tin whistle and flute, Ciaran on double bass and vocals, and Maire offering both harp playing and her distinct, other-worldly voice as the centerpiece. Joined by twin uncles Noel and Paidraig Duggan on guitar, mandolin, and other instruments, the Brennans christened themselves "an clann as Dobhar," meaning "family from Dore" in Gaelic.

Although the family quickly adopted the less cumbersome title Clannad, they otherwise showed no desire to smolder their strong Celtic pride. While the Brennan's parents were both musicians who specialized in more popular styles— father Leo had played a boisterous, accordion-peppered brand of big band jazz in a local tavern—their grandparents had been a reserve of time-worn tales and legends spun in original Gaelic. "The traditional songs and legends we used to learn when we were growing up had a lot of images of places and people's names," Maire stated on *The South Bank Show*, a program on the Bravo! network. "Like, there's an area in Donegal which is utterly gorgeous with a couple of legends attached to it as well. We tried to take in the various legends."

The history and landscape of Ireland permeated the world of Clannad's lyrics from the band's onset, but the family's penchant for tradition went further. Rather than adopting the styles of English and American pop music that had wafted from overseas, the Brennans and Duggans amassed a treasury of local songs from which they crafted a new sound. However, the fact that these songs remained in Gaelic did not win audiences over. "When we first started to actually play the traditional songs in our contemporary style, we weren't very encouraged by what we were doing, because people thought it was a bit mad that we were singing Gaelic songs," Maire told Lahri Bond in *Dirty Linen* magazine. "People used to say to us, 'Listen, you'll not get anywhere doing that'." As Clannad began playing live in nearby taverns, some locals were put off by the backwards, rural connotations of Gaelic, while purists of the culture found the group's addition of contemporary harmonies distasteful.

Having built up a repertoire of over 500 songs, Clannad made the unprecedented decision to arrange these traditional tunes for a full band, and began making forays into nearby villages for live performances. Despite initial friction, the Brennans and Duggans began to charm audiences, and soon found their first big break. To Clannad's surprise, they were awarded the first prize in the Letterkenny Folk Festival and as a result offered a chance to record with the Irish branch of the Phillips label. However, Clannad's uncompromising use of Gaelic was met by record executives with raised eyebrows. "That was in 1970 and we were still in college and school, but we didn't record the [first] record until 1973,

For the Record . . .

Members include **Ciaran Brennan** (born Ciaran—pronounced "Keeron" —O Braonain in Gweedore, Ireland, also the birthplace of other members), vocals, double bass, electric bass, guitar, synthesizer, piano); **Enya Brennan** (1980-82, born Eithne Ni Bhraonain, May 17, 1961), keyboards, vocals; **Maire Brennan** (born Maire —pronounced "Moya"— Ni Bhraonain, August 4, 1952), vocals, harp, keyboard; **Pol Brennan** (left band, 1989), tin whistles, flute); **Noel Duggan**, guitar (born Noel O Dugain); **Paidraig Duggan** (born Padarig pronounced —"Poric"— O Dugain), mandolin, harmonica, acoustic guitar.

Band formed in hometown of Gweedore, Ireland in the late 1960s by Duggan and Brennan families; won first prize at Letterkenny Folk Festival, leading to a deal with Phillips records, 1970; released self-titled debut album, 1973; toured Europe for the first time, 1976; released album *Dulaman*, 1976; embarked on first American tour, 1979; released first album with synthesizers, *Fuaim*, 1981; achieved European success with release of "Theme From Harry's Game," 1982; recorded hit single "In A Lifetime" with U2 vocalist Bono, 1986; achieved international fame with a second release of "Harry's Game," 1992; Maire released first solo record, 1992; scored heavily on world music charts with album *Lore*, 1996.

Awards: Ivor Novello Award for "Theme From Harry's Game," 1982; British Academy of Film And Television Arts Award for best soundtrack, *Legend*, 1984; Billboard World Music Song of the Year Award for "Theme From Harry's Game," 1992; Irish Recorded Music Award, lifetime achievement, 1998.

Addresses: *Agent*—Upfront Management Ltd., 14/15 Sir John Rogerson's Quay, Dublin 2, Ireland.

Maire told Bond, "because the record company didn't like the idea of us doing half the album in Gaelic. It wasn't heard of to sing Gaelic unless you were really heavy into folk, ethnic, and traditional music, and then for only a really small minority of people."

Clannad, the 1973 debut, was representative of the kind of folk-based arrangements the group would master throughout the rest of the decade. While tracks like the drinking song "Nil se'n la" ("It's Not Yesterday") demonstrated Clannad's willingness to season Celtic standards with alien jazz influences, it was the more rustic instruments like mandolin and bongos which dominated the overall flavor of the album. Their third album, *Dulaman*, released in 1976, was perhaps the most fully realized of Clannad's works to date, highlighted by the sprawling title track, a chronicle of two merchants of dulaman, or seaweed.

Despite the growing fan support these albums garnered, Clannad still considered themselves to be mere novices, and were uncertain of their band's future. When journalist Fachtna O'Kelly and recording engineer Nicky Ryan heard the band in the mid-1970s, though, they gave Clannad the needed push towards a professional career when they agreed to manage them. "After working with [Irish group] Planxty as an engineer in 1975, I was at loose ends," Ryan reflected to Peter Herbst in *Rolling Stone*. "Fachtna said, 'Why don't you give [Clannad] a listen,' and when I heard the double bass and those harmonies, I was just knocked out. But it was a big step for them, a family, to turn professional, leaving no children at home." After a standing ovation at a 1976 Berlin performance, that "big step" became significantly smaller.

By 1979, Clannad had drawn a strong following among folk devotees, recorded the impressive *Clannad in Concert* album, and crossed the Atlantic for their first American tour. More importantly, they had established a sound as unique as it was universally appealing, for in spite of the obvious language barrier, Maire's contralto vocals touched audiences at a more purely musical level. However, rather than becoming complacent merchants of folky charm, the Brennans and Duggans began to dabble in new kinds of arrangements, but did so by creating a truly new synthesis of musical sources rather than simply slapping Irish tunes into a modern setting.

The New Face of Clannad

With the release of the album *Fuiam* in 1981, Clannad showed the world their new face, and the reception was as positive as ever. Joined by younger sister Enya Brennan on keyboards and vocals, the group took on an electronic sound for the first time, but this only added to the rich, full sound they had already established. Enya's voice was a perfect counterpoint to older sister Maire's, and she took the lead duties on two songs, "An t Ull" and "Buaireadh An Phosta." However, Enya"s stay was short-lived as, after *Fuaim*, she launched a solo career that would make her perhaps the biggest celebrity of her time in new age music. Ironically enough, much of Enya's initial solo exposure was also due advertising, as her song "Orinoco Flow (Sail Away)" was employed in several advertisements.

If Clannad's music had always carried with it imagery of lush landscapes, then the addition of synthesizers bolstered that quality, and consequently the group was sought after to lend their atmospheric touch to film and television soundtracks. Their first, a theme for a television thriller titled *Harry's Game* was recorded in 1982 and would beget their most popular song ever. "When we wrote 'Harry's Game' we knew it was nice and it was special," Maire stated in a 1995 Public Broadcasting System interview. "It was very special to us. But honestly, I never thought it would accomplish what it has in any form. It was just other people that latched onto it.... We thought we'd just carried on with the next phase of our life as far as writing songs." This was the first of several releases given to *Harry's Game*, and this time around it broke the British Top ten sales chart, and won the Ivor Novello Award, the British equivalent to the Grammy Awards.

Became Minor European Stars

The success of "Harry's Game" made Clannad minor stars in Europe, and throughout the 1980s the Brennans and Duggans were seen as something like godparents by a new generation of acts who were proud of their Irish heritage. The impetus of their surprise hit single pushed their 1983 album *Magical Ring*'s sales to gold status, and *Legend*, a selection of music the band composed for the 26-part *Robin of Sherwood* television series, yielded a second gold record and a British Academy Award in 1984. Meanwhile, the Irish pop group U2 adopted "Harry's Game" as their theme music in live performances, and their outspoken singer Bono joined Maire for "In A Lifetime," a duet featured on the 1986 Clannad album *Macalla*. Despite all this, the group retained their sensibility, as well as their sense of humor. As Maire told Bond, "People were saying to us, 'What's it like to write a hit song?,' and we'd say, 'Oh, come on, if you were trying to write a hit song would you have written it in Gaelic?'"

The band's growing marketability led American rock producers Greg Ladany and Russ Kunkel to invite Clannad to Los Angeles to produce their next album. Collaborating with middle of the road singers like pianist Bruce Hornsby, J.D. Souther, and ex-Journey leader Steve Perry, the band created *Sirius* in 1988 with disappointing results. As Bond wrote, "[t]he resulting sound was typical of what American producers do with

ethnic music ... bland, over produced, and formulated for easy radio play." Although Clannad themselves were aware of the album's weakness, they did defend a few of its cuts, but did not continue to move in Sirius's direction.

Became Popular—Again

Throughout the late 1980s and early 1990s, Clannad found themselves in a flurry of activity, in spite of the amicable departure of Pol in 1989. In addition to releasing two retrospective compilations in 1990, *Past-present* and *The Collection*, the group had scored an animated feature called *The Angel and the Soldier Boy*. While still intact as a group, the members of Clannad also offered several solo albums, Pol's somewhat disappointing *Trisan,* released in 1993, and Maire's self-titled debut, released in 1992 with the help of sisters Deirdre, Olive, and Bridin. In 1992, the band proved that they had not been spreading themselves too thinnly with the release of *Anam,* their best album in years.

In addition to ten new compositions, the American version of *Anam* featured "In A Lifetime" and "Harry's Game," perhaps as selling points for listeners unfamiliar with Clannad's previous work. However, the inclusion of "Harry's Game" in a commercial for the Volkswagen Passat as well as in the soundtrack of the Harrison Ford film *Patriot Games* created an unexpected storm of demand for the song, and it became an even bigger hit the second time around. From the strength of one song, *Anam* became the first gold record for the band in America, and created new Clannad fans along the way. While Clannad was again mildly shocked by their mass success, they found Volkswagen's use of their music tasteful, and warmly welcomed overseas admirers. "We were really stunned by the public response," Maire told Bond. "It's funny, I was in Tower Records and they said, 'You wouldn't believe the amount of people who come in looking for the Volkswagen Song. It kind of worked out really well, being in the charts, for the first time. We thought America had passed us by."

Soon after their second big breakthrough, Clannad returned to the studio to create *Banba*, a rich work that was released to mark the twentieth anniversary of the group in 1993. Blending the band's earliest styles with its most recent innovations, *Banba* boasted a large selection of musicians in addition to the four piece core. Also that year, Clannad contributed yet another popular track to a film soundtrack, *Last of the Mohicans*. Showing their dedication to authenticity, the group did extensive research to write the song in the near-extinct language of the Mohican tribe.

For over two decades the Brennans and Duggans retained the same commitment to music that guided them from the start, notwithstanding any commercial success they may have found. "We're successful because we stuck from day one to the same thing ... we like doing things from our locality," Ciaran posited to Herbst. "And if people get off on it, we're just amazed."

Selected discography

Clannad, Phillips, 1973; re-released on Boot, 1997.
Clannad Two, Shanachie, 1975.
Dulamain, Shanachie, 1976.
Crann Ull, Tara, 1978.
Clannad In Concert, Shanachie, 1979.
Fuaim, Atlantic (repackage), 1981.
Magical Ring, Tara, 1982.
Legend, RCA, 1984.
Macalla, RCA, 1986.
Sirius, RCA, 1988.
Pastpresent, RCA, 1990.

Anam, Atlantic, 1992.
Banba, Atlantic, 1993.
Lore, Atlantic, 1996.
Rogha: The Best of Clannad, Atlantic, 1997.

Sources

Periodicals

Dirty Linen, August/September 1993.
Entertainment Weekly, March 17, 1995.
Newsweek, April 5, 1993.
Rolling Stone, November 29, 1979.
Vogue, May 1988.

Online

http://www.jtwinc.com/clannad

—Shaun Frentner

Tom Cochrane

Singer, songwriter

After spending 20 years building a solid following in his native Canada with a repertoire of mainstream rock 'n' roll, Tom Cochrane has been gratified in the 1990s with increased notice south of the border, in the United States. The hit singles "Life Is a Highway" and "I Wish You Well" have contributed to Cochrane's commercial success and growing notoriety, while his increasingly personal, more musically adventurous compositions have made him an intriguing, less predictable performer. "Early on, the raspy-voiced Cochrane developed the sort of gritty sound that epitomizes classic rock 'n' roll," *Maclean's* magazine wrote. "But critics now see a new maturity in the musician's lyrics ... and a winning combination of folk-rock and rhythm-and-blues influences in his songs."

Tom was one of three children of Tuck Cochrane, a bush pilot, and his wife, Violet. The family lived in a small mining town called Lynn Lake in the province of Manitoba and later moved to the Toronto area. "[Cochrane] began writing tunes at eleven," *Maclean's* reported, "soon after hocking a toy train set to raise money for his first guitar." He began playing his songs in bars across Canada in the early 1970s, and landed a recording deal with a small label, Daffodil Records, in 1974. However, his debut album, *Hang On to Your Resistance,* received little attention. He followed that up with the dubious achievement of writing and recording the theme song for a porn flick called *My Pleasure is My Business.* From there, Cochrane worked as a cab driver in Toronto, a crewman on a Caribbean steamer, and a dishwasher and deliveryman in Los Angeles—where he tried desperately to break into the music business. Unsuccessful, he returned to Toronto after a year.

Fate stepped in when Cochrane entered a downtown Toronto bar on a night the local band Red Rider was performing. He asked for an audition and soon became the group's lead singer. The band struck a deal with Vancouver manager Bruce Allen, the man who represented Canadian superstar Bryan Adams, and Red Rider's first album, 1980's *Don't Fight It,* sold 100,000 copies. From 1980 to 1989, Cochrane fronted Red Rider as the band released seven albums along with hit singles such as "White Hot," "Lunatic Fringe," and "Boy Inside the Man." Meanwhile, Cochrane gained a reputation as one of Canada's leading songwriters and entertainers.

In 1985 the band split from Allen after a falling-out, but its success continued. After renaming themselves Tom Cochrane and Red Rider, the group released four albums in four years and won the 1987 Juno Award—the Canadian equivalent of the Grammy—for group of the year. Two years later, Cochrane won the Juno for composer of the year. Despite the success, he could not escape the annoying references that characterized him as the Canada's Bruce Springsteen or John Mellencamp or Bob Seger. At the same time, Cochrane chafed at playing runner-up to Bryan Adams on his native soil; the two share a long-standing rivalry. In one interview, Cochrane criticized the England-dwelling Adams for "abandoning" Canada and even suggested that Adams' road crew sabotaged his sound system when they shared a venue.

Over the years, Cochrane has been active in a relief organization called World Vision. Before aligning himself with the agency, however, he traveled to five countries, including war-torn Mozambique, to examine World Vision in action. Upon his return, Cochrane penned the bouncy, infectious tune "Life is A Highway." It was included on his third solo album, 1991's *Mad Mad World,* and became a huge hit, giving Cochrane a foothold in the U.S. market that Red Rider had never achieved. "It was gratifying to finally break through in the U.S.," he was quoted in *Billboard.* "Previously, you had a lot of people saying, 'He's a success in Canada because he's Canada's own, and Canadians embrace him because of that.' There was the specter hanging over me that I was an esoteric artist, and people outside Canada couldn't relate to me. That was put to bed with *Mad Mad World.*" Not everyone was convinced, however. *Entertainment Weekly* reviewer Dave DiMartino decried the

Born May 14, 1953 in Manitoba, Canada and moved to Ontario; son of Tuck (a bush pilot) and Violet Cochrane.

Struggled as a musician in the years before he joined the popular Toronto band Red Rider. With Cochrane as lead singer, Red Rider released a string of popular albums in the 1980s. His solo career proceeded with *Victory Day,* 1988; *Symphony Sessions,* 1989; *Mad Mad World,* 1991; *Ragged Ass Road,* 1995; and *Song of a Circling Spirit,* 1997.

Awards: Juno Award, with Red Rider for best group of the year, 1987; Juno Award, for composer of the year, 1989.

Addresses: *Record company*—Capitol Records, 810 Seventh Avenue, 4th floor, New York, NY 10019.

album's "frighteningly commercial sound" and "well-crafted, extremely soulless radio fodder, a clever replica of music that wasn't even that interesting in the first place."

Cochrane followed *Mad Mad World* with 1995's *Ragged Ass Road,* one of the most eagerly awaited album's in Canada in years. It proved to be worth the wait: many critics and fans consider it Cochrane's most intimate, eclectic, and provocative record ever. "*Ragged Ass Road* is a rootsier, more rocking, more lyrically introspective piece of work than *Mad Mad World,*" Shawn Osler wrote in the *Southam News.* Sadly, it also is Cochrane's darkest album, as it recounts the disintegration of his marriage in painful detail. "I guess I use [songwriting] as a cleansing," Cochrane told *Billboard's* Larry LeBlanc. "It's unavoidable at this stage. You have to write about what you've gone through." The album's title is taken from a stretch of highway in Canada's Northwest Territories. "One thing I've learned is that if life is a highway, it's not paved with gold," Cochrane said. "It's more a quest of the heart and soul than anything. You can get dragged down by analyzing the past instead of looking into the future. I'm trying to live more in the now [and] make the music I want to make."

Cochrane's 1997 release, *Songs of Circling Spirit,* is something of an "unplugged" venture featuring mostly acoustic guitar-and-harmonica versions of many of his songs. That strategy can result in an uninspired regurgitation of an artist's past glories—but not this time. When Cochrane's music is pared down, they better demonstrate his subtle talents as a singer and songwriter, wrote Paul Cantin of the *Ottawa Sun.* "Free of all the ordinary heavy rock band accouterments," Mary Dickie reported in *Maclean*'s, "Tom Cochrane's direct, unpretentious songs come into sharp focus, and his raspy, world-weary voice makes them all the more affecting. The result is a record that feels more like a fresh view of a strong songwriter than a retread of past hits."

Selective discography

Albums

Victory Day, 1988.
Symphony Sessions (with the Edmonton Symphony Orchestra), 1989.
Mad Mad World, Capitol Records, 1991.
Ragged Ass Road, Capitol Records, 1995.
Song of a Circling Spirit, Capitol Records, 1997.

With Red Rider, on Capitol and RCA

Don't Fight it, 1980.
As Far as Siam, 1981.
Neruda, 1983.
Breaking Curfew, 1984.
Tom Cochrane and Red Rider, 1986.

Sources

Billboard, June 27, 1992; September 30, 1995.
Entertainment Weekly, July 10, 1992.
Maclean's, January 27, 1992; August 25, 1997.
Ottawa Sun, July 13, 1997.
Southam News, November 11, 1995.

Additional information was provided by Tom Cochrane's home page and press materials.

—*Dave Wilkins*

Vinnie Colaiuta

Drummer

Vince (Vinnie) Colaiuta is a versatile and well-rounded musician. A drummer by profession, Colaiuta's collaborations involve many of the great names in pop, rock, and jazz: Al Kooper, Chick Corea, John Patitucci, Herbie Hancock, the late Frank Zappa, and countless others. Colaiuta—a solo, studio, and live tour drummer—is the antithesis of flamboyance. He is not only content with the anonymous quality of studio session drumming, but Colaiuta lowered his visibility further during an early phase of his career when he habitually sawed several inches off the legs of his drummer's chair—not from shyness, but in order to get better leverage on the drum pedals.

Colaiuta grew up in Pennsylvania and decided at a young age to be a drummer. His original instruments were pots and pans from his parents' kitchen. He was only in grade school when his parents surrendered to his passion and gave their son his first set of drums. Colaiuta's musical talent was always evident. He exhibited a natural talent for playing his drums and he also took organ lessons and played electric guitar as well. Summer vacations were spent in music camp at West Virginia University.

In junior high school he added yet another instrument to his repertoire when he joined the junior high school band as a flutist for one year because the drummer's chair was already taken. Eventually the band's drummer vacated the spot and Colaiuta moved into the slot. At age 14, Colaiuta acquired a professional quality drum set and expanded his drum lessons and summer camp curriculum well beyond basic snare drum lessons. Colaiuta, by his own admission, was already very comfortable with a full set of drums at that point in time. He played every drum in the set and improvised with ease. He truly loved to play.

As a teenager Colaiuta's zeal for his drums and for music in general bordered on the fanatical. He practiced incessantly, everywhere—even at school, even during class, "I learned real fast because I was always practicing. I would go into English class and sit in the back of the room with a practice pad and practice double-stroke rolls and get kicked out of class," he confided to *Modern Drummer*'s Robyn Flans.

After high school, Colaiuta played his drums professionally with various bands around his home town. The following year he moved to Boston to attend Berkley School of Music. By then his technical interest in music including theory, notation, and technique was piqued. He loved the "nuts and bolts" music classes and he absorbed theory tirelessly. Colaiuta, in his eagerness to play, eventually lost enthusiasm for his classes at Berkley because it was too much like school. According to Colaiuta who said to himself at the time, "I'm not going to do this.... I'm a player." As a result he stayed only two semesters and the following year he accepted an opportunity to tour with organist/pianist Al Kooper, after which Colaiuta moved from Boston to California.

By January of 1978 Colaiuta settled permanently in Los Angeles. The following April he auditioned for the legendary musician and composer Frank Zappa who by that time had dissolved his band (Mothers of Invention) and was experimenting with new styles as a solo act. At the audition Colaiuta adeptly interpreted every strange and awkward rhythm that the eccentric Zappa threw the drummer's way. In the end Zappa was impressed with Colaiuta's drumming talent and the two worked together for over two years. Colaiuta experienced significant artistic growth during those years with Zappa. Zappa, for one thing, was drawn to odd rhythms of songs such as "Keep it Greasy" which switches from the off-beat meter of 19/16 to even more eccentric timing of 21/16. Colaiuta also developed the ability during his association with Zappa to play on a drum set with two bass drums without sacrificing other pieces of equipment. Colaiuta's extensive work with Zappa is best characterized on the 1979 album *Joe's Garage*.

According to Colaiuta, his inspiration to work hard professionally was essentially a matter of necessity, a

Born Vince Colaiuta, grew up in Pennsylvania; studied organ, electric guitar, flute, and drums; *Education:* attended Berkley School of Music, (Boston), studied with Gary Chaffee.

Toured with organist/pianist Al Kooper; played with the late Frank Zappa; was a regular feature on comedienne Joan Rivers's television talk show; 1994, directed Percussive Arts Society International Convention (PASIC '94) clinic; featured headliner at the "World Drum Festival, Paradiso Van Slag," (Netherlands) March of 1995; collaborated increasingly with Sting during the mid-1990s, toured and recorded with Sting, 1996; solo debut album, *Vinnie Colaiuta* 1997; contributing artist on *Songs from West Side Story,* for the NARAS Foundation, 1996.

Awards: *Modern Drummer,* #1 All Around Drummer, 1996; *Drumbeat* Drummie Award, Best Studio Drummer, 1998.

need to make music on the drums as well as basic logistics: "Once I left ... Berkley, I couldn't really practice ... still can't out here.... I can't play drums in my apartment. [So,] I practice when I work, ..." and he works very hard. It is a fact that Colaiuta has been heard on over 600 recordings made between 1983 and 1993. Despite a professed preference for jazz, his popularity and reputation was never confined to one solitary musical style; he played for and with an assortment of singers and instrumentalists: Natalie Cole, Billy Joel, Jose Feliciano, Judy Collins and Joni Mitchell. Additionally Colaiuta was a regular feature on comedienne Joan Rivers's television talk show.

In March of 1995, Colaiuta was a featured headliner at the "World Drum Festival, Paradiso Van Slag," in the Netherlands. He collaborated increasingly with Sting during the mid-1990s and they went on tour together in 1996. In 1997, the song "The Wind Cries Mary" by Colaiuta, Sting, John McLaughlin, and Dominic Miller was nominated for a Grammy award for the best pop collaboration with vocals.

His solo debut in 1997, an album aptly called *Vinnie Colaiuta,* featured guest spots by Colaiuta's professed idol, Herbie Hancock, as well as Chick Corea, Sting, and John Patitucci. Colaiuta always maintained a strong

jazz influence and modeled himself artistically after Steve Gadd, the legendary session drummer of pop, jazz, and folk idols of the 1970s and 1980s. Stylistically Colaiuta is unpredictable and hard to categorize. His eccentric drum-playing posture with his hard-hitting, foot-stomping bass style has caused some back problems and even a fractured foot from hitting the pedals too hard.

Colaiuta was named the number one All Around Drummer of 1996 by a readers' poll in *Modern Drummer.* He also received the *Drumbeat* Drummie Award for Best Studio Drummer in 1998. He is not at all enamored by success; instead he is pre-occupied with self-improvement. His friends respect him not only for his talent, but for his eagerness to help others. In 1994, he directed a clinic sponsored by the Percussive Arts Society International Convention (PASIC '94), and in 1996 he played behind pop legend Little Richard's "I Feel Pretty," as a contributing artist on *Songs from West Side Story,* a CD whose proceeds benefit the NARAS Foundation, an organization dedicated to fostering music among school children throughout the United States.

Colaiuta's musical likes and dislikes hinge on personal taste, and in general bear no relevance to his passion for drumming. His favorite songs are "Martha My Dear" by the Beatles and Samuel Barber's "Adagio for Strings." He just likes them, he said.

Selected discography

(with Frank Zappa) *Joe's Garage,* (includes "Keep it Greasy), 1979.
(with Joni Mitchell) *Dog Eat Dog,* Geffen Records, 1985.
(with Temptations) *To Be Continued,* Motown Records, 1986.
(with Nik Kershaw) *The Works,* MCA 1989.
(with Alan Holdsworth) *Secrets,* Intima Records, 1989.
(with Barry Manilow) *Barry Manilow,* Arista Records, 1989.
(with Bunny Brunel) Dedication, Musidisc, 1992.
(with Leonard Cohen) *The Future,* Columbia, November 17, 1992. (with Rodney Crowell) *Life is Messy,* Columbia, May 19, 1992.
(with Sting) *Ten Summoner's Tales,* A&M Records, March 9, 1993. (with Tim Weston and Shelby Flint) *Providence,* Soul Coast, 1994. (with SMAP) *SMAP 007 Gold Singer,* (Japanese) 1995.
(with Joni Mitchell) *Misses,* Reprise, October 29, 1996.
(with Little Richard) "I Feel Pretty" *The Songs of West Side Story,* RCA Victor, January 30, 1996.
(with Eric Marienthal) *Collection,* GRP Records, January 28, 1997.
Vinnie Colaiuta, Stretch Records, February 18, 1997.

Live from the Blue Note Tokyo, Stretch Records, 1997.
(with George Benson and Earl Klugh) *Collaboration.*
(with Joni Mitchell) *Wild Things Run Fast*, 1982.
(with Al Kooper), *"Championship Wrestling,"* 1982.

Sources

Books

Flans, Robyn, *Modern Drummer*, November 1982; May 1987; October 1993.

Periodicals

Hartford Courant, 8 January 1997.

—*Gloria Cooksey*

Color Me Badd

Pop group

Emerging in 1991 with the album *C.M.B.*, Color Me Badd helped to define the smooth R&B trend called "New Jack swing." Whether the band's actual influence upon later acts such as Boyz II Men was as decisive as Color Me Badd themselves would claim is debatable, but they were among the first in the 1990s to popularize a blend of rap, classic R&B, and harmonized ballads in one package. However, after their sudden appearance into the limelight, Color Me Badd slid back towards obscurity with a pair of follow albums that failed to recapture the chemistry of their debut.

Although born in different cities, all of Color Me Badd's members—Bryan Abrams, Mark Calderon, Sam Watters, and Kevin "KT" Thornton—grew up together in Oklahoma City, Oklahoma. Like many young singers, the foursome began vocal training within the setting of a church choir, and were able to create a local reputation before entering high school. After taking on the name Color Me Badd in 1987, they plied their trade in the halls of their school singing the doo-wop style of harmonizing made popular in the 1950s. After performing at several

Archive Photos, Inc. Reproduced by permission.

For the Record . . .

Members include **Bryan Abrams**, (born November 16, 1969, in Oklahoma City, OK), vocals; **Mark Calderon**, (born September 27, 1970, in Los Angeles, CA), vocals; **Kevin "KT" Thornton**,(born June 17, 1969, in MD), vocals; **Sam Watters** (born July 23, 1970, in TX), vocals.

Group formed in 1987 in Oklahoma City, Oklahoma; signed with Giant Records, 1990; "I Wanna Sex You Up" appeared on *New Jack City* soundtrack, 1991; released debut album *C.M.B.*, 1991; performed with Boyz II Men and Jodeci at Soul Train Music Awards, 1992; released second album *Time and Chance*, 1993; released *Now and Forever*, 1996.

Awards: Best R&B/soul song ("I Wanna Sex You Up"), American Music Award, 1991; Best R&B/soul song and Best R&B/soul song performed by a group, band, or duo, Soul Train Music Awards 1991.

Addresses: *Record company*—Revolution, 729 Seventh Avenue, 12th Floor, New York, NY 10019.

talent shows, it was not long before the quartet had gained enough credibility to audition for high-profile musicians, such as rocker Jon Bon Jovi, whose tours brought them through Oklahoma City.

When Robert Bell of the group Kool and the Gang saw the group perform, he was impressed enough to pull the necessary strings to land Color Me Badd their own manager. However, after relocating to New York City in hopes of making their break, the act found themselves back in a sea of show business contenders. "It was a struggle," Watters later told Bill Francis of *Billboard*. "For a year and a half, we slept on the floor of the one-bedroom apartment we were sharing with one of our managers." After that period of dogged perseverance, Color Me Badd was signed to Giant Records in August of 1990.

Having been struck by the sensual feel of Color Me Badd's demo tapes, Giant executive Cassandra Mills took decided to unveil her new signing act in an upcoming film soundtrack, *New Jack City,* a gritty 1991 crime film in need of a soulful, erotic number. After Mills delegated the writing duties to producer Dr. Freeze, who had given the group Bell Biv DeVoe their hit "Do Me,"

Color Me Badd delivered the song "I Wanna Sex You Up." Flavoring the cut with their own barbershop quartet nuances, Color Me Badd's result became the biggest hit of the *New Jack City* soundtrack and caused Giant to slate the group's debut album for as early a release as possible. The single release of "I Wanna Sex You Up" cut to the head of sales charts, and Color Me Badd was suddenly in demand.

As the *New Jack City* album offered no photos of Color Me Badd, many listeners were surprised to find that four-piece was comprised of various ethnic backgrounds. "A lot of people were surprised that we're not an all-black group," Abrams told Francis. "So when people listened to our song, they liked it for what it sounded like, not what we looked like." The band's blurring of color lines in the face of an often segregated market was refreshing, and in fact is at the heart of Color Me Badd's moniker. "The name Color Me Badd is a state of mind," said Thornton. "Color me 'bad' or don't color me anything at all. The type of music that we have doesn't have a color. It comes from within."

By summer of 1991, the group released *C.M.B.,* proving they were more than one-hit wonders. Expanding upon their self-named style of "hip-hop-doo-wop," Color Me Badd crooned a collection of ballads and funk-laced pop tunes such as "I Adore Mi Amor" and "All For Love," both of which were Number One singles. However, while *C.M.B.* was embraced by record buyers, critics found the record formulaic, if amiable enough. "[T]he group itself is fairly evidently fabricated to marketing specifications," wrote Mim Udovitch in *Village Voice*. "They don't play any instruments, they don't write most of their material, and though they sing and rap nicely, if unremarkably, for all I know it's not even their vocals. None of which detracts from the album's slight but satisfying charm in the least."

After "I Wanna Sex You Up" racked up statues at various music awards, Color Me Badd set themselves to work on their follow up album. Perhaps in response to charges of being studio pawns, the quartet helped pen the cuts for their next release, albeit under the guidance of a bevy of experienced producers that included DJ Pooh, David Foster, and the team of Jimmy Jam and Terry Lewis. The resulting songs, which appeared on the 1993 album, *Time and Chance,* bore a passing resemblance to the R&B groups of the 1960s that had influenced Color Me Badd, such as the Temptations and the Four Tops. "Once [our producers] heard tracks like 'Trust Me' and 'God Is Love,' Abrams told *Billboard's* David Nathan, "they got the direction we were going in. It's more of a an adult sound, because we're growing, and it reflects our love for older music." Unfortunately, few of *Time and Chance*'s 14 tracks were as catchy as the group's earlier singles, and the album withdrew from the public eye after a brief chart sojourn.

The group counted their losses and took some time off before returning to the studio, writing songs for other pop singers, including Paula Abdul. When Color Me Badd returned it was with an even larger arsenal of producers than on *Time and Chance*, most notably Grammy-winner Babyface and Narada Michael Walden, who was an uplifting force for Color Me Badd's members. "Working with Narada was an incredible experience," Watters remarked on the band's internet homepage. "He would light candles in the studio, set up props, do anything to make us really feel what the song was saying. It was very inspirational." In addition, the band prefaced their new album with a fairly successful live tour of Asia, where their popularity had not waned as radically as it had in North America. Nevertheless, the resulting *Now and Forever*, released in 1996, was Color Me Badd's biggest disappointment to date.

Almost completely ignored by critics, *Now and Forever* bore signs of being a calculated effort to recapture the formula that had made C.M.B. so popular. The first single, "Sexual Capacity," was another steamy soundtrack tune, featured in the film *Striptease,* but whereas the similarly themed "I Wanna Sex You Up" had became a summer anthem, "Sexual Capacity" was cast into the deepest reaches of the charts. In spite of such abysmal reception, Color Me Badd band remained undaunted In interviews at the time, and even claimed responsibility for the influx of male vocal groups that had recorded in the wake of *C.M.B.*. "We know a lot of groups have come along since we started recording in 1991," Watters claimed in a 1996 online interview, "and we know we were the first to hit it big. It makes us feel good when some of these newer groups let us know we inspire them."

Selected discography

C.M.B., Giant, 1991.
(Contributor) *New Jack City* (soundtrack), 1991.
Time and Chance, Giant, 1993.
Now and Forever, Giant/Revolution, 1996.

Sources

Periodicals

Billboard, May 11, 1991; May 25, 1991; March 21, 1992; December 4, 1993; April 6, 1996; August 10, 1996.
Village Voice, September 3, 1991.

Online

http://test.revolution-online.c

—Shaun Frentner

The Commodores

R&B/Pop group

Throughout the 1970s, the six-member Commodores grew into one of the biggest selling acts of all time. Breaking on to the scene with the album *Machine Gun* in 1974, the Commodores established a style of heavy funk, then moved on to score with a string of ballads. Although the band's members shared in songwriting duties, singer Lionel Richie was singled out into the limelight, so much so that he left the band in 1982. While Richie's subsequent solo career soared, a new incarnation of the Commodores that included vocalist J.D. Nicholas continued to make albums of lesser stature that veered increasingly toward a middle of the road style.

The Commodores' story began in 1968 on the campus of the Tuskeegee Institute in Alabama when business majors William King, Thomas McClary, and Lionel Richie banded together as the Mighty Mystics because, as Richie later told *Rolling Stone*'s Steve Pond, "the best way to get girls was to play every party on campus." The trio featured King on trumpet, McClary on guitar, and Richie taking up vocal duties, and were soon joined by

Archive Photos, Inc. Reproduced by permission.

Members include **William King, Jr.**,(born January 29, 1949, in Alabama), horns ; **Ronald LaPread** (born 1950, in Alabama, left group in 1986), bass, trumpet; **Thomas McClary** (born 1950 in Mississippi , left group in 1983), guitar; **James Dean "J.D." Nicholas**, (born April 11, 1952, in Paddington, England), vocals; **Walter "Clyde" Orange**, (born December 9, 1946, in Florida.), drums, vocals; **Lionel Richie** (born 1950, in Tuskegee, AL, left group in 1982), vocals and piano; **Milan Williams** (born 1949, in Mississippi, left group in 1988), keyboards, trombone, guitar.

Band formed in 1968 by Richie, King, and McClary at the Tuskeegee Institute, in Alabama; took on manager Benny Ashburn, later to be called "the seventh Commodore," 1968; signed with Motown and became opening act for the Jackson 5, 1971; released debut album *Machine Gun,* 1974; released *Commodores,* which featured several of the group's biggest hit singles, 1977; appeared in the disco film *Thank God It's Friday,* 1978; Richie departed for a successful solo career, 1982; released single and album *Nightshift* with new singer Nicholas, their last for Motown, 1985; signed to Polydor 1986; released *United,* 1986; released *Rock Sollid,* 1988; launched Commodore Records, 1992; released *Commodores Hits (Vols. 1 & 2),* 1992; released *Commodores XX—No Tricks,* 1993; Motown released definitive Commodores retrospective *Ultimate Collection,* 1997.

Awards: named best R&B Group in both *Rolling Stone's* critics' and readers' polls, 1978; named act of the year by *Performance* magazine, 1978; Grammy Award for Best R&B Song by a Group for "Nightshift," 1985.

Address: *Record Company*—Motown Records, 5750 Wilshire Blvd. #300, Los Angeles, CA 90036

keyboard player Milan Williams after his band, The Jays, dissolved. After randomly flipping through a dictionary, the foursome decided to dub themselves the Commodores, and adopted two more members, bassist Ronald LaPread and drummer Walter "Clyde" Orange. For over a decade, this lineup would not change.

Went Pro

Although Orange alone was a music major, all of the Commodores boasted rich musical backgrounds, as well as exposure to a wide variety of styles, as most of the sextet had relatives who were band leaders, composers, or performers. Richie, for example, had a grandmother who was a classical music teacher and an uncle who had arranged for the legendary big band leader Duke Ellington. Their earliest performances and recordings may have belied a similarity with upbeat funk acts like Sly and the Family Stone, but their appetite for a wide palette of sounds would soon lead them to form their own sound. "People always want to tag us by citing [R&B stars] James Brown and the Temptations as our main influences," Richie later told *High Fidelity's* Stephen X. Rea. "But we also grew up in a pop environment. We listened to [rock acts like] the Beatles, Jimi Hendrix, Led Zeppelin, [country singers] Glen Campbell and Merle Haggard as much as we listened to Brown."

The group continued to play an often exhausting number of shows, squeezed into their class schedule, and began to expand their touring orbit beyond Tuskeegee. After packing their equipment into a van and trekking to New York City, the Commodores managed to slate a gig at the nightclub Small's Paradise. Although the group's instruments were stolen shortly after pulling into the city, the Commodores managed to buy back the hijacked equipment and deliver a show that impressed audience member and talent agent Benny Ashburn. Ashburn immediately became the Commodores' manager, and remained in that position until his death in the early 1982.

Guided by Ashburn, the sextet capitalized on their own considerable business savvy and organized the Commodores into a no-nonsense corporation, complete with conduct guidelines and mission statements. The band's members prided themselves in their professional, drug-free behavior and aimed their sights at surpassing the success of the Beatles, one of the biggest selling pop group ever. After an impressive European tour in 1970 and a forgettable debut single was released for Atlantic Records, the Commodores signed with the Motown label in 1971 but refused to adopt the company's slick mode of packaging their acts and use of studio musicians. "We were different and Motown didn't know what to do with us," LaPread told *Billboard.* "We didn't fit the standard way of doing things and we'd started to write our own songs. When we met up with producer James Carmichael, things changed. Carmichael was won over by the Commodore's uncompromising attitude, and like Ashburn, continued to collaborate with the group for the next decade.

Became Pop Superstars

It took three years of finagling before the Commodores were able to release their debut album *Machine Gun,* but in the interim they continued to make a name for themselves on stage, often as the opening act for Motown label mates the Jackson 5. However, if the Commodores had taken their time getting started, success quickly caught up with them. *Machine Gun*'s title cut, a bass-fueled funk workout written by Williams, became a Top 30 single and the album itself went gold shortly thereafter. After more touring with acts like the Rolling Stones and the O'Jays, the Commodores were able to draw crowds on their own merits and found their name topping the marquis of increasingly larger venues.

For the next two albums, *Caught In The Act* and *Movin' On,* the Commodores stuck with their aggressive funk sound, which helped lay the foundation for the emerging trend of disco dance music. With all six members sharing the writing duties, the group produced a number of hits, such as "Slippery When Wet" in 1975 and "Brick House," released 1977,. However, by 1977 the group began having immense luck with ballads written and sung by Richie. Aside from their lack of dance appeal, songs like "Easy," written in 1977, showed Richie's graceful blending of country flourishes with R&B, and he rapidly became identified by the public as the center of the Commodores.

By the late 1970s, the Commodores had become veritable superstars, with each of their albums having sold anywhere from gold to triple platinum status. Much of this success continued to be credited to Richie's love songs, with tunes like the number one AThree Times A Lady" inciting other performers to seek Richie's services. Returning a favor to one of his influences, Richie penned the immensely popular ballad "Lady" for country singer Kenny Rogers, who also tapped Richie to produce his album *Share Your Love* in 1980. In addition to Richie's allure, the Commodores benefited from their ever-keen business sense. Creating the umbrella corporation Commodore Entertainment, the group had turned a college party band into a multi-million dollar empire. "I think of these guys more as businessmen than musicians," Richie confessed to Rea. "We're always thinking of the bottom line."

Bottom Line Began to Drop

As the next decade began, the Commodores' phenomenal success took a sharp dive, and for some critics, their growing corporate identity was to blame. For critics like *Rolling Stone*'s Stephen Holden, the emotion and energy of the group's earlier work had faded into albums like *Heroes,* released in 1980, which offered bland material intended to appeal to the widest demographics. Although *Heroes* was in fact the first "message" album to be released by the Commodores, Holden found the record to be full of unconvincing platitudes, as well as sloppy songwriting. "The title tune—which solemnly informs us that we are the heroes we're searching for in an unheroic age—is a pep talk that takes itself so seriously that it depresses more than it uplifts." Holden went on to say, "Wake Up Children' utilizes simplistic nursery rhymes about pollution and the fate of man in a genteel pop-funk idiom that has no bite."

If *Heroes* was a relative disappointment overall, the release of *In the Pocket* put the group temporarily back on track, producing two top ten singles, such as the memorable "Lady (You Bring Me Up)." Still, the band could not shake off claims of overly commercial, adult-contemporary banality from some critics. "[T]he Commodores' *In The Pocket* exhibits some of the worst traits of current MOR (middle of the road) R&B: most depressingly, the tiresome me-man, you-lady condescension of the love songs and a lust for upward mobility expressed in the distressing visual pun on the album cover—the Commodores' logo sewn onto the right hip pockets of the band members' designer jeans.' Nevertheless, the Commodores were still given a vote of confidence from record buyers.

Continued After Several Departures

After *In The Pocket,* the Commodores suffered a series of heavy losses. In 1982, longtime manager Ashburn died of a heart attack, and shortly thereafter Richie left to pursue a solo career. McClary left the following year, to be replaced by singer James Dean "J.D" Nicholas, but the group's stability was affected nonetheless. After the disappointing *Commodores 13* was issued in 1983, producer Carmichael also fled the Commodores' camp and the group waited a full two years before releasing their next record.

The album *Nightshift,* released in 1985, marked a relative comeback for the Commodores, if only on the strength of its title cut, a stirring lament over Jackie Wilson and Marvin Gaye, two R&B singers whose lives had been cut tragically short. The song was a major hit, winning Grammy Award, and winning over even the most hardened critics. As Mark Moses wrote in *High Fidelity,* "[w]hat's' distinctive about "Nightshift" is that this tribute doesn't simply rest on sentimentality: Its arrangements may coo softly, but its percussion ticks with relentless syncopations, its bass relishes long ominous slides." Still, many writers found the rest of *Nightshift* to be little more than filler material, as did *Rolling Stone*'s J.D. Considine. "That the remainder of the album fails to measure up to [the title song's] standard comes as no surprise. Because the Commodores have been unable either to resurrect the hard funk of their earliest hits or the sort of MOR ballads Lionel Richie once provided, the band continues to sound unsure of its musical direction and ends up wallowing in mediocrity."

As Richie grew to become one of the hallmarks of 1980s pop music with albums like the Grammy winning *Can't Slow Down,* the Commodores all but disappeared from mainstream eyes. By the latter half of the decade, the group was stripped down to a trio, with LaPread and Williams having retired to their families. After releasing the albums *United* and *Rock Solid* for Polydor, the enterprising Commodores once again showed their business know-how when they christened their own label in 1992. While the group did release an album of new material in 1993, *Commodores XX —No Tricks,* the trio primarily rested on the success of their past hits. With two greatest hits compilations released on Commodores Records, the group digitally re-recorded their standards, with Orange and Nicholas singing many tunes originally delivered by Richie. The trio also continued to perform live at state fairs and on nostalgia tours, and in 1998 celebrated what few pop acts can boast—thirtieth anniversary.

Selected discography

Machine Gun, Motown, 1974.
Caught In The Act, Motown, 1975.
Movin' On, Motown, 1975.
Hot On The Tracks, Motown, 1976.
Live, Motown, 1977.
Natural High, Motown, 1978.
Greatest Hits, Motown, 1978.
Midnight Magic, Motown, 1979.
Heroes, Motown, 1980.
In The Pocket, Motown, 1981.
Nightshift, Motown, 1985.
All The Great Love Songs, Motown, 1985.
Rock Solid, Polydor, 1988.
Commodores XX—No Tricks, Commodore Records, 1993.
Ultimate Collection, Motown, 1997.

Sources

Billboard, January 19, 1980; May 24, 1980; July 8, 1989; September 5, 1992.
Gramophone, September 1976.
High Fidelity, April 1980; August 1985.
Rolling Stone, August 21, 1980; September 18, 1980; October 1, 1981; June 20, 1985.
Village Voice, September 17, 1980; September 16, 1981.

—Shaun Frentner

Common

Rap artist

Hip hop artist Common—formerly known as Common Sense—is known for his emphasis on family values and departure from the "gansta rap" material and negative posturing sometimes found in popular hip hop or rap lyrics and videos. A video of his single "Rap City" on the BET network told the story of a young black man who decided to do the right thing by his pregnant girlfriend by staying with her and supporting her. Common, along with a few other high-profile rappers, was in the forefront of an unprecedented wave of family values in the hip hop community in 1998. He even featured his own father, Lonnie Lynn, on a single titled "Pop's Rap" from *One Day It Will All Make Sense*. The single is an apology from his father for not always being there. *Rolling Stone*'s Kevin Powell wrote, "Common could be the most thoughtful, lyrically skilled rapper you 've ever heard of.... Common's incisive observations offer a contrast to the materialism drowning today's hip-hop. "Ann Powers of the *New York Times* described Common as, "A gifted wordsmith ... Common honors a familiar hip-hop essential: storytelling. Like most rappers, he effortlessly discharges witty phrases; but he also weaves complicated, rich narratives. "

Common, born Lonnie Rashid Lynn in 1973, was raised in Chicago. An NBA hopeful, he was a ball boy for the Chicago Bulls. The first widely hailed MC to emerge from Chicago, Common aspired to be as lauded as KRS-1 or Rakim and he wanted to have something substantive to say through his music. He signed with Relativity Records in 1991 when the rock-oriented label first embraced rap and hip-hop music. The label's executive vice president of marketing and promotion, Alan Grunblatt, told Billboard 's Havelock Nelson, "We always wanted to be involved in cool, hip, alternative music. We feel that rap is part of that."

Common released *Can I Borrow A Dollar* in 1992, and *Resurrection* in 1994. In 1994, he was forced to abbreviate his name to Common from Common Sense due to a lawsuit by an Orange County-based reggae group called Common Sense. It him took three years to release *One Day It 'll All Make Sense,* which included a roster of rap and hip-hop's most talented artists. Erykah Badu contributed to the song "All Night Long, " and Cee-Lo Green of the Goodie Mob contributed to "G.O.D." (Gaining One's Definition). Lauryn Hill of the Fugees recorded with Common while both were expecting the birth of their first child in August of 1997. The single they worked on, "Retrospect For Life," dealt with the fragile topic of abortion and concluded, "315 dollars ain't worth your soul". Q-Tip joined Common on his third release as well in the single "Stolen Moments, Part 3," and De La Soul joined him for "Gettin" Down at the Ampitheatre". Black Thought of the Roots contributed to "Stolen

Moments, Part 2". Chantay Savage contributed to "Reminding Me (of Sef)", an upbeat remembrance of his of his youth, which was dedicated to his deceased best friend. Forrest Green 111 wrote in an article for the Detroit based *Metro Times,* "Common's newest release, *One Day It'll All Make Sense,* was easily one of the most inventive rap albums of 1997. It's loose, band-driven fusillade of rapping, poetry and musicianship revives the rap album format for real, but the piece de resistance, "Retrospect For Life," stuff's hip-hop's muses to the gill. "

When Common released *Resurrection* in 1994 he commented on the regretfully stagnant state of hip-hop and rap with the single, "i used to love h.e.r." The single was an allegory of hip-hop as an attractive but fickle woman, and it created discussion within the hip-hop/rap realm and drew attention to Common's talent. The single also prompted a lawsuit against Common by rapper Ice Cube, who felt he was maligned in the song. Common took on the gangsta rappers with the single and pointed out where hip-hop had grown tiring. The lawsuit did not end favorably for Common, and litigation slowed the production of *Resurrection.* Common explained to the *Orange County Register*'s Ben Wener why he was so disillusioned by rap when he wrote "i used to love h.e.r.". He said, "Everything became so old. The repetition of not just one sound but every sound, and all the samples

that came out were so tired.... In '88, '89, you had groups coming out in all different directions. Why did that suddenly stop "...I couldn't understand where hip-hop was going. I still can't, you know"

Common told Wener he knew he had to have a distinctive style to separate himself from other rap artists, and the impending birth of his daughter provided fuel for his imagination and creativity for his third release. Other noted rappers such as Snoop Doggy Dogg, LL Cool J, and Coolio turned to the joys of fatherhood and marriage in their material, and Common was among those ushering in a new lyrical and spiritual trend toward family values and adulthood. In a *Newsweek* interview with Veronica Chambers, he said, "A lot of my friends were getting turned off to hip-hop music because we were growing up ... Hip-hop lost part of its audience because of that. " Rapper Busta Rhymes, who doesn't rap about family values, told *Newsweek*'s Chambers, "I can really appreciate Common on a personal level. "

Common was the headline act for the Elements of Hip-Hop tour in 1998, which included Rahzel the Godfather of Noyze (of the Roots), four DJs from San Francisco known as the X-Ecutioners (Mista Sinista, Roc Raida, Total Eclipse, and Rob Swift), and Common 's four-piece band called A Black Girl Named Becky. After the release of *One Day it Will All make Sense,* Common decided to learn to play the piano and drums, and he took a music theory class and a course in the business of music in order to better appreciate his calling. In 1998, he aspired to eventually perform in a quartet and to someday look back on what he created with pride. In spite of his positive message and status as a "rapper's rapper," Common doesn't yet enjoy the mainstream success of commercial rappers such as Busta Rhymes or hardcore rapper Ice Cube. Common told Wener, "Sooner or later I'll catch the new people, even if I have to keep reinventing myself. I'll just keep doing what I'm doing and hopefully people will react. Eventually, I pray, they'll come to the songs."

Selected discography

Can I Borrow A Dollar?, Relativity Records, 1992.
Resurrection, Relativity Records, 1994.
One Day it'll All Make Sense, Relativity Records, 1997.

Sources

Billboard, February 26, 1994.
The Chicago Tribune, January 27, 1998.
The Los Angeles Times, February 4, 1998.

Metro Times (Detroit), January 21-27, 1998.
New York Times, January 23, 1998.
Newsweek, January 19, 1998.
Orange County Register, January 29, 1998.
Rolling Stone, January 22, 1998.

—*B. Kimberly Taylor*

Compulsion

Rock group

Announcing their arrival with a chainsaw buzz of guitars and an uncompromising attitude, the London-based four piece Compulsion began spreading their punk like brand of music in early 1992. The band was at first lumped together with a cluster of British groups reviving the sound of New Wave acts from a decade earlier but such labels quickly slid away with the release of their debut album, *Comforter,* in 1994. However, the band had a hot and cold relationship with the British press, as well as with their record label and was virtually ignored in America. "Fortunately for Compulsion, the lows are rivaled only by the depth of their talent," wrote Nisid Hajari in *Entertainment Weekly.* "They can't bear the next Beatles yoke any better than [British contemporaries] Oasis, but they do have the spunk (and more than enough chops) to be the next Sex Pistols." Unfortunately, any similarity to 1970s punk rock legends the Sex Pistols the group may have had included in its rocky existence, and after the release of a second album in 1996, Compulsion soon disbanded.

Compulsion's story began when two Irish natives, vocalist Josephmary and guitarist Garret Lee, relocated to London, England in the early 1990s. They formed Thee Amazing Colossal Men, a group firmly entrenched in the sound of classic 1960s guitar rock. After only one release, Thee Amazing Colossal Men called it quits.

Shortly thereafter they were joined by Sid Rainey on bass and Jan Willem on drums and emerged as Compulsion in January of 1992. From its onset, Compulsion's tolerance for record company politics was minimal and the band set up their own label, entitled Fabulon. Choosing spontaneous one-day spurts in the studio over drawn out overproduction, Compulsion committed to set their first two EPs to vinyl after one-take sessions. "The important thing is the song and the attitude," Josephmary explained in an internet article. "We can't imagine taking a week to record a song that takes three minutes to play."

Despite this attitude, Josephmary and company soon signed to the One Little Indian label, a company known for signing bands with unusual slants on pop music and released the hastily recorded *Safety* mini-album. The violent energy captured on *Safety,* as well as on the earlier *Compulsion* and *Casserole* EPs was matched by the band's live presence as they began appearing in the British club circuit in frenetic displays that resulted in a number of stage injuries. However, reviews of Compulsion's gigs were sometimes devastating, with many British critics seeing the band as a hollow and unoriginal attempt at 1970s style punk rock. "Compulsion ... are a band that should never have been signed in the first place," wrote *Melody Maker*'s Colm O'Callaghan in response to a London performance in the spring of 1990. "They haven't a song. Or a hope. Look, Compulsion really don't even deserve a critical boot in the groin. It's like stabbing a dead mule, really. Pointless."

To make matters worse, Compulsion was also unfairly thrown into the context of a musical "movement" that was in part created by hype alone within the pages of the British press. Called "the New Wave of New Wave (NWONW)," this small ensemble of groups that included Elastica and Menswear used dated keyboards and sported skinny ties in homage to post-punk groups of the early 1980s. Aside from Josephmary's spiky hair, Compulsion had little to do with most of these bands musically, yet for several years the group was hounded by the new wave tag.

Some of Britain's journalists slowly began to take a second look at Compulsion by the time of the group's full length debut *Comforter,* released in 1994. Musically, the album garnered more comparisons to the abrasive guitar sounds of groups like the Pixies and the Manic Street Preachers than to new wave acts of a decade earlier such as Devo or Wire. Through its lyrics, *Comforter* constructed fourteen disturbing snapshots of the warped cruelty often underlying the sober face of middle class society, on songs with titles like "Domestique" and "Mall Monarchy." "By now you'll have been

For the Record . . .

Members include **Jan Willem Alkema** (born c.1965 in Holland), drums; **Garret Lee** (born c.1968 in Dublin, Ireland), guitar; **Josephmary** (born c.1964 in Dublin, Ireland), vocals; **Sid Rainey** (born c.1968 in Ireland), bass.

Band renamed Compulsion after the dissolution of Thee Amazing Colossal Men in January of 1992; signed to One Little Indian , released the *Safety* mini-album, 1992; released debut album *Comforter* in 1994; rejected and sued American label Elektra weeks before the scheduled release of *Comforter* in the U.S., 1994; released final album, *The Future Is Medium* on One Little Indian, 1996; disbanded after being dropped from One Little Indian, 1997.

Addresses: *Record label*—Interscope, 10900 Wilshire Blvd., #1400, Los Angeles, CA 90024.

distracted by the NWONW tag," wrote Ian Watson in *Melody Maker.* "Or else you've been put off by the assertion that Compulsion are trading on someone else's—namely Pixies'—good idea. No matter. This distinclty deranged long player [*Comforter*] will iron out the creases.... Maybe it's time to start taking these guys *seriously.*"

Just as things were looking up for the group, a scuffle with Elektra, Compulsion's intended label for American release, set the overseas release of *Comforter* back for months. Although the band had made a verbal agreement with Elektra, Compulsion soon found problems with its corporate philosophies and signed a written contract with Interscope Records, leaving Elektra executives fuming. "Their lawyer said he would bury us so deep that no one ever knew the album existed," Josephmary admitted to Hajari with a smile. Elektra's threats proved to be idle, however, and Interscope was able to release *Comforter* in the fall of 1994.

Compulsion continued to make their live shows central to their music, embarking on a tour of the U.S. In response to the small teddy bear that graced the cover of *Comforter,* fans began pelting the group with stuffed animals during performances. Upon their return to the United Kingdom, critics still didn't know what to make of Compulsion and were, on the whole, equivocal towards the band. "There's something going on here that I can't quite put my finger on," wrote Jennifer Nine in *Melody Maker* in response to a subsequent gig. "I think it's called embarrassment. But only mine. 'Cos [sic] that's the Compulsion punk rock experience – pretty much shameless. Ninety per cent cheap laffs [sic], maybe, but 100 per cent dedication."

The band's misfortunes only snowballed for the following years, including MTV's rejection of the big-budget video Compulsion had made for "Mall Monarchy," a satire on American talk shows. Nevertheless, Compulsion forged ahead with their extensive touring, stopped only by the occasional injuries inflicted in and out of concert venues. In early 1996, several dates were scrapped when drummer Alkema cracked three ribs in a skirmish in the Netherlands.

In addition to the above flak, several British tabloids had followed their New Wave of New Wave hype with a celebration of "Britpop," bands like Blur or Pulp who had much in common with the style and self-consciously English songwriting of earlier groups like the Kinks. As Compulsion had already been associated with punk and new wave, they were again edged out of the latest national trend. In response to this, Compulsion released the single "Question Time For The Proles," a song which attacked the nostalgia for the past the Britpop fad incurred on many young workers, or proles. "Proles ... are being bombarded by these images of the Swinging Sixties, stuff they couldn't possibly remember because they were too young," Josephmary told *Melody Maker* in March of 1996. "I think Britpop is just another version of the New Wave of New Wave."

Compulsion's second album, *The Future is Medium,* was released by One Little Indian. Unreleased in America, *The Future is Medium* continued where they had left off on *Comforter,* satirizing the state of British society with songs like "Juvenile Scene Detective." Also as with *Comforter, The Future Is Medium* met with reviews that were positive, even if begrudgingly so, such as John Robb in *Melody Maker.* "Why be content with one guitar texture, when ten will do?," queried Robb rhetorically. "Why have just one vocal, when you can have two fighting crazily for the same space?.... *The Future Is Medium* is one huge war zone of guitar filth. Big, bright, and brassy, Compulsion are no spent force yet." Unfortunately, Compulsion were unable to prove their staying power to their naysayers, and by 1997 the band was dumped by One Little Indian in 1997, perhaps illustrating once again the chaos that punk rock and its offspring may carry. In Compulsion's aftermath, Lee and Alkelma went on to join the groups Sack and China Drum, respectively.

Selected Discography

Boogie Woogie, Elektra/Asylum, 1994 (compilation of early
    EPs).
Comforter, One Little Indian/Interscope, 1994.
The Future Is Medium, One Little Indian, 1996.

Sources

Periodicals

Billboard, October 22, 1994.
Entertainment Weekly, June 30, 1995.
Melody Maker, March 28, 1992; March 26, 1994; March 9,
    1996; April 27, 1996; May 25, 1996; July 6, 1996; July 13,
    1996.

Online

http://www.fortunecity.com/victorian/parkstreet/186/info.htm
http://www.interscoperecords.co/lrcompbio.html

—Shaun Frentner

Confederate Railroad

Country band

After a decade of playing in local saloons and honky-tonk bars, Georgia's Confederate Railroad achieved national success with their self-titled debut album released in 1992, largely on the basis of their somewhat controversial hit "Trashy Women." Although the band's overall image was another incarnation of the rowdy, Southern-boy spirit defined by acts like Hank Williams, Jr. and Lynyrd Skynyrd, Confederate Railroad soon found themselves popular among mainstream audiences, and even with demographic groups not stereotypically associated with country, such as Europeans and gays. In the meantime, the band released several follow-up albums that met consistently with mixed reviews.

Although Confederate Railroad did not assume their present name until the late 1980s, most of the band's six members began their working relationship in 1982, as country singer David Allan Coe's touring musicians. However, under the leadership of the boisterous singer/songwriter Danny Shirley, the future members of Confederate Railroad became the house performers at Miss Kitty's, a country bar in Marietta, Georgia. Embracing a rollicking, tongue-in-cheek style of rock-tinged country, Shirley and his cohorts established a strong local reputation. After their commercial breakthrough, energetic live shows continued to contribute to Confederate Railroad's popularity.

As a solo artist, Shirley had already released several records on the small Armor label, with whom he signed in 1984, but met with only minor successes, such as his debut "Love and Let Love". Upon the full realization of Confederate Railroad in 1987, however, the group sent a demo tape to executive Rick Blackburn at Atlantic Records' Nashville office signed with the label in 1991. Blackburn had hoped that the bands' demeanor, which suggested both good-natured fun and bar-room brawls at the same time, would be as successful nationally as it had been as Miss Kitty's.

The "band" released their debut album, *Confederate Railroad,* in 1992. The record was for all intents and purposes another Shirley solo album and featured none of Confederate Railroad's other members. In any case, the album produced a number of singles which scored heavily on the country charts, with the song "Jesus and Mama" hitting number five. However, it was "Trashy Women," the flip-side to the single "That Way You Can Never Go Back" that gave Confederate Railroad buzz outside the country charts, as well as some amount of notoriety.

"Trashy Women" was attacked by some both for its portrayal of women and its artistic merits, and in the process created a mild controversy. While critics like the *Village Voice*'s Eric Weisbard called the song "the sort of beer and babe anthem even heavy metal has gotten too sophisticated for," others were offended by its portrayal of big-haired, heavily made-up females. In general, however, the public took the song with a grain of salt, such as Houston, Texas disc jockey Dene Hallam. "I listened to it and found out that it wasn't a derogatory song," Hallam told *Billboard.* "It was just describing a (country singer) Dolly Parton type, just like a type of man or whatever. I believe even Dolly herself would describe herself as a trashy woman, and she's one of the classiest, most intelligent ladies in the business."

What little furor "Trashy Women" occasioned quickly passed and the song was released as a single in 1993, which outsold the record that had originally spawned it. A solid hit on the country charts, "Trashy Women" was also popular with those who rarely ventured beyond mainstream pop and was even reissued as a dance remix. In addition, the song's video, which featured the burly members of Confederate Railroad in drag, also warmed over audiences with the group's tongue-in-cheek attitude. Largely on the commercial pull of "Trashy Women," as well as the hit "Queen of Memphis,"

the band's debut had sold over a million copies by the end of the year.

The following year, Confederate Railroad demonstrated to some that they were more than more than a silly bar band with the release of their second album, *Notorious,* a collection of songs *Entertainment Weekly's* Alanna Nash characterized as "Dixie-fried satire and dead-serious takes on life and love." Indeed, the band's diversity of styles had often made casual listeners believe that Confederate Railroad's multiple hits were actually the work of as many different groups. In addition to "Elvis and Andy," a humorous song about a Southern woman's love for legendary singer Elvis Presley and television actor Andy Griffith, the album is highlighted by the title cut, a dark, moody piece. Still, other critics found even Confederate Railroad's straight-faced songs to be laughable, but such response did not prevent *Notorious* from going gold only weeks after its release.

The band proved to audiences outside of Georgia that their live presence was as engaging as their records, and after a successful European tour, Confederate Railroad returned to the studio. The result was their 1995 album, *When and Where,* which provoked yet another split decision from music press. On the one hand, *Entertainment Weekly* was fully won over by the spirit Confederate Railroad brought to their music. "Though it could have been another play-by-numbers outing, Shirley's redneck bark and some strong songwriting add soul. This Railroad is one of the year's classier models."

Conversely, other critics like Alanna Nash, writing in *Stereo Review,* found *When and Where* to show the group's limitations. "The love songs aren't memorable, and apart from a wry line or two in "Bill's Laundromat, Bar, and Grill," the songs aren't funny, running along the sappy, family-values of "Sounds of Home." Although Nash had earlier defended *Notorious,* she went on to say that "Confederate Railroad appears to be a one-shot wonder, a band whose time has come and gone." Such claims seemed unwarranted, given the amount of hits Confederate Railroad had scored on the country charts. While *When and Where* did not sell as well as the group's earlier efforts, it did receive several nominations at the 1995 British Country Music Awards ceremony.

Perhaps to further rebut claims of being a one-hit wonder, Confederate Railroad issued a seemingly premature *Greatest Hits* collection in 1997, which showcased the group's ballads as well as its more celebrated comedic tunes like "Trashy Women." In addition to previously recorded material, *Greatest Hits* also slipped in two new compositions. "I'm very happy with the way this album flows," Shirley stated on a Confederate

Railroad website. "The two new ones are kind of light-hearted, but middle of the road like 'Queen of Memphis.' So it's got the ballads we've had luck with and a couple of off-the wall tunes'... it's balanced out real nice." After the compilation release, Confederate Railroad continued to offer their robust live shows and planned their next contribution to the growth of contemporary country.

Selected discography

Confederate Railroad, Atlantic/Nashville, 1992.
Notorious, Atlantic/Nashville, 1994.
When and Where, Atlantic/Nashville, 1995.
Greatest Hits, Atlantic/Nashville, 1997.

Sources

Periodicals

Billboard, April 18, 1992; October 23, 1993; November 13, 1993.
Entertainment Weekly, March 11, 1994; June 30, 1995.
Stereo Review, October 1995.
Village Voice, May 3, 1994.

Online

"The big Butler Fair Presents: Confederate Railroad," http://www.butlercountry.com/Big (June 16, 1998).

—*Shaun Frentner*

Xavier Cugat

Bandleader, violinist

Archive Photos, Inc. Reproduced by permission.

Best-known for having popularized the rumba in the United States during the 1930s, Xavier Cugat's Latin-influenced band lead the way in a new music craze among the dancing and radio-listening public. A dramatic showman who often wore huge South American hats on stage and who led his band with the wave of a violin bow, Cugat performed in the ritziest of clubs, on the radio, and in the movies. Having made his professional start as a child prodigy playing classical violin, Cugat was never apologetic about his switch to popular music. He was quoted in the *Los Angeles Times* as saying, "I play music ... make an atmosphere that people enjoy. It makes them happy. They smile. They dance. Feel good—who be sorry for that?" Cugat's several marriages, extramarital affairs, and divorces made headlines, but these events did not cause him to repine. He credited his irrepressible interest in women to a Latin temperament and once said he'd marry each of his four wives over again.

Born on January 1, 1900 near Barcelona, Spain and christened Francisco de Asis Javier Cugat Mingall de Brue y Deulofeo, Cugat was two years old when his father moved the family to Havana, Cuba. Two years later, a neighbor and violin maker gave the boy a quarter-sized violin as a Christmas present. Cugat's exceptional talents were soon evident, as he developed into a musical prodigy. He played professionally when he was just nine years old, and at age twelve he became first violinist for the Teatro Nacional Symphonic Orchestra.

Tenor Enrico Caruso met Cugat in Havana when he was performing there with the Metropolitan Opera Company, and he enlisted the boy as his accompanist for an American tour. The subsequent events of Cugat's teen years are somewhat obscure. He is known to have played the violin on a WDY broadcast in 1917, which made him one of the first violinists to perform on radio, and some sources list Cugat as having moved to the United States with his parents in 1915. But the bandleader once told the *Los Angeles Times* a far different story, one where he began by working 14 hours a day for a room, meals, and no pay. "[Caruso died] shortly after I got to New York ... and there I was, no friends and not a word of English. And not much money," he said. In any case, Cugat was disappointed in his musical career. Although he played Carnegie Hall twice, toured the United States and Europe with a symphony orchestra, and became a soloist for the Los Angeles Philharmonic, the money—and critical response—was not satisfactory to Cugat.

He then gave up playing the violin for a job with the *Los Angeles Times* as a cartoonist. Caruso had taught

Born Francisco de Asis Javier Cugat de Bru y Deulofeo, January 1, 1900, Barcelona, Spain; died of arteriosclerosis, October 27, 1990, in Barcelona; son of Juan and Mingall (de Bru) Cugat; married Carmen Castillo, October 17, 1929 (divorced 1944); married Lorraine Allen, 1947 (divorced 1952); married Abbe Lane, 1952 (divorced 1966); married Charro Baeza 1966 (divorced 1978).

Began studying the violin at age four; began playing with a Havana symphony at six; was recruited to play for Enrico Caruso and toured with the tenor for five years; worded as a caricature artist for the *Los Angeles Times* 1924-25; formed his own Latin band in 1929; established the "Cugat Room" at New York City's Waldorf-Astoria hotel, 19302-402; appeared in several Hollywood musicals; often played Las Vegas venues during the 1960s and 1970s; retired at age 78, following an illness; subsequently formed a new band in Spain.

Cugat how to draw caricatures and the young man hoped to use this skill to improve his prospects. Cugat had considerable talents as an artist but soon grew tired of the situation. Quoted in a *Los Angeles Times* obituary, Cugat explained, "When they tell you to be funny by 10:30 tomorrow morning ... I can't do it—I finally quit, and get these six guys to play commercial music with me." Also joining Cugat on the bandstand was his wife-to-be Carmen Castillo as lead singer. The year was 1928 and Latin music was not yet popular. However, the band would land a gig playing during intermissions at the famed Coconut Grove in Los Angeles. At the time, a Gus Arnheim band with singer Bing Crosby was the main act. While in Los Angeles, Cugat also played the violin with two performers on a daily broadcast on KFWB radio.

The job that served as Cugat's springboard to fame was at the new Starlight Roof at the Waldorf-Astoria hotel in New York City. The bandleader made a modest start there in 1933, but was soon ensconced in the hotel's "Cugat Room." His dance band played at the posh hotel for 16 years and became the Waldorf-Astoria's highest-paid bandleader, making $7,000 a week plus a cut of the cover charge take. In 1934, Cugat's band played a three-hour network radio program on Saturday nights.

During a time when dance band leaders Benny Goodman and Glenn Miller were immensely popular, Cugat benefited from a conflict between the American Society of Composers, Authors and Publishers (ASCAP) and the radio networks. ASCAP withheld its music from broadcasts, forcing dance bands to play mostly tired public-domain songs. Cugat, however, had some 500 non-ASCAP Latin tunes at his disposal and had soon attracted a national audience. He became known as the "Rumba King." Some of the performers that Cugat in turn helped to popularize were Desi Arnaz, Dinah Shore, Lina Romay, and Miguelito Valdes. He wrote and recorded hundreds of songs, including "Chiquita Banana," "Rumba Rhapsody," "Kasmiri Love Song," "Rain in Spain," "Babalu," "My Shawl," "Rendezvous in Rio," "Walter Winchell Rumba," "Is It Taboo," and "I'll Never Love Again."

Cugat made the leap to the silver screen in 1942, appearing in "You Were Never Lovelier," which starred Rita Hayworth. Cugat had met the actress in California many years before, when she was a dancer known as Margarita Cansino. With his band, Cugat appeared in many more films—often as himself. He was repeatedly seen on screen with the swimming actress Esther Williams; among their motion pictures together were *Neptune's Daughter, Bathing Beauty, This Time for Keeps,* and *On an Island With You.* Cugat's caricatures were also featured in some of his films and on a "curtain of stars" in Grauman's Chinese Theater in Hollywood. These events followed an earlier interest in movie-making on the part of Cugat, who had previously made films including an ill-fated production during the early sound era. In 1928, he had spent $35,000 to produce a Spanish-language film, only to discover that there were as yet no sound projectors in Latin America.

Cugat's personal life made news many times, as he wed and divorced four times. His marriage to Castillo ended unhappily in 1944. The bandleader was married to Lorraine Allen from 1947 to 1952, when—with the help of private detectives—she caught him in a compromising position in a hotel room with the band's lead singer, Abbe Lane. Cugat wed Lane that same year, and stayed married some 14 years, until he found her with another man. In 1966 he married the much younger singer-guitarist Charro Baeza, who is better known by her first name alone. This marriage ended in 1978 and was said to be the only amicable divorce. Cugat's reflections on his love life were recalled in the *Los Angeles Times:* "I like women—all women.... Also, there is my temperament. I am Latin. I excite. For me, this is life."

Although the Latin music craze that had swelled in the 1930s and 1940s died down, Cugat remained extremely popular. His band was often booked in Las Vegas and he performed until 1969, when Cugat suffered a stroke and became partially paralyzed. The bandleader recovered from the stroke but his health was never the same. After his divorce from Charro, Cugat moved to Barcelona, where he lived for 18 years—until his death in 1990. He had been suffering from heart and lung problems and was in intensive care at the Quiron Clinic when he died.

Selected discography

Xavier Cugat [CBS], CBS, 1949.
Xavier Cugat [Mercury], CBS, 1952.
Quiet Music, Volume 6, Columbia, 1952.
Merengue, Sony Discos, 1986.
Adios Muchachos, Pro Arte, 1992.
La Ultima Noche, Triloka, 1992.
Me Gusta La Conga, Saludos Amigos, 1993.
El Negro Zumbon, Saludos Amigos, 1993.
Xavier Cugat & His Orchestra, Saludos Amigos, 1994.
Mambo No. 4, Columbia, 1995.
Golden Classics, Collectables, 1995.
Cugat's Favorite Rumbas: Leyendas/Legends, Sony Internati, 1995.
Say Si Si, Pair, 1995.
Latinissimo, Madacy, 1995.
Unheard Transcriptions & Air Shots, Harlequin, 1995.
Latin Dance Time with Xavier Cugat & His Orchestra, Fat Boy, 1996.
South America, Take It Away: 24 Latin Hits, ASV/Living Era, 1997.
Cugie A-Go-Go, Varese, 1997.
Cuban Mambo, International, 1997.
Cuban Love Song, Harlequin, 1997.

Sources

Books

Contemporary Authors, Volume 132, Gale, 1991.
Newsmakers, Gale, 1991.

Periodicals

Los Angeles Times, October 28, 1990, p. 1.
New York Times, October 28, 1990, p. 38.

Online

www.allmusic.com, All-Music Guide, 1998.

—Paula Pyzik Scott

Paul Desmond

Saxophone

Archive Photos, Inc. Reproduced by permission.

In the minds and hearts of music listeners, Paul Desmond and the Dave Brubeck Quartet are virtually inseparable. These innovators experienced an almost immediate mutual attraction. The underlying concept that melded them into this smooth, sometimes surprising, swinging unit began when they played together casually after being discharged from World War II service. Through seventeen ground-breaking years Desmond and Brubeck were the driving force behind the most commercially successful jazz group of its day, perhaps of any era. The quartet's bassists and drummers changed, but the vital, unique interplay between the altoist Desmond and the leader-pianist Brubeck were the constant key elements that drove the success of the group.

Desmond always claimed that he changed his name from Breitenfeld "because it sounds too Irish," and that he picked Desmond out of the phone book. His German father was an accomplished organist, playing in movie theaters and as a vaudeville accompanist. Into the 1960s, he was still doing arrangements for bands. When Paul's Irish mother became ill in about 1929 he moved to New Rochelle, New York, to live with relatives. He liked to tell of his grammar school experience there in which he played his first improvised solo (on vibes or chimes): "I was supposed to play one of those grisly semiclassical things.... I figured if I just went out and made up something as I went along, it couldn't be any worse. So that's what I did and it was a gas. It was the first thing I'd enjoyed doing. I didn't realize until about fifteen years later that you could make a living doing this."

After returning to San Francisco in 1936, Desmond later began playing the clarinet at Polytechnic High School, where he edited the school newspaper as well as played in the band. After some casual gigging on clarinet, Desmond took up the alto in 1943, the same year he entered the Army and was assigned to the 253rd AGF band. As he told pianist/radio host/writer Marion McPartland, "It was a great way to spend the war. We expected to get shipped out every month, but it never happened. Somewhere in Washington our file must be on the floor under a desk somewhere."

Stationed in San Francisco, he met tenorman/arranger Dave Van Kreidt, who in turn introduced Desmond to Brubeck for just a short session in their band room. Desmond's reaction to this first meeting has been reported using various "Desmondisms," the altoist's clever, off-beat observations. At the very least, Desmond was impressed by the pianist's far-out approach. The two did not meet again until after they were discharged from service when Brubeck was playing in saxophonist Darryl Cutler's trio at San Francisco's Geary Cellar. As Desmond recalled: "I went down and sat in, and the musical rapport was very evident and kind of scary. A lot of the things we've done since, we did then *immediately*—a lot of the counterpoint things, and it really impressed me. If you think Dave plays far out now, you should have heard him then. He made Cecil Taylor sound like Lester Lanin."

Quartet was Launched

Soon Desmond hired leader Cutler's pianist and bassist Norman Bates away from him, becoming the leader of his own group, playing near Stanford. "A lot of the things we did later with the quartet began there.... I have a memory of several nights that seemed fantastic, and I don't feel that way too often." Nevertheless, Desmond became disabused of the idea of being the leader. He entered San Francisco State College, aspiring to be a writer. He also joined the experimental Dave Brubeck Octet, mostly a rehearsal group. By June, 1950, related Paul, he had decided that writing could be learned but not taught. "My only jobs had been two concerts with the octet and a Mexican wedding," so he joined the band of Jack Fina, ending a tour in New York.

At about this time Brubeck, with assistance from disc jockey/promoter Jimmy Lyons, started his trio and established his own record company. Desmond returned to San Francisco and, in 1951, the Dave Brubeck Quartet was born. The earlier-evidenced rapport between them blossomed and the group began to draw the interest of a cadre of fans and critics. First Dave's trio recorded with Fantasy, followed by the full quartet, with Ron Crotty on bass and Cal Tjader on drums and vibraphone. In October of 1952, the quartet recorded a memorable set at George Wein's Storyville club in Boston, with Lloyd Davis now on drums. The group was making inroads with college audiences and in 1953 they recorded two concerts, *Jazz at Oberlin* and the equally sensational *Jazz at the College of the Pacific*, with Joe Dodge now the drummer. This signaled the beginning of a series of college concerts that culminated in a contract with Columbia Records.

Hail, Columbia!

Not surprisingly, Columbia's first Brubeck Quartet release was 1954's *Jazz Goes to College*. This blockbuster LP combined offerings from concerts at the University of Cincinnati, the University of Michigan and a return visit to Oberlin. Of Desmond's work on this album, George Avakian wrote: "... Desmond indulges in a favorite practice of his: to play what seem to be duets with himself. You will frequently hear Paul play passages in which he has two rapidly alternating melody lines in motion, which not only are independently valid, but which fit into one continuous line as well.... Desmond is nothing short of colossal in 'The Song is You"... A breathtaking flow of ideas carries the listener along from peak to peak, with a couple of exceptional examples of Paul's duet technique along the way."

In the early Columbia years Norman Bates and Bob Bates served as bassists; Joe Dodge continued on drums. The most memorable personnel lineup for the quartet began in 1956 when percussionist Joe Morello signed on for an eleven-year stint, with bassist Eugene Wright coming aboard in early 1958. Morello was an exceptionally gifted drummer, Wright a wonderful timekeeper and anchor for the rhythm section. Though Desmond and Morello initially clashed, in time they became close, and it was the drummer's versatility that allowed the quartet to experiment so successfully with several unusual time signatures. Desmond's 1960 composition, "Take Five,' in 5/4 time, became the most popular of all the Brubeck Quartet recordings and the first jazz recording to "go gold" when it appeared on their 1960 *Time Out* album. This meter may be the most difficult of all in which to make music swing, but this group managed it and this song, with a lyric added by lola Brubeck, crossed over to pop and other categories.

Styled for Success

In some ways Desmond and Brubeck were an odd match. Brubeck tended toward massive, heavy chords, whereas Desmond utilized a light, airy, "dry martini" sound. Both approached a melody obliquely, however, seeking to stake out new interpretations whenever possible. Perhaps the most important element of their playing together was their uncanny improvised fugues. Usually in the last chorus or more, one player would begin an invented phrase, only to have the other chime in with a perfectly matching counter phrase, in the manner of a perfectly conceived Bach fugue—swinging relentlessly. Desmond usually played in the upper range of his horn, beautiful of tone, always reaching. He was capable of playing extremely long phrases on one breath, allowing him to construct solos and fugues with majestic, flowing lines.

Once established, the Quartet traveled the world many times over, often composing new songs based on their travels, as found in the album "Jazz Impressions of Eurasia." Some of their concerts, such as those in Amsterdam and Copenhagen, were recorded. All the while they maintained a steady diet of performances in the United States—college concerts, concerts in halls such as Carnegie, club dates, studio recording, and jazz festivals such as Newport. Having established that he was no leader, Desmond was content to let Brubeck handle the business end. A financial agreement that they reached early in the partnership assured the altoist adequate compensation for his sizeable contributions to the group's success.

Brubeck and Desmond each credited the other with this success; they were both probably right. Jazz critics were not generally kindly disposed to Brubeck's playing and, perhaps by default, they sometimes found reason to carp about Desmond's. The New Yorker's Whitney Balliett points out that Desmond won the Down Beat Critics' Poll only once, while winning the Readers' Poll many times—"a rare instance of the public's having better ears than the professionals." Desmond had listened to three wonderful altoists when forming his taste, Pete Brown, Willie Smith and the incomparable Johnny Hodges, so long associated with Duke Ellington. Balliett wrote of Desmond's 1969 appearance at the White House, honoring Duke's seventieth birthday, in which Desmond "reproduced Johnny Hodges so perfectly during one of his solos that he startled the usually unflappable Ellington."

In their solos Desmond and Brubeck each made generous use of "quotes"—phrases from other songs that fit into the chord pattern of the song being played. Often the borrowed phrase was the title line of the tune and Paul and Dave would often communicate with one another through these exchanges. It is said that Brubeck could discern Desmond's mood or his immediate concerns by deciphering the altoists quotes. To amuse themselves, attuned to one another as they were, sometimes the musicians would engage in whole conversations in this esoteric manner.

Balliett wrote of Desmond's sound thus: "Desmond's tone was off-white, gentle—almost transparent and almost weightless. It had a brand-new, untouched sound, he used very little vibrato.... Desmond's solos thought; they had logic and clarity.... The quietness of Desmond's attack was deceptive.... But he always moved along the outer edges of the chords he was improvising on, atonality in sight. His rhythmic attack was equally deceptive.... He played behind the beat, on the eat, and ahead of the beat.... Like his friend Jim Hall, Desmond was one of he handful of jazz improvisers who demand total concentration. If the listener falters, he is lost; if he remains rapt, he is blessed."

From Notes to Quotes

After seventeen years of intensive travel the Dave Brubeck Quartet disbanded in 1967. Brubeck took some time to compose sacred words, but returned the following year with baritone saxist Gerry Mulligan as part of the Quartet. Desmond did some free-lancing and declared that he intended to return to his original goal by writing a book. This has been the subject of much mystery and speculation as, in his typical teasing mode, Desmond has variously declared this to be a serious project or a convenient excuse for not playing. The non-book bears the working title How Many of You Are There in the Quartet?, allegedly inspired by the frequent question asked of him in his travels. One hilarious chapter actually exists, having appeared in Punch. It was re- printed in the recent Reading Jazz, edited by Robert Gottlieb.

Desmond's friends were fond of collecting his often self-effacing witticisms. He called himself the world's slowest saxophonist and declared that when he played with unsupportive players he would "shrivel up like a lemoned clam." Of his own fame, Desmond claimed, "I was unfashionable before anyone knew who I was." He explained his failure to become a writer by stating, "I could only write at the beach, and I kept getting sand in my typewriter." He also purported to be discouraged by the fact that several of he fine writers whom he befriended and hung out with in the post-Brubeck days claimed that they were frustrated musicians.

Phasing Out

After 1967 Desmond concertized and recorded extensively with guitarists Jim Hall and Ed Bickert, both of whom were kindred musical souls. These pairings produced some notable recordings. He performed a Christmas Day concert with The Modern Jazz Quartet in 1971 at New York's Town Hall which fortunately was recorded. He also took part in a few reunion concerts with Brubeck and in a silver anniversary tour of the Quartet, re-uniting with Morello and Wright and resulting in the final recording of the famous group in March 1976.

Much of Desmond's semi-retirement was centered around his New York penthouse apartment, surrounded by books, and in the good company of musicians, writers, stylish women and friends. He ate and drank in congenial restaurants, notably Elaine's and Bradley's, where the talk and the Scotch were good. He developed lung cancer and underwent extensive therapy, taking great pains to avoid being a burden to his friends. From the early agreement with Brubeck, and with his royalties, especially from "Take Five,' Desmond was financially comfortable. He donated these royalties from his compositions and recordings to the American Red Cross. His attorney, Noel Silverman, estimated that this organization has received more than a million dollars from Desmond's estate since 1977.

Desmond's last appearance was with Brubeck at New York's Lincoln Center on February 4, 1977. In an interview on National Public Radio the day after Desmond's death, the pianist told of his partner propped in his familiar place at the crook of the piano, crafting his last duets before a full house. The altoist's beautiful playing brought great ovations. The audience begged for an encore. Too weak to continue, Desmond begged off and bowed out.

Selected discography

The Complete Recordings of the Paul Desmond Quartet with Jim Hall (1959-65); Mosaic, 1988.
The Dave Brubeck Quartet 25th Anniversary Reunion; A&M, 1976.
In Concert at Town Hall (with the Modern Jazz Quartet); DRG, 1971.
Jazz at Oberlin; Fantasy, 1953.
Jazz Goes to College; Columbia, 1954.
The Paul Desmond Quartet Live (with Ed Bickert); A&M, 1975.
Time Out; Columbia, 1959.

Sources

Books

Carr, Ian, Digby Fairweather, and Brian Priestley, *Jazz: the Rough Guide*; The Rough Guides, 1995.
Feather, Leonard, *The New Edition of the Encyclopedia of Jazz*; Bonanza Books, 1965.
Gottlieb, Robert, *Reading Jazz*; Pantheon Books, 1996.
Lyons, Len and Don Perlo, *Jazz Portraits*; Quill/William Morrow, 1989.
McPartland, Marion, *All in Good Time*; Oxford University Press, 1987.

Periodicals

Down Beat, August, 1977; March, 1988.
Esquire, October, 1988.
The New Yorker, September 16, 1991.
The New York Times, June 1, 1977.

Other

(Liner notes) *Jazz at Oberlin*; notes by James Newman.
(Liner notes) *Jazz Goes to College*; notes by George Avakian.

—Robert Dupuis

Dirty Dozen Brass Band

Jazz band

From the late 1970s until the middle 1990s, the Dirty Dozen Brass Band revitalized the New Orleans brass band sound. They mixed it with the contemporary styles of rhythm and blues and bebop to give it a different, more modern sound. Although they faced quite a bit of criticism from traditional brass band purists, they received universal praise from their audiences. After a three-year hiatus in the 1990s, the group shortened its name to the Dirty Dozen, as they had changed their style and instrumentation beyond the brass band format. "People come up to me sometimes, and they say, 'You're not playing real New Orleans music,'" said trumpet player and bandleader Gregory Davis in an interview with *Musician*'s Ben Sandmel. "And I tell them, 'I'm glad you noticed!'"

Throughout their career, the Dirty Dozen Brass Band recorded and performed as guest performers with a number of artists, spanning a wide range of musical genres including Elvis Costello, Buckwheat Zydeco, the Neville Brothers, the Black Crowes, the Grateful Dead, and David Byrne. Their influence spread throughout New Orleans, inspiring a new school of dancing known as "buckjumping," a triple-time dance done in large, all-male groups. They also performed at some of the most prestigious festivals around the world, such as the Montreux Jazz Festival and the Northsea Jazz Festival.

The Dirty Dozen Brass Band began playing around New Orleans in 1975, while most of the members had either just graduated or were still attending high school. They got the idea for their name from the Dirty Dozen Social and Pleasure Club in New Orleans. They continued to play in local clubs, parades, and funeral marches around town through the early 1980s. In 1984, the group released their debut album, *My Feet Can't Fail Me Now,* on Concord Jazz Records. It included recordings of the band's live performances of tunes such as Thelonius Monk's "Blue Monk," and Dave "Fat Man" Wilson's "I Ate Up the Apple Tree." At the time, the Dirty Dozen Brass Band was made up of eight members: Gregory Davis, trumpet; Roger Lewis, baritone and soprano saxophones; Kirk Joseph, sousaphone; Jennell Marshall, snare drums; Benny Jones, bass drum; Charles Joseph, trombone; Efrem Towns, trumpet; and Kevin Harris, tenor saxophone.

The following year, the Dirty Dozen Brass Band released another live album called *Live: Mardi Gras Montreux* on Rounder Records. In July of 1985, Benny Jones left the group, and was replaced by Lionel Batiste on bass drums. The band continued to perform live and increase their visibility, which would eventually lead to a contract with Columbia Records. Their major label debut, 1987's *Voodoo*—featuring guest appearances by such greats as Dizzy Gillespie on trumpet and vocals, Dr. John on piano and vocals, and Branford Marsalis on tenor saxophone. The album grabbed the attention of fans and the press, opening the door to future success.

"Once a staid, traditional style of music played by weathered old men at political rallies and shopping-mall openings, brass-band music has been radically modernized by the Dirty Dozen," Jeff Hannusch wrote in *Rolling Stone.* Hank Bardowitz wrote in his *High Fidelity* review, "They show expertise in everything from hard bop and free blowing to big band ensemble work, and even in their most up-to-date moments, there's just no room for such modern jazz appurtenances as guitar and piano."

The Dirty Dozen Brass Band expanded their fan base even more in 1989 when they performed on rock singer Elvis Costello's LP *Spike.* Costello reciprocated later in the year with a guest appearance on "That's How You Got Killed Before" on the Dirty Dozen Brass Band's next release *The New Orleans Album.* The album also included collaborations with pianist Eddie Bo, and Danny Barker, who sang and played guitar on the song "Don't You Feel My Leg."

Again, the group received positive feedback from the press and their fans. "The [Dirty Dozen Brass Band] is undeniably fun listening, churning out those infectious good-time grooves with a sense of humor and laid-back nonchalance that is endemic to the Nawlins experience,"

Members included **Keith Anderson**, sousaphone/trombone; **Revert Andrews** (joined 1993), trombone; **Lionel Batiste** (1985-1996), bass drums; **Gregory Davis**, trumpet/vocals; **Kevin Harris**, tenor saxophone; **Terence Higgins**, drums; **Benny Jones** (1975-1985), bass drums; **Charles Joseph** (1975-93); **Kirk Joseph** (1975-93); **Richard Knox**, keyboards; **Roger Lewis**, soprano and baritone saxophones; **Jenell Marshall** (1975-1996), snare drums; **Julius McKee** (joined 1993), sousaphone; **Efrem Towns**, trumpet.

Band formed as the Dirty Dozen Brass band in New Orleans, 1975; released debut *My Feet Can't Fail Me Now*, 1984, Concord Jazz, singed with Colimbia Records, 1986; released major label debut, *Voodoo*, 1987; *The New Orleans Album*, 1989; *Open Up (Watcha gonna do for the Rest of Your Life?)*, 1991; *Jelly*, 1991; changed name to Dirty Dozen, signed to Mammoth Records, and released *Ears to the Wall*, 1996; released *This is Jazz*, 1997, Sony Music.

Addresses: *Record company*—Mammoth Records, 101 B Street, Carrboro, NC 27510.

Bill Milkowski wrote in *Down Beat*. They continued to expand and diversify their repertoire in their live shows, too, as Jeff Hannusch wrote in a performance review in *Billboard*, "Who else but the Dozen could get away with paying the Rolling Stones classic 'It's All Over Now' and Thelonius Monk's 'Blue Monk' during the same show?"

Spirited Music

Two years later, the Dirty Dozen Brass Band returned with another Columbia release *Open Up (Whatcha Gonna Do for the Rest of Your Life?)*, featuring guest drummer Raymond Webber, and it continued to reflect the band's theme of fun and spirited music. "In a funny way, this may presently be the most 'radical' popular group around," Joseph Woodard wrote in his *Down Beat* review. "With the [Dirty Dozen Brass Band], there's camaraderie, safety—and also danger—in numbers." Al Pryor wrote in *Audio*, "*Whatcha Gonna Do for the Rest of Your Life* is another excellent contribution from an ensemble that has managed to instill a sense of joy and revelry into their music."

Moved into New Directions

The Dirty Dozen Brass Band embarked on another tour before returning to the studio. Before the release of their next album, Charles Joseph was replaced by Revert Andrews on trombone and Kirk Joseph left the band, as well. In 1993, their next album *Jelly* arrived in stores. Its name reflected its content—an album of the Dirty Dozen Brass Band's interpretation of songs by Jelly Roll Morton. Kenyatta Simon and Big Chief Smiley played percussion on the LP, and Barker and George French contributed vocals.

After *Jelly*, the Dirty Dozen Brass Band took a three-year break, and underwent several changes. First, they changed their lineup along with their instrumentation. Julius McKee stepped in to replace Kirk Joseph on sousaphone. Terence Higgins took over as the single trap-set drummer after the departure of both Lionel Batiste and Jennell Marshall, and Richard Knox was added to the group on keyboards. Although they continued to use the sousaphone, they occasionally replaced it with electric or acoustic bass guitar on some of their new material. As they began writing and recording, the band decided to change their name to the Dirty Dozen, since their direction no longer fit into the basic brass band format.

New Name and New Sound

The newly formed Dirty Dozen also signed a new record contract with Mammoth Records and released *Ears to the Wall* in 1996 to mixed reviews. "The Dozen has drifted in the direction of generic, crossover soul-jazz, a move that makes a lot of commercial, but very little musical, sense," Geoffrey Himes wrote in the *Washington Post*. The album included a rearranged and re-recorded version of their early song "My Feet Can't Fail Me Now," which appeared on the album and in the film *Sgt. Bilko*. Sony Music also released a compilation of the Dirty Dozen Brass Band's earlier material in 1997 called *This Is Jazz*.

Despite the group's new name and new direction, their influence on New Orleans brass band music was undeniable. "A lot of people couldn't adjust at first, and they disapproved of us," Kirk Joseph had told Sandmel in *Down Beat* at the height of their popularity. "They thought we were abolishing our heritage. But then they got into it. And someone else will come behind us, and expand it even more."

Selected discography

My Feet Can't Fail Me Now, Concord Jazz, 1984.
Live: Mardi Gras Montreux, Rounder Records, 1985.
Voodoo, Columbia Records, 1987.
The New Orleans Album, Columbia Records, 1989.
Open Up (Whatcha Gonna Do for the Rest of Your Life?), Columbia Records, 1991.
Jelly, Columbia Records, 1993.
Ears to the Wall, Mammoth Records, 1996.
This Is Jazz, Sony Music, 1997.

Sources

Books

Cook, Richard and Morton, Brian, *Guide to Jazz on CD,* Third Edition, Penguin Books, New York, 1996.
Wynn, Ron, editor, *All Music Guide to Jazz,* Miller Freeman Books, San Francisco, 1994.

Periodicals

Audio, July 1987, August 1992.
Billboard, April 28, 1990.
Down Beat, June 1984, July 1989, July 1990, April 1992.
Essence, March 1985.
High Fidelity, February 1987, June 1989.
Maclean's, March 6, 1989.
Musician, August 1989.
New Yorker, July 23, 1984; July 22, 1985; April 24, 1989.
People, December 10, 1984; April 24, 1989; July 23, 1990.
Rolling Stone, April 20, 1989.
Stereo Review, February 1985, July 1992, August 1993.
Washington Post, August 16, 1996.

Online

http://www.rosebudus.com/dozen/

—Sonya Shelton

Dr. Demento

Disc jockey

As with most forms of culture, rock music sometimes takes itself a bit too seriously, with overly somber critics taking time to notice only "serious" musicianship. For decades, Barret Hansen, better known as Dr. Demento, has trampled over such pretensions, sharing pop music's offbeat novelties to listeners of his highly rated syndicated radio program. After years of airing the wackiness of musicians like Spike Jones as Frank Zappa, Dr. Demento became a cult figure with a devoted following, and the top hat clad disc jockey was invited to make numerous cameo appearances in videos and television programs. However, such inspired silliness often obscures another side of Dr. Demento. "People know him for his goofy stuff," Rhino Records president Jim Neill told Kathy Gronau in the online *Radio Guide Magazine*. "But he's a very serious musical scholar. He knows everything about music. He has a barn somewhere just filled with records."

Born in Minneapolis, Minnesota in 1941, Barret Hansen was surrounded by music from the beginning. The son of a talented pianist, the young Hansen was encouraged to follow in his father's footsteps. Instead he was seduced by his passion for recorded music. Although he had begun raiding thrift shops for dusty phonographs containing all styles of music, a practice he never abandoned, his taste for the bizarre was already evident. "I suppose you could say it started when I was four years old and my dad brought home a record by [outrageous bandleader] Spike Jones," Demento told Terry DuFoe in *Outre* magazine. "This would be at the time when Spike was at the peak of his career in the forties, so all the gun shots and all the noise and chaos and the liveliness of it certainly excited me. So that planted the seed of the taste for funny music that has never left."

While Dr. Demento's collection of records grew, he was captured by the first wave of rock and roll music that exploded across America in the 1950s. His first job as a disc jockey came in 1957, when he was hired to play rock and R&B records at high school dances but his commitment to the musical form ran much deeper. Soon after, Dr. Demento moved to Reed College in Portland, Oregon where he earned a degree in classical music. During that time had tried his hand at writing essays on rock and blues, which he began playing on Reed's campus radio station, KRRR. In the late 1960s, Dr. Demento relocated to Los Angeles, California to continue his education at UCLA and here he wrote his master's thesis on the growth of blues music in the 1940s. As Dr. Demento has suggested, if his career as a disc jockey had not taken off, he would most likely have continued this academic path.

Los Angeles proved to be a fertile environment for Dr. Demento, and has served as his base of operations to this day. After obtaining a spot on the city's KPFK radio station, Dr. Demento filtered into the bustling scene of music production by becoming a roadie for the groups Canned Heat and Spirit, for whom he engineered a demo tape. This association, along with his scholastic credibility, led to a job with Specialty Records for whom he assembled over thirty compilations of out of print blues artists. Specialty Records, in turn, introduced Dr. Demento to the lively atmosphere of the underground radio station KPPC, where a format of groundbreaking rock and an often irreverent attitude gave Barret Hansen the final push towards becoming Dr. Demento. "We really felt we were doing something revolutionary;" Demento said of the station to Gronau, "We were the main missionaries for Jimmy Hendrix, Elton John, and The Who."

Falling in step with KPPC's free-form school of broadcasting, the newly dubbed disc jockey began *The Dr. Demento Show* in 1970 when the airing of novelty songs such as "Monster Mash" by Bobby "Boris" Pickett and "Transfusion" by Nervous Norvis received numerous calls of support on the disc jockey's earliest Los Angeles shows. In 1972, the show moved to KMET FM for Sunday evening broadcasts, where it became the highest rated program among the area's teenagers, who would often send him absurd petitions requesting

For the Record . . .

Born **Barret Hansen**, 1941, in Minneapolis, MN, son of an amateur pianist; wife Sue. *Education:* Reed University, Portland, OR; UCLA, Los Angeles, CA.

Made Los Angeles radio debut at the blues and country station KPFK in the late 1960s; compiled 35 reissue records of blues and gospel music for Specialty Records, 1968-70; assumed the name Dr. Demento, 1970 after moving to the underground station KPPC FM; moved to KMET, Los Angeles , 1972; *The Dr. Demento Show* went into syndication, 1974; released first compilation of novelty records as *Dr. Demento for Warner Brothers,* 1976; appeared with actor Bill Paxton in the video for "Fish Heads" by Barnes and Barnes, 1980; began *The Demento Society News,* 1986; received tribute special for twenty years of broadcasting by the Comedy Central cable network, 1991; completed book, *Heavy, Man: A Cruise Through the World of Blues,* 1998.

Addresses: *Fan club*—The Demento Society, P.O. Box 884, Culver City, CA, 90232; *Syndication contact*—On The Radio Productions, 3250 Ocean Park Blvd., Suite 206, Santa Monica, CA 90405.

equally absurd music. "They would make up a funny name like 'Psychotic Pineapples of Pasadena'," Dr. Demento recalled to Gronau. "The kids would get a charge out of it." As his fan constituency grew to include many adults as well, demand for his weekly salad of oddities resulted in the syndication of *The Doctor Demento Show* in 1974.

As more stations added Dr. Demento's show to their schedules throughout the 1970s, the disc jockey's own role in the world of bizarre music became more involved. Along with requests, some fans of the program were inspired to send their own creations, and the *Dr. Demento Show* became a way-station for those out to amuse, shock, or simply perplex. In 1978, for instance, Robert Haimer and ex-child actor Bill Mumy, once famous for his work on television's *Lost In Space,* sent Dr. Demento a cassette containing the potentially offensive "Vomit Song," under the name Barnes and Barnes. As Demento later remembered to DuFoe, "I wrote back to them and said, 'It's brilliant, but I can't use it on the air. Do you

have any other material?' A month later they sent me 'Fish Heads'." That song, a comically nightmarish tune sung by a chorus of chipmunk-pitched voices, became one of Demento's signature cuts, as well as one of the most popular novelty songs of all time.

In the early 1980s, Dr. Demento made what may have been his biggest discovery, "Weird Al" Yankovic. Later to become a million-selling artist, Yankovic started sending Dr. Demento his parodies of popular pop songs, sometimes accompanied with an accordion, when he was only sixteen. Demento saw potential in Yankovic's offerings, giving the young comedian much needed exposure on his radio show. "He was not an overnight discovery," Dr. Demento told DuFoe. "I mean fisrt there was the one song I played on my show, then there was a better song I played on my show, then there was something that a record company noticed and put out on a record, then there was something that was good enough to get him a major label record deal." Yankovic's fame eventually eclipsed that of Dr. Demento himself, but the latter's role as mentor was not forgotten, as Yankovic asked Dr. Demento to appear in almost half of his videos, as well as in his weekly television series.

Dr. Demento's cult status only continued to grow throughout the decade, as did his personal archive of records, which at one point caused the floor of his apartment to collapse. In 1986, a fan club started the *Demento Society News,* a newsletter that offered readers release updates, lyrics, and other miscellaneous tidbits concerned with novelty music or Dr. Demento himself. While not a star in the strictest sense, Dr. Demento obviously had gained clout with many American pop culture fanatics, and consequently he was contacted to endorse or annotate a number of new collections of bizarre music. As one of the few on-air champions of gimmicky pop songs, Dr. Demento began a fruitful association with Rhino Records, a company at the time known almost exclusively for unusual re-releases.

Over the years, *The Dr. Demento Show* added new features to its format, such as the satirical "Demented News," a four-minute segment in which "Whimsical" Will Simpson peppered accounts of current events with ironic sound samples. Expectedly, the program also inducted timely songs of the day into its vaults, such as "Sensitive New Age Guy" and "Weird Al" Yankovic's send-ups of contemporary hits. However, while Dr. Demento's show had never been wholesome family fare, he chose not to capitalize on the trend of on-air obscenity for its own sake popularized by shock DJs' like New York's Howard Stern. "I do not find Howard Stern funny often," Demento admitted to Gronau. "[But] I have to hand it to him: Anyone who can just blab on the radio about whatever crosses his mind for five hours a day and get millions of listeners to slavishly listen to him has to be smart."

In the 1990s, Dr. Demento's show was picked up by the On The Radio network, which continued its syndication in an increased number of locales. As he continued to do his own research and tribute records to artists of the past, he was given his own commemoration when in October of 1991, the Comedy Central cable network aired a one hour special in honor of *The Dr. Demento Show*'s twentieth anniversary, which featured appearances by novelty favorites like Bobby "Boris" Pickett as well as Dr. Demento himself. While not intending to return to a life of scholarship, Dr. Demento completed his first full length book in 1998, entitled *Heavy, Man: A Cruise Through the World of Blues*. Published under his real name, the book demonstrated that after almost thirty years of embracing lunacy, Dr. Demento was still cultivating a love of all music.

Selected discography

Dr. Demento's Delights, Warner Brothers, 1975.
Dr. Demento's Dementia Royale, Rhino, 1980.
Demento's Mementos, Eccentric, 1982.
Dr. Demento Presents the Greatest Novelty Records of All Time, Rhino, 1985. (Six-CD box set)
Dr. Demento Presents the Greatest Christmas Novelty Records of All Time, Rhino, 1989.

Dr. Demento's 20th Anniversary Collection, Rhino, 1991.
Spooky Tunes and Scary Melodies, Rhino, 1994.
Dr. Demento's 25th Anniversary Collection, Rhino, 1995.
Country Corn, Rhino, 1995.
Holidays In Dementia, 1995.

Selected writings

Hansen, Barret, *Heavy Man: A Cruise Through the World of Blues,* 1998.

Sources

Periodicals

Outre, 1996.
Rolling Stone, October 14, 1993.

Online

Dr. Demento, The Doctor Speaks, http://www.rhino.com/Albums/721, (6/22/98)
Radio Guide Magazine, http://amp.electriciti.com/benj, (6/22/98).
http://home.earthlink.net/~tafu
http://php.indiana.edu/~jbmorri

—Shaun Frentner

Dream
Theater

Rock band

Influenced by the progressive rock music of the 1970s, New York's Dream Theater managed to combine the technically difficult, heavily orchestrated style of their mentors with the heavy metal power of the 1980's. From the mid-1980s and all the way through the alternative grunge rock scene of the 1990s, Dream Theater stayed true to their heavy-metal-meets-progressive-rock direction without swaying with the trends. "It's like an unwritten rule that we don't chase trends," guitarist John Petrucci told Michael Mehle in Denver's *Rocky Mountain News*. "The music scene changes so often—what's popular, what's on top of the charts—that it's best just to stay focused."

The spark of what eventually ignited the formation of Dream Theater happened in September of 1985. Longtime friends John Petrucci and bassist John Myung were attending the prestigious Berklee School of Music in Boston, where they met drummer Mike Portnoy and discovered they had many things in common. Not only did they have the same musical interests, but all three hailed from Long Island in New York. "It was obvious that all our heads were in the same place," Portnoy said in the band's record company biography, "and to find that they were from home was amazing because [there're] people from all over the world at Berklee."

When the trio returned to Long Island for their winter break, they began rehearsing with keyboardist Kevin Moore, who was attending the Fredonia School of Music and had played with Myung and Petrucci in their high school band Centurion. "There weren't many real keyboard players performing in rock when I broke in," Moore told Robert L. Doerschuk in *Keyboard,* "and that left it wide open for me."

Early the next year, the group found singer Chris Collins and the five musicians formed a band called Majesty. After the summer of their first year in music school, the members decided to leave their education behind and focus on their band. They took regular jobs and spent much of their free time writing, rehearsing, and performing. Later that year, they recorded a six-song demo tape, which they sold to local fans and sent out to record labels. In November of 1986, the group decided that Collins didn't have enough of a vocal range to fit the music they were writing, and they began to search for a new singer.

After auditioning nearly 100 singers, they settled Charlie Dominici in 1987. Dominici was quite a bit older than any of the other members, but seemed to fit their requirements at the time. In 1988, a fledgling record label, Mechanic Records, signed Majesty as their first artist, but after the ink was dry, they discovered that another band owned the trademark to the name Majesty. While the band brainstormed to find a new name, Portnoy's father called them from California to suggest Dream Theater, the name of a movie theater in Monterey, California. Petrucci recalled their surprise at the perfect suggestion to Valerie Potter in *Metal Hammer,* "It's not too often that your father thinks of the name of your band!"

With their new moniker in place, Dream Theater released their debut *When Dream and Day Unite* in 1988. Since Mechanic Records had just started, the company didn't have the budget for a video or tour for the band, so the group continued to play shows throughout the New York tri-state area and work their regular jobs. Despite the lack of exposure, Dream Theater received critical praise and word-of-mouth fans. "To say the least, this is a bit different from the norm, and it certainly explores the musical spectrum," wrote Brian Pithers in Metal Hammer. Tom Mulhern wrote in his *Guitar Player* review, "*When Dream and Day Unite* features speedy licks and complex interplay by the guitarist and bassist as keyboards swirl and the drums tear through the songs like a Ferrari down a narrow alley."

In 1990, Dream Theater fired Dominici from the group, and began another search for a singer. "He had the experience that Chris [Collins] didn't, but after awhile, it became evident that he wasn't the singer we were looking for," Portnoy said in the band's record company

For the Record . . .

Members include **Chris Collins** (left band, 1987), vocals; **Charlie Dominici** (joined band, 1987; left band, 1991), vocals; **James LaBrie** (born Kevin James LaBrie), vocals; **Kevin Moore** (joined band, 1986; left band 1994), keyboards; **John Myung**, bass; **John Petrucci**, guitar; **Mike Portnoy**, drums; **Derek Sherinian**, keyboards.

Band formed as Majesty in New York, 1985; vocalist Chris Collins was replaced by Charlie Dominici, 1987; signed to Mechanic Records and released *When Dream and Day Unite,* 1988; Kevin LaBrie replaced Charlie Dominici, 1991; signed to EastWest Records, 1991; released major label debut, *Images and Words,* 1992; Derek Sherinian replaced Kevin Moore, 1994.

Addresses: *Record company*—EastWest Records, 75 Rockefeller Plaza, New York, NY 10019.

biography. The remaining members thought they would be able to find a replacement relatively quickly, however, the search ended up taking almost two years. "We were very picky," continued Portnoy, "because the four of us set such high standards for each other, we didn't want to sell ourselves short on the fifth member."

Dream Theater continued to write new songs and perform in the New York area as an instrumental four-piece band. After auditioning around 200 singers, they found Kevin LaBrie, who was playing in a Toronto band called Winter Rose. When LaBrie joined Dream Theater, he decided to use his middle name, James, since the band already had two members named John and having two Kevins would be even more confusing.

With their lineup solidified, Dream Theater signed a record contract with EastWest Records. In 1992, their first major label release *Images and Words* arrived in stores. The album was produced by David Prater, and this time, the band was able to increase their fan base. Their videos appeared on MTV, and Dream Theater embarked on their first world tour called "Music in Progress." *Images and Words* went gold in Japan, and the group played a sold-out tour there, as well as dates throughout Europe and in Korea. "The Japanese are so devoted to music; it's really inspiring," Petrucci told Andy Widders-Ellis in *Guitar Player.* During their European tour, Dream Theater recorded a live album at London's famed Marquee nightclub called *Live at the Marquee.*

In March of 1994, the group returned to the studio. Two months later, they temporarily relocated to Los Angeles to work with producers John Purdell and Duane Baron on their next album. Halfway through the recording, keyboardist Kevin Moore decided to leave the band citing musical differences. "I came to the decision that I needed to concentrate on my own musical identity and that a split with the band would be the best thing for both the band and myself," Moore stated in a press release. After his departure, Moore moved to New Mexico and began working on a solo project.

On October 4, 1994, Dream Theater released *Awake* and the single "Lie." The album debuted at number 34 on *Billboard*'s album charts, sold 50,000 copies in Germany within the first week of its release, and reached platinum sales in Japan. Before they took off on their next world tour, Dream Theater found keyboardist Derek Sherinian to fill in for Moore. Sherinian had played with Alice Cooper, Kiss, and would eventually join Dream Theater on a full time basis.

The group released an EP later that year called *A Change of Seasons.* Produced by Prater, the title track clocked in at about 22 minutes in length and became legendary among Dream Theater's fans. "The way that we write is maybe somewhat different," said singer LaBrie. "We start a song, and we don't end that song until we feel the message has been completed." The other songs on the record were live recordings from Ronnie Scott's Jazz Club in London, England.

In 1996, Dream Theater played five shows on what they called "Fix for '96," where they played some of the new material they were working on at the time. They did the same sort of mini tour in Europe the following year called "Fix for '97." On September 23, 1997, they released the Kevin Shirley produced *Falling Into Infinity.* Writing for *Bass Player,* Karl Coryat wrote, "*Falling Into Infinity* is an intense listen— at times fatiguing to the ear, but still highly enjoyable. If you can move someone with something simple or beautiful, or play something so complex that it makes someone nervous—that's the allure to me," Petrucci told Mehle in the *Rocky Mountain News.* Throughout their career, Dream Theater ignored the passing trends and continually stayed in touch with their own musical direction. "The minute you try to fit a trend, it's going to change, and you're going to be left in the dust," Portnoy told Sparky in *Loudmouth Magazine.* "If you just do what you do, that's where you create your own sound, and that's the kind of stuff that's timeless."

Selected discography

When Dream and Day Unite, Mechanic Records, 1988.
Images and Words, EastWest Records, 1992.
Awake, EastWest Records, 1994.
A Change of Seasons, EastWest Records, 1995.
Falling Into Infinity, EastWest Records, 1997.

Sources

Periodicals

Bass Frontiers, November/December 1997.
Bass Player, January 1998, April 1998.
Guitar Player, June 1989; January 1990; December 1993;
    January 1998.
Kerrang!, March 11, 1989.

Keyboard, April 1993.
Loudmouth Magazine, November 1997.
Metal Hammer, No. 5/1989; October 1994.
Music Street Journal, March 1998.
Rocky Mountain News (Denver, Colorado), November 5,
    1997.
Shockwaves, Number 2, 1997.

Online

http://www.dreamtheater.net

Additional information for this profile was obtained from
Mechanic Records press materials, 1988; and EastWest
Records press materials, 1997.

—Sonya Shelton

Michael English

Singer, songwriter

AP/Wide World Photos. Reproduced by permission.

From prodigal son to pariah and back again, Michael English has been successful in both the contemporary Christian and pop music industry. English's success in these two different industries made him a rarity in the music business, whose strict divisions between its music categories usually blocks any attempts for such crossover success. Yet it was how English entered the pop music world, not his crossover success that made him famous.

Michael Dewayne English was born in 1962 in Kennansville, North Carolina. Before English was big enough to be seen from its pews, he began singing with his father, Aubine and his brother, Biney in their Pentecostal Church in Wallace, North Carolina. By the age of 13, English and Biney became members of The Singing Samaritans, a southern gospel quartet. After graduating high school, English toured professionally for two years with the gospel group, The Singing Americans. In 1982, English continued his singing career by joining another gospel group, The Goodmans. According to his online web page biography, English said that "singing with The Goodmans was a dream come true [because] Vestal Goodman is my favorite singer in the whole world. When I get to Heaven, I want her voice." In 1986, English was asked to join the respected gospel group, The Gaither Vocal Band and for the next five years they recorded the albums *1 X One*, Wings,, and *Homecoming.*

During these years, though, English was not just professionally singing, he was also battling a panic disorder. As Lyla Akouri noted in his online web page biography, English suffered from panic attacks that were "brought about by years of internalized stress and sense of worthlessness." Some of these attacks became debilitating to the point where he would experience heart palpitations, shortness of breath, and tunnel vision. When English lost his voice for seven months, he sought help from a familiar source. "Michael turned to God to help him through a time when he says he was 'out of hope'," wrote Akouri. By "turning to God," English regained his hope and took a giant step forward and began his solo contemporary christian music career.

In 1991, Christian record label Warner Alliance Records released English's first solo album, Michael English. This album, with such hits as "Do You Believe in Love", "Mary Did You Know", and "Heaven" won English two Gospel Music Association (GMA) Dove awards. By the end of 1992, *Michael English* was also the thirteenth best selling album on *Billboard*'s Contemporary Christian album chart. In 1993, English released his second album *Hope*. The GMA awarded *Hope* and English six Dove awards including Contemporary Album of the Year

For the Record . . .

Born Michael Dewayne English, 1962 in Kennansville, NC; son of Aubine and Grace English; Married Lisa Bailey in 1983 (later divorced); children: one daughter, Megan.

Performed as group member of gospel's Singing Americans, Bill Gaither Trio, and Gaither Vocal Band; provided background vocals for a variety of Christian artists in the early-to-mid-1990s; released first solo album, *Michael English,* 1991; released second solo album, *Hope,* 1993; dropped by Christian music recording label Warner Alliance because of extramarital affair, signed with Curb, 1994; released first pop album, *Healing,* 1995; recorded duet with country singer Wynonna Judd, 1995; produced albums for numerous Christian artists throughout 1990s; released second pop album, *Freedom,* 1996; contributed background vocals for *The Apostle* movie soundtrack, 1998; launched return to contemporary Christian music in summer 1998.

Awards: Gospel Music Association's (GMA) Dove Award for Best Male Vocalist and New Artist of the Year, 1992; GMA Dove Award for Artist of the Year, Best Male Vocalist, Best Inspirational Recorded Song of the Year, Contemporary Album of the Year, 1994.

Addresses: *Management*—Trifecta, 209 10th Ave. S., Suite 302, Nashville, TN 37203; The William Morris Agency, Inc. 2100 West End Ave., #1000, Nashville, TN 37203. *Record Company*—Curb Records, 47 Music Square East, Nashville, TN 37203. *Online*—www.michaelenglish.com.

in 1994. *Hope* was also the fifth best selling record on *Billboard*'s Contemporary Christian album chart for 1993. As *People*'s Cynthia Sanz stated, English had "secured a place among gospel's most successful singers." The spotlight of fame and success had finally shone brightly on English perhaps a little too brightly.

On May 6, 1994, English and Warner Alliance announced in *Billboard* magazine that English "would be withdrawing from the Christian music industry because of mistakes he has recently made." The spotlight that had so brightly shone fame and success on English was now about to illuminate a public scandal—his affair with Marabeth Jordon, the married singer of the gospel group First Call. Two days before the Dove Awards, English had learned that Jordon was expecting his child (she later miscarried). English admitted his affair to his wife, Lisa, then one week later moved out of their house. English also admitted the affair to Warner Alliance. According to Sanz, Warner Alliance record executives then "stopped promotion of his music and pushed him to make a public confession." English also returned his half-dozen Dove awards to the GMA.

Although English had planned to simply retire without an explanation, he honored his record company's wishes and publicly confessed to the affair. Sanz wrote that, as a result of this public confession, "Christian radio stations stopped playing English's music, and some Christian bookstores pulled his tapes and CDs from their shelves." Warner Alliance, as stated in *Christianity Today,* then announced that it had decided to "dissociate itself from English due to his actions that were contrary to the very ideals he had been espousing." Thus, just three years after his first solo album, English had been dropped by his record label, had been shunned by Christian radio stations and bookstores, and had left his home.

However, English's fans had not left him. *Newsweek* reporters Paul O'Donnell and Amy Eskind said that these fans "made a distinction between English's sin and his songs." O'Donnell and Eskind also noted that fans had "snatched up any of his albums still on the racks," and barraged radio stations with "nasty calls" against banning English's music. Nashville's WNAZ radio disc jockey Mark DeYoung told *Newsweek* that "they [fans] were more angry with us [radio stations] than with Michael English. They weren't condemning him at all." Yet, despite continued fan support, English told Sanz: "I felt as if scandal was written across my forehead. I was depressed and sick. I thought my life was over."

Healing

In May of 1994, English told *Newsweek* that "I grew up singing Christian music and Christian music is where my heart is. I'd like to sing [Christian] music again, but I don't know if I will be allowed to." Yet a mere seven months later, *Billboard* reported that the contemporary Christian music industry had "urged English to return ... to share his tribulations and potentially reach an even larger Christian audience." English told *Billboard* that he would not return to the industry because, "I'd have to talk about it [the affair], preach about it, testify about it for Lord knows how long, and I choose not to do that. I choose not to have a tool like that to make myself huge in the Christian industry. I think that's ridiculous. I think that's nasty, and I think that's dirty. I don't have a gimmick. I've just got a voice, and I just want to use that voice."

English chose to use his voice by signing with Curb Records, a secular music label who had offered English a record deal the same day he was dropped by Warner Alliance. Curb chairman Mike Curb told *Billboard*, "I feel he's one of the greatest artists I've ever heard, and I feel his artistry should be allowed to continue." In October of 1994, Curb Records released English's first pop single, "Healing". This song, a duet with country singer Wynonna Judd, was featured on the *Silent Fall* movie soundtrack. In 1995, Curb released *Healing*, a compilation of previously released material along with two new songs.

In July of 1994, English fully declared his freedom from the constraints of the contemporary Christian music industry by debuting his first mainstream pop album, *Freedom*. He told *Billboard* that pop music allowed him, "the freedom to sing and not worry if this [song/album] is going to offend anyone. I'm free to say whatever I feel there is to say. I hope people feel the pain that I have been through and the freedom of expression I have in these songs." Most of the original songs on *Freedom* have a common lyrical theme—freedom. In "Freedom Field", which English co-wrote, he sings: "Old man religion, I've got your name; the best part of my years were wrapped up tied up in your thang." English explained to *Billboard* that the idea for this song came from a "recurring dream that I've had of that place, the freedom where all my dreams come true, the place where everything is right and everything that is wrong is made right." However, English had not totally severed his ties with the contemporary Christian music industry. He produced albums and wrote songs for southern gospel artists such as J.D. Sumner and the Stamps, the Gaither Vocal Band, and The Martins. English acknowledged in *Billboard* that "Christian music will always be part of my life, because that's how I grew up.... I'm never going to shut the door on it."

The doors for English's return to contemporary Christian music was opened in 1996 by his friend, Sumner. Sumner and his band The Stamps were performing at the National Quartet Convention when he asked English to join him on stage, and asked him "to forgive those times when he was judged by the church." English, genuinely honored, sang "I Bowed On My Knees," his signature and classic contemporary Christian song.

In May of 1997, the contemporary Christian music industry's door opened even wider for English when he was asked to be a guest on Trinity Broadcasting Network's (TBN) popular religious TV program, *Praise The Lord*. English thought hard about performing, fearing that Christian audiences would still not accept him, but eventually decided to do it. Afterwards he told *The U.S. Gospel News*, "I'm overwhelmed with gratitude. [People] have been gracious enough to forgive, and now I want to give something back to them."

Struggled for Re-acceptance

The controversy surrounding English's return to contemporary Christian music led to the establishment of two internet web sites devoted to English. Robin Parrish, general editor of one web site, told Jill Doss-Raines from *The Dispatch* that the Christian media and mainstream media had ignored English, even in the wake of his comeback attempt. Writing for the second web site, Akouri agreed with Parrish. In an editorial, Akouri stated that there were "radio stations who still refuse to play his music; one we know of requiring an apology in person before they will do so." Similarly, music product buyer for Berean Christian Stores, Rick Anderson told Carol Chapman Stertzer of *Contemporary Christian Music (CCM) Update* that stores " have a responsibility to our customers and, more importantly, to the Lord, to carry a product that is recorded by artists whose lifestyles are examples of what Christ wants for us: lives of self-control." Therefore, Anderson had not yet decided whether the Berean Christian Stores would carry English's forthcoming Christian album.

English was aware of the hostility over his return to Christian music, telling Stertzer that "there have been some down times dealing with radio stations that won't play my music and say they never will. But I'm not bitter or angry about those things anymore. I'm just thankful for the ones that do play my music." Not to mention the Christian retail stores who never stopped selling English's music. "I felt Warner went overboard," explained Joe Oakley of Family Christian Stores, to Stertzer. "I understand the need to discipline the guy, but to pull everything off the shelves because he sinned? That is tantamount to pulling Psalms out of the Bible because David sinned." Or as Ken Farley, program director at Oklahoma City's KOKF-FM, told Stertzer, "If the criteria for playing a song or stocking a CD was based purely on whether an artist had sin in his or her life, then we'd have nothing to play or sell." Thus, it seemed that English had found some acceptance for his return to contemporary Christian music.

As for why he decided to return to his Christian music, English told Sertzer, "[I] felt a tugging to go back in and do what I know that God has called me to do. I've gone through the fire and made it, so I have something to tell. I'm just me now—there's nothing to hide. People accept me, or they don't."

Selected discography

Michael English, Warner Alliance, 1991.
Hope, Warner Alliance, 1993.
Healing, Curb Records, 1995.
Freedom, Curb Records, 1996.

With The Singing Americans

Hymntime, 1983.
Live and Alive, 1984.
Something Old, Something New, 1984.
Black and White, 1985.

With The Gaither Vocal Band

1 X One, 1986.
Wings, 1988.

A Few Good Men, 1990.
Homecoming, 1991
Peace of the Rock, 1993
Can't Stop Talking About Him, 1995.

Sources

Periodicals

Billboard, May 21, 1994; October 15, 1994; May 25, 1996; June 6, 1996.
CCM Update, April 13, 1998.
Christianity Today, June 20, 1994; December 12, 1994; September 16, 1996.
Newsweek, May 30, 1994.
People, December 12, 1994.
The Dispatch (NC), July 31, 1997.
The Grand Rapids Press, November 6, 1997.
The U.S. Gospel News, September, 1997.

Online

http://www.michaelenglish.com

—*Ann M. Schwalboski*

4Him

Gospel group

The multiple award-winning gospel group 4HIM are noted for their upbeat, beautiful harmonies and poignant, message-laden lyrics. The band is comprised of vocalists Mark Harris, Kirk Sullivan, Andy Chrisman, and Marty Magehee, all of whom were previously with the seminal Christian pop group Truth. *Billboard*'s Deborah Evans Price wrote, "4HIM has built one of the biggest followings in Christian music—on the strength of its polished pop sound and Harris' songwriting prowess." The Christian "Fab 4" is especially noted for superb vocals and sophisticated pop sensibilities.

4HIM sold more than two million records, enjoyed twenty number one radio singles, and was nominated for more than 30 Dove Awards. They won for Group of the Year from 1993-95. The foursome won the Gospel Music Association's Group of the Year accolade in 1993, 1994, and 1995, and each new album for the group was part of an improved musical progression. Laura Harris of *Contemporary Christian Music* described their sound as, "lightly seasoned with tastefully placed distorted electric guitar, while on the other hand it often lends itself to an unmistakably acoustic sound. One thing that sets 4HIM apart from other groups is its vocal mix ... (featuring) only one or two vocalists per song while the others provide seamless, substantial background vocals."

Mark Harris, Marty Magehee, Andy Chrisman, and Kirk Sullivan were all former members of the group Truth and worked together for three years before forming 4HIM.

Harris is the primary songwriter for the group but Magehee contributes songwriting talent as well. The group released their debut album *4HIM* in 1990, which featured the hit single "Where There is Faith," and after their debut *Christian Research Report* poll voted the group Best New Artist. The following year the group released *Face the Nation* and garnered a Dove Award for Best New Artist, and a *Christian Research Report* poll voted the group Best Group. Face the Nation saw five hit singles, including "Why," "He Never Changes," and "Chisel Meets the Stone". In 1992, the group released *The Basics of Life,* which was RIAA-certified as gold and, again, the *Christian Research Report* poll voted the quartet Best Group. The group also received Impact Awards from the Christian Bookseller Association for Cassette Jacket Design and Total Promotional Campaign for *The Basics of Life.*

The Season of Love was released in 1993 as a Christmas album. Subsequent albums were also released including *The Ride* in 1994 and *The Message* in 1996. All received raving reviews and various awards and award nominations including a Grammy Award nomination for *The Message.* Twenty of the group's songs have reached the top spot on the charts and the group has received sponsorships from the American Bible Society and Compassion International.

In 1994, the group took a trip to Russia to distribute Bibles and reach Russian audiences; the trip was planned in conjunction with the American Bible Society. The trip was documented in the video for the single "Real Thing" from *The Ride*. In 1996, 4HIM toured 40 cities with the all-female group Point of Grace, followed by another 40-city tour with Point of Grace six months later in 1997. In 1998, their seventh release, *Obvious,* was cross-promoted with a devotional book titled *The Basics of Life,* which was written by the group. 4HIM took a 23-city city tour to launch the release in 1998. Sullivan told *Christian Retailing* magazine, "As believers we should live a life in front of other people that would make it obvious to them that we 're different. We don 't have to wear a cross and carry a big Bible around all the time."

One of the group's main strengths is a common musical goal and shared perspective, and the most difficult aspect of creating new material is finding producers and arrangers who understand the group's sound. Group members remain flexible—as to which member sings on which song—when recording in the studio, preferring to opt for what sounds best at the moment. The members of 4HIM feel that delivering God's message has been the driving force behind their music; as a result, they choose songs of encouragement with pertinent religious messages, and are noted for being very straightforward contracted a rare, debilitating form of arthritis in 1994 which required 11 different specialists to diagnose, and he was given a 25 percent chance of ever walking again. Six months later, after a concert in Fort Wayne, IN, he felt healed and knew it was from God's hand. The single "Sacred Hideaway" was a reference to this experience. Chrisman told *New Music Magazine* 's Jerry Williams, "We know that 4HIM, that every artist, has a shelf life. And we've decided that we can't waste any time talking about stuff that's fluff.

After working together for more than ten years, the group's members acknowledge that they go through periods of renewal, much like a long-married couple. In a 1998 interview, Harris told Williams, "I think our purpose has changed a little ... God revealed to us that we really need to go one step further with one another and minister to one another. And then the ministry we have on stage is just going to be an overflow of what happens every day within the lives of the four of us toward each other." Asked how long he thought the group would stay together; Chrisman responded, "We try not to put any pressure on ourselves to keep going longer than we should, and we try not to limit God."

Selected discography

4Him, Benson, 1990.
Face The Nation, Benson, 1991.
The Basics of Life, Benson, 1992.
The Season of Love, Benson, 1993.
The Ride, Benson, 1994.
The Message, Benson, 1996.
Obvious, Benson, 1998.

Sources

Periodicals

Billboard, May 2, 1998; May 25, 1996.
Christian Retailing, March 24, 1998.
Contemporary Christian Music, April 1998.
New Music Magazine, Spring 1998.

Online

http://www.4him.net/
Contemporary Christian Music Magazine Online:
http://www.ccmcom.com/ccmmag/96sept/09964HIM_cover.html

—B. Kimberly Taylor

about their faith in Christianity. They also bring different strengths and talent to the group. Chrisman, the father of two, is considered the perfectionist in the group, the member who wants to try something repeatedly until it's perfect. Sullivan is the most communicative, passionate member and Harris is the primary songwriter and a devoted family man with two children. Magehee

Bob Gibson

Singer, guitarist, arranger

Bob Gibson was one of the original troubadours of the American folk music revival of the 1950s. His creative, sensitive style was inspired by classic country folk music; Pete Seeger was one of his heroes. Gibson re-invented the old standard folk songs, revitalized them, and developed his own arrangements. He is credited with kindling a resurgence in that genre of music among his own generation, as well as for generations after. Gibson is especially remembered for his collections of folk songs from the Ohio Valley and from the North Atlantic. He also popularized the 12-string guitar among the new folk singers of the 1960s. Gibson successfully combined his warm and generous nature with a freewheeling image, endearing himself as one of America's best loved folk artists.

Robert "Bob" Gibson was born on November 16, 1931, in New York City. He always liked to sing and was inspired by his family, all of whom loved music; his father at one time sang professionally. Gibson grew up in New York and, as an adolescent, was drawn to the music at the small clubs and coffee houses. He collected records and memorized the words to his favorite songs. Eventually, he learned to play both guitar and banjo and went on to perform at local functions on an amateur basis. In time, Gibson realized that music was his calling. He traveled the northeast in search of both songs and an audience. He sang at concerts and in clubs,

learning new songs and accumulating material for his performances. He developed his own trademark sound on the 12-string guitar, and he frailed and picked his banjo. Before long, Gibson, with crewcut hair and clean cut appearance, developed a following of fans. Initially, he made a name for himself in Cleveland and in the college town of Oberlin, Ohio. From Ohio he traveled to Chicago.

Gate of Horn

Sometime in the mid-1950s Gibson arrived in Chicago. Eventually, he connected with Albert Grossman, owner of a brand new nightclub, the Gate of Horn, which was struggling to survive. Gibson brought his fresh new face and folk styles to the club. Soon, the Gate of Horn was a showcase for Gibson and his songs, and his reputation spread nationwide. Television appearances, a rarity for many stars in the 1950s, were bread and butter for Gibson. He was a regular guest on television's "Arthur Godfrey Time," and he appeared on the "Hootenanny" show among others over the years. So wide was his appeal that he performed even at New York's prestigious Carnegie Hall. His performances were at times whimsical, and many of his songs were truly flippant. His *Ski Songs* album, released by Elektra Records in 1959, was a collection of novelty songs, typical of his wit.

Gibson's contemporaries admit to their admiration for him. Some confided that they emulated Gibson's style before they acquired one of their own. Folk singer Gordon Lightfoot and guitarist Tom Paxton were both influenced by the unique Gibson style. Tom Paxton marveled at Gibson's special style in *Artists of American Folk Music* when he commented "[Gibson] actually did his rhythm work with his fingers, something like a frailing banjo player." Roger McGuinn, founder of the 1960s folk-rock quartet the Byrds, revered Gibson as both a friend and mentor. Gibson indeed was a generous and patient advisor who thought nothing of sharing his own spotlight in order to help launch the career of a talented but unknown performer. Among others, he sang frequently with Bob Camp (later Hamilton Camp), and the two recorded an album together, all of which helped to promote Camp's career. Gibson is widely credited with introducing singer Judy Collins to the American public as well.

Of all of the young singers to whom Gibson gave a helping hand, he is widely remembered for launching the career of folk singer Joan Baez in 1959, at the first Newport Folk Festival in Rhode Island. Gibson first met Baez, a virtually unknown teen-ager, in the spring of 1959 when Grossman engaged her to perform at his club for two weeks. By the time Baez arrived on the scene,

Gibson himself was well tenured at "the Horn." Baez at that time had recorded one album, albeit obscure, and was known chiefly to frequenters of the college coffee house crowds around Boston and Cambridge, Massachusetts. A friendship gelled between Gibson and Baez, who in her 1987 memoir *And a Voice to Sing With* reminisced fondly and described Gibson: "I got a crush on Bob, of course, and was terrified of him because he was at home in a den of sin called a nightclub, was marvelously sarcastic and funny, drank too much, sang both serious and silly songs, and cracked jokes in between them." After becoming acquainted with Baez, Gibson invited her to accompany him to Newport that summer for the first Newport Folk Festival. Gibson was already scheduled to appear, although Baez was not on the program. On July 11 at the festival, Gibson took the stage and sang a song. Then he introduced Baez and ushered her onto the platform to join him. The two sang a pair of gospel tunes together: "Virgin Mary Had One Son," and "We Are Crossing Jordan River." The Gibson and Baez duet left the audience elated; both artists received excellent reviews. Vanguard Records released a live recording of the event on the *Newport Folk Festival Recording, 1959, Volume 2,* and the landmark performance of "Virgin Mary Had One Son" was re-released in a subsequent Vanguard collection, *Greatest Folksingers of the Sixties.*

Curiously, the same historic performance at Newport that thrust Joan Baez into the public eye also marked the beginning of a slow denouement in the career of Bob Gibson. Gibson persistently suffered from health problems associated with exhaustion; he also experienced intermittent loss of his voice. Except for one album, *Where I'm Bound,* released in 1964, the mild natured Gibson faded from public view for a decade. It was rumored that Gibson suffered from drug addiction during those years.

Gibson reappeared later in the 1970s with a fresh new collection of songs and styles. During those later years, Gibson performed on tour with his friends Tom Paxton and Odetta. In 1984, he wrote and released a musical, *The Courtship of Carl Sandburg.* The play was produced in Evanston, Illinois.

A Fondness for Children

Gibson, with his smooth voice and kind heart, was especially fond of younger audiences. In 1988, he recorded and released *A Child's Happy Birthday* for preschool children, described by *All Music Guide* as "A gentle record for younger kids." He later collaborated in writing songs with children's author Shel Silverstein. Gibson's final album, released two years before his death in 1995, was *Makin' a Mess: Bob Gibson Sings Shel Siverstein.*

Gibson was diagnosed with progressive supranuclear palsy in 1994. After 35 years in the Chicago area, he lived out the final years of his life in Portland, Oregon, with one of his daughters. Late in 1996, Gibson returned briefly to Chicago, and on September 20, 1996, in his characteristic wry and friendly manner, he hosted a spirited party, a reunion for his many friends and associates. Gibson's friends affectionately remember the reunion as the "farewell party" that took place one week before his death. Most agree that the party was Gibson's clever means of attending his own wake. After the party, he returned to Portland where he died on September 27, 1996.

Throughout his life, Bob Gibson shunned the commercialism of show business; he was a "singer's singer," who counted other singers and performers among his most loyal fans. He loved his music, and he loved his songs. Gibson's unpretentious musical career predated the Kingston Trio and Peter, Paul, and Mary. Gibson's musical arrangements were recorded by folk artists everywhere, from Odetta to John Denver to the Serendipity Singers. Upon his death, Gibson was remembered by his friend and admirer Roger McGuinn in the song, "Sweet Bobby from Chi."

Selected discography

Singles

"I'm Never to Marry," 1956.

Albums

Folksongs of Ohio, Stinson, 1956.
Offbeat Folk Songs, Riverside Records, 1956.
I Come for to Sing, Riverside Records, 1957.
Carnegie Concert, 1957.
Ski Songs, Elektra Records, 1959.
(with Joan Baez and others at Newport) *Folk Festival at Newport, Volume 2,* Vanguard, 1960.
Yes I See, Elektra, 1961.
Bob Gibson and Bob Camp at the Gate of Horn, Elektra, 1961.
Where I'm Bound, Elektra, 1964.
Greatest Folksingers of the Sixties, Vanguard, 1972.
Funky in the Country, 1974.
(with Bob Camp) *Homemade Music,* Moon Rail, 1978.
Perfect High, Mountain Railroad, 1980.
Uptown Saturday Night, Hogeye, 1984.
Courtship of Carl Sandburg, 1984.
A Child's Happy Birthday, Big Records, 1988.
Makin' a Mess: Bob Gibson Sings Shel Silverstein, Asylum, January 24, 1995.
Serics Vol. 1, Riverside Records, (originally recorded 1957-58) December 3, 1996.
Joy Joy! The Young and Wonderful Bob Gibson: The Riverside Folklore The Perfect High, (re-release) Drive Archive, May 19, 1998.

Sources

Books

Baez, Joan, *And a Voice to Sing With,* Summit Books, 1987.
Baggelaar, Kristin and Donald Milton, *Folk Music: More than a Song,* Thomas Y. Crowell Company, 1976.
Erlewine, Michael, ed., *All Music Guide,* Miller Freeman Inc., 1992.
Fuss, Charles J., *Joan Baez: a Bio-Bibliography,* Greenwood Press, 1996.
Hood, Phil, ed., *Artists of American Folk Music,* GPI Publications, 1986.
Larkin, Colin, ed., *The Guinness Encyclopedia of Popular Music,* vol. 2, Guinness Publishing, 1992.
Okun, Milton, *Something to Sing About!,* Macmillan Company, 1968.
Stambler, Irwin and Grelun Landon, *Encyclopedia of Folk, Country and Western Music,* St. Martin's Press, 1969.

Periodicals

New York Times, July 19, 1959, p. II-7.

Online

Dresser, Michael and Benjamin H. Cohen, "Bob Gibson Discography," Version 4, <http://users.aol.com/McGuinn742/Gibson.html/> 1997.

—*Gloria Cooksey*

Gravediggaz

Rap group

The hip-hop foursome Gravediggaz is comprised of Frukwan da Gatekeeper (or Fruitkwan, formerly of Stetsasonic), Poetic da Grym Reaper (formerly Too Poetic), Prince Paul a.k.a. Dr. Strange (formerly of De La Soul and Stetsasonic), and RZA the Rzarector (also part of the Wu-Tang Clan). The foursome assembled to pool their musical talents and experiences for their debut 1994 release, *6 Feet Deep*. Originally lumped into the genre of "horrorcore" rap because of their name and grisly themes, they took a three-year hiatus and eventually transcended the narrow confines of "horrorcore hip-hop" by releasing *The Pick, the Sickle and the Shovel* in 1997, which featured a return to positivity, hip-hop's original sound, and intention to educate the disheartened and the street-wise. Andrew Emery of *Hip Hop Connection* wrote, "The central metaphor of the Gravediggaz project (is) the struggle for recognition of the everyday horror of life, of the black plight in America and world-wide."

Gravediggaz formed in 1992 with the intent to hoist themselves out of a musical slump. All of the group's members had been signed to Tommy Boy Records but, by 1992, none of them had a record deal, so they joined forces to usher in a change. They spent two years shopping the Gravediggaz material around to various record companies before Gee Street Records picked up the group up in 1994. Prince Paul told E. Brennan of the U.K.'s *Trace* magazine, "I had all this music and I didn't

know how to get it out there. So I tried to get brothers who I felt were in the same predicament.... I called Poetic ... RZA ... Frukwan." Prince Paul's original intention was to make a compilation album, but when the foursome met for the first time the chemistry worked so well that they ended up creating a song on the spot.

Before Prince Paul created the Gravediggaz, he was enjoying gold and platinum record sales from his work with De La Soul and more specifically, from their release *3 Feet High and Rising*. He had a label deal with Tommy Boy Records, but the label didn't release his albums and Prince Paul was bound exclusively to the label. His Dew Doo Man records imprint didn't meet with success, and Def Jam didn't want to pay him for his work with 3rd Bass. He told Brennan, "I was at the bottom of the barrel. I didn't have the reputation of an LL Cool J or an EPMD. I just got put on the back burner." The other members of Gravediggaz felt similarly stifled or overlooked, so the foursome had a common bond apart from music from the start. Poetic released "God Made Me Funky" with part of the duo Too Poetic, but his record deal soured. Frukwan left the band Stetsasonic on less than good terms, so he fell back on making custom-tailored clothes to make ends meet. RZA, formerly known as Prince Rakeem, was a struggling solo artist who felt he had been given the short-shrift more than once. After the foursome met and created the Gravediggaz, they held fast to their respect for one another and have prided themselves on their ability to work together without having to grapple with inflated egos or foolish pride. Poetic told Alan C. Page of *Rap Sheet,* "You're dealing with Fruitkwan and Prince Paul. That's 13, 13 years of hip-hop. You're dealing with me...you got 10 years of hip-hop right there. RZA, same thing. Between us all, you got 40 years of hip-hop."

RZA became part of the wildly successful Wu-Tang Clan shortly after forming the Gravediggaz, and divides his time between both band , freelance music projects, and even a clothing line business. *Rolling Stone*'s Neil Strauss described RZA as, "the calm in the center of the Wu-Tang storm...(who) is currently masterminding some 13 records in the coming year (1998)."

"We came up with the Gravediggaz," Frukwan told Page, "because we still dwell in the ghetto, where a lot of people need knowledge and wisdom, meaning that a lot of people are walking around mentally dead, who don't know their purpose on this earth." The connotations associated with grave diggers and physically burying people led to immediate typecasting for the band shortly after their first release, *6 Feet Deep*. Bands and musicians like Crustified Dibbs (a.k.a. RA the Rugged Man), the Flatlinerz, and Half Pit Half Dead were

For the Record . . .

Members include **Anthony Berkely** (Poetic the Grym Reaper); **Robert Diggs** (RZA the Rzarector, born 1968 in New York City, also part of the Wu-Tang Clan); **Arnold Hamilton** (Frukwan da Gatekeeper); **Paul Hanson** (Prince Paul A.K.A. Dr. Strange).

Released debut album *6 Feet Deep,* 1994; released *The Pick, the Sickle and the Shovel,* 1997.

Addresses: *Record company*—Gee Street Records, 14 East 4th Street, New York, NY 10012, (212) 320-8690, fax (212) 777-0764. E-mail—jennifer.hondru@v2music.com.

part of the "horrorcore" music scene, and the Gravediggaz were slated as part of this "new rap movement". Prince Paul told *Hip Hop Connection*'s Emery, "If we came out with the album when we first started working on it—it took us two-and-a-half years for that album to come out—it would have been a totally different arena.... Unfortunately, we came out at a bad time, where everybody was coming out with "horror-core" and ... that put us in the middle of it." The band waited three years after the release of their first album to allow the "horror-core" smoke to clear before releasing *The Pick, the Sickle, and the Shovel.* Poetic told Page, "We were waiting for the snakes to kill themselves. We let those groups (horror-core groups) qualify or disqualify themselves. In three years, they couldn't come back with anything." In the three-years the band took to release their second album, group members were also surprised to see that the record companies that had shunned their material began looking for groups that could emulate them.

The dark tone of the band's debut release, coupled with the band's misunderstood name and imagery, obscured the artistry and deeper meaning of *6 Feet Deep,* but the band's second release met with lavish praise. Page wrote that *6 Feet Deep* was misunderstood even by their imitators, as the band was simply reflecting reality instead of making up horror-raps. He wrote, "*The Pick, the Sickle,* and the Shovel focuses on more positivity than the first, especially on joints such as "Hidden Emotions" and "The Night the Earth Cried.""

Band members view the darkness of the first album as akin to being inside of a cocoon, drawing an analogy between a cocoon and the ghetto. They feel the second album reflects their metamorphosis musically and spiritually. Poetic told Page, "On this album (*The Pick, the Sickle, and the Shovel*), the caterpillar develops into what it was supposed to be, a black butterfly."

Spin magazine's Armond White wrote, "*The Pick, The Sickle, and the Shovel* ... is actually meant to be death defying.... Poetic attempts to wake hip-hop from it's venal trance...." *Vibe*'s David Bry wrote, "This second offering from Gravediggaz...finds (RZA) moving away from production and immersing himself fully in the power of words. Standouts like "Twelve Jewelz" remind us that RZA is a master MC." A review in *Details* sums up the band's second effort with, "(the album) raises the stakes with some serious elegiac rhyming," and *Billboard* dubbed the release "a new mythology that shocked and amazed as it bounced across ear space." The group also contributed the title song to the film *Dangerous Mindz.*

Selected discography

6 Feet Deep, Gee Street Records, 1994.
The Pick, the Sickle, and the Shovel, Gee Street Records, 1997.
(Contributor) *Dangerous Mindz (soundtrack),* Gee Street Records, 1997.

Sources

Billboard, November 22, 1997.
CMJ, October 13, 1997.
Details, November 1997.
Entertainment Weekly, October 31, 1997.
Hip Hop Connection, November 1997.
New York Times, October 26, 1997.
Rap Pages, December 1997.
Rap Sheet, November 1997.
Request, November 1997.
Rolling Stone, September 4, 1997; September 18, 1997.
Spin, December 1997.
The Source, September 1997.
Trace Magazine, September 1997.
Urb Magazine, September/October 1997.
Vibe, November 1997.

—B. Kimberly Taylor

Guess Who

Rock band

One of Canada's most successful and prolific rock groups of the 1960s and 1970s, the Guess Who produced a string of hits and more than a dozen albums. All natives of Winnipeg, Manitoba, they proudly marketed their image as hard rockers from the Canadian prairies and scored their biggest success with a song that portrayed the United States as a seductive, villainous woman.

The Guess Who was spawned from two teenage bands in Winnipeg, Manitoba, in the early 1960s. Guitar player Randy Bachman and drummer Garry Peterson were in a band called the Velvetones. Guitarist and vocalist Allan Kobel, bass player Jim Kale and pianist Bob Ashley were in Allan & the Silvertones. Kobel changed his name to Chad Allen and the merged group was first known as Chad Allen & the Reflections. They learned most of their repertoire from British singles by the likes of Cliff Richards and the Shadows, and their first recording was a cover of Mike Berry's British hit "Tribute to Buddy Holly." The song made the local Winnipeg radio station's top ten and led to the group signing with Canada's largest record label, Quality.

By early 1964, the group had copied the Beatles and perfected the popular Mersey beat sound, and they changed their name to Chad Allen & the Expressions. Two singles, "Shy Guy" and "A Shot of Rhythm and Blues," failed to generate many sales. However, in 1965, with the British Invasion in full swing, the band released a cover of "Shakin' All Over" which rose to the top of the Canadian charts. Officials at Quality credited the single and an album of the same name to "Guess Who?"—a ploy to suggest that the music was the work of an anonymous British super-group. The name stuck, the song reached number 22 on the charts in the United States, and the band toured America with the Turtles and the Crystals.

Unfortunately, the pressure of touring overwhelmed Ashley's nerves, and he quit the business. He was replaced by Burton Cummings, a member of the Winnipeg group the Deverons. Cummings had a lilting, soulful and powerful voice that could cover several octaves, and he would eventually share lead vocal duties with Allen. The group's version of "Tossin' and Turnin'" hit the top of the Canadian charts. Scepter Records, the U.S. licensee for Quality, took the band to New York to record more material for release in the United States but the session produced only flops. One song, "Hurting Each Other," with lyrics by Cummings, later became a hit for the Carpenters, though.

In 1966, the Guess Who virtually disappeared from view in the United States, though they remained popular in Canada. Allan left the group due to voice problems. He was briefly replaced by Bruce Dekker before Cummings became sole lead vocalist and the group became a quartet. Cummings, Bachman, Kale and Peterson would be the group's most successful lineup, but not without more struggle. In 1967, the Guess Who's Canadian release "His Girl" was a minor hit in England, but a promotional tour of Britain was canceled due to a contract dispute, and the group returned to Canada $25,000 in debt.

Back home the Guess Who remained popular. In 1968, they started appearing on a CBC-TV music show, "Where It's At." Their efforts so impressed producer Jack Richardson that he mortgaged his house to start a record label, Nimbus 9, and produce a Guess Who album, *Wheatfield Soul*. The third single released off the album, "These Eyes," hit big, topping the charts in Canada and rising to number six in the *Billboard* ranking, eventually selling more than a million copies in the United States. The song, a soulful, bluesy ballad about a broken relationship, featured the haunting refrain, "These eyes have seen a lot of love but they're never gonna see another one like I had with you," repeated at increasingly higher octaves by Cummings. "These Eyes" became a ballad standard but had enough soul to be a hit when covered by Motown's Junior Walker & the All-Stars. That song earned the Guess Who a contract with RCA Records and started their remarkable run.

Members include **Chad Allen,** (left band 1966), vocals; **Bob Ashley,** pianist; **Randy Bachman,** (born September 27, 1943, Winnipeg; left band 1970), guitar; **Burton Cummings,** (born December 31, 1947, Winnipeg, Manitoba; joined band 1965), vocalist; **Jim Kale,** (left band 1972), bass; **Greg Leskiw,** (1970-72), guitar; **Don McDougall,** (1972-74), guitar; **Garry Peterson,** (born May 26, 1945, Winnipeg), drums; **Bill Wallace,** (1972-75), bass; **Kurt Winter,** (1970-74), guitar.

Group formed in Winnipeg, Manitoba in 1962, as Chad Allen & the Reflections; signed to Quality label, 1963; changed name to Chad Allen & the Expressions in 1964; changed name to Guess Who in 1965; released *Wheatfield Soul* for Nimbus 9 label in 1968; signed with RCA in 1969; released Top 10 singles "These Eyes" and "Laughing," and album *Canned Wheat Packed by the Guess Who* in 1969; Released "No Time," "American Woman" and "Share the Land" in 1970; "Clap for the Wolfman" in 1974; Cummings disbanded group and embarked on solo career in 1975.

Addresses: *Website*—www.theguesswho.com

In 1969, the band moved to Los Angeles but remained based in Winnipeg, and by the end of that summer they had a second U. S. hit single with "Laughing," a more upbeat song about lost love, which peaked at number ten on the *Billboard* charts. With Cummings' writing and voice providing a signature style, and the band's tight musicianship, the Guess Who became a phenomenon—rockers from the prairie who played the Seattle Pop Festival with the likes of the Doors, Led Zeppelin, and Santana.

In early 1970, the Guess Who logged its third consecutive million-selling single, "No Time," which hit number five on the *Billboard* charts. In May, its biggest hit, "American Woman" and the flip side "No Sugar Tonight," climbed to number one on the charts and stayed there for three weeks. "American Woman" was the eighth most popular record of the year and charted as number 235 on the top 1,000 singles of the rock era, according to a 1992 *Billboard* compilation. "American Woman" was one of the group's first songs with an overt message—in this case, a thinly veiled put-down of crass American commercialism and an anthem of Canadian independence. When the group was invited to play at the White House, First Lady Pat Nixon asked that the song be removed from the play list.

The group's third album, *Canned Wheat Packed by the Guess Who,* continued the band's massive popularity, but even as the group enjoyed its success it was unraveling. Bachman and Cummings feuded frequently. In 1970, Bachman quit, saying the group's hedonistic lifestyle was incompatible with his Mormon religion. He would later achieve similar success with Bachman-Turner Overdrive. With Bachman gone, Cummings took total control of the Guess Who, recruiting two new guitarists, Kurt Winter and Greg Leskiw. By the end of 1970, the group had charted twice more with songs that had an anti-materialistic, pro-environment message: Hand Me Down World," and "Share the Land." The album *Share the Land* reached number 14 on the album chart.

Now past its peak, the Guess Who in 1971 had marginal success with the songs "Hang On To Your Life," "Albert Flasher," "Rain Dance," and "Sour Suite". The album *So Long, Bannatyne* softened the group's rock edge with more piano ballads by Cummings, and a greatest hits compilation, *The Best of the Guess Who,* did well, reaching twelve on the charts. The next year saw the band's popularity wane further still with the album *Rockin' and Live at the Paramount* achieving only mild success. Don McDougall replaced Leskiw and Bill Wallace replaced Kale, leaving Peterson—the drummer—as the only original member of the Guess Who.

The band continued its downward spiral in 1973 with two less than memorable albums, *Artificial Paradise,* and *#10*. The 1974 hits compilation, *The Best of the Guess Who Volume II,* did not manage to register on the *Billboard* Top 100, but the novelty song "Clap For the Wolfman" hit number 6 on the singles chart, their best showing since "American Woman." Later that year, Cummings fired Winter and McDougall and replaced them with Domenic Troiano, the only group member not from Winnipeg. In 1975, the Guess Who released two more albums, *Flavors* and *Power in the Music,* before Cummings disbanded the group and started a solo career. His first solo release, "Stand Tall," was his biggest hit, charting at number ten in 1975.

In 1979, Kale and McDougall led a revival of the Guess Who, adding vocalist Allan McDougall, guitarist David Inglis, drummer Vince Masters and horn player David Parasz. They released an album *All This For a Song* and a single "Sweet Young Thing," both of which flopped.

Several subsequent efforts to regroup the Guess Who also failed until the 1990s, when the group found new life playing concerts at fairs, casinos and amusement parks across North America. Only two members of the original group, Kale and Peterson, remained to lead the nostalgia tours. Joined by Dale Russell on lead guitar, Leonard Shaw on keyboards, and lead vocalist Terry Hatty, they signed with Atlanta's Intersound label and, in 1995, released first new Guess Who recording in 15 years, *The Lonely One*. The title cut got some airplay on adult contemporary radio stations, but the Guess Who's legacy remained its "wheatfield soul" from the golden era of rock.

Selected discography

Shakin' All Over, Quality/Scepter, 1965.
Wheatfield Soul, Nimbus 9/RCA, 1968.
Canned Wheat Packed by the Guess Who, RCA, 1969.
American Woman, RCA, 1970.
Share the Land, RCA, 1970.
The Best of the Guess Who, RCA, 1971.
So Long, Bannatyne, RCA, 1971.
Live at the Paramount, RCA, 1972.
Track Record: The Guess Who Collection, RCA, 1988.
The Lonely One, Intersound, 1995.
The Guess Who: The Ultimate Collection, RCA, 1997.

Sources

Books

Clarke, Donald, editor, *The Penguin Encyclopedia of Popular Music,* Viking, 1989.
Einarson, John, *American Woman: The Story of the Guess Who,* Quarry Press, 1995.
Erdewine, Michael, editor, *All Music Guide to Rock,* Miller Freeman Books, 1997.
Hitchcock, H. Wiley and Stanley Sadie, editors, *New Grove Dictionary of American Music,* Macmillan, 1986.
Larkin, Colin, editor, *The Guinness Encyclopedia of Popular Music,* Guinness, 1992.
Rees, Dafydd, and Luke Crampton, *Rock Movers & Shakers,* Banson, 1991.
Whitburn, Joel, *Billboard Top 1000 Singles of the Rock Era 1955-1992,* Billboard, 1992.

Periodicals

Amusement Business, November 27, 1995.

Online

http://www.theguesswho.com/theguesswho/

—Michael Betzold

Harry Hepcat

Rockabilly singer, writer, disc jockey

Reproduced by permission.

Harry Hepcat, an original 1950s rock and roll performer, has been keeping rockabilly music alive for over 40 years, or as Hepcat told *Northport Journal* reporter Doug Reina, "I've been doing rock and roll since some of the oldies were newies." Yet, Hepcat, unlike his well-publicized love for rock and roll, has kept his personal history a mystery. Hepcat told Reina that he couldn't say where he is originally from "because they're still after me, the sheriffs, irate boyfriends, and husbands, all after the ol' Hepcat." However, Hepcat is not only known for his quick wit and uncommon name, but also for his dedication to perform and preserve, what he thinks of as an American art form in music.

Born sometime in the early 1940s, Harry Hepcat grew up in a house blasting with music. His grandfather, played trumpet with a band, and his mother, wanting to dance in a chorus line, took tap dancing lessons. Around this musical house, Harry's mother also sang along to old 78 rpm records. Unfortunately, Harry's father was sent to Europe to fight in WWII, and never returned. According to his online web page biography, Hepcat, became infatuated with the guitar in the early 1950s listening to guitar pioneer Les Paul. "I dug [Paul's] sound and his records. I would never miss his 15 minute TV show." In 1955, Hepcat, like many teenagers of that era, had also fallen in love with rock and roll, and by 1958 was playing the guitar, performing live with bands, and recording albums. Hepcat told reporter James Turner that he "even cut a record that year, but I broke my copy."

Times would change, however, and so would the music that defined them. The rock and roll of the 1960s, with it's Mersey Beat, psychedelic, and acid rock off-shoots, would little resemble that which had so enraptured Hepcat as a teen. Undaunted, Hepcat continued to perform the rhythm and blues influenced rock and roll of his youth at clubs and colleges. Playing music, though, was not the only thing he did at colleges. He also studied, earning a Bachelor of Arts degree in Literature from Iona (NY) College and a Master of Fine Arts degree in Communications from New York University.

In 1974, popular radio shows like Wolf Man Jack discovered Hepcat's single, "Streakin' USA". That summer, along with rock and roll legends Chubby Checker, Ben E. King, and the Shirelles, Hepcat jammed at the "Rock and Roll Spectatcular" in Long Island, NY. As a result, Hepcat's popularity soared and he and his Boogie Woogie Band toured the northeastern US, and released many albums for numerous record labels—including one in Germany under the name "Harold Jackson". Hepcat has used many different names and told Reina that he has stuck with "Hepcat" because "Allen Freed [infamous radio disc jockey] appeared to me in a dream and said, 'Go forth and carry the gospel of rock and roll and henceforth be Harry Hepcat'."

Hepcat preached his rock and roll gospel throughout the 1980s, co-hosting various radio shows such as WNHU FM's (Connecticut) "Rockin' Richard Show," and WCBS FM's (New York) "Do-Wop Shop". In 1988, Hepcat began hosting his own show on WNYG in Babylon, New York. Hepcat also took his act into the video realm, appearing on several TV shows, like New York's "Joe Franklin Show" (1978-84), and Long Island's "People Plus" (1983). He also wrote, directed, produced and edited six short films, including *Teen Beat*, his documentary about how teens growing up in the 1950s were treated by society. That documentary earned Hepcat the Suffolk County (New York) Motion Picture/Television Commission's video award at the 1988 Suffolk County Film and Video Festival.

However, it was Hepcat and his Boogie Woogie Band's performances that continued to delight audiences. Founder and President of the Rhythm and Blues Rock and Roll Society, Bill Dolan told James Turner, "Jerry Lee Lewis could not do 'Great Balls of Fire' better than Harry Hepcat.... He isn't an imitator; he is an original." That originality shined through Hepcat and the Boogie Woogie Band's 1981 four song, extended-play (EP) release, *The Sunrise Special*. That offering displayed Hepcat as the living, breathing, guitar strumming artifact of 1950's rockabilly that he undoubtedly was. One album reviewer crowned Hepcat the king of "50s rockabilly nowstalgia. (Nowstalgia is the practice of surrounding oneself with the trappings of another decade but paying the bills in the the late 1980s)." And by the late 1980s, Hepcat had surrounded himself in the 1950s so much so that Joe Franklin of New York's WOR-TV named him, " the official archivist and historian of the 1950's rock and roll scene."

Through a series of high school and college lectures during the 1990s, Hepcat shared his love of first generation rock and roll with a new generation of teenagers. The gist of his lectures, he told Reina, was thus: "Rock and Roll is pure American, historical art form. The 1950's spawned a revolution in music, clothing styles, and attitudes which is still reverberating and evolving today." Yet, Hepcat has not only opened the ears of the MTV generation through his speeches, he has reminded everyone of rock and roll's history through his writings.

In *History of Rock and Roll,* a three-part essay available on Hepcat's web site, Hepcat tells how rock and roll originally began when disc jockey Allen Freed started airing songs by popular black rhythm and blues artists. In Part II, Hepcat continued tracing rock and roll's history, and in Part III, he revealed that "certain elements were out to kill the [rock and roll] movement," and described the legal battles that many of rock and roll's prominent figures, including Freed, faced in the 1950s. In 1998, Hepcat, for his dedication to preserve rock and roll, was inducted into the Rockabilly Hall of Fame. He and his Boogie Woogie Band continued to perform and record albums, like 1997's *Real to Reel.*

Selected discography

The Sunrise Special, 1981.
Go Cat Go!, 1988.
Real to Reel, 1997.

Sources

Periodicals

Good Times, June 30-July 13, 1981.
Northport Journal (New York), August 2, 1985.

Online

http://www.mjet.com/hepcat

Additonal information was provided by Hepcat publicity materials, 1998 and by materials provided by Gale Research, 1998.

—Ann M. Schwalboski

Ben Heppner

Opera singer

Canadian opera singer Ben Heppner has been described as one of the outstanding tenors of his generation, and his voice "an instrument of arresting brilliance and flexibility," according to *New York Times* opera critic David Mermelstein. Since the late 1980s, Heppner's growing prominence inside the rarefied world of opera superstars has increased so rapidly that *Wall Street Journal* writer Solange DeSantis described it as a career "suddenly brilliant." Still in his mid-forties, Heppner is esteemed for his talents as a "heldentenor," or heroic tenor in the tradition of the great male leads in the operas of nineteenth-century German composer Richard Wagner. "This man is a phenomenon," the artistic director of the Metropolitan Opera of New York, James Levine, said of Heppner to Mermelstein. "His voice is extraordinarily big, with a Classical ring and Romantic expression to it. He is unique."

Heppner was born in Murrayville, British Columbia in 1956, and was the last of nine children in a close-knit Mennonite farm family. He grew up in another rural British Columbia town, Dawson Creek, and displayed only an average predilection for music and performing country-and-western music which was popular in his home, not the European classical canon. Heppner sang in church and played the trumpet and euphonium in the band at South Peace Secondary School. His friends thought he had a good voice, and Heppner was often encouraged to sing and in college he began singing for special occasions. He then decided to make music his major.

Heppner received his degree in vocal performance from the University of British Columbia School of Music, and headed east. He took a job with a professional choir, the Tudor Singers, in Montreal, and in 1979 won top prize in the Canadian Broadcasting Company (CBC) Radio Competition for Young Performers. "That gave me the courage to think I could make a living as a singer," Heppner later told the *New York Times*' Mermelstein. However, success was not immediately forthcoming, Heppner moved to Toronto, and studied opera at the University of Toronto; he then won a spot with the Canadian Opera Company Ensemble, a training program affiliated with the Toronto Opera. Yet Heppner, who had married a piano teacher and begun a family by this time, often worked several jobs to make ends meet, including teaching music and doing carpentry; with his wife Karen, he served as music director for Toronto's Rexdale Alliance Church for a time in the mid-1980s.

Performing with the Canadian Opera Company Ensemble, Heppner gradually began to fulfill the promise of his 1979 CBC award. A turning point in his career came with his performance in *The Lighthouse* at the 1986 Guelph (Ontario) Spring Festival. The festival director had cast

The new strategy was a success. In the preliminary auditions for the Metropolitan Opera of New York held in Cleveland in late 1987, Heppner took first place and went on to win in the next rounds in Toronto, advanced to the New York finals, and there won first prize with "Prize Song" from Wagner's *Die Meistersinger von Nuernberg.* Moreover, at the Met finals Heppner was awarded the Birgit Nilsson Prize from the American-Scandinavian Foundation. It was the inaugural year of the prize, named after the Met's longtime star of Swedish heritage and presented to an American opera singer thought considered ready to embark upon an international career. This honor also brought with it a debut at Carnegie Hall the very next month in a command performance for the King and Queen of Sweden and a European debut with the Royal Swedish Opera of Stockholm. In the fall of 1988, Heppner made his formal American debut with the Lyric Opera of Chicago in *Tannhäuser,* an early Wagner opus.

Offered the Great Lead Roles

It was an auspicious start for Heppner. Unlike many opera singers, who often spend years performing with regional opera houses, his path to stardom was a relatively brief one. Early on, Heppner first gained renown for singing parts such as the title role in *Lohengrin,* classic Wagner, based on an epic poem from medieval German times, which he performed in both Stockholm and San Francisco in 1989. The following year, he appeared on the stages of two of the world's leading opera houses, Milan's La Scala and Covent Garden, on both occasions in *Die Meistersinger.* By 1992, he had made his debut at the distinguished Salzburg Festival in Austria and preeminent opera houses around the world began to press him for performance commitments.

Heppner's style has earned him comparisons to another great Canadian heldentenor, Jon Vickers, who rose to prominence in the 1950s; Heppner has also been compared favorably to such stellar dramatic tenors as Lauritz Melchior and Wolfgang Windgassen. A heldentenor must possess, according to the *New York Times*'s Mermelstein, a "loud, ringing and indefatigable" voice as well as a similarly impressive stage presence. It is not an easy category in which to excel. "Some heldentenors can be accused of having a 'bark'; to their sound, but not Heppner," wrote Rick Phillips in *Maclean's.* DeSantis, writing in the *Wall Street Journal,* wrote that Heppner's "big, burnished voice, marathon-like stamina ... and power in the Wagner repertoire has persuaded some fairly cool heads to call him the best *heldentenor* of his generation."

Heppner somewhat over his head in this opera, which Heppner later admitted forced him into realizing his potential. Afterward, Heppner headed back to Toronto and signed on with two opera coaches for private study. His teachers, William Neill and Dixie Ross Neill, first suggested that Heppner steer his vocal talents toward the heldentenor repertoire. Relatively rare in opera's modern era, "heroic" tenors, sometimes referred to as "dramatic" tenors, possess a strong voice of great amplitude and an ability to reach the upper registers. Many of the operas written by the German composer Wagner center around these imposing roles.

Earned Praise for Portrayals

"Like the great singers before him, Heppner has a rare ability to change his sound and style according to the repertoire he is singing," wrote Phillips in *Maclean's*. In addition to excelling in the Wagner repertoire, Heppner has performed in William Bolcom's *McTeague,* directed by Robert Altman at the Lyric Opera of Chicago, as well as Benjamin Britten's *Peter Grimes* at the same company in 1997. Heppner's casting in the title role in what is considered a rather tough modern opera was anything but "heroic": "Grimes" is a coarse and cruel fisherman who incurs the wrath of villagers in an English coastal town after two of his apprentices die.

Indeed, as *New York Times* writer Conrad L. Osborne wrote in 1996, Heppner's one shortcoming seems his inappropriateness for romantic leads,"he's a bit of a lummox," wrote Osborne, but noted that in some roles the awkwardness of his bulky size works to his dramatic advantage on stage. Osborne singled out his performance in the *Queen of Spades* at the Met,"his clumsiness became a dangerous quality, part of a brooding shiftiness.... Best of all, a bitter intensity invaded the singing, giving it color and bite and the kind of startling life that only the fully engaged operatic star can summon."

Heppner is notoriously careful about preserving his voice. Many promising heldentenors of previous decades seemed to lose their talents early on, and the lucrative offers thrown to rising opera stars such as Heppner to record and perform are tempting. Like many opera singers, he believes his voice only has a certain number of good years in it, and is cautious about not overworking it and thus shortening that span. He only began to make solo recordings in 1995, releasing *Ben Heppner Sings Richard Strauss* on CBC Records and *Great Tenor Arias* on the RCA Victor Red Seal. "They display his formidable talent and skill," opined Phillips in *Maclean's*. "On both CDs, Heppner's wonderful musicality, complete understanding of the text and ability to pass on its full meaning are always present."

Missed Opportunity with Solti

Heppner has paid a price for his prudence, however. His work with the Chicago Symphony Orchestra had earned the respect of its famed conductor, Sir Georg Solti, and in 1997 Solti asked Heppner to record a famed role in the heldentenor repertoire, "Tristan" in *Tristan und Isolde*. In a rather unusual occurrence, Heppner asked the elderly Solti to wait another year, since he did not think his voice was quite ready for such a role; Solti agreed, but passed away before they could work together in the studio. Heppner was scheduled to debut in *Tristan und Isolde* in August of 1998 at the Seattle Opera; many other top opera houses around the globe were requesting that he sing the popular Germanic love story at their venue as well, but Heppner was adamant about performing *Tristan* only once a year from then on.

Still, Heppner has concert engagements scheduled well into the twenty-first century. Once comfortable in Tristan, it is assumed Heppner will tackle the other great heldentenor roles in the Wagner repertoire, including "Siegfried" in *Der Ring des Nibelungen* and the title role in *Parsifal;* Verdi's *Otello,* thought to be the most difficult of the genre, is likely on the distant horizon too. Despite the accolades, Heppner is described by most interviewers as refreshingly deflated, devoid of "the temperamental personality of an international super-ego," as *Maclean's* writer Chris Wood put it, that many renowned tenors seem to possess. Back in his former hometown of Dawson Creek, he is a celebrity, and Heppner remains modestly delighted that a street was named after him. Heppner continues to call Toronto home, living in a suburb of the metropolis with family, and when not touring or recording enjoys the typical suburban family pursuits, such as attending his children's sports activities. He sings every Sunday at the First Alliance Church in Scarborough,along with his family and the rest of the congregation,and has said that if his voice gave out he might like to become a minister instead.

Selected discography

Ben Heppner Sings Richard Strauss, CBC Records, 1995.
Great Tenor Arias, RCA Victor Red Seal, 1995.

Sources

Periodicals

American Record Guide, November-December 1993.
Maclean's, February 13, 1995; November 13, 1995.
New York Times, May 19, 1996, ; May 8, 1998.
Wall Street Journal, February 21, 1996, p. A12.

Online

http://www.bmg.classics@bmge.com

—Carol Brennan

The Incredible String Band

Folk group

The Incredible String Band was one of the most engaging groups to emerge from the esoteric 1960s. Comprising the duo of Mike Heron and Robin Williamson, its sound was haunting Celtic folk melodies augmented by a variety of Middle Eastern and Asian instruments. In *The British Invasion,* Nicholas Schaffner describes them so, "Take two exceptionally talented purveyors of traditional music from Scotland, immerse them in an underground cauldron of occult secrets, Eastern spells, and LSD in Swinging Sixties London, and you have an approximation of what The Incredible String Band were about."

Mike Heron was a member of several rock bands in England in the early 1960s, while Robin Williamson and Clive Palmer played as a bluegrass and Scottish folk duo. Heron was asked to join as rhythm guitarist, and the trio began playing as The Incredible String Band. The band was spotted at a club by Joe Boyd, who was opening a British wing of Elektra Records. The trio gave Boyd a demo tape of mostly American bluegrass standards with a few original songs at the end. Boyd

Archive Photos, Inc. Reproduced by permission.

For the Record . . .

Members include **Mike Heron** (born December 12, 1942, Glasgow, Scotland), vocals, guitar, sitar, organ, dulcimer, harpsichord, recorder, harmonica, percussion; **Robin Williamson** (born November 24, 1943, Glasgow, Scotland), vocals, guitars, sitar, oud, flute, gimbri, sarangi, chahanai, whistle, bass, violin, piano, organ, percussion. Other members include **Gerald Dott,** (joined, 1972), clarinet, sax; **Graham Forbes,** (joined, 1974), guitar; **Jack Ingram,** (joined, 1973), drums; **Stan Lee,** (joined, 1973), drums; **Malcolm LeMaistre** (joined, 1970), bass, vocals; **Christina "Licorice" McKenzie,** (joined, 1967, left, 1970), violin, keyboards; **Clive Palmer,** (joined, 1965, left, 1966) vocals, guitar, banjo; **Rose Simpson,** (joined, 1968, left, 1970), bass, percussion.

Formed in Edinburgh, Scotland, 1965; recorded first album *Incredible String Band* for Elektra, 1966; appeared at Newport Folk Festival, 1967; appeared at Woodstock Festival, 1969; recorded *Be Glad For The Song Has No Ending* for Island, 1970; appeared in film *Rehearsal,* 1974; disbanded, 1974.

recalled to *Melody Maker,* "[The original songs] blew up my mind. Immediately I forgot about bluegrass and started planning an album of original material."

The Incredible String Band, released in 1966, featured mostly original numbers enthusiastically played in American and Celtic folk styles. Following the album's release, Williamson spent several months studying music in Morocco, and Palmer left the band to travel to Afghanistan. For the String Band's second album, *The 5000 Spirits Or The Layers of the Onion,* exotic touches such as the Middle Eastern oud or Indian sitars and tambouras began to permeate the Incredibles' sound. The band's lyrics also became more whimsical; highlights include Williamson's tale of insomnia, "No Sleep Blues," and Heron's amorous "Painting Box."

The press raved about The Incredible String Band. A *Melody Maker* review of a live performance in 1967 stated, "Their songs, backed by guitars, sitars, gimbri, drums, rattles, and battery-driven mini-organ, range from the beautiful to the bizarre and from weird to whimsical. Yet they are all impressive individually in one

way or another and the Incredibles are two of the most original and exciting songwriters on any scene."

The 1968 album *The Hangman's Beautiful Daughter* was Incredible String Band's brief flirtation with stardom. Although the music was less commercial than its predecessor, it reached the top ten in the British album charts and was also the group's highest *Billboard* chart placing in America. The songs became less structured, as the opening "Koeeoaddi There," which changed tempo frequently as it cascaded joyously with sitars and jaw harp. The album's centerpiece, "A Very Cellular Song," was a suite of short pieces sewn together with the folk song "Bid You Goodnight."

For *Wee Tam and The Big Huge,* The Incredible String Band was augmented by Williamson and Heron's girlfriends Licorice McKenzie and Rose Simpson. The group also began to electrically amplify its instruments. This expanded lineup performed at the Woodstock Festival in 1969, but due to circumstances was not one of the band's most memorable performances. The Incredibles' slot was originally to be Friday night after Joan Baez, however, due to heavy rain, the band opted not to perform. Manager Joe Boyd recalls on the String Band web site, "I [told them], 'you don't know what's going to happen - you may never get on stage' but they wanted to wait for the rain to stop and so someone else went on - Melanie - who triumphed in that slot and wrote 'Candles In The Rain' about that exact moment! ... It sort of haunted me, that moment because I should have pushed - just dragged them to the stage and said 'forget the amps, just play acoustically.' ... We ended up going on the following afternoon after Canned Heat in the baking sun. People were ready for something heavy and loud and they came on and just-died."

At the turn of the seventies, The Incredible String Band began to lose some of its momentum. The album *Changing Horses* was not as engaging as the band's previous collections, and the group's eclecticism became a liability rather than an asset. A 1971 concert review in *Melody Maker* stated that, "Curiously, although Mike Heron and Robin Williamson have been together with various satellites since before the days of [British psychedelic club] the U.F.O., when they first really made their name, the moods and form of their music, far from coalescing and solidifying, have fragmented and become even more diverse.... They have always been a band eager to draw on all sources, but this eclecticism, I think, is being taken too far."

Joined by bassist and pantomimist Malcolm LeMaistre in 1971, The Incredible String Band's project entitled *U* was a well-received stage show that did not translate as easily to record. The band made the transition to electric rock 'n roll in 1972. Mike Heron explained the change in sound to *Melody Maker,* "[When the band first started], we couldn't have a big orchestra ... so the way to do it was to colour a song ... we learned to play a basic amount of a certain instrument to give the colour of that instrument to a song. Now what we tend to do is use slightly more conventional instruments and try to get the music, since we're slightly more technically advanced now than nine years ago.... We don't use quite so many weird instruments now."

In 1974, following the album *Hard Rope And Silken Twine,* The Incredible String Band disbanded. Both founding members had prolific solo careers; Heron's took him in a rock direction, while Williamson explored his Celtic roots. For several years the band was seen as a dated anachronism. Recently, with the resurgence in interest the psychedelic 1960s as well as "world" music, The Incredible String Band's music has been rediscovered by new audiences won over by its mystical charm.

Selected discography

The Incredible String Band, Elektra, 1966, reissued Hannibal/Rykodisc, 1995.
The 5000 Spirits Or The Layers of The Onion, Elektra, 1967, reissued Hannibal/Rykodisc, 1995.
The Hangman's Beautiful Daughter, Elektra, 1968, reissued Hannibal/Rykodisc, 1995.
Wee Tam and The Big Huge, Elektra, 1969, reissued Hannibal/Rykodisc, 1995.
Changing Horses, Elektra, 1969, reissued Hannibal/Rykodisc, 1995.
I Looked Up, Elektra, 1970, reissued Hannibal/Rykodisc, 1995.
Be Glad For The Song Has No Ending, Island, 1970.
U, Elektra, 1971.
Relics of The Incredible String Band, Elektra, 1971.
Liquid Acrobat As Regards The Air, Island, 1971.
Earth Span, Island, 1972, reissued Edsel, 1991.
No Ruinous Feud, Island, 1973, reissued Edsel, 1991.
Hard Rope and Silken Twine, Island, 1974.
Seasons They Change, The Best of The Incredible String Band (rec. 1970-74), Island, 1976.
Live In Concert (rec. 1971), Windsong, 1991.

Sources

Books

Hardy, Phil & Dave Laing, *The Faber Companion To 20th Century Popular Music*, Faber & Faber, 1990.
Joynson, Vernon, *A Tapestry of Delights: The Comprehensive Guide To British Music of the Beat, R & B, Psychedelic, and Progressive Eras 1963-1976*, Borderline, 1995.
Schaffner, Nicholas, *The British Invasion*, McGraw-Hill, 1982.

Periodicals

Billboard, December 14, 1967; May 10, 1969.
BMI, October, 1968.
Melody Maker, June 24, 1967; August 29, 1967; September 30, 1967; May 1, 1971; November 25, 1972; June 15, 1974
Sing Out!, Volume 18, 1969.
Stereo Review, June, 1969; December, 1972.

Online

http://dspace.dial.pipex.com/town/square/ac455/feature3.htm

—Jim Powers

Incubus

Alternative band

Funk, thrash-rock, and hip-hop band Incubus combine elements of various music styles to forge their own unique musical identity. Incubus mixes speed rock with funk and hip-hop, metal music with rap, jazz with thrash-rock, and 1970s-sounding riffs with chanting and funk music. The band is comprised of vocalist Brandon Boyd, guitarist Michael Einziger, bassist Alex Katunich (DJ Killmore), and drummer Jose Pasillas. Band Members purposely avoid musical categorization, preferring instead to play a combination of whichever musical styles inspire them. Mike Savoia of the *Rocket* described Incubus as, "a '90s melting pot of the Red Hot Chili Peppers, Sugar Ray, War, Faith No More, Devo, Average White Band and the kitchen sink." Pete Prown of *Guitar Shop* wrote, "Picture a funkier, more street-savvy Alice in Chains, and you'll be on the right Incubus track. This ain't your father's heavy metal."

Vocalist/percussionist Brandon Boyd and drummer Jose Pasillas went to elementary school together in Calabasas, California, a semi-rural bedroom community north of Los Angeles. In middle school, they met guitarist Mike Einziger and in high school the three became friends with bassist Alex Katunich, who was playing in a jazz band at the time. They formed Incubus in 1991 when they were all fifteen.

As teens, the four members of Incubus loved a variety of music. They listened to and were influenced by Iron Maiden, Ella Fitzgerald, Slayer, Santana, Steve Vai, Primus, and Rage Against the Machine. The band played for parties for a year and, by 1992, they began playing at all-ages clubs in the San Fernando Valley and at the Roxy on the Sunset Strip. One day Einziger found a hundred-dollar bill on the ground. "That's when you had to buy tickets and sell them in order to play the Strip," Einziger is quoted in and Epic press release. The day he found the money, he went to the Roxy, bought tickets, booked a show, and the result was an expanded audience for Incubus.

DJ Lyfe joined the band in 1995 and was later replaced by DJ Killmore. Band members prefer to use the turntable as an instrument with its own distinct sound as opposed to the sound of someone scratching a snare drum. In 1995, the band released the EP *Fungus Among Us* on Red Eye Records with Jim Wirt as producer. Only 1,000 copies were released and the EP has been unavailable since. The band's high-energy live performances, growing fan base, and flexible amalgamation of musical styles sparked a bidding war between labels. Immortal/Epic Records signed the band, and Incubus released the EP *Enjoy Incubus* in early 1997. The EP contained six remixed songs that were previously recorded as demos, and the band toured with Korn, the

Members include **Brandon Boyd**, vocals; **Micha-el Einziger**, guitar; **Alex Katunich**, (DJ Kill-more), bass, turntable; **DJ Lyfe**, bass, turntable, (joined band in 1995); and **Jose Pasillas,** drums; all born c. 1976 and raised in Calabasas, CA

Band was formed in 1991 when they were all fifteen; began playing at all-ages clubs in the San Fernando Valley and at the Roxy on the Sunset Strip; released the EP *Fungus Among Us* on Red Eye Records, 1995; released the EP *Enjoy Incubus,* on Immortal/Epic Records, 1997; toured with Korn, the Urge, 311, and Sugar Ray; featured on the soundtrack for the film *Spawn,* 1997; released *S.C.I.E.N.C.E.,* on Immortal/ Epic Records, 1997.

Addresses: *Record company*—Immortal/Epic Records, 2100 Colorado Avenue, Santa Monica, CA 90404; (310) 449-2870, fax (310) 449-2559.

Urge, 311, and Sugar Ray to support the release of their EP and their debut album *S.C.I.E.N.C.E.,* as well. Incubus was also featured on the soundtrack for the film *Spawn* in 1997.

S.C.I.E.N.C.E., the band's 1997 debut release, featured an underlying positive theme through stories of space, relationships, and socio-political issues. The lyrics were penned by Boyd and his views were most strident in "My Favorite Things" a song about the constricting influence of organized religion, "New Skin" addresses the benefit of creation through chaos, and "Redefine" is about the importance of taking control of your life. *Sliver Magazine*'s Z.A. wrote of *S.C.I.E.N.C.E.,* "In my opinion, this is up for album of the year. Just flat out amazing.

Combining brutal, funkesque slap bass, slick drums with a slight jazz influence and thick, hard-hitting guitars, Incubus is playing a sound pioneered by the Red Hot Chili Peppers, but are beating the innovators at their own game.... Overall, this album is one of the best of 1997."

Savoia wrote, "*S.C.I.E.N.C.E.* is high-energy ... with phat beats and grooves ... psycho pop rock ... smooth low-rider sounds ... and jazzing soulful rock overtones ... they boldy go where many rock bands have feared to tread in rock music. Don't let a friend borrow this CD, I

guarantee you won't see it again for a long time!" Prown mused, "Bands like Run D.M.C. and San Francisco's Mordred pioneered the coming together of hip-hop and metal, and today that legacy can be heard in Incubus.... Clearly, there's no shortage of fine musicianship in this quintet."

Incubus is part of a new generation of bands that are creating alloys with a diverse spectrum of influences; bands such as Limp Bizkit, Deftones, Sevendust, Coal Chamber, and System of A Down also reflect far-reaching influences and a trend toward "melting pot" music that fuses rap, rock, jazz, hip-hop, funk, metal, and ska. Boyd told *Alternative Press'* J.P., "I think that the vast majority of youth today are into a lot of different things—and not just metal, or just rap. There are certain scenes, but I think that this generation is more eclectic." Most musicians usually have one style in mind when they start a band, but Boyd told *Alternative Press* that he and his bandmates got together to play "any" music.

The band's live performances have warranted media attention, primarily because of their high energy levels, teeming mosh pits, and exuberant, head-banging fans. Boyd's vocal style is a combination of singing, screaming, and even screeching—which seems appropriate for a band with such diverse influences as Ella Fitzgerald and Iron Maiden. *Sliver Magazine*'s Z.A. wrote, "If you get a chance, catch their live show, as you will not regret it." Jennifer Clay of *Guitar For The Practicing Musician* summed up the Incubus performing style when writing, "What separates this SoCal-based group apart from the others is the charismatic stage presence of vocalist Boyd and the quirky guitar bites Einziger creates. In fact, some of the freaky noises the guitarist makes—like the bird chirps in 'My Favorite Things'—ring like they're coming from a disc.... While not traditional guitar rock with traditional guitar solos, Einziger still gets his metal 'solo' in on 'Shaft,' his rock moves on in 'Hiliku,' and his jazz noodle on in 'Deep Inside.'"

Boyd told J.P. of *Alternative Press,* "Incubus will always be a work in progress because we are constantly evolving, and we're not really conscious of direction." He then added, "I think because we've never had just one sound, our audience respects us. We're out to take them on a little adventure that's just ours."

Selected discography

EPs

Fungus Among Us, Red Eye Records, 1995.
Enjoy Incubus, Immortal/Epic, 1997.

Albums

S.C.I.E.N.C.E., Immortal/Epic, 1997.

Sources

Alternative Press Magazine, July 1998.
Billboard, December 6, 1997.
Guitar For The Practicing Musician, June 1998.
Guitar Shop, May 1998.
The Rocket, November 5, 1997.
Sliver Magazine, Winter 1998.

Additional source material was provided by the public relations department at Epic/Immortal Records.

—B. Kimberly Taylor

The Ink Spots

Vocal quartet

A number of black male quartets have billed themselves as the Ink Spots, cashing in on the tremendous success of the original singing group which performed during the 1930s and '40s. Famous for their song "If I Didn't Care," with its smooth tenor lead and spoken refrain, they were the best known act of their kind and served as a huge influence on later rhythm and blues groups. The Ink Spots were also one of the first black acts to become a hit with white audiences. The Ink Spots made numerous recordings, had regular radio shows, and performed with the biggest musical stars of their time, including Count Basie and Ella Fitzgerald. While they were at their peak of popularity, the group appeared in two Hollywood movies.

After the quartet split up, however, their reputation became blurred by the splinter groups that were created. And so the Ink Spots have lost some of the recognition they deserve, according to David Hinckley of the *Daily News;* he reflected in 1995 that "the Ink Spots are too often relegated to the wallpaper of pop music history as if they were one more group that was

Archive Photos, Inc. Reproduced by permission.

For the Record . . .

Members include **Jerry Daniels** (died November 7, 1995, in Indianapolis, IN), tenor and guitarist; **Charlie Fuqua** (born 1911, died 1971), tenor and guitarist; **Orville Jones** (born February 17, 1905, in Chicago, IL; died October 18, 1944, in Chicago, IL), bass singer and cellist; **Bill Kenny** (born in 1915, in Philadelphia; died of respiratory illness in March 23, 1978, in Vancouver, British Columbia), tenor; **Herb Kenny** (born in 1915, in Philadelphia, PA, died of cancer on July 11, 1992, in Columbia, MD), bass; **Ivory Watson** (born 1909, died 1969), baritone and songwriter.

Daniels, Jones, and Watson formed trio King, Jack and the Jester in the early 1930s; with the addition of Fuqua and an "s" on "Jester," became a quartet; struggled to establish the singing group in New York City; changed name to the Ink Spots before touring with Jack Hylton in England; signed recording contract with RCA Victor, 1935; debut record *Swing High, Swing Low,* ASV/ Living Era, 1936; Daniels became ill and was replaced by Bill Kenny in 1939; Jones died in 1944, and was replaced by Herb Kenny; founding members dissolved group in 1951, but proceeded to form own groups under the same name.

bright and new for a while, then got covered over by something brighter and newer." Original members of the Ink Spots struggled for many years to distinguish themselves from copycat acts and to perpetuate the reputation of the group, but were often fighting amongst themselves. Now that all of these men have passed away, several "Ink Spots" groups continue to perform, and if they do not have an authentic pedigree, they do serve to keep the many songs popularized by the Ink Spots in the public's ear.

Founding Members

The group's founding members were all from Indianapolis. They were Jerry Daniels, who played guitar and sang lead tenor; Orville "Hoppy" Jones, who sang bass and played the cello; Ivory "Deek" Watson, a baritone and songwriter; and Charlie Fuqua, the second tenor and guitarist. The Ink Spots are sometimes described as having evolved out of the Percolating Puppies, a group that Deek Watson performed with on street corners in Indianapolis. Watson was on the road when he met up with Fuqua and Daniels, whom he knew from Indianapolis. This meeting resulted in the formation of a trio that went by the name King, Jack and the Jester; the addition of Jones and an "s" to the name made a quartet.

This foursome moved to New York with hopes of making it big, but struggled to make a living. For a time, all worked as ushers at the Paramount Theater. Subsequently, the quartet billed themselves as the Riff Brothers until one day in 1932 when, according to Deek Watson in his book *The Story of the 'Ink Spots,'* the group happened upon the idea of the "Ink Spots." Watson told of how he was inspired by a splash of ink from a fountain pen and how he had to overcome the protests of his fellow members. He remembered Jones as saying that he was "always wanting us to be something colored. 'Black Dots,' 'Ink Spots'—next thing you know he'll be wanting to call us the 'Old Black Joe's'." But the members agreed to try the new name, and its adoption coincided with better fortunes for the struggling quartet.

During the 1930s, the Ink Spots specialized in singing up tempo jazz or jive music. Early in the decade they traveled to England under contract with promoter and bandleader Jack Hylton, and in 1935 the group signed a recording contract with RCA Victor. The Ink Spots had made about a dozen records by 1939, when Daniels left the group. He was ill and could not keep up with the hectic pace of traveling and performing. Tenor Bill Kenny was then hired to take his place. This transition resulted in a major stylistic change for the group, as they turned to the slower tempo heard in their first big hit, "If I Didn't Care." The song featured a solo guitar introduction, Kenny's fluid tenor lead, and a talking refrain. This became the group's signature sound, although they did have several up tempo hits. At about this time, the quartet signed a five-year recording contract with Decca Records and soon had additional hit songs with "Address Unknown" (1939) and "We Three (My Echo, My Shadow, and Me)" (1940).

1940s was a Successful Decade

The Ink Spots were highly successful in the 1940s, when they worked with Ella Fitzgerald, Count Basie, Lena Horne, Nat King Cole, Cab Calloway, and Dinah Washington. The group appeared in the films *The Great American Broadcast of 1941* and *Pardon My Sarong* (1942). The men were cast as Pullman porters in the first film, in which they performed "Swing, Gates, Swing," "If I Didn't Care," "Java Jive," and "Maybe." Watson recalled the experiences of making these film with great enthusiasm in his book. He said of *Pardon My Sarong,*

"We really had a ball. Abbot and Costello were fine people to work with." In this film, the group repeated "Java Jive" and performed "Do I Worry?" and "I've Got a Bone to Pick with You." By this time, the United States had entered World War II and the quartet was also traveling around the country preforming at army camps. Fuqua was soon enlisted in the army and Bernie MacKay filled in for the tenor until he was discharged.

The next permanent change in the Ink Spots lineup came when Hoppy Jones, who suffered from epileptic seizures, died of a brain hemorrhage in 1944. He was replaced by Herb Kenny, Bill's twin brother. This version of the group stayed together until 1951. Watson credited the breakup of the Ink Spots to the meddling of booking agents and managers and said in his book, "They got us so confused, and caused so much conflict among us, that at last even we realized that we could no longer make it as a group.... Many people actually cried when they heard the news that we had split up. I know it was one of the saddest days in my life, and I believe it was in Charlie's and Kenny's too." The multiplicity of Ink Spots groups began when both Bill Kenny and Charlie Fuqua led quartets using the name. Deek Watson—who had worked in Fuqua's split—had a further spinoff and would be forced to use the name The Brown Dots. Soon the argument over use of the Ink Spots name would be in the courts, as others—including members of these splinter groups—began performing under the name. Such litigation went on for many years.

Most of the former Ink Spots tried to continue working in the music industry, although they did so with mixed success. The exception was Jerry Daniels, who—having left the group before its first big hit—became a state excise officer; he died at age 79 in Indianapolis. Deek Watson, who had performed with groups in Las Vegas and toured Australia, had hopes of reuniting the remaining original members of the Ink Spots when he published *The Story of the Ink Spots* in 1967. However, he died in 1969 without having realized this dream.

Solo Careers

The Kenny brothers each worked at solo careers. Herb had a hit with "It Is No Secret" in 1951 and he continued to perform until 1957, when he became a disc jockey in Washington. At one time, he was program director for WJMD. In the mid-1960s, he returned to his singing career, but he also worked as a car salesman in Washington. Herb retired to Columbia, Maryland and made his last public performance in April 1992, when he sang at a ceremony inducting him into the Hall of Fame of the United in Group Harmony Association. He died at home just a few months later, on July 11, of cancer.

Herb's fraternal twin Bill moved to Toronto to begin a solo career and later relocated to Calgary, Alberta where he recorded three albums. Bill would tour with the Harlem Globetrotters as a half-time entertainer and he worked as a solo performer into the late 1960s. His career and indeed his life seemed over, when in 1969 he was almost killed; he lit a cigar in an underground garage where there were gas fumes coming from his car's overfilled gas tank. He returned to performing, but in 1971 was diagnosed with myasthenia gravis, an autoimmune disease that weakens the muscles. When Kenny surprised his doctors by recovering from the effects of the disease, he hoped to again pick up his music career, but audiences were now caught up with Ink Spot copycats. Bill Kenny died in March 1978 in Vancouver of a respiratory illness.

Sadly, the individual members of the Ink Spots never regained their place in the spotlight. However, the music they performed has had a lasting impact on contemporary music. During the early 1950s, rhythm and blues artists such as the Drifters, Coasters, Penguins, Temptations, and Platters all were indebted to the Ink Spots for their style of performance. Elvis Presley's "Are You Lonesome Tonight" also copied techniques perfected by the Ink Spots. The group's recordings continue to be reissued and the original members were inducted into the Rock and Roll Hall of Fame in 1989. In 1992, on the occasion of the death of Herb Kenny, former Baltimore radio program director Steve Cochran concluded that "The Ink Spots were an important chapter in modern American music.... They defined what a vocal group could be, substituting beautiful voices for instruments."

Selected discography

Swing High Swing Low, ASV/Living Era, 1936.
The Ink Spots, Vol. 1, Decca, 1950.
The Ink Spots, Vol. 2, Decca, 1950.
Time Out for Tears, Decca, 1956.
Ink Spots, K-Tel, 1956.
Something Old, Something New, King, 1958.
Torch Time, Decca, 1958.
Songs That Will Live Forever, King, 1959.
Sincerely Yours, Vocalion, 1964.
Lost In a Dream, Vocalion, 1965.
The Best of the Ink Spots, MCA, 1980.
Just Like Old Times, Open Sky, 1985.
Whispering Grass, Pearl Flapper, 1992.

Sources

Books

Watson, Deek, with Lee Stephenson, *The Story of the "Ink Spots,"* Vantage, 1967.

Periodicals

Calgary Herald, May 4, 1996, p. B7.
Daily News, (New York) December 28, 1995, p. 56.
Newsday, July 15, 1992, p. 107.
New York Times, July 15, 1992, p. 19; November 11, 1995.
Times, August 13, 1992.
Washington Post, July 14, 1992, p. B5.

Online

www.allmusic.com, All-Music Guide, 1998.

—Paula Pyzik Scott

Jesus Jones

Rock band

The end of the 1980s saw a flowering of British acts that fused the unlikely combination of club inspired electronic beats and samples with guitar riffs that might easily find a home on a hard rock record, and the London, England centered band Jesus Jones was among the most visible of these. However, unlike many of these groups, Jesus Jones struck deep into sales charts worldwide, and eluded falling into the traps of mere faddism. After the solid successes of their first and second albums *Liquidizer* in 1989 and *Doubt,* in 1990. The swaggering, often inflated public persona of frontman Mike Edwards reached a fever pitch and the singer made grandiose claims of the band's importance and influence. Perhaps victims of their own arrogance, Jesus Jones fell into a relative slump with their third record, *Perverse,* and the future of the band seemed dubious. Such doubts were appeased with *Already,* released in the U.K. after a several year hiatus, which returned the outfit to their prior exploits of politically engaged, high-energy pop music.

Jesus Jones formed in 1988, when London born Mike Edwards, longtime friend and drummer Gen, born Simon Matthews, and guitarist Jerry De Borg were vacationing on the beaches of Spain. Despite all appearances, their moniker was chosen not as a mark of anti-Christian blasphemy, but merely as a humorous cultural clash. "We were surrounded by people called Jesus," Edwards told *People Weekly.* "So we just put it with something very English. We could have followed in Salman Rushdie's footsteps and called ourselves Mohammed Jones." In England, the trio was rounded out by keyboardist Barry D (Iain Baker) and bass player Al Jaworski. Given the teetering careers of the group's members–Edwards had been variously an unemployment check writer, a building mechanic, and a city council worker–committing to Jesus Jones full time presented little problem.

After Andy Ross, then head of the semi-independent Food Records, heard a cheaply produced demo cassette of what was to become Jesus Jones' "Info Freako," the band was snatched up by the label immediately. When that demo became the groups's debut single in February of 1989, Jesus Jones was suddenly nearing the British Top 40 charts and gracing the covers of music magazines. Edwards, who christened himself Jesus H. Jones, supplied the British press with the perfect kind of sassy quips to keep him in the limelight. Nevertheless, this marked the beginning of a sometimes strained relationship between Jesus Jones and British critics, who found an easy target in the mouthpiece's bravado.

After the release of several more singles, the group had amassed enough material for the album *Liquidizer,*

Members include **Jerry De Borg**, (born Jerry Simon de Abela Borg Born, October 30, 1960, in Kentish Town, London), guitar, backing vocals; **Michael James Edwards**, (born June 22, 1964, in London, England), vocals, lead guitar, sampling; **Iain Richard Foxwell Baker**, (also known as Barry D, born September 29, 1965, in Carshalton, Surrey, England), keyboards; **Al Jaworski**, (born Alan Leon Doughty, January 1, 1966, in Plymouth, England), bass guitar, backing vocals; **Simon Matthews**, (also known as Gen, left band in 1996), drums.

Band conceived on the beaches of Spain and formed in London, England, 1988; signed with Food Records, 1988; released debut album *Liquidizer,* 1989; played a series of dates in Romania, 1990; released *Doubt,* which established the band as global stars, 1991; perform at MTV's giant outdoor *Rock In Rio* festival in Brazil, 1993; released *Perverse,* 1993; guitarist De Borg began side project, *The Feely Room,* 1997; made their "comeback" with the release of *Already,* 1998.

Awards: MTV Music Award, Best Video ("Right Here Right Now"), 1991.

Addresses: *Record company*—Food Records/EMI, 810 Seventh Avenue, New York, NY 10019; *Fan club Email*—jimbo@jesusjones.com

---

which hit British stores in the fall of 1989. As the title may suggest, *Liquidizer* was an impressive amalgam of the band's sundry influences, 38 of whom are thanked in the album's liner notes, ranging from the earsplitting noise outfit Big Black to the rapping Eric B. However, it was hip hop and rap styles that dominated the record's landscape, and electronic sampling that gave it a special flavor. While hardly an innovation within dance music as such, the use of sampling was a fresh innovation to a band with strong rock underpinnings. "The sampler is the ultimate instrument to access sounds," Edwards later told *People* magazine. "With it, your imagination is not limited by your natural abilities. Without it, you'd be a boring guitar band like everyone else."

Peppered with Top 50 singles including "Info Freako" and "Bring It On Down," *Liquidizer* itself peaked at the 32 position, but perhaps more importantly gave the

band high visibility and star status in the U.K. While playing live, supporting Tin Machine, then a vehicle for veteran singer David Bowie, Jesus Jones demonstrated that despite their penchant for electronic equipment, their stage presence was not bogged down with the prerecorded quality of which techno groups are sometimes guilty in concert. The band soon headlined their own tour in support of *Liquidizer,* which included a critically lauded show at the London Town and Country Club. In step with the political tone that was emerging in their lyrics, Jesus Jones continued their tour and ushered in the 1990s with a series of gigs in the revolution-torn country of Romania.

If the sudden success of Jesus Jones in their home country left the band mildly bemused, then their virtual conquering of America was a total befuddlement. Throughout 1990, the group released a string of singles in Britain that became their biggest sellers yet, with "International Bright Young Thing" cresting at Number Seven. Subsequently, when the accompanying album, *Doubt,* entered the British charts in the top position, it was not without fanfare. However, when these same singles were released in the U.S., their popularity was even better, and Jesus Jones a bona fide overnight success. The song "Right Here Right Now," a perfect encapsulation of the uncertain but inspiring state of affairs in Eastern Europe, peaked at number two, and was later adopted by a major network's news program as a theme song.

After the overwhelming success of *Doubt*, the less than modest Edwards, who had become something of a teen heartthrob in the U.S., continue to teeter between self-confidence and campy arrogance. "We are influential now over a lot of bands, throughout the world," Edwards averred to Kim Neely in *Rolling Stone.* "It isn't just England; there are bands in Japan and Australia, and soon they'll be Jesus Jones-influenced bands in America." While the fusion of rock and dance was perhaps contagious at the time, beyond a handful of acts, most notably the British EMF, Jesus Jones' status of pop music missionaries was at best doubtful. However, such boasting had surely been part of the band's allure from the beginning, as with so many pop stars. "Rock music is there for people to be pompous, to make possibly stupid statements," Edwards told Neely. "These are not opportunities you get if you're an accountant. I chide myself for not taking advantage of this....With the next album, I probably will do that sort of thing. It's time for Jesus Jones to be pretentious and outrageous—not just solid and worthy."

While the next album, *Perverse,* may not have been pretentious or outrageous, it did mark a diversion from

Jesus Jones' guitar driven flavor and was a partial disappointment. Pushing their love of techno to the extreme, songs like *Magazine* and *Yellow Brown* used electronic sounds to critique life in an electronically mediated world. As Gil Griffin wrote in *Time,* "*Perverse* is rather perverse about the electronic age: with lucid and ironic lyrics that lurk beneath the surface's maelstrom, it examines politics, pop culture, love, and hypocrisy in a world that has become overly high tech." Other critics found the new album halfhearted, and even many fans agreed that the gigs which supported it "only seldom overcame the lazy craftsmanship that made the album somewhat disappointing," as Elysa Gardner penned in *Rolling Stone.* Nevertheless, *Perverse* still managed to break the Top Ten in the U.K. In retrospect, Edwards caustically quipped to internet writer Shaun Phillips that "the album was really good. It was our most adventurous and most principled, that's why it failed. If you call half a million failing."

The mixed reception of *Perverse* avalanched into a career slump for Jesus Jones, and for several years the existence of the band seemed bleak during the mid-1990s. While Edwards had written at least an album's worth of material, a divorce in 1994 soured the songwriter, and the departure of Gen, who joined the band Baby Chaos in the fall of 1996, only made matters worse. Still, although Jesus Jones was collectively dormant, issuing only remixes of earlier singles, band members were rustling with activity. Jaworski moonlighted in the in the southern-fried Chicago, Illinois outfit the Waco Brothers, De Borg and Baker were busy with various technical jobs, and Edwards offered his engineering services to recordings made by acts as unlikely as the Swedish duo Roxette and ex-porn star Traci Lords.

Recording in the house of ace producer Martin Phillips, whose credits included dance groups Erasure and the Beloved, Jesus Jones was a coherent band once again, and the result was a return to form with the album *Already,* released in the U.S in the spring of 1998.

"*Already* is unashamedly reminiscent of old school Jesus Jones," wrote Shaun Phillips. "Edwards' vocal style, for instance, is as unforgettable as it is consistent – albeit exploring new sonic territory, especially on the self-explanatory "Wishing It Away" and "February," a tune about seasonally adjusted depression." In spite of the similarity to earlier material and a world tour, the album did not generate the fervor of fans as around *Doubt.* Ironically, by the time of the band's return many dance rock bands had achieved immense acclaim, but this time around Edwards kept his bragging in check. "I don't want to get into that 'I invented rock 'n' roll,' because I've had it with all those soundbites and grandiose claims," Edwards told Phillips. "That's another thing that bores me about our past." Whether such boredom will inspire Edwards to take new chances with Jesus Jones remains to be seen.

Selected discography

Liquidizer, Food, 1989.
Doubt, Food, 1991.
Perverse, Food, 1993.
Already, Food, 1998.

Sources

Periodicals

Entertainment Weekly, June 13, 1997.
People Weekly, August 26, 1991.
Rolling Stone, May 16, 1991; June 24, 1993.
Time, March 1, 1993.

Online

http://www.jesusjones.com
http://www.jesusjones.zao.net/f

—*Sean Frentner*

Steve Lacy

Saxophone, composer

Anybody who cares about the soprano saxophone, the straightest and most nasal-toned member of the sax family, knows that Sidney Bechet pioneered its use in jazz. Current listeners of light jazz and pop music probably associate it most commonly with Kenny G. But to hardcore jazz fans willing to listen to more challenging music, no soprano sax player has been more important or influential than Steve Lacy. From the 1950s to the present, Lacy's work on that instrument, combined with his unique talents as a composer, has earned him a reputation among genuine jazz buffs, as a true giant of jazz. To trace his career, through his sequential forays into dixieland, bebop, free jazz, and postmodern hybrids, is to retell the modern history of jazz itself.

Lacy was born Steven Lackritz on July 23, 1934, in New York City. As a youngster, Lackritz studied piano and clarinet. Inspired by Bechet, he eventually switched to soprano sax, and began specializing in old-time New Orleans-style jazz, which at that time was about all you heard played on the archaic soprano horn. He began to study with clarinetist and tenor saxophonist Cecil Scott, and took classes at the Manhattan School of Music and the Schillinger School of Music. Schillinger later changed its name and became famous as the Berklee School of Music. Lackritz also changed his name, in 1952, to Lacy.

Lacy spent the early 1950s playing dixieland and other early jazz styles, mostly with a group of older musicians that included Red Allen, Dickie Wells, Vic Dickenson, Zutty Singleton, Joe Sullivan, and Pops Foster. During a performance in New Orleans one day in 1953, pianist Cecil Taylor, an unknown upstart at the time, introduced himself to Lacy, and asked him why such a young man was wasting his time playing such old music. The question posed by Taylor represented a crucial turning point in Lacy's career. He did not immediately give up the old styles, but he became friends with Taylor, and together the pair began exploring a new brand of jazz that stretched the boundaries of harmony and structure to a degree that was not yet common in jazz.

From 1955 to 1957, Lacy performed in a quartet led by Taylor, whose futuristic ideas about music were so advanced that Lacy had to struggle just to keep up. Taylor eventually dropped Lacy from his band, but not before launching him on a career path that emphasized originality and imagination. In the late 1950s, Lacy hooked up with Gil Evans and Mal Waldron, musicians with whom he continued to perform on and off into the 1980s. About this time, Lacy become keenly interested in the music of pianist and composer Thelonious Monk. He joined Monk's band in 1960. After a short stint there, Lacy formed a group with trombonist Roswell Rudd that was dedicated to interpreting Monk's music. He continued to focus on Monk and Monk-inspired music throughout the first half of the 1960s. Lacy's immersion in Monkness was so complete that it moved German jazz writer Joachim Berendt to call him "one of the few horn players—and probably the only white among them—who fully understood and assimilated Monk."

In the mid-1960s, Lacy's interest shifted toward the burgeoning free-jazz scene. He joined forces in 1965 with trumpeter Don Cherry and pianist Kenny Drew to perform for a month at a Copenhagen club called Montmartre. That group then went to France and Italy in search of gigs. He also worked with Carla Bley during this period. In 1966 Lacy formed an ensemble in Italy with trumpet player Enrico Rava. That was also the year he met Swiss vocalist and cellist Irene Aebi, whom he eventually married.

Later in 1966, Lacy, Aebi, and Rava, with the addition of bassist Johnny Dyani and drummer Louis Moholo, embarked on a disastrous tour of South America, after which they returned to New York. Lacy and Aebi stayed in New York for about a year, but work for experimentalists like themselves was hard to come by. Frustrated, the pair moved to Rome, and they lived in Europe ever since. For the next few years, Lacy dabbled in a variety of musical forms, with influences ranging from rock, to contemporary art music, to free jazz. He performed with many different Italian musicians of varying abilities, and

Born Steven Norman Lackritz, July 23, 1934, in New York, NY; married Irene Aebi, c. 1966; *Education:* attended Schillinger School of Music, 1953; attended Manhattan School of Music, 1954.

Performed with a variety of New York-based bands, playing dixieland and other old-time jazz styles, 1953-54; member of band led by pianist Cecil Taylor, 1955-57; began ongoing collaborations with Gil Evans and Mal Waldron, 1957-59; member, Thelonious Monk's band, 1960; co-led Monk-inspired band with trombonist Roswell Rudd, 1961-65; performed in Europe with Enrico Rava, Carla Bley, Kenny Drew, and others; toured South America, 1966; began playing solo soprano sax concerts, 1972; formed and led quintet, which performed worldwide and recorded prolifically, 1970-79; expanded to become sextet, 1981; toured U.S. with trio, 1997; over the course of his career, has produced more than 100 recordings as a bandleader or collaborator.

Awards: Frequent winner of *Down Beat* poll as "Best Soprano Saxophonist;" MacArthur "Genius Grant" Fellowship, 1992.

Addresses: *Residence*—Berlin, Germany; *Booking agent*—Steppin' In Artist Development, 1802 15th St., San Francisco, CA 94103.

worked with the experimental electronic group Musica Electronica Viva.

Lacy's own composing began to mature around this time. His music began to veer away from free jazz toward more structured compositions. Many of his pieces were settings of poetry or other words to music, including his first major composition, "The Way," a suite based on the ancient Chinese text the *Tao Te Ching.* In 1969 Lacy and Aebi moved to Paris, where the avant-garde jazz scene was in full bloom. There Lacy found an enthusiastic audience for his work, and he had little problem hooking up with good musicians and finding decent work.

For the next twenty years, Lacy churned out an astonishing catalog of albums, over 100 in all. Most often, he has toured and recorded as the leader of a sextet, often featuring long-time associates Aebi, drummer Oliver Johnson, and alto saxophonist Steve Potts. Other frequent collaborators have been bassists Jean-Jacques Avenel and Kent Carter, and pianist Bobby Few. During the 1970s, inspired by the work of saxophonist Anthony Braxton, he began performing occasionally as a solo act. At other times, he has performed as half of a duo with any of a number of musicians, including Potts, Mal Waldron, and Gil Evans.

At some point during the 1970s, Lacy dubbed his musical style "poly-free," alluding to its connections to both free jazz and more concretely structured forms. By the mid-1980s, Lacy's sextet was a finely-honed musical machine. The string of albums recorded around that time, including *Prospectus, Futurities, The Gleam,* and *Momentum,* represents the band at is peak. In addition to his own compositions, Lacy continued to throw in the occasional Monk piece, and to this day he remains one of Monk's chief interpreters.

Lacy is the type of musician who thrives on collaborations with artists of other ilks. He likes to work, for example, with poets and dancers, and the textual sources for his lyrical compositions are amazingly diverse, ranging from Herman Melville to obscure Islamic verse. In 1992, Lacy received a MacArthur Foundation "genius grant" in recognition of his brilliant and prolific work in jazz. As the 1990s continued, Lacy more or less pressed on with his continuing mission; namely, to create works of art with his horn and his pen, incorporating as influences whatever moved him at the time, be it poetry, painting, movement, philosophy, or a mundane life event.

After more than two decades based in Paris, Lacy moved to Berlin in the mid-1990s. From there, he has continued to churn out new material at an impressive pace. In 1997 Lacy broke up his sextet and toured the United States as a trio with bassist Avenel and drummer John Betsch. Now in his sixties, he remains as innovative and active as ever. Steve Lacy may never become a household name, but his status as the most important modern soprano sax player, one of the most important interpreters of Thelonious Monk, and simply one of jazz's more intriguing figures, is already beyond debate.

Selected discography

Soprano Sax, Prestige, 1957.
The Straight Horn of Steve Lacy, Candid, 1960.
Evidence, New Jazz, 1962.
Disposability, RCA, 1965.
Sortie, GTA, 1966.

The Forest and the Zoo, ESP, 1967.
Epistrophy, BYG, 1970.
Moon, BYG, 1970.
Roba, Saravah, 1971.
Wordless, Futura, 1971.
Lapis, Saravah, 1971.
Steve Lacy Solo, Emanem, 1972.
The Gap, America, 1972.
Estilhacos (Chips) Live in Lisbon, Guilda da Musica, 1972.
The Crust, Emanem, 1973.
Scraps, Saravah, 1974.
Saxophone Special, Emanem, 1974.
Flakes, RCA Vista, 1974.
School Days, QED, 1975.
Dreams, Saravah, 1975.
Lumps, ICP, 1975.
Trickles, Black Saint, 1976.
Torments, Morgue, 1976.
Clangs, Ictus, 1976.
Stabs, FMP, 1976.
Stalks, Denon, 1976.
The Wire, Denon, 1976.
Distant Voices, Nippon Columbia, 1976.
Sidelines, IAI, 1977.
Threads, Horo, 1977.
Raps, Adelphi, 1977.
Straws, Cramps, 1977.
Clinkers, Hat Hut, 1977.
Follies, FMP, 1978.
Points, La Chand du Monde, 1978.
Catch, Horo, 1978.
The Woe, Quark, 1979.
Troubles, Black Saint, 1979.
Stamps, Hat Hut, 1979.
Shots, Musica, 1980.
Alter Ego, World Artists, 1980.
New York Capers, hat Art, 1981.
Tips, Hat Hut, 1981.
Ballets, hat Art, 1982.
The Flame, Soul Note, 1982.
Prospectus, hat Art, 1983.
Blinks, hat Art, 1984.
Futurities, hat Art, 1985.
The Condor, Soul Note, 1986.
Outings, Ismex, 1986.
The Kiss, Lunatic, 1987.
The Gleam, Silkheart, 1987.
Only Monk, Soul Note, 1987.

Momentum, RCA, 1987.
One Fell Swoop, 1987.
The Window, 1988.
The Door, 1989.
Anthem, 1990.
Itinerary, 1991.
Remains, 1992.
Weal and Woe, Emanem.
Vespers, Soul Note.
We See, hat Art.
Revenue, Soul Note.
Findings, CMAP.
Blues for Aida, Egg Farm.
Bye-Ya, Freelance.

With Mal Waldron

Mal Waldron With the Steve Lacy Quintet, America, 1972.
Snake Out, hat Art, 1982.
Herbe de L'oubli, hat Art, 1983.
Let's Call This, hat Art, 1986.
Sempre Amore, Soul Note, 1987.
Hot House, 1991.

With Cecil Taylor

Jazz Advance, Blue Note, 1956.
Masters of Modern Piano, Verve.

Sources

Atlantic, November 1989, p. 120.
Boston Herald, December 4, 1997, p. O63.
Down Beat, May 1980, p. 20; May 1987, p. 30; April 1988, p. 30; October 1989, p. 32; June 1996, p. 56; February 1997, p. 18.
Jazziz, July 1997, p. 55.
Jazz Times, December 1997.
Rolling Stone, March 5, 1981, p. 53.
San Francisco Examiner, November 18, 1997, p. B3.
Seattle Times, November 27, 1997, p. I11.

Additional material for this profile was provided by Steppin' In Artist Development.

—*Robert R. Jacobson*

Lisa Lisa

Singer/songwriter

Shooting from the New York City club circuit to the national singles charts in 1985, singer Lisa Lisa helped to prove that hip hop need not be confined to the underground. With the assistance of keyboard player and guitarist Alex "Spanador" Mosely and drummer Mike Hughes, together known as Cult Jam, and the production team Full Force, Lisa Lisa created a debut album full of dance numbers and ballads that evoked comparisons to classic 1960s girl groups such as the Supremes. *Spanish Fly,* the outfit's sophomore effort, a potpourri of musical styles including salsa and doo-wop, was even more impressive than the previous album, producing a slew of singles that peaked on multiple charts in 1987. After falling into a relative slump with two albums that passed little muster with critics, Lisa Lisa returned to form in 1994 with the satisfying solo debut *LL-77.*

The youngest of ten siblings in a large Latino family, Lisa Lisa (born Lisa Velez) grew up in the tough New York City neighborhood called Hell's Kitchen, where she discovered a talent for singing in her church's choir. As a young teenager, Velez continued her budding career in high school musical theater and made her inauspicious professional debut as a singing prune for a company of local fruit growers. However, it was in the vibrant world of the Fun House, one of New York's most celebrated dance clubs, that Velez would find her first real break.

Having heard that pop star Madonna had emerged from the Fun House herself, Velez donned the lace and corset couture of that singer and became a fixture of the club scene. Velez quickly caught the eye of musicians Mike Hughes and Alex "Spanador" Mosely in 1983, who also saw the potential for Velez to capitalize on the sound of New York's underground. "We clearly thought, 'Madonna left the market,'" Hughes reflected to *People* magazine in 1987. "The Latin female thing started with Madonna.... She was accepted and became the Latin queen." While Madonna's complete lack of Latino heritage made such an acceptance something of an irony if not an outright cultural appropriation, the trio began promoting Velez in hopes of becoming Madonna's successor.

Within a year, Velez was introduced to the street gang turned music group Full Force, who had scored heavily as producers with the rap hit "Roxanne Roxanne" by the act UTFO in 1984. Although at the time it was Madonna that Velez sought to imitate, for Full Force her voice invoked legendary soul singer Diana Ross, who had defined a generation of all-female vocal acts with the Supremes in the 1960s. As Velez told *People* magazine, it was precisely that "Supremes type of feel" that won Full Force over. "They wanted that innocent, girlish

For the Record . . .

Born Lisa Velez, January 15, 1967, New York, NY.

Lisa Lisa joined Cult Jam, 1983; song "I Wonder If I Take You Home" released on the *Breakdancin'* compilation, 1984, and as a single, 1985; released debut album *Lisa Lisa and Cult Jam with Full Force,* Columbia Records, 1985; released *Spanish Fly,* Columbia, 1987; toured with David Bowie, 1987; left Cult Jam, 1991; released first solo album *LL-77* for new label Pendulum, 1994.

Addresses: *Record company*—1290 6th Ave., New York, NY, (212) 397-2244, fax (212) 347-2240. *Home*—New York, NY.

voice, yet womanly." Doubling up her first name in homage to "Roxanne Roxanne," Velez assumed the handle Lisa Lisa, with Hughes and Mosely backing her up as Cult Jam.

With Full Force's credibility, attracting a major label posed little problem and, in the fall of 1985, Columbia released the cumbersomely titled debut *Lisa Lisa and Cult Jam with Full Force,* with the latter writing, arranging, and producing the whole affair. While critics such as *Rolling Stone*'s Debby Bull reserved much of their praise for Full Force's impressive behind-the-scenes work, it was clearly the still teenage Velez who was the center of public attention. Comparisons to Ross and Veronica of the 1960s group the Ronettes were again made favorably on cuts like the hit single "I Wonder If I Take You Home," which Bull assessed as "girl-group innocence married to a big street beat.... What a perfectly conceived pop perfection." While the single made the group a favorite across the U.S. in dance clubs, the follow-up "All Cried Out" broke the Top 10 pop chart and proved Velez's mastery of emotive ballads.

Fly Popped to the Top of Charts

After a two year interval, Velez and company returned with the album *Spanish Fly,* a more diverse ensemble of influences that dominated both pop and R&B charts, in addition to impressing critics. *Newsweek*'s Jim Miller echoed the majority of writers, summing up *Spanish Fly* as "a clever synthesis of Motown-style melodies,

girl-group nostalgia, and the robotic funk pioneered by [singer/songwriter] Prince and his proteges," featuring "the girlish doo-wop of "Lost in Emotion" and the upbeat hip-hop of 'Everything Will B-Fine'." "Lost In Emotion" hit the number one position in two charts, as did the infectious dance cut "Head To Toe," and the album became Lisa Lisa and Cult Jam's second platinum-selling effort. Although such success resulted in an invitation to accompany veteran pop singer David Bowie on his world tour and massive media exposure, Velez retained her humility. "I don't consider myself a star," she confessed to *Newsweek* in the summer of 1987. "I'm an entertainer. I like to do my job. If I'm a star, it shows that I'm doing my job right."

After the enormous popularity of *Spanish Fly,* the reception of their third album in 1989 was a major disappointment. Despite the autobiographical hints of rags to riches success in its one minor hit "Little Jackie Wants to Be a Star," as well as the ascendant outlook of its title, *Straight to the Sky* showed signs that Velez had seen her fame come and go. While a moderate seller in R&B charts, the record was attacked in many reviews. "*Straight to the Sky* is a conflict of interests," asserted one *Melody Maker* critic. "The electro and Latino hip hop roots are in evidence, but Full Force's polished production, more than ever, is part of Lisa Lisa and Cult Jam's attempt to maintain their pace in the pop straights. It's neither gracious nor glamorous, [and] tepid in comparison to the spartan spontaneity of their earlier work."

Made Impressive Solo Debut

In response to the claims of blandness leveled at *Sky,* Velez and her cohorts aimed at an edgier sound for their next release, entitled *Straight Outta Hell's Kitchen.* For this 1991 release, the group secured hit-making producers David Cole and Robert Clivill&eaccutes of the outfit C&C Music Factory to handle half of its cuts, in hopes that the duo's finesse with club tracks would spark a new chemistry. Although Clivill&eaccutes and Cole's efforts gave shape to the memorable "Let the Beat Hit 'Em," a single that hit the top of the R&B charts, the group's status as a "crossover" act in the mainstream did not recover. Still, the record testified to Velez's increasing scope as a singer, which no critic would have denied. "I wanted everyone to realize that I'm a true vocalist," Velez told *Billboard* upon the release of *Hell's* Kitchen. "I'm not one of those rinky-dink girls that come out of nowhere and makes a little money and is here for a little while. No"

After leaving her longtime collaborators Cult Jam and Full Force, Velez made good on her promise of being a long-term artist with her solo debut *LL-77,* released on the Pendulum label in 1994. For the first time, Velez co-wrote her songs with an impressive lineup of partners including co-producer guru and funk vocalist Nona Hendryx. While not a radical break from her work with Cult Jam, *LL-77* evidenced that Velez was able to take on more subtle, adult-oriented material without sacrificing the energy that had made her famous. "The lyrics on this album are all a reflection of me and my life," Velez told *Billboard* in early 1994. "My darker side came out [on this album], I guess because it had the opportunity. There's always been a hunger inside me to do this kind of music, and now I can finally do what I want to do."

LL-77 was on the whole overlooked by record buyers, with its single "Skip To My Lu" barely skimming the R&B Top 40, but it was probably Velez's most critically acclaimed album yet. Both *Rolling Stone*'s Paul Evans and the *Village Voice*'s Rob Sheffield praised the album for its remodeling of earlier club sounds, the latter critic proclaiming it was "not really a dance record, but a fantasy of how yesterday's dance-pop mainstream might sound dressed up in today's studio tricks." In addition to the album's diversity of instrumentation, thanks largely to co-producer Giovanni Salah, *LL-77* showcased Velez's most refined singing to date. "Lisa Lisa plays it cool vocally," wrote Sheffield, "so that where her voice once sounded charmingly thin, she now sounds lazily ethereal." If Velez had needed to make a comeback, *LL-77* was critically more than an ample one,

paving the way for a reinvented career as a mature pop chanteuse.

Selected discography

With Cult Jam and Full Force

Lisa Lisa and Cult Jam with Full Force, Columbia, 1985.
Spanish Fly, Columbia, 1987.
Straight to the Sky, Columbia, 1989.
Straight Outta Hell's Kitchen, Columbia, 1991.
Lisa Lisa and Friends, Alex, 1995 (compilation).
Head to Toe, Sony, 1995 (compilation).

Solo

LL-77, Pendulum/ERG, 1994.

Sources

Billboard, May 23, 1987; August 19, 1989; September 21, 1991; January 15, 1994.
Melody Maker, June 3, 1989.
Newsweek, June 22, 1987.
People, September 14, 1987.
Rolling Stone, October 10, 1985; May 5, 1994.
Village Voice, March 15, 1994.

—*Shaun Frentner*

Lisa Loeb

Singer, songwriter

© Ken Settle. Reproduced by permission.

Alternative pop singer and guitarist Lisa Loeb is noted for her thoughtfully crafted melodies and original songs that contain compelling narratives. Her songs are akin to setting short stories to music, and she initially garnered a lot of unexpected exposure when her single "Stay (I Missed You)" was featured on the soundtrack for the film *Reality Bites* in 1994. According to Jeff Colchamiro of *Guitar World Acoustic*, the single "Stay (I Missed You)" holds the distinction of being the sole Number One single by an unsigned artist. Loeb told Colchamiro, "For a long time, being a songwriter and a girl meant that you were considered a folk singer.... I felt like I was doing something more in the genre of Elvis Costello--a person who plays with a band sometimes and plays all different kinds of songs, and it's not folky. They're just songs." Colchamiro described Loeb's style as, "slick pop arrangements and orchestral instrumentation with ... layered vocals, straightforward rock strumming and jazzy acoustic fingerpicking."

People magazine's Alec Foege described Loeb's chart-topping "Stay (I Missed You)" as, "an unabashedly sweet acoustic ballad ... she seemed daringly different." Loeb explores the mentality of various characters in her music, and has appeared as an actress in two films and a television show. She told Sharon Steinbach of *Hits* magazine, "Music is my business, it's my life, but I can schedule stuff around it."

Loeb was born in 1969 in the San Francisco area, and was raised in Dallas, TX, along with her older brother Ben. Her father, a physician, used to play the piano at home frequently, as did her brother, and her brother eventually became a classical musician. Loeb was immersed in music lessons and performance experiences before the age of fourteen. When she was eight, she won an award for a song she composed for the piano and she played it in a recital. Her high school had a minimum of two mandatory shows per year, and at the local Jewish Community Center Loeb played Musetta in *La Boheme,* a postman, a young Mexican girl, an Oscar Meyer wiener in a musical fashion show, and the character Linus in *You're A Good Man Charlie Brown*. Loeb began playing the guitar at the age of fourteen—primarily because her brother was always using the piano when she needed it—and she discovered that she enjoyed being able to carry an instrument around with her and take it to the privacy of her room. Loeb's first live, acoustic guitar performance occurred at sleep-away summer camp, where she performed a unique version of Led Zeppelin's "Stairway to Heaven". She began writing songs for the guitar at age fifteen, figuring that composing an original song was preferable to remembering the Rush and John Cougar songs that her guitar teacher hoped she would master.

Loeb's early influences were the Cure, Brian Eno, David Bowie, Jimi Hendrix, Kiss, Elton John, the musical *Annie,* Led Zeppelin, Olivia Newton-John, and the Police. Queen's *A Night At The Opera,* including the release's cover art, was another early influence for Loeb, along with other top 40 rock and pop hits from the 1970s and early 1980s. She learned to finger-pick as a teenager, and developed an interest in acoustic music. She eventually relied upon a hybrid finger-picking style, using a flatpick and finger picking with her other three fingers.

Loeb went to Brown University in Providence, Rhode Island after high school, and found that she was more interested in playing and recording music than pursuing her studies in comparative literature. She created a group called Liz and Lisa in college with her friend Liz Mitchell, and the musician Duncan Sheik played with them for a year. Loeb and Mitchell performed often and spent their last two years in school mostly in the recording studio. A few years after graduating from Brown, Loeb pursued a solo career in earnest and Mitchell founded a band called Ida.

Loeb moved to New York City after college and played as many shows as possible. She tirelessly performed at clubs, coffeehouses, and music festivals until she began to see results. She recorded a demo called *The Purple Tape* with producer/engineer Juan Patino in his home studio, and during this period of time in the early 1990s, Loeb made a lot business contacts and visited numerous record company offices with her demo tape in hand. Record company A & R executives began requesting her tapes—and the listening public began to purchase them as well. It was serendipitous that actor Ethan Hawke was Loeb's neighbor and then friend, because he heard "Stay (I Miss You)," requested a copy, played it for actor/director Ben Stiller, and it was featured on the soundtrack for the enormously popular film *Reality Bites* in 1994. Ethan Hawke then directed a video for the song, and it reached the top of the charts. Loeb didn't release her debut album, *Tails,* until 1995, because the popularity of the single entailed touring, extensive promotional work, signing with a label, and appearing on the "David Letterman Show". "Stay (I Missed You)" was nominated for a Grammy Award and won a Brit Award in 1995.

Tails was released worldwide and Loeb toured with her band, Nine Stories, and alone with her acoustic guitar. Nine Stories is comprised of bass player Joe Quigley, guitarist Mark Spencer, and drummer Ronny Crawford. For the release of Tails, Loeb used Juan Patino on drums, JR Robinson of Chaka Khan, and musician Leland Sklar. She played with Lyle Lovett and Sarah McLachlan in the U.S., and toured Europe with the Counting Crows. She also toured with the Lilith Fair in 1997 and 1998, singing with Lyle Lovett, Emmylou Harris, Shawn Colvin, the Indigo Girls, and Bill Janovitz from Buffalo Tom. She told Calchamiro, "It was a real community and there was a lot of encouragement and good will towards people.... It was a learning experience ... A lot of times when you play music, you're on tour and you don't get to see what other artists are doing or get inspired by their ideas."

Loeb appeared in the film *Black Circle Boys,* which was screened at the 1997 Sundance Film Festival, and in the independent Arroyo Studios film *Serial Killing for Dummies.* She also appeared in an episode of the television show *The Nanny.* She then released *Firecracker* in 1998 and used classical orchestration in her material for the first time. She told Steinbach, "It takes the songs to a different place than they would normally go. It gives a deeper cinematic quality to songs like "Falling In Love" or "Furious Rose." They're not standard pop arrangements. That's the part of the album I really love." Firecracker has a more intimate sound than Tails, but features the same storytelling themes as her previous work, a theme that has now become Loeb's trademark—along with her large, black, cat-eyed glasses. Leob told Steinbach, "I love playing shows. I love being there and relating to the audience and I love when people are singing along at concerts. That feels good. it's so immediate."

Selected discography

(Contributor) "Stay (I Missed You) (soundtrack), RCA, 1994.
Tails, Geffen Records, 1995.
Firecracker, Geffen, 1998.

Sources

Guitar World Acoustic, January 1998.
Hits, February 20, 1998.
People, November 17, 1997.
React, December 29, 1998.
Rolling Stone, February 5, 1998.
Teen People, April 1998.

—B. Kimberly Taylor

Chuck Mangione

Flugelhorn

AP/Wide World Photos. Reproduced by permission.

Writer, band leader, and horn player Chuck Mangione emerged into the music scene in the early 1960s to quickly mark himself as an anomaly among most jazz performers. His unshakably positive persona stood in contrast to the often tragic stereotype of many jazz legends, but perhaps even more importantly, Mangione found a place in the hearts of mainstream listeners—a fact that caused some cynical critics to write Mangione off as a commercial panderer. While it is true that aside from popularizing the flugelhorn, Mangione broke few barriers in his style, his devotion to making emotionally outreaching music consistently resulted in albums which were lauded both by the public and critics until the end of the 1970s. "Chuck Mangione's band hasn't changed that much from the days he was playing small jazz clubs instead of concert halls," critic Herb Nolan wrote in *Down Beat* upon seeing Mangione live in 1978. "It's simply Chuck Mangione, a musician who came up playing with band like Art Blakey's Jazz Messengers, being Chuck Mangione, a performer who probably brings more jazz to more people than any other."

Born in upstate New York in the city of Rochester, on November 29, 1940, Mangione was raised by very supportive parents, although they had little interest in music themselves. Willing to accomodate whatever interests their son might develop, Mangione's mother and father enrolled the boy in music lessons at age eight. It was after seeing the film *Young Man with a Horn,* starring Kirk Douglas, that Mangione decided to take up playing the trumpet. Along with his brother Gap, himself a budding pianist, Mangione began improvising at home.

Rather than lamenting the possibility of having two sons taking up the unsteady life of jazz musicians, Mangione's father instead escorted him to the nearby Ridgecrest Inn, where famed jazz musicians such as Miles Davis, Art Blakey, and Dizzy Gillespie often performed. After repeated visits, Mangione, then fifteen, was introduced to Gillespie, and gradually the two became friends. "We'd be playing every Sunday afternoon with Dizzy—in fact, that's where I got to know Dizzy and he gave me [his] upswept horn—and there were sessions at our house practically every night of the week," Mangione remembered to *Down Beat* writer Jim Szantor.

By the late 1950s, the aspiring Mangione was juggling an academic career at the Eastman School of Music and a role in the Jazz Brothers, a combo he had formed with Gap during his final year of high school. While a university education bolstered Mangione's musical knowledge and exposed him to the flugelhorn, later to

For the Record . . .

Born Charles Frank Mangione, November 29, 1940, in Rochester, NY. *Education:* attended Eastman School of Music.

Formed first group, the Jazz Brothers, with brother Gap in 1957; recorded self-titled album with the Jazz Brothers, 1960; joined Art Blakey's Jazz Messengers in New York City, 1965; wrote the Top 10 single "Time Won't Let Me" for rock group The Outsiders, 1966; signed a four record contract with Mercury Records, 1970; released the album *Friends and Love,* cut from a concert of the same name, 1970; performed at Montreaux International Jazz Festival in Switzerland, 1972; released *Land of Make Believe,* 1973; signed with A&M and released label debut *Chase the Clouds Away,* 1975; released double platinum *Feels So Good*; 1977; issued soundtrack double album for the never - released *Children of Sanchez,* 1979; wrote theme song for 1980 Winter Olympics; signed to Columbia, 1982; launched reunion tour with *Feels So Good* quartet, 1997.

Awards: Grammy Award, Best Instrumental Composition, for song "Bellavia," 1976; double platinum status for *Feels So Good,* 1977; named Top Instrumentalist by *Billboard* magazine, 1979; voted Instrumentalist of the Year by *Performance* magazine, 1979; named Composer/Arranger of the Decade by *Cashbox* magazine, 1979.

Addresses: *Record company*—Columbia Records, 51 West 52ⁿᵈ St., New York, NY 10019.

become his pet instrument, Mangione found the environment too rigid and concentrated on his extracurricular jamming. "I did what a lot of young people do when something is not their way: I rebelled against everything," Mangione later told Lee Underwood in *Down Beat.* "Because of that, I didn't really take advantage of the four years I spent as an Eastman student. I never studied composition, and I never studied orchestration—the very things that would have been extremely beneficial to me today."

When Mangione graduated from Eastman in 1963 he had already cut three albums with the Jazz Brothers, but he was still a long way from being an established artist.

In 1965, he decided to join the ranks of Art Blakey's Jazz Messengers, one of the foremost names in the New York City club circuit, for whom he played trumpet until 1968. In the meantime, Mangione tried his hand at teaching, first at parochial schools, then at the Hochstein School of Music in Rochester, an institution that offered first rate training to underprivileged youths. Remembering his own experiences as a student, Mangione also served as the chair of a jazz program at his alma mater, where he pushed students to connect their performance of jazz with experiences and feelings outside the academy. "I used to teach courses on how to ride a bus and how to check into an airport," Mangione later quipped to Nolan. "No kidding, there's so much missing from reality in relationship to young musicians and where they are going that somebody has to tell them what's coming."

Created Special Image

In addition to his unconditional placement of personal feelings in music, Mangione had also become known for his trademark style. While many performers at the time still donned formal gear on the stage, Mangione chose to maintain a casual look, topped off by a wide brimmed, floppy hat given to him by friends Bill and Marie Tedeschi in 1965. "Everybody was so uptight with all those [black ties and] tails," Mangione told Underwood. "That had to be wiped away so musicians could feel free like they *naturally* feel." In addition, his complete abandonment of the trumpet in favor of the flugelhorn in 1968 struck some as unusual, but gave Mangione's music its own special flavor.

Nearing his thirtieth birthday, Mangione decided to take the full plunge towards being a professional musician. Although he had formed his own quartet in 1969, he found that many of his compositions begged for the sound of a large orchestration. After a largely unsuccessful concert performance called Kaleidoscope, Mangione directed a show at Eastman in 1970 called "Friends and Love," a fifty person arrangement that was simulcast on a local television channel. The performance was committed to a double record set, and after local sales took off, Mangione was offered a four album contract with Mercury Records.

It was during his years at Mercury that Mangione's fame erupted towards international proportions, with both *Friends and Love* and *Land of Make Believe,* recorded in 1973, garnering Mangione's first Grammy Award nominations. While still experimenting with larger arrangements, Mangione also continued with his quartet, which was comprised of Gerry Norwood on saxophone and flute, Chip Jackson on bass, Joe LaBarbera on drums, and of course Mangione himself playing flugelhorn. However, Mangione felt that despite his popularity, his music still was not reaching far enough beyond circles of jazz buffs and he decided to move to the A&M label.

Jerry Moss and horn-player Herb Alpert, A&M's co-owners, ran their company with loose reins, and Mangione was allowed to handle his next album exactly as he saw fit. The result was *Chase the Clouds Away,* released in 1975, an album that paired intimate cuts played by Mangione's quartet with expansive, forty-member orchestrations. Mangione was yet again graced with several Grammy bids for the record and he was fully satisfied with the studio conditions at his new label. "All the music was done live in the studio," Mangione told Underwood of *Clouds.* "There was no overdubbing. We were playing eight and nine minute takes with an orchestra, and they were *all* good. It was like picking between red wine and white wine."

As the 1970s drew to a close, Mangione had reached his commercial and critical peak through his A&M efforts. With *Bellavia,* his 1976 follow-up to the million-selling *Chase the Clouds Away*, Mangione finally snared his first Grammy win for the album's title cut in the category of Best Instrumental Composition. However, it was the release of Mangione's fourth A&M album *Feels So Good* that inscribed him in the annals of popular music history. The record's title track climbed to the Number Two position on the pop charts, a feat almost unheard of for a jazz musician, and the album itself went double platinum. In addition, Mangione scored again with his double record soundtrack for *The Children of Sanchez* in 1979, in spite of the fact that the film was never released.

Continued Despite Critical Backlash

In the wake of Mangione's crossover into the mass market, some critics pessimistically assumed that such popularity could only be accounted for by Mangione's debasement of jazz. Despite his own favor for Mangione's music, Nolan noticed that it had "been dismissed by some as something like 'bubblegum jazz' with the content of a Bazooka [Gum] wrapper cartoon." Others claimed that whatever claims Mangione made of passionate performing, his own style lacked the powerful eroticism many associate with jazz. "His sexuality has all of the rage and passion of a Continental breakfast," one critic was quoted as saying to Underwood after seeing Mangione play live. "Let's face it: Chuck Mangione's audience came to be lulled and caressed,

to be held close to mama's breast, to be lovingly patted all over with Johnson's Musical Baby Powder. He picks up his horn and spills out Cream of Wheat laced with dollar signs."

Mangione himself was nonchalant towards such scathing criticism, as he had also been towards fervent praise in equal measure. "It seems there is always something wrong, maybe from a critic's or musician's point of view, when the public begins to accept something," Mangione told Schaeffer. "They think it must be 'commercial;' it must be 'watered down;' it must be this or that. To me the musician who's performing is usually the guy who can best evaluate whether it is good or bad." Mangione felt that such critics were blinded by preconceptions of musical categories, to their own detriment. "It's like spaghetti sauce," he analogized to Schaeffer. "You get twenty Italian mothers to cook a sauce and each sauce is going to taste different. However, you can have a good time with all of them."

In the early 1980s, Mangione enjoyed his position as an entertainment figure to dabble in unexpected new terrain. In 1980, he was given the impressive task of composing a theme for the Winter Olympics, held in Lake Placid, New York, and from then on he was frequently invited to play the American National Anthem at major sporting venues. Mangione also provided theme music for other, less prominent outings, such as the film *The Cannonball Run* and television's *Larry King Show.* Mangione even turned out an acting performance for an episode of the action-drama *Magnum P.I.* in February of 1984.

Although it seemed at the time that Mangione's career was an unstoppable force, as the decade wore on he quickly slipped out of mainstream visibility. In 1981, Mangione's contract with A&M had run its course, and he decided to sign with Columbia. Unfortunately, most of his work for Columbia, as well the occasional releases on his own Feels So Good label, was largely forgettable, and failed to pass muster from either critics or fans. Nevertheless, Mangione held fast as a master showman, and continued to give live performances, if on a somewhat smaller scale.

The 1988 release *Eyes of the Veiled Temptress* was a slight return to form, and at the very least proved that Mangione had more in store for him than greatest hits packages and reissues alone. Still, it was a return to his past that gave Mangione's career its biggest boost in years. In 1997, Mangione organized a comeback tour that reassembled his quartet from the recording of *Feels So Good*, during which he delivered well received takes on his most memorable compositions.

Selected discography

Friends and Love, Mercury, 1970.
The Chuck Mangione Quartet, Mercury, 1971.
Alive!, Mercury, 1972.
Together, Mercury, 1973.
Land of Make Believe, Mercury, 1972.
Chase the Clouds Away, A&M, 1975
Bellavia, A&M, 1975
Main Squeeze, A&M, 1976
Feels So Good, A&M, 1977.
The Best of Chuck Mangione, Mercury, 1977.
Children of Sanchez, A&M, 1979
Fun and Games, A&M, 1980
Tarantella, A&M, 1981
Love Notes, Columbia, 1982.
Live at the Village Gate, Feels So Good, 1987.
Eyes of the Veiled Temptress, Columbia, 1988.
Compact Jazz, The Best of Chuck Mangione Live, Verve, 1992.
Greatest Hits, Feels So Good, 1996

Sources

Down Beat, November 25, 1971; May 24, 1973, May 8, 1975; March 23, 1978

—*Sean Frentner*

Billy Mann

Singer, songwriter

With a richly soulful voice and a songwriting sensibility straight out of Motown's heyday, singer-songwriter Billy Mann sounds like an artist from a bygone era. But, while his music may evoke memories of radio staples from days of yore, the Philadelphia native has only been a force on the national music scene since the mid-1990s, when he released his first record. A relative newcomer, Mann has carved out a niche for himself by attempting to mix his influences with more modern sounds, crafting catchy pop songs rooted in soul.

Like many musicians-to-be, Mann was introduced to music as a child. He started to play the piano at the age of five, and soon thereafter took up bass, flute, and guitar as well. Majoring in vocal music and creative writing at his hometown's High School for Creative and Performing Arts, Mann wrote songs, sang in a gospel choir and played in local bands. A precocious young talent, Mann slipped surreptitiously into nightclubs to listen to professional performers at work. He reportedly hid inside the legendary Sigma Sound studio during a recording session with Patti LaBelle until he was discovered and promptly kicked out.

Following a performance in honor of songwriter Linda Creed at the Philadelphia Music Awards, the 20 year old Mann met the famed jazz and R&B saxophonist Grover Washington Jr., a Grammy-winner and Philadelphia session musician who was impressed with Mann's vocal prowess. "Grover gave me no choice but to be inspired to keep on with it [music], even when I ran out of confidence ... which I did ... a lot," Mann was quoted as saying of the encounter.

Even as a novice performer, Mann seemed determined to make a living making music. Harking back to his days singing R&B tunes on street corners as a 12-year-old, an early twentysomething Mann branched out to street performances in cities like San Francisco, New York, Miami, and London. During those globe-trotting days, he also frequented nightspots with open microphones.

His love for an aspiring actress (immortalized under the fictional name of "Daisy" in "Killed by a Flower," a single from Mann's debut album) took him to New York at the age of 23. While the romance eventually faltered, the move enabled Mann's career to blossom—thanks to a chance encounter with star producer Ric Wake in the stairwell of an apartment building in Manhattan. Wake, who has worked with the likes of Mariah Carey and Hall and Oates, heard Mann singing and was struck by his musical talent. Mann soon found himself cutting a demo with Wake's help in a professional studio. It was also Wake who brought Mann to the office of A&M label head Al Cafaro, where Mann's performance led him to be the first musician signed to Wake's DV8 label, a division of A&M. As Mann recalled of the experience to Nathan Brackett in *Musician,* "'I was terrified. I did one of those Bruce Springsteen auditions where you go into the president's office with your guitar.... You can't hide at that point."

As it turned out, Mann didn't have to. Although he has been criticized by some for being a bit derivative, his self-titled first album, released on April 2, 1996, got a number of positive notices, with critics likening his sound to the 1960s and 1970s pop-soul of Stevie Wonder, the Spinners, and Hall and Oates, among others. In *Entertainment Weekly,* Tony Scherman echoed a sentiment expressed by other rock writers when he praised Mann's "beautifully supple voice." Reviewing the record for the *Chicago Sun Times,* Jae-Ha Kim called Mann a "pensive writer" whose songs "are a potent blend of folky melancholy and stripped-down rock 'n' roll."

To generate interest in the record, Mann's label sent him out on the road, as is typically done with musicians who have new releases in stores. However, one leg of the tour was a bit unique: In 1996, Mann played a series of Borders book and music store acoustic shows around the country, opening up for fellow singer-songwriters Patty Griffin and headliner Jann Arden. Larry Weintraud, vice-president of artist development/artist relations for

A&M, told Bradley Bambarger of *Billboard* that the bookstore tour was part of a development plan the label had for the artists.

Mann's emerging success on the music scene came at a time when his personal life was dealt a sharp blow. Shortly after completing his debut album in 1995, his girlfriend, Rema (to whom he had already proposed) was diagnosed with cancer. They married soon thereafter but she died within a year. The experience inspired the content and tone of *Earthbound,* Mann's second record, released in May of 1998. As Mann observed in his record company biography, *"Earthbound* came from the up-and-down life juggling that I've been through.... In my own way, sharing my experience helps me honor Rema, and that feels good to me."

Recorded with well-known producer David Kershenbaum (Tracy Chapman, Joe Jackson) in only three days, *Earthbound* teamed Mann with a group of childhood musician pals from Philadelphia, including bassist Adam Dorn, background vocalist Brett "Dig" Laurence, guitarist Paul Pimsler, and drummer Steve Wolf. The fact that they performed in a band together when they were 12-year-olds made the recording process easier—and more enjoyable. "After recording, we were all so wired nobody could sleep," Mann said in his biography. "What was mind-boggling was that it got to tape so naturally. Knowing each other so well, I think, made it all come together."

The record not only teamed Mann with old friends, but also allowed him to work with newer acquaintances, perhaps most notably, the renowned singer-songwriter Carole King. King added back up vocals to the songs "Mary on My Mind" and "Numb Heart," as well as piano and vocals to "What Have I Got to Lose?", which she co-wrote with Mann and Mark Hudson. "Having Carole as a mentor has taught me many lessons, but mostly to rely more on a song's emotional impact and less on the production," says Mann.

While Mann has made a host of inroads for himself as a solo artist, he has continued to focus on songwriting and collaborations with others as well. His credits include penning tunes for the likes of Diana King and Chaka Khan, and he co-wrote the song "Treat Her Like a Lady," which appeared on Celine Dion's 1997 album, *Let's Talk About Love.* As he told Brackett, "If I could say anything to anybody trying to make music their business, I'd say write songs. You can have the voice and the act and you can have the vibe, but ultimately, you have to have those songs."

Selected discography

Billy Mann, DV8/A&M, 1996.
Earthbound, DV8/A&M, 1998.

Sources

Periodicals

Audio, July 1996, p. 81.
Billboard, June 8, 1996, p. 8.
Chicago Sun Times, March 31, 1996.
Entertainment Weekly, April 5, 1996, p. 80.
Glamour, June 1996.
Musician, November 1995.
Philadelphia Daily News, April 2, 1996.
Time Out New York, May 8, 1996.

Additional information provided by A&M Records publicity materials, 1997 and 1998.

—K. Michelle Moran

Malcolm McLaren

Singer, songwriter, producer

Malcolm McLaren has been described as the "P.T. Barnum" of modern rock for his talent in promoting a number of new musical trends, and while the term "Impresario" has been usually found next to his name since his first success with the late Seventies British punk rockers the Sex Pistols, McLaren has also enjoyed a successful solo recording career on his own. Because of his legendary connection to the early days of punk, McLaren is both a reviled and revered figure—one who might be viewed, as art critic Michael Boodro put it in *ARTnews,* as "an impresario of frustration and energy and anger, and his service, if any, has been to endow lost an struggling youth with an outlet and an affirmation of their embittered feelings. He paid attention when no one else did...."

McLaren was born in London in 1946, and grew up in the household of his grandmother. As a young adult, he studied art at several London-area schools, including St. Martin's School of Art, Chiswick Polytechnic (from which he was expelled in 1966), and Harrow Art College. He was greatly influenced by the student riots in Paris in May of 1968, in which radical youths literally took over some streets of the French capital and a number of labor strikes brought it to a standstill. As a result of this, McLaren became involved in radical art movement known as Internationale Situationist, which staged "happenings" and utilized slogans designed to provoke outrage. It was around this time that he met Vivienne Westwood, an aspiring fashion designer.

As a college student—his last foray was Goldsmiths' College from 1969-71—McLaren admittedly spent much of the stipend he received from the government on rock records. When his collection began to number into the thousands, he decided to open a store on King's Road, a hip street in London. That store evolved into Let It Rock in 1972, which sold not just vinyl but outrageous clothing created by Westwood. Another reincarnation of the store with Westwood opened in 1973: Too Fast Too Young To Die. McLaren and Westwood were determined to create their own "anti" fashion. They destroyed brand-new t-shirts, for instance, and put up them for sale; they were also purveyors of rubber fetish gear and dog collars. Such items, common in most suburban shopping malls by the 1990s, were considered shocking and rather perverted at the time. Disaffected urban youth in England, living under some of the worst economic conditions since World War II, were drawn to such politically-charged, anti-establishment fashion statements in large numbers.

The growing fame of his store lured rock stars and iconoclasts of all stripes, and an American band visiting London, the New York Dolls, made a great impression on McLaren. They dressed in outrageous, glitter-bedecked costumes and teetered on platform heels, and even wore makeup. For a time in 1974, McLaren went to New York City to manage them; he wanted to make them Mao-inspired revolutionary rockers, but the band was less than enthusiastic about the idea. Back in London, he and Westwood opened another version of their store, which they called Sex, and McLaren began looking for a band to work with who could serve as fronts for his ideas about music—it would be a band possessing little musical talent, but with a propensity for stirring up public outrage—in other words, "a group whose music was so bad that everybody wanted to hear it," as McLaren explained in a 1997 *New Yorker* article.

"A Lovely, Deadly, Sexy Chaos"

In 1975, he found half his band by corralling two young men who sometimes brought stolen music gear to his Sex shop for resale, according to the *New Yorker* article; one day one of them, John Lydon, sang an Alice Cooper song along with the jukebox in the store. "He was angry and the anger was clearly masking a shyness that made him appear vulnerable and, in some way, cool," McLaren wrote. Lydon, soon to be known as "Johnny Rotten," would become the lead singer for the Sex Pistols. "The sound he brought to the group wasn't melodic.... He

For the Record . . .

Born January 22, 1946, in London, England; children: one son, Joe. *Education:* Attended St. Martin's School of Art, Chiswick Polytechnic, Croyden College of Art, Harrow Art College, and Goldsmiths' College.

Owned the London boutiques Let It Rock, 1972-73; Too Fast Too Young To Die, 1973-74; Sex, 1974-76; and Seditionaries, (1976; he was also involved in documentary filmmaking and costume design; served as head of development for CBS Theatrical Productions, 1985; manager of New York Dolls, 1974; manager of Sex Pistols, 1975; released first solo effort, "You Need Hands," 1979; manager of Bow Wow Wow and Adam Ant, 1980; released single "Buffalo Gals," 1981; released first LP, *Duck Rock,* on Island Records, 1983.

Awards: Gold Lion, Cannes International Advertising Film Festival, 1989.

Addresses: Record company—Atlantic Records, 75 Rockefeller Plaza, New York, NY 10019.

created anthems of despair—loud, relentless, unforgiving," he wrote in the *New Yorker*. McLaren rounded out the band with Steve Jones, Paul Cook, and a guitar player who took the name Sid Vicious. Early Sex Pistols shows attracted attention for their disgusting stage antics. Rotten and Vicious insulted the audience and were known to spit on them; fans went wild. "Their sounds was raw, noisy, and poorly played, and always on the verge of collapsing entirely," McLaren wrote in the *New Yorker*. "It was chaos—a lovely, deadly, sexy chaos, wicked and nihilistic and, at the same time, utterly cataclysmic."

McLaren was skilled in stirring up publicity for the band, which soon joined a growing musical movement in England that came to be collectively termed "punk"; punk followed the same principals as McLaren's clothing—to do it yourself, and make it as ugly as possible. In the summer of 1977, during the national holiday celebration of Queen Elizabeth II's silver jubilee, McLaren chartered a boat to cruise down the Thames River past thousands of spectators; the Sex Pistols were on board and played their own version of England's national anthem, "God Save the Queen"; the most famous lines in the Sex Pistols' version were "No future.... and England's dreaming!" McLaren was arrested for this stunt. The record featured a cover depicting the Queen with a safety pin through her nose; the single was banned from radio airplay but sold millions.

Pistols went Out with Bang

McLaren engineered generous contracts record labels in England and the United States for the band, but both companies fired them, which launched a legal tangle that would last several years. In 1978, they embarked upon an American tour, which attracted massive publicity, but McLaren was unable to keep the quartet, barely out of their teens, from self-destructing. Later that year Rotten launched a court battle against McLaren over use of the band's name, and also made accusations of financial mismanagement. Then Vicious, a known heroin addict, was suspected of killing his American girlfriend in New York City; he was free on bail when he died of an overdose in early 1979.

Over the next few years McLaren occupied himself with writing a film about the Sex Pistols, titled *The Great Rock & Roll Swindle,* and was involved in the early Eighties music acts Adam Ant and Bow Wow Wow, which featured a 14-year-old singer. When he traveled to the U.S. with the latter act, McLaren discovered urban music and the fledgling rap genre. He began making recordings on the street, particularly in the South Bronx, which was ground zero for the trend during this era. He also began traveling to Africa and recording live performances there. The result was the 1983 album *Duck Rock,* which was a radical blend of traditional pop with world-beat music; later in the decade, more established musicians such as Peter Gabriel and Paul Simon would follow in his wake to far greater commercial success. "Punk It Up," a McLaren song on *Duck Rock,* would be cited at the time by Robert Palmer of the *New York Times* as "one paradigm for what is shaping up as an important pop-music trend—cross-cultural fusion, the meeting of ethnic and street cultures with Western technology and pop sensibility."

Operas and Waltzes

Another track, the square-dance inspired "Buffalo Gals," became a huge dance club hit. McLaren followed with two more albums along the same vein, *D'ya Like Scratchin'* and *Scratchin',* but in 1984 again broke new ground with the album *Fans.* Its genesis lay with his obligation to Island Records to make one more record: the label wanted him to do love songs, but McLaren won approval to adapt classic arias from famous operas instead. His hip-hop beat/blues-inflected reworkings of songs from composers Georges Bizet and Giacomo Puccini, among others, were loosely grouped around a tale of zealous groupies who kidnap their favorite rock star; he hoped to one day create an actual work for the stage. *Fans* became a huge international seller, and McLaren's version of Puccini's *Madam Butterfly*, on which McLaren himself sang the part of a World War II-era American soldier, gave the unlikely singer another chart hit.

By the mid-1980s McLaren had separated from Westwood and relocated to Hollywood, where for a time he served as head of development for CBS Theatrical Productions. He also began writing music for television advertisements and even won an industry award in 1989 for a British Airways spot. That same year, he attempted to re-create the success of *Fans* with an adaptation of an even catchier musical form—the waltz. His Epic release, *Waltz Darling,* was described as "Strauss meets house," and featured guitarist Jeff Beck and P-Funk's Bootsy Collins. It failed to achieve the success of *Fans,* however. By the mid-1990s, McLaren was living in France, and released the *Paris* record in 1995. It was a homage to the sultry French chanteuses of 1950s, and he sang a duet with Francoise Hardy titled "Revenge of the Flowers." It sold well in Europe. In 1998, McLaren was back behind the scenes with his launch of the Asian girl-group Jungk, whose music was disco-influenced but with a modern "jungle" twist. He also planned to re-release the *Buffalo Gals* album later in 1998.

McLaren's influence on the culture of alternative music is undeniable, especially in relation to its dependency on fashion and style to sell records and promote new trends. He was even feted with a 1988 exhibit, "Impresario: Malcolm McLaren and the British New Wave," at New York's New Museum of Contemporary Art. "He is the underside of the dream of youth, a Dick Clark from hell who has left in his wake not just the punk paraphernalia ... but a legacy of cynicism and destruction in which the role of the artist is fundamentally changed and debased," wrote Boodro in *ARTnews.*

Selected discography

D'ya Like Scratchin', Island, 1983.
Duck Rock, Island, 1983.
Scratchin', Virgin, 1984.
Fans, Island, 1984.
Swamp Thing, Island, 1985.
Waltz Darling, Epic, 1989.
Round the Outside! Round the Outside!, Virgin, 1990.
Paris, V2, 1994.
The Largest Movie House in Paris, Noi, 1996.
World Famous Supreme Team Show, Atlantic, 1996.

Other

Appears on Sex Pistols, *The Great Rock & Roll Swindle,* 1979.
(Producer) Bow Wow Wow, *Girl Bites Dog,* EMI, 1993.

Sources

Periodicals

Advertising Age, November 18, 1990, p. 51.
ARTnews, January 1989, pp. 114-117.
Billboard, March 9, 1985, p. 50.
New York, September 12, 1988, pp. 28, 32.
New York Times, July 13, 1983, p. C20; November 7, 1984, sec. III, p. 25.
New Yorker, September 22, 1997, pp. 90-102.
Village Voice, November 28, 1995, p. 53.

Online

"The Roughguide to Rock," *Malcolm McLaren,* http://www.roughguides.com/rock,
(May 2, 1998).
"Malcolm McLaren--An Autochronology," http://www.malcolmmclaren.com, (May 2, 1998)

—Carol Brennan

Ian McCulloch

Singer, songwriter

Ian McCulloch has had a difficult time separating himself from the band he fronted for most of the eighties, Echo and the Bunnymen. The Liverpool post-punkers achieved phenomenal success as a pop band in England in the 1980s and simultaneously as a proto-alternative band on North American shores; their music was often compared to U2. McCulloch, however, emerged as the classic new wave sex symbol, adored for his big messy haircut and pouty lips as much as his bewitching voice. His talent for penning arty, pensive lyrics also brought renown but McCulloch became known for his excess of words in his dealings with the press; he often launched diatribes against other bands—most notably U2. In 1997, McCulloch reunited with his band after several years as a solo artist for the first Echo and the Bunnymen studio album in almost a decade and he used the occasion to revisit the topic of U2: "I said that they appealed to the lowest-common-denominator emotions and were flag-waving born-agains, and now they're the born-again Village People," he told *Billboard* writer Craig Rosen.

McCulloch was born in 1959 and grew up around the Liverpool area. He knew fellow alternative musician Julian Cope as a teen and at one point was in a band called the Crucial Three with him; later McCulloch would say that Cope—whom many in the music industry despise—took songs of his and put them on later solo albums. McCulloch went on to form a band with a local guitarist, Will Sergeant, and a bass player named Les Pattinson; they took their name from the "Echo" label on their drum machine, but later replaced it with actual drummer Pete DeFreita. By 1980, they had a contract with Sire and had released *Crocodiles,* which brought them extraordinary acclaim. A string of other commercially successful and critically lauded releases followed, such as 1983's *Porcupine* and *Songs to Learn and Sing* from 1985. As with other British acts such as the Smiths, U2, and the Cure, Echo and the Bunnymen were well received on American shores and acquired a loyal fan base during the 1980s—though few American radio stations during this era had playlists that accommodated such "alternative" acts.

From these early days, McCulloch emerged as the photogenic, talkative, sometimes inebriated lead singer whom some compared to the late Doors singer Jim Morrison. McCulloch would later admit to using his looks to his advantage, after only becoming narcissistic and conceited as self-defense against his own insecurity in the first place. He sometimes endured criticism from his bandmates, who, as he recalled in an interview with *Melody Maker*'s Simon Reynolds, would say "'Oh, look at the state of you.' I'd sit back and think, 'If it wasn't for my haircut and my lips, we wouldn't have the houses that we've got.'"

Still, though Echo and the Bunnymen never achieved the mainstream, international success that U2 or Simple Minds did during the eighties, McCulloch and his bandmates would later be termed, by *New York Times* writer Ann Powers, as "leaders in the early-80s romanticization of punk that became New Wave." She also noted that "Echo and the Bunnymen's appeal always rested in its ability to mix a certain loutish charm with an artier aura," and found their Nineties heirs in Oasis; McCulloch professed in another interview to admire that band's lead singer, the similarly loutish, handsome, opinionated, and unabashed substance abuser Liam Gallagher.

Yet as the eighties neared to a close, McCulloch grew dispirited with the lack of creative progression in Echo and the Bunnymen. Songs such as "Bring on the Dancing Horses," from 1985, and "Lips Like Sugar, a single released two years later, achieved Top 40 success but were not considered representative of the band's talents. In 1989, McCulloch went into the studio alone to record a solo effort, *Candleland.* Released that same year, its making was interrupted by two tragedies: the death of McCulloch's father and the fatal motorcycle accident that killed Echo and the Bunnymen drummer Pete DeFreita. Not surprisingly, *Candleland* had some somber moments. *Melody Maker* reviewer Ted Mico

For the Record . . .

Born May 5, 1959; married; wife's name, Lorraine; one child, a daughter, born in the early 1990s.

Member of the Crucial Three with Julian Cope in the late 1970s; became lead singer for Echo and the Bunnymen, released debut album *Crocodiles* on Sire, 1980; released first solo LP, *Candleland* on Reprise, 1989; reunited with former Echo and the Bunnymen guitarist Will Sergeant to form Electrafixion, 1995; reunited with Sergeant and a third Echo bandmate to re-form the Bunnymen, 1997.

Addresses: *Record company*—London Records, 825 8th Ave., New York, NY 10019.

found praise for McCulloch's lyrics, but faulted the songs and delivery he tagged with words such as "lugubrious" and "insufferable." Guest musicians McCulloch invited to help out on *Candleland* included the drummer for Cure and Liz Fraser of the Cocteau Twins. "The good news for McCulloch fans is that a sizeable chunk of his solo album sounds like a fair facsimile of the Bunnymen," opined Mico—but added, "the bad news for McCulloch fans is that a sizeable chunk of his solo album sounds like a fair facsimile of the Bunnymen."

The following year, Sergeant, Pattinson, and a new drummer released an album under the Echo and the Bunnymen name, an act that was met with rancor by the outspoken McCulloch. He recalled in a 1995 interview with Rosen of *Billboard* that the betrayal hurt. "I felt let down. It was the worst idea possible." Not surprisingly, the McCulloch-less *Reverberation!* was largely ignored, and McCulloch himself fared better with his second solo effort, 1992's *Mysterio. Melody Maker* writers the Stud Brothers termed it "a far cry from the morbid excesses of his first solo venture." One track, "Lover Lover Lover," did well on the charts and on newly-emergent alternative radio in North America, but it was actually a cover of a Leonard Cohen song. The legendary Canadian songwriter, along with Lou Reed and David Bowie, are usually cited by McCulloch as the most profound influences on his own efforts.

Next, McCulloch collaborated with former Smiths guitarist Johnny Marr, but the tapes from their studio hours were supposedly stolen; there were rumors that the pair simply argued so badly that little came of it. Yet

McCulloch told Rosen in the 1995 *Billboard* interview that the experience "showed me again that writing with someone is more enjoyable." It led McCulloch back to Sergeant and a reconciliation—the two had not spoken to one another in four years—and they created a new band they called Electrafixion. It debuted in 1995 with the *Zephyr* EP and then the full-length *Burned*. "Far funkier than anything the Bunnymen had attempted," opined *Addicted to Noise* writer Johnny Walker, "this fine effort features a new, more lyrically down-to-earth Mac and a more prominent, and a more wildly inventive than ever Sergeant." *Billboard*'s Rosen asserted that "the album rocks harder than most of the Bunnymen's recordings."

McCulloch came full circle in 1997 with a regrouping of the surviving Bunnymen. He and Sergeant invited Pattinson back into the fold and borrowed drummer Michael Lee from the Jimmy Page and Robert Plant tour. The first new Echo and the Bunnymen album in nine years, *Evergreen* was released that same year. Their new corporate home, London Records, allowed them full reign in the studio to produce it themselves. The label switch was the result of perhaps a too-long relationship with Sire—part of the Warner/Elektra family—as McCulloch explained to Rosen in *Billboard,* "when you're with someone like that for that long, they kind of lose the sense of what they are supposed to do with you." *Evergreen* was well received. Rosen declared it "evokes the lush atmospherics of late-period Bunnymen," and in a review of a live performance in support of the record later that year, *New York Times* writer Powers found the stage show lacking, but McCulloch's voice the best part--"a still compelling, hearty working man's tenor."

McCulloch's ill-fated collaboration with Johnny Marr did result in one unusual release—one song, "How Does It Feel (To Be on Top of the World)," was selected as England's theme song for the World Cup '98 soccer games. McCulloch recorded it under the name "England United" along with the Spice Girls. He apparently has little desire to retire. "Music gives me a reason to handle everyday life," McCulloch said in the 1992 interview with the Stud Brothers in *Melody Maker*. "It gives me a position, and it lets me feel like I did when I was 13, when I felt apart from all my mates who were into Queen. So I can't seem myself stopping, really ... not ever."

Selected discography

Solo

Candleland, Reprise, 1989.
Mysterio, Sire, 1992.

With Sergeant as Electrafixion

Zephyr (EP), Spacejunk/WEA, 1995.
Burned, Sire/EEG, 1995.

With Echo & the Bunnymen

Crocodiles, Sire, 1980.
Heaven Up Here, Sire, 1981.
Porcupine, Sire, 1983.
Echo and the Bunnymen (EP), Sire, 1983.
Ocean Rain, Sire, 1984.
Songs to Learn and Sing, Sire, 1985.
Echo & the Bunnymen, Sire, 1987.
Evergreen, London Records, 1997.

Sources

Books

Weisbard, Eric with Craig Marks, eds., *Spin Alternative Record Guide,* Vintage Books, 1995.

Periodicals

Billboard, April 4, 1992, p. 46; August 12, 1995, p. 9; June 14, 1997, pp. 11, 14.
Guitar Player, July 1995, p. 23.
Melody Maker, July 30, 1983, p. 24; September 29, 1984, pp. 24-26; September 23, 1989, p. 33; September 30, 1989, pp. 32-34; January 25, 1992, pp. 30-31.
New York Times, October 29, 1997, p. E5.

Online

An Addicted to Noise feature interview with McCulloch; *Mac the Mouth is Back,* http://atn.addict.com/issues/2.01/Features/Electrafixion/, (June 1, 1998).
A June 1996 interview with McCulloch published in the Vancouver-based magazine Dropd
at http://www.dropd.com/issue/12/Electrafixion/index.html, (June 1, 1998).
The official Echo and the Bunnymen site at http://www.bunnymen.com, (June 1, 1998).

—Carol Brennan

Anne Sophie Mutter

Violin

German violinist Anne Sophie Mutter's trademark qualities were described by Anthony Tommasini in the *New York Times* as, "rich yet focused (in) tone, striking varieties of sound, articulate yet supple rhythmic play.... Her increasing work in recent years with living composers has brought a new kind of intellectual energy to her playing." Mutter performed magnificently throughout a "Beethoven: Face to Face" world tour in 1998, performing and simultaneously recording for Deutsche Grammophon all ten of Beethoven's violin sonatas. Mutter is lauded for her imaginative and accomplished playing, but she is also noted for her sophisticated beauty. Tommasini wrote, "Special lighting onstage drew attention to Ms. Mutter's glamour. In her sleek, shoulderless gown, with her auburn hair pulled back, she could have turned heads on Oscar night. But, as usual, it took just a few phrases for Ms. Mutter to establish that she is a thoughtful, dedicated artist." James R. Oestreich wrote in the *New York Times*, "The more Ms. Mutter trades on a glamorous image, it seems, the more surely she is recognized for her essential seriousness as an artist and a person."

Mutter was born in 1964 and spent her teen years and early 20s as a protegee of famed Austrian conductor Herbert von Karajan. She is often described as intense, an adjective she often uses to describe herself both artistically and personally in interviews as well. Much of her musical intensity was derived from her time spent with von Karajan, as he would rehearse tirelessly at an elderly age—with painstaking precision—to improve upon an already acceptable piece. His absolute will and determination impressed Mutter at a young age, and she is now known for being equally precise with herself and for devoting herself entirely to her music. She told Oestreich, "It was incredibly touching to see (Karajan), who was not very young anymore, going on stage at ten o'clock in the morning and rehearsing the piece the orchestra had played so gloriously the evening before. Nobody would have thought there was anything you could possibly do better, and he started again from scratch."

American pianist Lambert Orkis, Mutter's musical partner, has attested to the fact that Mutter shares von Karajan's work ethic. He told Oestreich, "There's something to be said for this endless polishing. What comes to mind is Michelangelo and the Pieta ... how he would be on his way to something else and go by and give it a few more polishes. It's never quite finished. That's the beauty of this music." Much of Mutter's work throughout the 1990s was dedicated to contemporary music, playing works by Witold Lutoslawski, Norbert Moret, Wolfgang Rihm, and others. She anticipates new works from Andre Previn, Pierre Boulez, and Sofia Gubaiduline. Change and growth have marked Mutter's professional course even though she was blessed with a pure, beautiful tone at the onset—which would have allowed her to coast effortlessly through a lucrative career. The fact that she kept expanding her repertory and technique and searched for ways to grow defines her more than anything else.

Kurt Masur led the New York Philharmonic in Mutter's recording of the "Brahms Violin Concerto" in 1997; he told Oestreich in 1998, "I followed her in those early years, but her playing today has nothing to do with her childhood. She is not only serious but deeply profound. Very few people could do what she does in Beethoven and Brahms, not just playing it but bringing a depth of philosophy to understand what these composers wanted to tell us. And yet there is still a kind of innocence in her playing." Mutter has attributed her style to her time spent working on contemporary music which provided the impetus for her deep interest in analyzing, understanding, and reading a score. She told Oestreich, "When you have to learn a completely new piece, a foreign language for which you have nearly no clue at all, you have to be much more precise in your research than you would in approaching a style period with which you have grown up.... Much of what we have grown up with we don't analyze anymore. We don't put question marks."

Born 1964; married Detlef Wunderlich, 1989; two children, daughter named Arabella.

Spent her teen years and early 20s as a protegee of famed conductor Herbert von Karajan; began recording with Karajan, 1978; released more than 22 recordings since then; collaborated with American pianist Lambert Orkis, 1988; performed the "Beethoven: Face to Face" world tour with Orkis, 1998; simultaneously recorded world tour for Deutsche Grammophon

Addresses: *Record company*—Deutsche Grammophon/ Polygram, 825 Eighth Avenue, New York, NY 10019, (212) 333-8000.

confided with Oestreich saying, "The wonderful thing about playing these sonatas in the composed order is that you really get into the right state of mind. In the 'Sonata No. 10', for example, after having played all nine of the others, you are physically stressed, and therefore you have the peace of mind, the tranquillity you need for the last sonata. It's like climbing the mountain for real, not just faking that you did it when you actually got there by helicopter."

Mutter has planned a program of song and dance anchored by the forthcoming new piece by Andre Previn in 1999 and, in the year 2000 she plans to present a five-program retrospective of the musical 20th century, complete with a new sonata by composer Penderecki. She also plans to become involved in a piano trio if she can find the right cellist, and her standards are exacting. When speaking to Oestreich about the incredible energy Rostropovich still has at the age of 71, she revealed a bit about herself by saying, "It's obviously something he was born with, but it's also something which is essential to his playing and essential to music altogether. If you don't burn from both ends, then why do it? Why bother?"

Mutter married Karajan's former lawyer, Detlef Wunderlich, in 1989. He died in 1995, leaving her alone with two young children. Mutter guards her private life zealously, but Kurt Masur speculated when speaking to Oestreich that personal difficulties may have had a deepening effect on her musical interpretations. Mutter did tell Oestreich that she was delighted when she saw her six year old daughter Arabella dancing to the "Berg Violin Concerto." An English reviewer found Mutter's Deutsche Grammophon recording of Sarasate's "Carmen Fantasy" and other supposedly light pieces far too overpowering and intense. Mutter's response to the reviewer when speaking with Oestreich was, "Poor man. The singer of Carmen is a very intense woman. Maybe a woman with whom some men cannot deal, but that doesn't make her too intense." In a way, this sentiment sums up Mutter's approach to her work and life as well. She highlights her glamour, knowing full well it couldn't overshadow her artistry and talent, and she throws herself into her work as passionately as she guards her private life. She's a professional in every sense of the word.

Mutter has worked with her collaborator, American pianist Lambert Orkis, since 1988. For their "Beethoven: Face to Face" tour, they decided to perform at least five of Beethoven's ten violin sonatas in one performance, which constitutes a solid two hours of weighty music. Mutter and Orkis wanted to present the body of music not only in chronological order but also in coherent stylistic groupings, disregarding their physical ease of performance or the audience comfort level. Mutter

Selected discography

with von Karajan

Mozart, Berliner Philharmoniker-Karajan, Deutsche Grammophon, 1978.

Beethoven, Berliner Philharmoniker-Karajan, Deutsche Grammophon, 1980.

Mendelssohn and Bruch, Berliner Philharmoniker-Karajan, Deutsche Grammophon, 1981.

Brahms, Berliner Philharmoniker-Karajan, Deutsche Grammophon, 1982/1983.

Vivaldi: The Four Seasons, Wiener Philharmoniker-Karajan, EMI, 1984.

Tschaikowsky, Wiener Philharmoniker-Karajan, Deutsche Grammophon, 1988.

Romance, Berliner Philharmoniker-Wiener Philharmoniker-Karajan, Deutsche Grammophon, 1995.

Masters, Berliner Philharmoniker-Karajan, Deutsche Grammophon, remastered older recordings from 1981 and 1982.

with Others

Philharmonia Orchestra-Muti, EMI, 1982.
Brahms: The 3 violin Sonatas, EMI, 1983.
Bach: Violin Concert, EMI, 1983.
Lalo and Sarasate Orchestre National de France-Ozawa, EMI, 1985.
Strawinsky and Lutoslawski, Deutsche Grammophon, 1988.

Prokofiev (National Symphony Orchestra-Rostropovitch), Erato, 1989.

Beethoven: Die Streichtrios (The String Trios), Deutsche Grammophon, 1989.

Academy of St. Martin in the Fields-Marriner, EMI, 1991.

Bartok and Moret Boston (with Symphony Orchestra-Ozawa), Deutsche Grammophon, 1991.

Berg and Rihm (withChicago Symphony Orchestra-Levine), Deutsche Grammophon, 1992.

The Berlin Recital, Anne-Sophie Mutter and Lambert Orkis, piano, Deutsche Grammophon, 1993.

Carmen-Fantasie (with Wiener Philharmoniker-Levine), Deutsche Grammophon, 1993.

Sibelius (Staatskapelle Dresden-Previn), Deutsche Grammophon, 1995.

Sources

Periodicals

The New York Times, April 24, 1998; April 16, 1998; April 12, 1998.

Online

http://www.silcom.com/~craig/anne-sophie.
http://www.cdnow.com/cgi-bin/mserv and http://www.allmusic.com/cg/amg.exe

—B. Kimberly Taylor

Iggy Pop

Rock singer

Often dubbed "the godfather of punk rock" by critics and fans, singer Iggy Pop became an immediate cult figure in the late 1960s as a member of the Stooges, a boundary-breaking rock band known for its ear-splitting guitars and nihilistic attitude. Although never a major commercial draw, the Stooges' influence on later generations is inestimable. After the Stooges dissolved in the early 1970s, Pop went on to create a number of striking solo albums with the aid of British pop innovator David Bowie. However, by the end of the decade it seemed to many that Pop had begun to mellow and had been eclipsed by the very decadent thrash of punk rock that the Stooges had helped inspire. By the mid-1980s, Pop impressed listeners once again with a string of albums that were still angst-ridden, if somewhat slicker than before.

Iggy Pop, born James Jewel Osterberg, grew up in a trailer park in the college town of Ann Arbor, Michigan. As a teenager, the disenchanted Pop played drums in a garage band called the Iguanas, and after dropping out of the University of Michigan, in a blues band called the Prime Movers. He moved to the South Side of Chicago in 1966 to take in that city's rich blues scene but returned to Ann Arbor the following year. Christening himself Iggy Stooge, Pop then joined brothers Ron and Scott Asheton, who played guitar and drums respectively, and bassist Dave Alexander to form the Stooges.

The Stooges made their live debut on Halloween in 1967 and made no haste in raising the eyebrows of local rock fans. Aside from the New York band Velvet Underground and fellow Ann Arborites the MC5, few rock bands could have prepared listeners for the Stooges' brand of potent, feedback-edged guitar crunch. Perhaps even more shocking, though, was Pop's riotous onstage antics which more than matched the fury of the group's music. Screaming, diving into broken glass, and smearing his body with raw meat, Pop marked the dawn of a new chapter of disillusionment and outrage in the history of rock. Nevertheless, Pop later told Kurt Loder in *Rolling Stone* that "I never felt like a self-destructive person when I started out. I admit that I may have been the first performer to vent his immediate angers in this format —if I was pissed off, I sang about it. But that was only part of it."

After gaining a regional reputation, the Stooges were signed to Elektra in 1968, and a year later their self-titled debut hit record stores. Although the record sold only marginally, it developed a strong cult following but, more importantly, *The Stooges* was a revelation for the next generations of young musicians tired of the often banal nature of commercial rock. The Stooges would become a key influence for the first wave of punk rock

For the Record . . .

Born James Jewel Osterberg, April 21, 1947, in Ann Arbor, MI.

Joined the Stooges in 1967, who released their self-titled debut two years later; released *Funhouse* in 1970; recorded last Stooges album *Raw Power*, 1973; traveled to Berlin, Germany with David Bowie where the two recorded Pop's solo albums *The Idiot* and *Lust For Life,* 1977; Pop tours the U.S. and Europe with Blondie, 1977; signs with Arista in 1979 and records *New Values*; published autobiography *I Need More,* 1982; performed the title song for and made a cameo in the film *Repo Man,* 1984; returned to recording with *Blah Blah Blah* on A&M, 1986; recorded critically acclaimed album, *Brick By Brick,* 1990; released *American Caesar,* 1993; released *Naughty Little Doggie,* 1996.

Awards: Brick Video Music Awards, Best Video by a Male Vocalist and Best Rock Video for "Home;" Hall of Fame Award for *Brick By Brick,* 1990.

Addresses: *Record company*—Virgin, 30 west 21st Street, New York, NY 10010.

groups, both in form and content. To wit, one can easily draw a direct line between the "no future for you" chorus of punk legends the Sex Pistols' 1977 "God Save The Queen" and the Stooges' "1969," in which Pop drones: "Another year for me and you/Another year with nothing to do."

Although *The Stooges* was nothing short of a musical revolution—with tracks like "No Fun" and "I Wanna Be Your Dog" later becoming standard cover fare for underground bands—its sequel, *Funhouse,* released in 1970, was even more impressive. Subsequently noted by many critics as one of the rawest, most energetic rock albums ever, *Funhouse* showed Pop's vocal style to have grown from the first album, ranging from his drawling, near-monologue singing to an ear-splitting wail. From the opener "Down On The Street" to the finale of "L.A. Blues," the album provided still more classic tunes to the underbelly of rock.

After *Funhouse,* the Stooges temporarily broke up, and Pop spent over a year trying to shake his growing heroin addiction for the first of many times. Relocating to London, England—where the Stooges had developed a sizable following—Pop met the esoteric singer David Bowie, who decided to assist Pop on his next effort. The two managed to corral all of the Stooges except for Alexander, who was replaced by Ron Asheton on bass. With new recruit James Williamson taking up lead guitar and co-writing with Pop, the newly dubbed Iggy and the Stooges recorded *Raw Power* for Columbia. At least on par with previous releases, *Raw Power* pushed the band's fixation on sex and death in the atomic age to new extremes, and once again provided a share of proto-punk anthems like "Gimme Danger," "Search and Destroy," as well as the catchy title cut. Although the album might have marked the acme of the Stooges' career, within the year the group disbanded permanently and Pop returned to his heavy heroin habit.

Solo Career Launched

In 1974, Pop moved to Los Angeles to untangle a number of legal problems left in the wake of the Stooges' breakup. After checking in and out of a mental hospital, during which time he and Williamson recorded what would later be issued as the slapdash album *Kill City,* Pop again left the U.S., this time to Berlin, Germany, with Bowie as his guide. Pop was considerably influenced by Bowie, who allegedly cajoled Pop into opting out of an early retirement. Fully collaborating with Bowie, Pop released his first two official solo albums in 1977, *The Idiot* and *Lust For Life,* revealing a persona strikingly more subdued than Iggy Stooge. Although songs like "Sister Midnight," "Lust For Life," and "The Passenger" were edgy and engaging, overall the two records had more in common, not surprisingly, with Bowie's Berlin-inspired landscapes of European decadence than with the Stooges. Despite this shift, or perhaps because of it, *The Idiot* and *Lust For Life* became the most commercially and critical successful Iggy Pop albums.

Although Pop's solo albums were a clear sign of Pop's maturity as a performer and songwriter, his onstage habits of self-mutilation, exhibitionism, and audience-heckling swelled to new proportions. Touring the U.S. and Europe with Bowie as a band member and New York's New Wave/disco group Blondie as openers, Pop demonstrated that writing catchy tunes need not entail a compromise of energy. "Rock's oldest adolescent, Iggy, wrote the book of punk and continues to do it better than most of the children he spawned," wrote *Rolling Stone*'s Kristine McKenna in response to a 1980 Los Angeles gig. "Busting the evening open with a rabid version of [1960s rock group] the Animals' 'I'm Crying,' he proved himself the consummate showman and the unstoppable animal boy he's always claimed to be." The 1978 live album *TV Eye* captured the previous year's tour, but most critics agreed that its middling audio quality did not do Pop justice.

In 1979, Pop signed to the Arista label and released a trio of albums there before moving on. The first, *New Values,* showed the singer in fine form and even yielded a minor hit within the confines of the budding medium of college radio, "Five Foot One." Unfortunately, the following releases, *Soldier* and the pseudo-dance record *Party,* were much weaker and commercially abominable. Subsequently all of Pop's Arista output was deleted in the U.S. After the Arista debacle, Pop submerged himself into heroin and alcohol while living in a squalid hotel room near New York City's Times Square. "I would try to play without drugs, and I'd get so depressed I'd just beat up on people," Pop later admitted to Rob Tannenbaum in *Rolling Stone.* "It was a disaster."

Pulling himself together and signing with the Animal label, Pop created the more satisfying *Zombie Birdhouse* in 1982, a more experimental effort that saw the singer dabbling in beat-oriented tunes with almost rapped vocals. Nevertheless, *Zombie Birdhouse* was to be Pop's last record for the next four years, although a myriad of bootleg Stooges live albums began to surface during this hiatus. While his bootleggers were busy, Pop spent time in Switzerland with Bowie and in 1984, married a Japanese woman named Suchi. In the meantime, Pop's legacy was influencing another wave of bands who pushed the drone and feedback of the Stooges to unimagined new levels, such as New York City's Sonic Youth and England's Spacemen 3 (who later covered *The Stooges*' tracks "I Wanna Be Your Dog" and "Little Doll," respectively).

Another Comeback for Pop

When Pop returned to the studio in 1986 to release the album *Blah Blah Blah,* he shocked many listeners once again, but this time around the shock stemmed from the commercial direction Pop had chosen. Produced by Bowie and featuring ex-Sex Pistol Steve Jones on bass, the mainstream oriented *Blah Blah Blah* alienated some fans who looked to Pop for abrasive, even offensive attitude. However, the majority of listeners and critics applauded the album. "*Blah Blah Blah* is no wholesale sellout," defended Kurt Loder in *Rolling Stone.* "Iggy still sings like a lion, and 'Cry For Love,' the first single, illuminates his existential stance as clearly as anything on *Raw Power* did thirteen years ago. But in its sonic details, the album is frankly designed as a crossover move — one for which Iggy has never been readier."

After *Blah Blah Blah,* Pop increased the commercial viability of his albums with guest producers and session musicians, yet still retained his cocky, sometimes adolescent, verve. Although he had finally become a bona fide mainstream rock star, Pop became outspokenly venomous towards the contemporary entertainment business. On his 1990 effort *Brick By Brick,* for example, which featured star producer Don Was and heavy-metal guitarist Slash of the heavy metal group Guns N' Roses, Pop lampooned the sleazy, show-biz world of Los Angeles with the song "Butt Town." Despite the juvenile leanings such a title suggests, critics could not fail to see Pop's maturity. As Tannenbaum wrote of *Brick By Brick* in the *Village Voice,* "[t]he mixes as clear, the tempos remain consistent even during the hard-rock interludes, the arrangements are varied, and the range of expression includes a sentimental duet with Kate Pierson of the B-52s and a marital ballad set to David Lindley's bouzouki. Almost like a real adult!"

Stooges Sound Returned

With *American Caesar,* released in 1993, Pop took a step backwards towards the sound of his earliest work, albeit while keeping his high profile as a performer. On songs like "Wild America" and "Perforation Problems," the latter about quitting heroin, Pop once again gave listeners snapshots of the seedier side of life in the U.S. with instrumentation slanted towards his classic Stooges work. "*Brick By Brick* showcased [Pop] as a classic rocker, with plenty of loud but clean guitars," posited *Stereo Review.* "*American Caesar* lets him play in the dirt. The solos here are nasty, brutish, and short — distortion and reverb rule. Iggy is definitely back, the noblest punk of them all." Mark Kemp, writing in *Rolling Stone* gave the album even greater praise: "What elevates *American Caesar* from merely a good album to a great one is that the songs are sequenced in a way that sharpens the record's dynamics—musically, stylistically, and thematically. By all appearances, this is a concept album—but the good kind."

Pop released another album in 1996, *Naughty Little Doggie,* which in comparison to *American Caesar* was less stinging in its music, if not its content. "The lyrics are twisted, but there's a lot of longing," Pop told Jim Bessman in *Billboard.* "They're about a guy in middle age who goes 'Jesus Christ! I haven't got that long, but I still want to touch people and I don't know how—or if I can get away with it!'" However autobiographical the album might have been, critics continued to marvel over Pop's ability to indeed get away with it at almost fifty years of age. "If Iggy had died ahead of schedule, he would be just another rock & roll martyr," *Rolling Stone*'s

David Fricke wrote in his review of *Naughty Little Doggie*. "Instead, the funhouse is open for business.... Celebrity is great, but survival is the best revenge."

Pop's survival alone was in fact incredible, if not miraculous, given his decades of heavy barbiturate, alcohol, and heroin intake. Still more impressive was the vitality his recorded work retained, as well as the influence it wielded. By the mid-1990s, Pop was embraced by a third generation of youth culture, this time in the form of the so-called American "grunge" scene of fuzzy guitars and flannel sweaters. And yet Pop remained as nonchalant about his laurels as ever. "I think I'm lucky I didn't get paid enough to drown in the syrup of success; I'm still really hungry," he told Kim Neely in *Rolling Stone.* "I could to relax more, I will say that. You know, if you're going to hold a bird, you still have to hold it with a certain tension, or it will fly away. But if you crush it, you're gonna kill it. I gotta learn how to hold the bird."

Selected discography

The Idiot, RCA, 1977.
Lust For Life, RCA, 1977.
TV Eye Live, RCA, 1978.
New Values, Arista, 1979.
Soldier, Arista, 1980.
Party, Arista, 1981.
Zombie Birdhouse, Animal, 1982.
Blah Blah Blah, A&M, 1986.
Instinct, A&M, 1988.
Brick By Brick, Virgin, 1990.
American Caesar, Virgin, 1993.
Naughty Little Doggie, Virgin, 1996.

with the Stooges:

The Stooges, Elektra, 1969.
Fun House, Elektra, 1970.
Raw Power, Columbia, 1973.

Sources

Billboard, October 26, 1991; January 27, 1996.
Rolling Stone, November 20, 1986; September 20, 1990; September 30, 1993; October 14, 1993; February 22, 1996.
Stereo Review, November 1993.
Village Voice, July 19, 1988; August 14, 1990; September 17, 1996.

—Shaun Frentner

Baden Powell

Guitarist

For almost half a century, the Brazilian born guitar player Baden Powell has been one of the key musicians among his country's jazz scene. However, Powell's work demonstrates a mastery of many classical guitar styles, from the South American tradition of flamenco to interpretations of the composer Johann Sebastian Bach. Nevertheless, on the whole Powell built his reputation as an innovator of bossa nova or the marriage of Brazilian sambas and jazz, often aided by the poet and lyricist Vinicius de Moraes. Although his popularity in the United States has never truly expanded beyond jazz and guitar aficionados, Powell's name has been virtually a household word in Europe from the early 1960s, when he relocated to that continent for several decades.

Born in the a small shantytown, called a *favela* in Portuguese, Powell grew up amongst a musical family. His father Lino de Aquino was a fairly successful violinist, and his grandfather had been an important orchestra leader. Seeing that the young Powell had an attraction to musical instruments—he had been caught stealing his aunt's violin—Lino decided to sent his son to study with the nationally famous composer and guitarist Jaime Florense. Florense, under the stage name of Meira, had made a name for himself in the 1940s as an accompanist for many Brazilian radio stars and immersed Powell in a vigorous diet of trade secrets of the classical musician. All the while, the budding musician was seduced by the sounds of jazz musicians such as saxophone player Charlie Parker and pianist Thelonius Monk.

By the mid-1940s, Powell had become something of a minor child star in Brazil, largely through the help of Florense. "When I was nine, my father entered me in a radio amateur hour contest—without telling me," Powell remembered to *Guitar Review* writer Brian Hodel in 1990. "I had been playing only two years, but I played well." Powell won the contest, and the publicity gave Florense a lever with which to boost his protégé into other engagements. In 1947, Powell appeared in the first ever Brazilian television program, performing jazz pieces on an electric guitar. After this point, Powell would carry out his work almost exclusively through acoustic instrumentation.

Although Powell began playing professionally at the age of fifteen, it was not until the late 1950s that he began to take himself seriously as a composer, after his song "Samba Triste" became a popular hit for the singer Lucio Alves in 1956. However, it was not until his experience with the congealing school of bossa nova found in the Bar Plaza district of Rio de Janeiro that helped Powell develop his own flavor of songwriting. While the exact origin of bossa nova is debated, it gained international fame in the 1960s through the work of artists such as Antonio Carlos Jobim, Joao and Astrud Giberto, Chico Buarque de Hollande, and Powell himself.

Became Hero among European Jazz Buffs

In the early 1960s, Powell began his partnership with Vinicius de Moraes, who was already Brazil's foremost poet. With the delicate, sometimes nostalgic mode of Powell's music accompanied by the understated lyrics of Moraes, the duo became instrumental in defining what bossa nova meant to the world. Although his reputation in his own country had peaked upon his teaming with Moraes, Powell was celebrated even more in Europe, where the cool jazz flavor of bossa nova raged in many clubs. "In Brazil the audience [for my music] is affectionate, but it is a very select group," Powell told Hodel. "In Europe, the same people who attend a rock concert will listen to [composer] Artur Rubenstein, jazz, everything. There is just so much culture!" As a result, in 1963 Powell moved to Europe, which remained his base of operations for three decades.

In Europe, Powell made a number of important bossa nova recordings, beginning with a duet recorded with

For the Record . . .

Born Roberto Baden Powell de Aquino (named after Boy Scout founder Lord Robert Baden Powell), August 6, 1937, in Rio de Janeiro, Brazil. *Education*—Studied with famed musician Jaime "Meira" Florense, 1944-1949.

Toured Brazil playing guitar at Florense's suggestion, 1947; had first success with Lucio Alves's recording of song "Samba Triste," 1956; met lyricist and partner Vinicius de Moraes, 1961; moved to Europe to record with artists such as Herbie Mann, 1963; toured Europe as a band leader, beginning in 1966; recorded in New York City with American saxophonist Stan Getz, 1967; performed at the Berlin Guitar Festival, 1967; recorded bossa nova styled album *La Grande Reunion* with Stephane Grappelli, 1974; recorded acclaimed album *Seresta Brasiliera*, 1994; released retrospective record *The Guitar Artistry of Baden Powell,* 1998.

Awards: second place in first Festival of Brazilian Popular Music for song "Valsa do Amor Que Nao Vem), written with Moraes, 1965; fourth place in Festival of Brazilian Popular Music for song "Cidade Vazia," written with Lula Freire, 1966; won French Golden Disc Award for album *Le Monde Musical de Baden Powell,* 1967; won Biennial Samba Competition with "Lapinha," written with P.C. Pinheiro, 1968.

Addresses: Record company—Iris Records, Box 422, Port Washington, NY, 11050, (516) 944-7905; *Home*—Rio de Janeiro, Brazil.

---

flutist Herbie Mann. In the meantime, bossa nova had become synonymous with a chic, cosmopolitan lifestyle, and infiltrated the rock-dominated charts in both Europe and the United States as pop groups like Sergio Mendes and Brazil '66 fused bossa nova with contemporary pop. Powell and Moraes' own composition "Samba da Bencao" ("My Heart Loves The Samba"), featured in French director Claude Lelouch's 1966 film *A Man and a Woman,* accompanied images of a young, attractive couple galloping on horseback through Brazilian grasslands and helped create an almost mythical image of Brazil for a generation of foreigners.

As one of the few guitarists in Europe who had mastered the bossa nova style, Powell was in high demand during

the 1960s and extensively toured Europe throughout that decade. Nevertheless, Powell confined himself neither to the bossa nova genre nor to the European scene. In addition to recording a number of jazz and classical guitar pieces, he shuttled back to Brazil to compete in a number of competitions, including the very first Festival of Brazilian Popular Music in 1965, where his "Valsa do Amor Que Nao Vem" placed second. Still, it was his intense take on the often laid-back bossa nova that demonstrated Powell's greatest inspiration, such as on *Afro-Samba,* an album actually recorded in a flooded studio in Rio. "The water was nearly up to our knees and we were getting shocked by the microphones, so we went to a nearby bar and borrowed wooden beer crates to stand on," Powell remembered to Hodel. "The great thing about the bossa nova days was great love – more love than professionalism. That doesn't exist anymore."

Distinguished Classical Guitarist

Throughout the 1970s, Powell continued to cut diversely styled albums in Europe, highlighted by the efforts *Solitude on Guitar* in 1971, *La grande reunion* in 1974 (recorded with vocalist Stephane Grappelli), and *Brazilian Rhythm* in 1977. While never abandoning the bossa nova, Powell made sure to offer listeners the full scope of traditional Brazilian music. As *Gramophone* said of *Brazilian Rhythms,* Powell's recorded efforts were "a delightful array of his own works and those of some fellow countrymen, demonstrating the beauty of the guitar in its pristine, unamplified state." Powell's devotion to his instrument was so great that in 1979, he needed surgery to repair parts of his rib cage that had worn away from tightly cradling his guitar. Although Powell sometimes needed to spend days lying on his back to recuperate, he chose to keep playing.

Powell began to take further steps away from the jazzier side of bossa nova in favor of an even more refined classical execution. Likewise, his live performances of the period contained less of the spontaneous musical license associated with jazz gigs. "I improvise," Powell explained to Hodel, "but I lost that jazz style improvisation because I lost the habit. I improvise well, but it's not totally jazzistic. It is in accord with the kind of music I am performing." Although Powell's new material did not place him on the vanguard of stylistic experimentation, he was respected nevertheless by jazz and classical critics alike. "With his clean, consummate technique and, more importantly, abiding musicality, Powell animates these songs with a kind of emotive power that crosses the line between classical and folk sensibilities," Josef Woodward wrote in *Down Beat.* "The intent here is not to overwhelm with virtuosity, but to find a path between twilight-like melancholy and controlled passion."

In addition to creating new albums, Powell re-released some of his back catalogue during the 1990s, making the full legacy of his work available to newer listeners. As Powell's popularity in the United States had never been level with what it was in Latin America and Europe, he also expressed interest in relocating to New York City, where Powell performed several special engagements in the early 1990s. With many young Americans delving into diverse styles of world music as an alternative to the monopoly of mainstream rock, it would not be unlikely if Powell's guitar mastery were to be embraced by yet another generation.

Selected discography

Tristeza on Guitar, Verve, 1966.
Berlin Festival Guitar Workshop, Pausa, 1967.

Le Monde Musical de Baden Powell, Barclay, 1967.
Solitude on Guitar, Columbia, 1971.
La Grande Reunion, Festival, 1974.
Brazilian Rhythms, Phillips, 1977.
Baden Powell, WEA/Atlantic, 1979 (live).
Melancolie, Accord, 1985.
Three Originals, Polygram, 1993.
Seresta Brasiliera, Milestone, 1994.
Afro Samba, Iris, 1996 (re-release).
Live In Rio, Iris, 1996,
Guitar Artistry of Baden Powell, Dom, 1998.

Sources

Down Beat, June 1994.
Gramophone, May 1977.
Guitar Review, Fall 1990.
Jazz Journal International, October 1995.
Jazz Times, May 1994.

—Sean Frentner

Prong

Rock band

In the late 1980s, New York's Prong hit the scene with a vengeance, blending their own combination of thrash, industrial, and post-punk doom. Their sound made it difficult for critics to classify them into any one particular genre, as Chris Gill wrote in *Guitar Player,* "In a world where music is segmented into countless sub-genres, Prong defies categorization." Singer and guitarist Tommy Victor, one of the group's founding members, says the group doesn't try to limit themselves by writing and recording music that fits into a particular category. "I don't want to align myself with some kind of subculture in order to get popular," Victor told *HM.* "I just want to feel good about myself ... and avoid these classifications."

Victor started his career in music as a bass player for local R&B, ska, and funk bands. He switched to guitar as he moved toward more aggressive rock music, and when he joined Prong, he decided to take on lead vocal duties, as well. At the time, he was a sound engineer at the famed CBGB's nightclub in New York. He formed the band with bassist Mike Kirkland and drummer Ted Parsons. Kirkland, who used to play with the band Damage, worked with Victor at CBGB's as a doorman, and before joining Prong, Parsons played for heavy art-rockers the Swans and studied art at the Pratt Institute in Brooklyn, New York.

The newly formed Prong trio began rehearsing together in 1986. By the following year, they had released their first album, *Primitive Origins,* on their own British label, Spigot Records. They continued to write, perform, and record, releasing their second album, *Force Fed,* the following year, this time with a U.S. distribution deal through Relativity/In-Effect Records. In 1989, Prong released *The Peel Sessions* on the Strange Fruit label, featuring four re-mixed tracks from their first two albums. The BBC originally broadcast the sessions on the John Peel show on Radio One. That same year, Prong signed their first major record label contract with Epic Records.

When they released their 1990 LP, *Beg to Differ,* Victor and Kirkland still held their jobs at CBGB's. The album included one live track, "Third from the Sun," which was recorded at CBGB's. The widespread distribution of a major label deal increased the exposure of their unique sound. Kim Neely wrote in *Rolling Stone,* "Prong's musical approach is a schizophrenic minimalism; the band pares its songs down to skeletal form and then grafts meat back onto the bone."

The following year, founding member Kirkland left the group and was replaced by former Flotsam & Jetsam bassist Troy Gregory. Once Gregory was firmly in place, Prong joined forces with producer Mark Dodson for their next release *Prove You Wrong.* Before the album was released, Gregory left the band for personal reasons. Former Killing Joke bass player Paul Raven quickly stepped in to fill Gregory's spot. It started as a temporary replacement, but the chemistry worked so well that Raven soon joined the band on a permanent basis.

Prong's next project broke new ground. *Whose Fist Is This Anyway,* included five re-mixed versions of Prong's songs recorded by various artists, plus a new song called "Talk, Talk." Once Prong released the EP, the idea took off within rock music circles. Other bands, including Nine Inch Nails, Megadeth, Pantera, and White Zombie, used the same guest re-mix concept on their own albums, yet Prong never received any recognition for the idea. "We never got any notoriety for that," Victor told Chris Gill in *Guitar Player.* "That EP went nowhere, and the label is still apologetic about it, because they realize how a lot of groups picked up on that afterwards."

Undaunted, Prong continued to tour and record, releasing *Cleansing* in 1994. *Cleansing* featured guest keyboardist John Bechdel who played in the group Murder, Inc., and was produced by Terry Date, who had previously worked with hard rockers Pantera and Soundgarden. The album showed Prong to be able song writers, as Tom Sinclair wrote in his *Entertainment Weekly* review, "What renders Prong's fury more engaging is the way it sometimes pulls honest-to-God songs out of the

For the Record . . .

Members include **Charlie Clouser**, keyboards; **Troy Gregory**, bass; **Mike Kirkland**, bass; **Ted Parsons**, drums; **Paul Raven**, bass; **Tommy Victor**, vocals and guitar.

Band formed in New York, 1986; released *Primitive Origins* on their own label, Spigot, 1987; signed to Epic Records, 1989; released major label debut, *Beg To Differ*, 1990; *Prove You Wrong*, 1991; *Whose fist is This anyway*, 1992; *Cleansing*, 1994; *Rude Awakening*, 1996.

Addresses: *Record Company*—Epic Records, P.O. Box 4450, New York, NY 10101-4450

din, proving that metal and melody don't have to be mutually exclusive." *Cleansing* begins with a song called "Another Wordly Device." According to Tommy Victor, the song establishes the concept of the rest of the album. Its lyrics revolve around the theme of eliminating outside interventions and personal obstacles from one's life. "I think there's a unique fairness to society," Victor told Chris Gill in *Guitar Player*. "I live by my own values, do my own thing, and do away with the things that are unnecessary. I'm more confident about myself because I've eliminated many obstacles."

After *Cleansing*, Victor began to reflect on his musical growth, as well. Since he had not performed as a singer before he joined Prong, he decided to spend some time developing his voice, and by the time their next album, *Rude Awakening*, was released, he had improved his abilities enough to highlight the vocals more throughout the album. In addition to Victor's vocals, Prong hooked up with Nine Inch Nails keyboardist Charlie Clouser to play on the album, which added a new dimension to their sound. "Prong has always walked the tight rope between hard rock and industrial," Sheila Rene wrote in *Rocknet*. "There's just enough on this album to keep those industrial folks happy."

After the release of *Rude Awakening*, Prong headed out on a world tour, playing throughout the U.S., Japan, and Europe. Continuing in the vein of the album, Prong hired a guitarist to perform on the tour, allowing Victor to concentrate more on his vocals in concert. During the tour, bassist Paul Raven was injured and could not continue to perform with the band in 1996. He was temporarily replaced by World of Pain bass player Vince Dennis until he could return.

Although Prong had not attained the huge commercial success of hard-edged contemporaries Nine Inch Nails or Soundgarden, they continued follow their own artistic path. They had just enough popularity to keep going without having to compromise their musical direction in order to maintain their fan base. "I'm just looking to reinvent the group constantly, without completely abandoning all that we've done," Victor told Rene in *Rocknet*.

Selected discography

Primitive Origins, Spigot, 1987
Force Fed, Relativity/In-Effect, 1988.
The Peel Sessions, Strange Fruit, 1989.
Beg to Differ, Epic Records, 1990.
Prove You Wrong, Epic Records, 1991.
Whose Fist Is This Anyway, Epic Records, 1992.
Cleansing, Epic Records, 1994.
Rude Awakening, Epic Records, 1996.

Sources

Periodicals

Billboard, December 14, 1991.
Entertainment Weekly, January 21, 1994.
Guitar Player, April 1994.
Rolling Stone, March 22, 1990; May 3, 1990.
Wilson Library Bulletin, June 1990.

Online

http://www.geocities.com/CapeCanaveral/7839/inter1.html
http://www.place2b.org/cmp/hmmag/Prong.htm
http://www.rocknet.com/may96/prong.html
http://www.xs4all.nl/~sveneric/prong/

—Sonya Shelton

Psychedelic Furs

Punk rock band

For a generation of alternative music fans in the days when the genre barely existed commercially, the Psychedelic Furs defined a particular moment of the eighties with their distinctively arty, half-pop/half-punk sound. Fronted by singer/songwriter Richard Butler, whose unique voice delivered acerbic lyrics in a less-than-perfect yet still emotionally resonant pitch, the Furs were more a superb studio band than a great live act. They also possessed a talent for being able to mine the talents of several esteemed producers early in their careers and engineer great commercial appeal. Later they seemed to lose themselves in that prosperity, especially after becoming indelibly associated with Molly Ringwald. James Hannaham, writing about the Furs' career in the *Spin Alternative Record Guide,* called them "the self-conscious post-punks who listened hardest to their marketing departments and paid for it."

The Psychedelic Furs formed in England inside the Butler household, a family headed by an iconoclastic father who, although he was a British civil servant, was also a Communist and an atheist. His sons—Simon, Tim, and Richard—inherited some of that peevishness and, around 1976, when they were nearing or past the age of about 20, they grouped together around Richard Butler's arty ideas about music. At art school he had cultivated a passion for sixties pop painter Andy Warhol, as well as for the surrealist art of the 1920s. Warhol's attempt to create the most uncommercial, unlistenable

band imaginable, evoking the ideas of the surrealists and dada artists, spawned the Velvet Underground. Butler loved the word "psychedelic" and all that it implied, and teamed the adjective with "furs," from the Velvet Underground song "Venus in Furs."

Yet in late-1970s England, anything recalling the sixties was extremely uncool and they suffered as a result when potential fans were scared off by their name. The rest of the band—most of whom were Simon Butler's friends—were admittedly talentless, as were many "punk" bands of this era and the combination of these two factors usually resulted in jeers. Their first show at a London pub, the Duke of Lancaster, was a disaster; to distance themselves they had to call themselves "The Europeans" for a time but audiences derided them nevertheless. They also had problems keeping a drummer, but managed to find a good guitarist, John Ashton, to replace Simon Butler when he quit.

Richard Butler began to display a talent for writing songs with pithy, sharp lyrical content and the band slowly gained a minor following. They obtained a steady gig at a London venue called Windsor Castle, where producer Steve Lillywhite first saw them. Soon A&R people began to show an interest and they recorded a demo, for which their new drummer showed up four hours late. They did manage to put down the tracks "Sister Europe"—which Butler had written about his girlfriend away in Italy at the time—as well as "Pulse," "We Love You," and "Fall." The demo got them a live session in June of 1979 on the famed BBC radio program hosted by John Peel. Again, their drummer was late and Peel helped them advertise for another. Once Vince Ely joined to fill that slot, things coalesced musically and they suddenly sounded much better. Ely contributed greatly to the Furs' early sound, and during the first hour of their initial meeting they all wrote "India" together. It would be the first track on their first album.

By the fall of 1979, the Furs were the hot band in London to see and soon signed to CBS/Columbia. "I don't think the record company signed us on musical abilities at all," Richard Butler told J.D. Considine in a 1987 interview in *Musician*. "It was a good time to be a band and get signed. The business didn't understand punk rock at any point, and all of a sudden they didn't know what to sign. That was when they signed some of their most interesting things." The first Furs single was "We Love You/Pulse." Their self-title debut was released in 1980. Produced by Lillywhite, who helped them define their sound in the studio, *The Psychedelic Furs* was "an album that mixed a drone-laden wall of noise (two guitars, sax and/or keyboards) and an odd adaptation of the quieter Bowie Low-style sound over which Butler rasped his lyrics in a bored, asthmatic drawl," wrote Jim Green and Ira Robbins in the *Trouser Press Record Guide.*

Butler was criticized, however, for an inability to sing on key, but he later explained to Considine in the 1987 *Musician* interview that in addition to usually being drunk for studio sessions, "I refused to go in and do [the takes] more than once.... I felt like I meant it when I sang it and that's what was important." Lillywhite also produced the next Furs album, the acclaimed *Talk Talk Talk* released in 1981. It displayed deep Velvet Underground influences and critics praised them for finally hitting solid ground musically with tracks like "Dumb Waiters" and "All of This & Nothing." The first track was "Pretty in Pink," a song about a group of young men who deride their ex, Caroline, for her "promiscuity." The melody and Butler's ironic lyrics were so catchy that both title and track were borrowed for a 1986 teen film that starred Molly Ringwald.

Their third record, 1982's *Forever Now,* was an even greater critical success, and made a heavy dent in the charts as well. Produced by Todd Rundgren, its biggest hit was "Love My Way." In the *Spin Alternative Record Guide,* Hannaham remarked that *Forever Now* "made it shockingly apparent that Butler wished to emulate not Iggy Pop but David Bowie." One fan of the record was

Melody Maker writer Steve Sutherland, who lauded the album for the way "it secretes strange, melancholy melodies ... [proving] once again, that the Furs are unique in their use of drastically damaged and reassembled past pop artillery-even their own!"

The title "Forever Now" also reflected a less astringent, perhaps even somewhat romantic Butler. He seemed to write less songs with the word "stupid" in them, and more with "love." This about-face culminated in 1984's *Mirror Moves,* for which the band enlisted the production talents of Keith Forsey, who had recently worked with Billy Idol but had great success in 1979 with the Donna Summer disco album *Bad Girls.* Tracks like "The Ghost in You" and "Heaven" did have somewhat of a disco sound, yet still sounded fresh in their day. The record was a commercial success in both the U.K. and North America, especially on some of its new "alternative" radio stations. Sutherland, reviewing it for *Melody Maker,* called *Mirror Moves* "sparkling," and noted their new producer tapped into the band's talent with a "dynamic production perfectly complementing the transparent, ozone purity of the songs."

Around this time Butler and the rest of the band moved to New York City. It would be three years before their next studio release and one that came out after the 1986 *Pretty in Pink* film made them a huge hit among the teen set. Perhaps to capitalize on this, 1987's *Midnight to Midnight* seemed to be, as Hannaham wrote in the *Spin Alternative Record Guide,* "a bid for higher sales so thinly disguised as an album that even Butler later admitted the error of his ways." The song "Heartbreak Beat" would become the Furs' biggest commercial hit, and a decade later was still a staple on alternative radio. Reviewing *Midnight to Midnight* for *Musician,* Jon Young called it "a treatise on the ever-popular anguish of amour, rendered in a suitably sophisticated Roxy-Bowie style," but he faulted Butler for "keeping an emotional distance that leaves his music dead at the center."

Perhaps the Furs' last distinctive gasp was the mid-1988 single "All That Money Wants;" they rarely played live anymore and began to fulfill some contractual obligations by putting out compilations and B-side collections. After the 1988 compilation *All of This and Nothing,* they did another studio album, *Book of Days,* released in 1989 and quickly forgotten. Its production had severely toned down Butler's voice, which had been the charm of their music in the first place. After *Crucial Music: The Psychedelic Furs Collection* in 1989, they recorded and released the studio LP *World Outside* in 1990, which had some nominal success with the single "Until She Comes." But reviewers expressed disappointment that Butler and his bandmates had not grown musically. *Rolling Stone*'s Christian Wright noted the effort's inadvertently retro appeal, and wrote of Butler's "accent still strong like a memory of England when it was somehow exotic, a little dangerous and cool." Parke Puterbaugh, critiquing *World Outside* for *Stereo Review,* echoed the sentiment, noting its reliance on evoking a black mood. "Once again, [Butler] declaims in an asthmatic, catatonic, monotone," and the rest of the band put forth "the musical equivalent of an overcast sky."

The Psychedelic Furs officially disbanded in 1993, and Richard and Tim Butler went on to form Love Spit Love shortly afterward. A 1997 retrospective, *Should God Forget: A Retrospective,* helped give the band some of their long-overdue credit as a seminal eighties presence that mixed guitars with synthesizers and emphatic, real percussion—a combination that, in its day, was practically revolutionary. Several other bands have covered their classics, including the Counting Crows ("The Ghost in You") and Live ("Love My Way").

Selected Discography

The Psychedelic Furs, Columbia, 1980.
Talk Talk Talk, Columbia, 1981.
Forever Now, Columbia, 1982.
Mirror Moves, Columbia, 1984.
Midnight to Midnight, Columbia, 1987.
All of This and Nothing, Columbia, 1988.
Book of Days, Columbia, 1989.

Crucial Music: The Psychedelic Furs Collection, CBS Special Products/Relativity, 1989.
World Outside, Columbia, 1991.
Should God Forget: A Retrospective, Columbia/Legacy, 1997.

Sources

Books

Larkin, Colin, editor, *The Guinness Encyclopedia of Popular Music,* Guinness Publishing, 1992.
Weisbard, Eric and Craig Marks, eds., *Spin Alternative Record Guide,* Vintage, 1995.

Periodicals

Melody Maker, September 25, 1982, p. 15; October 9, 1982, pp. 24-25; May 5, 1984, pp. 20-21, 27; May 12, 1984, p. 22;
Musician, February 1987, p. 106; March 1987, pp. 62-66.
Rolling Stone, August 8, 1991, p. 87.
Stereo Review, November 1991, p. 95; December 1991, pp. 112-113.

Online

http://www.talktalktalk.com ("A Shrine to Richard Butler, Love Spit Love & The Psychedelic Furs")
http://www.trouserpress.com

—*Carol Brennan*

Quicksilver Messenger Service

Rock group

Quicksilver Messenger Service was one of the most acclaimed San Francisco psychedelic rock groups from the 1960s. At its best, the band's bluesy flights of fancy were propelled by the interplay between guitarists John Cipollina and Gary Duncan. Their origins lie in the folk and rock and roll scenes in San Francisco during the early 1960s, two musical circles that rarely mixed. Cipollina recalled in *Guitar Player*, "The folk scene was going strong in San Francisco in the early 60s, and rock and roll and electric guitars were pretty much identified with greasy hair, beer, and teenage trauma." Folk singer and guitarist David Freiberg, intent on forming a band with New York folk singer Dino Valenti and singer Jim Murray, began playing with rock guitarist John Cipollina. Drummers came and went, and Freiberg switched to bass guitar. After Valenti was arrested for possession of marijuana in 1965, he was replaced by two members of the San Francisco rock group The Brogues, drummer Greg Elmore and guitarist Gary Duncan.

Freiberg explained the origin of the band's name in *Rock Names*. "Originally there were four Virgos in the band, and one Gemini. Of the four Virgos, there were only two birthdays: John and I were born on August 24, and Gary and Greg were born on September 4.... The ruling planet for Virgo in astrology is Mercury, and it is for Gemini also. So in searching for a name, we said, 'Well, let's see - mercury's the same as quicksilver, right? Mercury's the messenger god? Quicksilver Messenger Service.'"

Late in 1965, Quicksilver began rehearsing and playing live gigs. It opted, however, not to record immediately. The band had a strong local reputation, playing the Monterey Pop Festival and an appearance in the film *Revolution* in 1967 spread it's name nationally. That year, Quicksilver finally signed a recording contract with Capitol Records. At that point, Murray left, tiring of the hours of rehearsal time.

Quicksilver's self-titled debut album, released in 1968, opened with a scorching version of folksinger Hamilton Camp's "Pride of Man" and closed with the extended instrumental, "Gold and Silver." Although the album was generally well received, the band felt that its best work occurred on stage. Quicksilver Messenger Service recorded its second album *Happy Trails* live at the Fillmore West in San Francisco and the Fillmore East in New York.

Revered as a classic American psychedelic album, *Happy Trails* displayed the individual band members' strengths on the sidelong version of Bo Diddley's "Who Do You Love", while Quicksilver's ensemble playing was showcased on "Mona". It became the first of four consecutive Quicksilver records to reach the top 30 of *Billboard's* Album Charts. Following its release in 1969, Gary Duncan left the band.

In an interview on the Quicksilver Messenger Service web page, David Freiberg explained the effect of Duncan's departure, "We were trying to find a replacement for Gary.... Of course nobody showed up that could [replace him].... Duncan was the 'engine' man, it just didn't work without him ... for me." The band soldiered on with recording sessions, aided by veteran English pianist Nicky Hopkins, famous for his work with The Beatles and The Rolling Stones. Hopkins got along so well with Cipollina that he was invited to join the band. Those sessions resulted in *Shady Grove*, a new sound for Quicksilver. Gary Von Tersch commented in *Rolling Stone*, "The old Quicksilver was immediate, instrumentally flashing, and frenzied. The Quicksilver on *Shady Grove* has had its collective head turned around by Nicky Hopkins. The result is a more precise, more lyrical, more textured Quicksilver. But they pull it off quite well."

Gary Duncan returned to Quicksilver for its New Years Eve, 1970 Fillmore West show; he also agreed to return to the band provided Dino Valenti could join as well. The band agreed and relocated to Hawaii to record its next album *Just For Love*. On the runway just prior to the band's departure, bullets were found in one of the entourage's luggage. Further search revealed marijuana, resulting in the arrest of David Freiberg. Freiberg recalled about the conditions during that trip, "We picked a place to build a studio that doesn't have

Members include **John Cipollina**, (born August 24, 1943, Berkeley, CA; left group c. 1971; rejoined c. 1975; died May 29, 1989 of emphysema, San Francisco), guitar, vocals; **Gary Duncan**, (born September 4, 1946, San Diego), guitar, vocals; **Greg Elmore**, (born September 4, 1946, San Diego), drums; **Greg Errico**, drums; **David Freiberg**, (born August 24, 1938, in Boston; left group c. 1972), bass, vocals; **Jim Guyett**, bass; **Nicky Hopkins**, (born February 24, 1944, London, England; joined group, 1969, left, 1971; died September 6, 1994 of stomach illness, in Edgham, Surrey, England), piano; **Michael Lewis**, (joined, mid 70s), keyboards; **Jim Murray**, vocals, harmonica; **Mark Naftalin**, (joined group, 1971, left, 1972), keyboards; **Sammy Piazza** (joined, mid 80s), drums; **Mark Ryan**, (joined group, 1972, left, 1974), bass; **Chuck Steaks**, (joined group, 1972, left, 1974), keyboards; **Dino Valenti**, (born October 7, 1943, New York City; left group c. 1966; rejoined c. 1970; died November 16, 1994 of brain tumor, in Santa Rosa, CA), vocals, guitar, percussion; **Bobby Vega**, bass.

Group formed in San Francisco, 1966; played at Monterey Pop Festival, 1967; appeared in film *Revolution*, 1968; released first album *Quicksilver Messenger Service*, on Capitol Records, 1968; disbanded, 1975; reformed, 1986; disbanded, 1986; reformed as Quicksilver 98, 1998.

Awards: Gold album 1997 for *Happy Trails*.

electricity ... So we gotta get a generator for the electricity and it was THREE weeks before we even got started on [the album]." *Just For Love* featured Quicksilver's highest charting single, "Fresh Air."

The title track to Quicksilver's 1971 album, *What About Me*, with its socially conscious lyrics was a minor hit single. Due to Valenti's increasing domination of the band, Cipollina and Hopkins left. Freiberg was arrested once again for possession of marijuana and also left the band; following his jail sentence, he joined Jefferson Starship.

On July 3, 1971, Quicksilver Messenger Service participated in the closing week concerts at the Fillmore West in San Francisco. Judging by the two songs which appeared on the album commemorating the event, *Fillmore: The Last Days*, Quicksilver had a harder edge in live performance than in its studio albums of that period. Throughout 1971 and 1972, a period of high bandmember turnover, Quicksilver recorded two disappointing albums *Quicksilver* and *Comin' Thru*, afterwhich the band was inactive for almost two years. In 1975, the original lineup of Quicksilver, including Valenti, reunited for an album and tour before officially disbanding.

Gary Duncan reunited Quicksilver briefly in 1986 for the album, *Peace by Piece*. He has been leading a band called Quicksilver 98, playing in the spirit of the band's classic material. John Cipollina was involved in many musical activities following his tenure with Quicksilver, though he never again enjoyed as high a profile as he had with the band. He died of heart failure related to asthma in 1989. Quicksilver Messenger Service's improvisational style of its early years, the embodiment of the psychedelic San Francisco sound, as well as the folk-pop styles of later albums, assures the band of its place in rock history.

Selected discography

Quicksilver Messenger Service, Capitol, 1968.
"Stand By Me"/ "Bears", Capitol, 1968.
Happy Trails, Capitol, 1968, reissued BGO, 1992.
Shady Grove, Capitol, 1969, reissued One Way, 1992.
Just For Love, Capitol, 1970, reissued BGO, 1992.
What About Me, Capitol, 1970, reissued BGO, 1992.
Quicksilver, Capitol, 1971, reissued BGO, 1992.
(with John Cipollina), Papa John Creach, "Janitor Drives A Cadillac", Grunt, 1971.
"Fresh Air", "Mojo" and (with others) "Final Night Jam Session" (rec. 1971) from *Fillmore: The Last Days*, Fillmore, 1972, reissued Epic/Legacy, 1992.
Comin' Thru, Capitol, 1972, reissued BGO, 1992.
Anthology, Capitol, 1973, reissued BGO, 1992.
(with John Cipollina), *Copperhead*, Columbia, 1973.
Solid Silver, Capitol, 1975.
(with John Cipollina), Man, *Maximum Darkness*, United Artists, 1975, reissued BGO, 1992.
(with John Cipollina), Terry & The Pirates, *Wild Bunch*, Legend, 1979.
Peace By Piece, Capitol, 1986.
"Fresh Air", from *Electric Sixties*, JCI, 1986.
(with John Cipollina), *Dinosaurs*, Relix, 1988.
(with John Cipollina), Merrell Fankhauser, *Dr. Fankhauser*, D-Twon, 1986.
"Fresh Air", from *The Golden Age of Underground Radio*, DCC, 1991.
*The Best of Quicksilver Messenger Service 1968-1975*Son

Sons of Mercury, Rhino, 1991.
Shape Shifter, Pymander, 1996.
Live At Fieldstone 1997, Pymander, 1997.

Sources

Books

Dolgins, Adam, *Rock Names*, Citadel Press, 1993.
Erlewine, Michael, Vladimir Bogdanov, and Chris Woodstra, *The All Music Guide To Rock*, Miller Freeman, 1995.
Frame, Pete, *The Complete Rock Family Trees*, Omnibus Press, 1993.
Joynson, Vernon, *Fuzz, Acid and Flowers: A Comprehensive Guide To American Garage, Psychedelic, and Hippie Rock (1964-1975)*, Borderiline, 1994.

Periodicals

Billboard, February 7, 1970.
Guitar Player, January, 1973; August, 1989.
Melody Maker, November 7, 1970; June 10, 1989.
Rolling Stone, May 14, 1970.
Variety, February 4, 1970; November 25, 1970; March 17, 1971.

Online

"Shady Grove,' *The Quicksilver Missenger Service Web page,* www.penncen.com/quicksilver.

Additional information was gathered from the film *Survivors* and Shady Grove,

—*Jim Powers*

Bonnie Raitt

Singer, guitarist

AP/Worldwide Photos, Inc. Reproduced by permission.

Inspired by politically-themed folk music and rhythm and blues, vocalist and guitarist Bonnie Raitt perfected her own style of crossover music for some twenty years before becoming a superstar. In fact, Raitt was dropped by her record company because of poor sales prior to releasing her 1989 breakthrough album, *Nick of Time.* Soon thereafter, Robert Hilburn commented in the *Los Angeles Times,* "At 44, an age when many pop-rockers are in the twilight of their careers, Bonnie Raitt exudes the energy and ambition of someone just entering her prime—which she may well be." A performer who loves to tour, Raitt is also a tireless champion of social issues. Within the musical realm, this includes encouraging women to play the guitar and helping aging, financially-distressed blues musicians.

Raitt's husky vocals and slide guitar playing are the core of a musical style that defies categorization. As she explained in *Guitar Player,* "I'm certainly blues-based, but I've never felt that I was totally a blues artist. I've been doing the same mixture of rock and roll songs, ballads by contemporary songwriters, [and] off-the-wall jazz songs." Raitt is famous for playing bottleneck slide guitar, a technique she taught herself. And while Raitt is modest about her playing abilities—she demurred in *Guitar Player,* "I play the same Muddy Waters lick over and over"—she placed first in the magazine's readers poll for four consecutive years. For many years, Raitt specialized in playing and singing other people's songs, performing only a few of her own. But the overwhelmingly positive response to Raitt's own songs on *Nick of Time* has given her a new confidence and interest in songwriting.

Raised a Quaker, Raitt grew up in New York and Los Angeles. She began playing guitar at age nine and learned to play, in part, by copying her favorite blues recordings. Another important musical influence was, as Raitt described it in the *Los Angeles Times,* "this sort of progressive Quaker camp in the early '60s that had a lot of counselors from the East Coast colleges where a lot of interest in folk music and civil rights and the peace movement was mushrooming.... So that kind of tied music and politics together for me." The experience led Raitt down a far different musical path from that of her father, John Raitt, a musical theater star who had leading roles in the first Broadway productions of *Carousel* and The *Pajama Game* during the 1940s and 1950s. Father and daughter have widely different professional interests but have great respect for each other's talents and a mutual understanding of the desire to perform. Raitt said to her father in a New York Times interview titled "Like Father, Unlike Daughter," "I think we have the same dedication. I don't want to get another job and neither do you. We'll do anything to keep this

For the Record . . .

Born Bonnie Lynn Raitt, November 8, 1949 in Burbank, CA; daughter of John (a musical theater actor) and Marjorie (Haydock) Raitt; *Education:* Radcliffe College, Cambridge, MA; married Michael O'Keefe (actor) in April 1991.

Dropped out of college to pursue a musical career; began by performing in Boston clubs; signed with manager Dick Waterman who introduced her to legendary blues musicians; signed a recording contract with Warner Bros. and released debut album *Bonnie Raitt,* 1971; earned first gold album with *Sweet Forgiveness,* 1977; was dropped by Warner Bros. during work on her ninth album, which the company eventually released as *Nine Lives;* with a new manager and record contract with Capitol, Raitt produced *Nick of Time* with Don Was, 1989; released first live album, *Road Tested,* 1995.

Awards: Album of the year, best female rock vocal, best female pop vocal, best traditional blues recording (with John Lee Hooker), 1990; Grammy Awards, best female pop vocal, best rock performance by duo or group, 1992; Grammy Award, best pop album, 1994.

Addresses: *Record company*—Capitol Records, 1750 N. Vine St., Hollywood, CA, 90028, (213) 871-5197, fax (213) 871-5836; *Office*—P.O. Box 626, Los Angeles, CA 90078-0626.

gig." The two have performed together on "An Evening at the Pops," a 1992 concert broadcast on public television.

In 1967, Raitt began attending Boston's Radcliffe College but she soon found a greater interest in the local music scene. She met Dick Waterman, a manager who introduced her to blues greats John Hurt, Fred McDowell, and Sippie Wallace. Waterman eventually became Raitt's manager. Within a couple of years, Raitt dropped out of college to perform in folk and blues clubs. While other artists speak of the inspiration they have found in the recordings of blues musicians, Raitt met and performed with her idols, a practice she has continued throughout her career. In 1971, Raitt signed with Warner Bros. Records and released her debut album, *Bonnie*

Raitt. It was not until 1974 that Raitt began playing lead guitar, beginning with the album *Streetlights,* and touring with her own band. The next year, Raitt bought a home in Los Angeles.

Raitt produced five albums from 1971-75, containing mostly covers of blues, folk, and pop songs. Tracks included several Sippie Wallace tunes ("You Got to Know How," "Mighty Tight Woman," and "Woman be Wise") as well as songs by Joni Mitchell, John Prine , Jackson Brown, and Randy Newman. In 1977, Raitt's LP *Sweet Forgiveness* turned into her first gold album and produced a hit cover of Del Shannon's "Runaway." Raitt's interest in linking music and social causes was evident in her 1979 participation as a founding member of Musicians United for Safe Energy (M.U.S.E.). Joining M.U.S.E. co-founders John Hall, Jackson Browne, and Graham Nash, she performed in a series of five benefit concerts at Madison Square Garden, which were recorded and released as a three-album set.

The albums that followed, *The Glow* (1979) and *Green Light* (1982), did not perpetuate increased album sales for Raitt. She was working on an album tentatively titled *Tongue and Groove* for Warner Bros., only to be told that the record company refused to release it. While the material was eventually released as by Warner Bros. as *Nine Lives* in 1986, Raitt parted ways with the company in 1983, sought new management, and later signed a contract with Capitol Records. The upheaval in Raitt's life was personal as well as professional. In 1987 she joined Alcoholics Anonymous, feeling that she had hit bottom physically and emotionally. Raitt looked back on the experience in a *New York Times* interview, noting, "I'm really grateful that I didn't either kill myself or somebody else. I really used to think I needed to be messed up to sing the kind of music I sing.... I don't regret all those years, but I was one of the lucky people that could say no to [alcohol] and not miss it that much."

Working with producer Don Was, Raitt rebounded professionally when she recorded *Nick of Time.* The album surprised many with its hit songs "Thing Called Love," "Nick of Time," and "Have a Heart." Raitt won four Grammys in 1990, three for Nick of Time, and one for best traditional blues recording, for her duet with John Lee Hooker, "In the Mood." *Nick of Time* went on to sell more than four million copies and the album catapulted Raitt into super-stardom. By comparison, her previous albums had each sold in the ballpark of several hundred thousand copies. In 1991, Raitt recorded a follow up album with Don Was, *Luck of the Draw,* which included the hit singles "Something to Talk About," "I Can't Make You Love Me," and "Not the Only One."

The media attention generated by these two break-through albums gave Raitt new opportunities to promote political and social causes as well as to express her views on the music business. In 1991, Raitt co-founded the Rhythm and Blues Foundation, an organization devoted to assisting aging and often poor musicians. She frequently appears at political benefits, such as a 1998 fund-raiser for Democratic California senator Barbara Boxer. In the *New York Times,* Raitt commented on using fame to advance causes: "You just do what you can.... As long as I've got a mouth, somebody's going to be hearing about it. I'm just glad I won those Grammys, so now I get on a better page when the newspapers cover these things."

Raitt has also used the spotlight to remark on the youth-oriented and male-dominated music business. Speaking to the *New York Times* she said, "I thought that after I won those Grammys, people like Delbert McClinton and John Hiatt would then start having hit records.... I though maybe it would mean that age-ism wasn't going to happen, but everything's too bucks-driven." Regarding her own experiences as a woman in the industry, she told *Rolling Stone,* "I've been lucky in that people haven't judged me primarily by my appearance; they've judged me by how I sing and play. Women like Tracy Chapman and Chrissie Hynde and me—we're all gonna be OK. But the Spice Girls probably won't be able to do what they're doing now when they're 45."

Raitt is working to encourage other women to play the guitar, which led to the Bonnie Raitt-signature Fender guitar. The only Fender instrument to honor a woman, it's production resulted in a giveaway program and provided women with an instrument that features a slimmer neck—which is more suited to smaller hands—and a copy of a guitar that Raitt plays. Raitt was enthusiastic about the future of women guitarists in *Guitar Player,* saying, "I'm waiting for the next Stevie Ray Vaughan to be a woman.... We're like a sneeze away from a great lead guitar player with that kind of attitude.... We just have to make sure [women] get the exposure they deserve."

Her interest in such issues has not diminished Raitt's devotion to performing or her desire to grow as an artist. In 1994, she again worked with Don Was, recording *Longing in Their Hearts* and the hit "Love Sneakin' Up on You." In 1995 Raitt issued the live, two-CD recording *Road Tested,* capturing her passion for performing on stage with excerpts from five concerts. This album ended Raitt's string of collaborations with Was. Raitt's 1998 release, *Fundamental,* was produced by Mitchell Froom and Tchad Blake, who have worked with artists including Elvis Costello, Los Lobos, and Richard Thompson. The album was described by Neill Strauss in the *New York Times* as "11 stylistically diverse songs that value raw musical immediacy over pop polish. Throughout the album, Ms. Raitt... sings of the search for love and the struggle to keep love alive."

Writing for *Billboard,* Melinda Newman observed that at the time of *Fundamental*'s release, Raitt had already enjoyed "household name" status for nearly ten years. With appearances on The *Oprah Winfrey Show, The Tonight Show With Jay Leno,* and *The Late Show With David Letterman,* in addition to being highlighted on VH-1, the album's promotion showed that Raitt continued to keep a high profile. She was also scheduled to take part in several concerts in the 1998 Lilith Fair festival, which features an eclectic mix of female performers. Raitt expressed both appreciation for her good fortune and a yearning for the smaller, intimate performances of the past in *Billboard,* saying, "I've been playing these sheds because there's 15,000 people a night who want to see [me] luckily, and that's great for me. Except, I'm sure those longtime fans sure get tired of only getting to see me in a big place." And she concluded that her time onstage was still her greatest thrill: "The time when you're actually getting onstage and playing makes it all worth it. If you can have a life where you get to travel around and control when and where you work and have that much fun and make that many people happy'. I'm not complaining for one minute."

Selected discography

Bonnie Raitt, Warner Bros., 1971.
Give It Up, Warner Bros., 1972.
Takin' My Time, Warner Bros., 1973.
Streetlights, Warner Bros., 1974.
Home Plate, Warner Bros., 1975.
Sweet Forgiveness, Warner Bros., 1977.
The Glow, Warner Bros., 1979.
Green Light, Warner Bros., 1982.
Nine Lives, Warner Bros., 1986.
Nick Of Time, Capitol, 1989.
The Bonnie Raitt Collection, Warner Bros., 1990.
Luck Of The Draw, Capitol, 1991.
Longing In Their Hearts, Capitol, 1994.
Road Tested, Capitol, 1995.
Fundamental, Capitol, 1998.

Sources

Billboard, March 14, 1998, p. 12-14.
Guitar Player, August 1, 1994, p. 43-52.
Los Angeles Times, March 20, 1994, p. 66.

New York Times, February 2, 1994, p. C1; May 6, 1998, p. E1.
Rolling Stone, November 13, 1997, p 157.

—*Paula Pyzik Scott*

REO
Speedwagon

Rock group

AP/Wide World Photos. Reproduced by permission.

REO Speedwagon emerged from Champaign, Illinois in the early 1970s with an amiable, if unremarkable, brand of pop-laced hard rock that failed to gain either commercial or critical recognition for nearly a decade. In 1977, the group finally earned their first gold record with *You Get What You Play For,* a live album that captured the sound that the band had been delivering doggedly around the Midwest. Several years later, REO Speedwagon's *Hi-Infidelity* became one of the biggest selling rock albums of the decade, entering the number one chart position on three separate occasions. However, the group's shift towards middle-of-the-road ballads, while probably the key to REO's newfound fame, did not impress critics any more than had earlier material. After releasing several more albums, REO Speedwagon slid back into the obscurity of regional touring.

REO Speedwagon was formed on the campus of the University of Illinois by drummer Alan Gratzer and keyboard player Neal Doughty in 1968, who for the most part would remain the core of the band throughout years of lineup changes. Rounded out by bassist Greg Philbin, guitarist Gary Richrath, and vocalist Terry Luttrell, the band had become a fixture at local venues when they were noticed by agent Irving Azoff. After Azoff was able to slate the group as the opening act on a number of Midwestern tour bills, most notably with Bob Seger, REO had gained enough stature to cut their self-titled debut album for Epic. Although the record captured the rollicking fun of live bar music, *REO Speedwagon* produced no hits and flew underneath the radar of most critics.

Until the late 1970s, there was little that distinguished each REO album from the next, aside from an occasional replacement of a member. The most important of these was Kevin Cronin, who took over as lead vocalist with *R.E.O./T.W.O.* The group's sophomore effort was released in 1972. Cronin departed after that album but returned in 1975 to relieve substitute Michael Murphy. Although Cronin's style of singing is not recognized for its innovations, his knack for writing ballads later became an integral part of the band's commercial day in the sun. Still, although they borrowed their name from a fast-paced fire truck, REO Speedwagon was slow in reaching the charts.

Oddly enough for a group that had not yet warmed the public over with studio favorites, REO at long last achieved their first gold album with the two-record live effort, *You Get What You Play For,* released in 1977. With Cronin and Richrath taking over at the production helm, the group capitalized on *Play For*'s momentum with the whimsically titled studio album *You Can Tune A Piano But You Can't Tuna Fish* in 1978. The record was REO's

For the Record . . .

Members include **Dave Amato,** guitar; **Kevin Cronin** (born October 6, 1951, in Evanston, IL),vocals; **Neal Doughty,** (born July 29, 1946, in Evanston, IL, core member), keyboards; **Alan Gratzer,** (born November 9, 1948, in Syracuse, NY, core member), drums; **Bruce Hall** (born May 3, 1953, in Champaign, IL), bass; **Jesse Harms** (joined in 1991), keyboards; **Bryan Hitt,** drums; **Graham Lear** (joined in 1990), drums; **Terry Luttell,** vocals; **Michael Murphy,** vocals; **Greg Philbin,** bass; **Gary Richrath,** (born October 18, 1949, in Peoria, IL), guitars, vocals.

Band formed in by Doughty and Gratzer in Champaign, IL, 1968; signed to Epic and released self-titled debut album, 1971; released first gold record *You Get What You Play For,* 1977; dropped longtime manager Irving Azoff, 1977; released multi-platinum album *Hi-Infidelity,* 1980; found a brief comeback with single "Can't Fight This Feeling," 1985; released third compilation album *The Second Decade of Rock and Roll,* 1991.

Awards: National Academy of Recorded Music Awards Best Selling Album, *Hi-Infidelity,* 1980; Best Selling Album by a Group, *Hi-Infidelity,* 1980.

Addresses: *Record company*—Epic, P.O. Box 4450, New York, NY, 10101-4450.

first to produce a million-selling single, "Roll With the Changes," and tempered the group's hard rock leanings with catchier, pop-oriented hooks. With the subsequent release of *Nine Lives* in 1979, it grew clear that this fusion was the group's new direction.

Found National Success at Last

While REO's transformation into easy to take pop-rock balladeers began to rack points with audiences, it was clear that critics saw the band's newfound success to be indicative of the public's embrace of bland, unimaginative music. As the 1980 release *Hi-Infidelity* made itself comfortable in the number one album slot for almost five months, selling over six and a half million copies, music journalists gave REO kudos, grudgingly. J.D. Considine's comments written for *Rolling Stone* in July of 1981 are representative. "For the most part, the

formula REO Speedwagon follows is simple and dependable. Kevin Cronin croons a melodic, slightly naïve pop song, underpinned by strumming acoustic guitars and a lot of echo. Classic MOR [middle-of-the-road] production, except that instead of strings there's the familiar crunch of Richrath's guitar. In a way, it's almost too neat–the most obvious something-for-everyone formula since [1970s bubblegum pop group] the Partridge Family."

In addition to the hooky nature of *Hi-Infidelity*'s songs, the inclusion of ballads was also decisive in the band's turn toward success, as the slow-tempo "Keep On Loving You" and "Take It On The Run" were the biggest of the album's four chart hits. REO themselves attributed the change in popularity simply to hard work and maturity. When asked by the skeptical *Stereo Review* critic Steve Simels why it was only after a decade that REO caught on, Cronin replied, "Because we're better songwriters. I don't think, five years ago, I could have written 'Keep On Loving You.' Plus, we've gotten better as producers. This time out, we had a chance to really rehearse the album before we did it, to really learn the songs."

Whether *Hi-Infidelity*'s runaway popularity was a question of the public's mood or time-tested craftsmanship, REO began to slip from its commercial crest almost upon its arrival. REO's 1982 follow up album *Good Trouble,* like *Hi-Infidelity,* worked to strengthen the once-generic band's identity as songwriters and producers, but wallowed in hackneyed, forgettable lyrics. "The question is whether lack of content will hurt REO," mused Considine in *Rolling Stone* in August of 1982. "Not so much losing their instincts, I'd guess, because unlike the majority of bands cashing in on the hard-pop sound, REO seems to have arrived there almost by accident, after years of touring the heartland. Now that they've made the big time, we'll see how deep their roots run, Don't get your hopes up, though: *Good Trouble* already finds them piling on the fertilizer." Although both the album and its single "Keep the Fire Burnin" both broke the top ten charts, such critical prophesies would soon come to pass.

Failed to Match Earlier Success

Before hitting their terminal sales slump, the group had one more giant hit with "Can't Fight This Feeling," a single from REO's 1985 *Wheels Are Turnin'* album. Once again it was a melodramatic ballad that gave the group a hit, this time about a platonic friendship that gets sparked into romance. As the subject matter may suggest, Cronin's lyrics had not become any more imaginative, and the groups record continued to be critically panned. However, after being panned for over a decade, REO had learned to take reviewers' potshots in stride. "For a while it was very important to me to be accepted by critics," Croni confessed to *Rolling Stone*'s Michael Goldberg in 1985. "We've gotten some reviews on this record [*Wheels Are Turnin'*] –if the record was actually *that* bad, the record company would have never released it. I don't think we deserve all the abuse we get. But I'd rather be abused than ignored."

Unfortunately for Cronin, his fears of being shunned completely were just around the corner. With *Life As We Know It,* a studio album released in 1987, REO enlisted outside songwriters Tom Kelly and Billy Steinberg to take a stab at a more adult oriented kind of pop, but impressed neither listeners or critics in the process. As *Rolling Stone*'s Jimmy Gutterman reflected, "[o]n the surface, this ostensibly ambitious move makes sense: after a dozen-odd albums of peppy midtempo love songs and rockers, the group must have wanted to try something new, if only from boredom. But REO acts as if starting anew is a simple equation that can be solved by pushing the right buttons ... *Life As We Know It* replaces one used-up formula with another." After this album, REO's efforts rarely were given even a passing nod from major music journals.

By the early 1990s, REO had seen the retirement of core members Richrath and Gratzer, and were largely resigned to releasing compilations of earlier material, such as *The Second Decade of Rock & Roll,* released in 1991. However, with new guitarist Dave Amato and drummer Bryan Hitt in tow, REO were able to remain intact. Finally coming to a full circle, the band's career again consisted of regular touring on smaller stages and state fairs throughout the Midwest, where diehard fans still filled out sizable audiences.

Selected discography

REO Speedwagon, Epic, 1971.
R.E.O./T.W.O., Epic, 1972.
Ridin' The Storm Out, Epic, 1973.
Lost In A Dream, Epic, 1974.
This Time We Mean It, Epic, 1975.
REO, Epic, 1976.
You Get What You Play For, Epic, 1977,
You Can Tune A Piano, But You Can't Tuna Fish, Epic, 1978.
Nine Lives, Epic, 1979.
A Decade of Rock 'n' Roll, Epic, 1980.
Hi-Infidelity, Epic, 1980.
Good Trouble, Epic, 1982.
Wheels Are Turnin', Epic, 1984.
Life As We Know It, Epic, 1987.
The Hits, Epic, 1988.
The Earth, A Small Man, His Dog, And A Chicken, Epic, 1990.
The Second Decade of Rock & Roll, Epic, 1991.

Sources

Billboard, April 10, 1982.
Musician, February 1985.
Rolling Stone, July 8, 1981; February 4, 1982; August 19, 1982; March 14, 1985; April 23, 1987.
Stereo Review, September 1981.

—Shaun Frentner

Ricochet

Country group

The six-member, contemporary country music group Ricochet combines seamless ensemble harmonies with irresistible, up beat dance music and delivers a sound with depth and passion. The band achieves its vocal trademark by layering two tenor parts atop the lead, then adding a baritone and low tenor beneath. Ricochet has been compared favorably to the Eagles, Restless Heart, and Southern Pacific, and the band's sixstring-and-fiddle exuberance, combined with their memorable balladry, has garnered numerous music awards since the band's inception in 1993. Ricochet was described by Stephen Thomas Erlewine on the web-based All-Music Guide as, "one of the most successful new country groups of the year [1996], spending the better part of the year in the Top 40 of the country charts."

In 1993, drummer Jeff Bryant asked lead guitarist/singer Heath Wright to join his band Lariat, which included Bryant's brother, fiddle and mandolin player Junior Bryant. Shortly after Wright joined Lariat, the group disbanded, but the Bryant brothers and Wright decided to form another band. They called their new band Ricochet and, by 1994, they had found bassist/vocalist Greg Cook, steel guitar player Teddy Carr, and keyboardist/rhythm guitarist/saxophonist/vocalist Eddie Kilgallon. From 1994-96 Ricochet toured the southern states and the west coast, slowly developing an ardent fan base and developing a uniquely energetic, edgy, and neo-traditional sound. They also devoted their time to writing original songs and rehearsing, which paid off when they cut their first demo.

Ricochet's first manager was a friend of record producer Ron Chancey, noted for his work with the Oak Ridge Boys. After hearing them, he arranged for the band to cut a demo, and subsequently sent the tape to his son, Blake Chancey, Artist and Repretoire director for Columbia Records in Nashville, Tennessee. After hearing the band perform live, Blake Chancey and a group of Columbia Record's executives decided to sign Ricochet to a development deal under the direction of producer Ed Seay, who had worked with Martina McBride and Colin Raye. By 1995, the development deal turned into a full-fledged record contract, and during the spring of 1995, the band recorded their debut album, *Ricochet*. During the remainder of 1995, the band toured the country as a supporting act for Merle Haggard, Doug Stone, and Charlie Daniels, which increased their exposure and fan base. *Ricochet* was released in early 1996 to vast acclaim, and remained on the charts for most of the remainder of the year.

Ricochet's self-titled debut release sold over 500,000 copies and garnered the Academy of Country Music's Top New Vocal Group of the Year award. In addition, the band was named Group of the Year by the *Radio & Records* readers poll, and Ricochet was registered by SoundScan as the number one-selling group in country music for 19 weeks straight. After touring exhaustingly throughout 1996, the band released its second album *Blink of an Eye* in 1997. The album won *Country Weekly* magazine's Favorite New Group Award at their Golden Pick Awards, and further underscored the fact that Ricochet was a talented new band with staying power.

Blink of an Eye—released 18 months after *Ricochet*—was a more confident album than the band's first release, due in part to the band's extensive touring. The release featured stronger songs and offered a more strident approach to country music balladry. The band had grown more comfortable with their producers after working with them for over a year, and band members felt freer to make suggestions, changes, and to experiment. As a result, their second release was truer to their musical intentions and the material emphasized their vocal strengths more effectively. Singles such as "He Left A Lot to be Desired," "Blink of an Eye," and "You Can't Go By That" married breathtaking balladry with rollicking dance rhythms. Ricochet's overall style, however, often defied description and was characterized by it's contemporary, country, folk, dance, and melodic ballad approach, presented in a vigorously energetic style. Chris Rimlinger of *Country Weekly* described

For the Record . . .

Members include **Jeff Bryant**, drums; **Junior Bryant**, (brothers born in Texas), fiddle and mandolin; **Teddy Carr**, (raised in Lafayette, TN), steel guitar; **Greg Cook**, (raised in Vian, OK), bass and vocals; **Eddie Kilgallon**, (raised in East Greenbush, NY), keyboards, guitar, saxophone, and vocals; and **Heath Wright**, (raised in Vian, OK), guitar and vocals.

Band formed in 1993; signed a development deal with Columbia Records in 1994; signed a record deal with Columbia Records, 1995; toured the U.S. as a supporting act for Merle Haggard, Doug Stone, and Charlie Daniels, 1995; released *Ricochet*, 1996; signed with Sony Music, released *Blink of an Eye,* 1997.

Awards: Academy of Country Music's Top New Vocal Group of the Year award for 1996; Group of the Year by the Radio & Records readers poll in 1996; Country Weekly magazine's Favorite New Group Award at the magazine's Golden Pick Awards in 1997.

Addresses: *Record company*—Sony Records Nashville, 34 Music Square East, Nashville, TN 37203; (615) 742-4321, *Website*—website www.sony.com.

Blink of an Eye as, "Fresh, featuring songs that look at common scenarios from slightly out of the ordinary perspective."

After the release of *Blink of an Eye* in June of 1997, 24,000 country music fans flocked to see the band at the 26th Annual Country Music Fan Fair event held in Nashville, Tennessee. The group was the biggest selling act for the second consecutive year at the Fan Fair, and their second release outsold projects by country music notables such as George Strait and Tim McGraw.

Another key to the band's success and ability is their cohesiveness and shared musical perspective. The Bryant brothers were raised in a small town in Texas, where their father was a keyboardist who once worked

with Roy Orbison, and their mother was a bass guitar player. Junior Bryant's influences were Vassar Clements, Bob Wills, Roy Rogers, and Jean-Luc Ponty. Jeff Bryant was influenced by Tex-Mex music, 4/4 shuffles, and rhythm-and-blues. Teddy Carr was raised in Lafayette, Tennessee, and worked with Clay Walker, Little Jimmy Dickens, and Jack Greene. He was inspired by Chet Atkins. Multi-talented Eddie Kilgallon was raised in East Greenbush, New York, and is a self-described "glissando freak." Wright and Cook were childhood friends in their hometown of Vian, Oklahoma, and offer inventive guitar and bass interchanges. Cook was influenced by Johnny Cash's guitarist Luther Perkins and by Don Rich, who played with Buck Owens.

The kinship the six band members share provides the ultimate strength of Ricochet. The band members view music as a shared adventure and a joy, and it is this enthusiastic perspective that can take an audience by surprise. Sony Nashville senior vice president of sales and marketing, Mike Kraski, told *Billboard*'s Deborah Evans Price, "They are, in my mind, the best band in country music today. I just don't know that it could get any better than to have that depth of talent, that kind of work ethic, and that kind of personality and charm all in one mix of ingredients."

Selected discography

Ricochet, Columbia Records, 1996.
Blink of an Eye, Sony Records, 1997.

Sources

Periodicals

Billboard, May 3, 1997.
Country Weekly, July 29, 1997.
The Courant, Febuary 25, 1997.

Online

http://205.186.189.2/cg/amg.exe?sql=2PIDP///182058 (All-Music guide)
www.imusic.com (CDNOW)
www.Sony.com

—B. Kimberly Taylor

Rolling Stones

Rock band

Arguably the most successful band in the history of rock music, the Rolling Stones enjoyed unmatched fame—and infamy—for the better half of the 20th century. In an effort to distinguish the band from the multitude of early 1960's pop/rock groups, the Rolling Stones were marketed as a sort of anti-Beatles. Whereas the Beatles were viewed as relatively clean cut, wholesome pop artists, the Rolling Stones were considered sex crazed, wild and dangerous men who would do unmentionable things to wives and daughters, all the while espousing their love of, what was then considered wickedly sinister African-American blues music. The Rolling Stones used their nefarious image to not only arouse the sexually charged youths of the 1960s and 1970s, but to promote and hype themselves as the greatest rock and roll band in the world.

The Rolling Stones was founded by singer Mick Jagger and guitarist Keith Richards in 1962. The two had attended the same primary school in their home town of Dartford, England, but it wasn't until a chance meeting at a London train station in 1960 that they realized they

AP/Wide World Photos. Reproduced by permission.

Members include **Mick Avory**, (left group, 1962), drums; **Mick Jagger**, vocals; **Brian Jones**, (died, 1969), guitar; **Darryl Jones**, (joined group, 1994), bass; **Keith Richards**, guitar; **Ian Stewart**, (left group, 1962), piano; **Dick Taylor**, (left group, 1962), bass; **Mick Taylor**, (1969-74), guitar; **Charlie Watts**, drums, **Ron Wood**, (joined group, 1975), guitar; and **Bill Wyman**, (left group, 1992), bass.

Group formed in London, England, 1962; signed to Decca and released *Rolling Stones*, 1964; released *December's Children*, 1965; released *Aftermath*, 1966; released *Their Satanic Majesties Request*, 1967; released *Beggar's Banquet*, 1968; Former guitarist Jones found dead in pool, band released *Let it Bleed*, 1969; formed Rolling Stone Records and released, *Sticky Fingers*, 1971; released *Exile on Main Street*, 1972; released *It's Only Rock and Roll*, 1974; released *Black and Blue*, 1976; released *Some Girls*, 1978; released *Emotional Rescue*, 1980; released *Tattoo You*, 1981; released *Undercover*, 1983; released *Dirty Work*, 1986; released *Steel Wheels*, 1989; signed to Virgin and released *Voodoo Lounge*, 1994; released *Stripped*, 1995; released *Bridges to Babylon*, 1997.

Awards: Platinum Certification for *Black and Blue*, 1976; Platinum Certification for *Emotional Rescue*, 1980; Platinum Certification for *Tattoo You*, 1981; Grammy Award for Best Rock Album for *Voodoo Lounge*, 1994.

Addresses: *Record company*—Virgin, 30 West 21st Street, New York, NY 10010.

both shared a love for the blues and decided to start a band. Jagger and Richards met up with guitarist Brian Jones, who had played with the band Blues Inc. before leaving them to start up his own band with Ian Stewart on piano. Jones and Stewart would later join Jagger and Richards, along with drummer Mick Avory and bassist Dick Taylor to form the original incarnation of the Rolling Stones. After playing their first concert at London's Marquee Club, Taylor and Avory quit and were replaced by bassist Bill Wyman and drummer Charlie Watts.

With their line-up intact, the Rolling Stones began an eight month residency at the Crawdaddy Club, which not only increased their exposure but introduced them to Andrew Loog Oldham, who would soon become their manager. Oldham had a knack for promotion, and it was he who solidified the image of the rough and ready Rolling Stones. He told the band to dump Stewart because he did not fit into the lean, mean, street fighting image of the Rolling Stones. The band acquiesced and reluctantly made Stewart their road manager. According to John Lahr of *New Republic*, the Rolling Stones appropriated "the black truculence of the early blues forms they scrupulously imitated. They gave off none of the familiar signals of the buttoned-down establishment culture; and what's more, these lower middle class white boys wanted, even strained to sound black. And they succeeded ... the Stones were blues shouters who flayed the bourgeoisie, only to become the new hipoisie. They epitomized the White Negro."

The Rolling Stones signed a recording contract with Decca in the spring of 1963 and began to record singles in earnest. Their first was "Come On," a Chuck Berry cover that almost made the Top 20, but it was their second single, "I Wanna Be Your Man," that would put the Rolling Stones on the rock and roll map. That song, which became a Top 15 hit in England, was given to the band by none other than the Beatles' John Lennon and Paul McCartney. What may have appeared as supreme irony at first glance, the nice Beatles helping the nasty Rolling Stones, was in reality a sort of mutual appreciation society between the two bands. As Richards told Jas Obrecht of *Guitar Player*, "We [the Rolling Stones and the Beatles] would work with each other instead of against each other, which is very interesting, because for the most part people were either a Beatles or a Stones man."

Into the Kitchen

In the spring of 1964, they released their debut album *Rolling Stones*, which contained their first British number one single, "It's All Over Now." Oldham told the Rolling Stones that they needed to write their own material because the reservoir of covers would eventually run dry. To facilitate the process, he locked Jagger and Richards in a room until they came out with a song. Richards described the incident to Obrecht: "Andrew locked Mick and myself in a kitchen in this horrible little apartment we had. He said, 'You ain't comin' out,' and there was no way out. We were in the kitchen with some food and a couple of guitars, but we couldn't get to the john so we had to come out with a song.... In that little kitchen, Mick and I got hung up about writing songs."

Their second album, *12X5*, released in 1964, contained the band's first two American hits "Tell Me" and "Time is on My Side," which managed to crack the American top ten. 1965 saw the release of *Rolling Stones Now!* and their first self-penned number one British hit, "The Last Time," which also made the top ten in America. The seminal track, however, was "(I Can't Get No) Satisfaction" which announced the coming-out party for the Jagger/Richards songwriting team. The smash hit of 1965, "(I Can't Get No) Satisfaction," was the first of a long line of bluesy, riff driven rock anthems that the Rolling Stones would become famous for. Three more albums were released that year, *December's Children*, *Out of Our Heads*, and *Got It Live If You Want It*.

1966 saw the continuing maturation of the Rolling Stones as a band, and Jagger and Richards as songwriters. They released *Aftermath,* their first entirely original, and most complex, album to date, which included the hit "Paint It Black." With it's Indian influenced, sitar laced riff, "Paint It Black" was proof that even the mighty Rolling Stones were not free from the Beatles sphere of influence, as that band had begun recording with sitar earlier that year. A year later, and despite the arrests of Jagger, Jones, and Richards on drug possession charges, the Rolling Stones remained prolific, and by now eclectic, in their output, releasing the overtly pop *Between the Buttons*, *Flowers*, and the tepidly received psychedelic experiment, *Their Satanic Majesties Request*.

Triumph and Tragedy

Although the success of singles like "(I Can't Get No) Satisfaction," "Get Off Of My Cloud," and "As Tears Go By" would place the Rolling Stones among the very elite of British rock, major upheaval and tragedy would greet the band in 1968. Allen Klein was brought in to manage the band after the dismissal of Oldham. "Jumpin' Jack Flash" hopped to number three on the charts and it's parent album, *Beggar's Banquet* was the band's biggest critical success to that point. Unfortunately, where *Beggars Banquet* was the high water mark for the Rolling Stones, it saw the demise of guitarist Jones. Craving the spotlight occupied by Jagger and Richards, Jones developed an inferiority complex, not to mention a drug habit. As Richards explained to *Playboy*'s Stanley Booth, "Brian and I were at odds from, oh, '65 through '66. At the time, Brian was in bad shape, far away from the rest of the band. He needed help." Throughout the sessions for the album, Jones' insecurity fueled an escalating drug problem which further alienated him from the band. He was kicked out of the band on June 9, 1969 and, in less than a month, was found dead in his swimming pool.

Having replaced Jones with ex-John Mayall Bluesbreakers guitarist Mick Taylor, the Rolling Stones released *Let It Bleed*, which featured the work of both Jones and Taylor, and the single "Gimme Shelter." The attendant tour for *Let It Bleed,* the band's first American tour in three years, spawned more tragedy when a fan was stabbed to death by a member of the Hell's Angles Motorcycle Club, who were providing security for the free show at California's Altamont Speedway in December, 1969. The subsequent live album, *Get Yer Ya Ya's Out* was the last the Rolling Stones release on Decca, and for the next 20 years they would record for their own label, Rolling Stone Records, beginning with 1971's *Sticky Fingers.* 1972 saw the release of double album *Exile on Main Street* which, despite early poor reviews, would eventually be regarded as the band's watershed album.

Drugs, Fame, and Credibility

Drugs and fame consumed Richards and Jagger,, throughout the 1970s. *Goat's Head Soup* came out in 1973 and was followed by *It's Only Rock and Roll* the following year. Taylor left after that album and was replaced by former Faces guitarist Ron Wood. While Jagger spent the middle years of the seventies jetsetting, Richards was busy feeding his heroine addiction, and the Rolling Stones released several forgettable albums, as did Wood and Wyman. In 1978, a rejuvenated Rolling Stones released *Some Girls* which featured the disco-influenced, number one single "Miss You." *Some Girls'* 1980 follow up, *Emotional Rescue*, was a critical disappointment, but was certified platinum none the less. With 1981's *Tattoo You* and the arena rock anthem, "Start Me Up," the band regained some of the credibility it lost with *Emotional Rescue*, but would see it vanish once again with 1983's *Undercover* and 1986's *Dirty Work*.

Jagger and Richards spent much of the 1980s feuding but, by 1988, had started to make amends, and 1989's *Steel Wheels* had the positive reviews to prove it. The resulting tour provided the material for 1991's live album *Flashback*, after which Wyman left the band. The Rolling Stones signed to Virgin in 1994 and released the album, *Voodoo Lounge*, which continued the success of its predecessor. *Voodoo Lounge* also earned the Rolling Stones their first ever Grammy Award, for Best Rock Album of 1994.

After replacing Wyman with Darryl Jones in 1994, the band recorded *Stripped*, an acoustic live album, and 1997's *Bridges to Babylon*, and with Jagger and Richards at the helm, continued headlong through their fourth decade of rock and roll. Richards once quipped to Obrecht that, "when we started the Rolling Stones, we were just little kids, right? We felt we had some of the licks down, but our aim was to turn other people on to Muddy Waters. I mean we were carrying flags, idealistic teenage sort of stuff. There was no way we thought anybody was really going to seriously listen to us. We just wanted to get a few people interested to listening to the sort of stuff we thought they ought to listen to ... but that was our aim—turn people on to the blues. If we could turn them on to Muddy and Jimmy Reed and Howlin' Wolf and John Lee Hooker, then our job was done."

Selected discography

Rolling Stones, Decca, 1964.
12X5, Decca, 1964.
Rolling Stones Now!, Decca, 1965.
December's Children, Decca, 1965.
Out of Our Heads, Decca, 1965.
Got It Live If You Want It, Decca, 1965.
Aftermath, Decca, 1966.
Between the Buttons, Decca, 1967.
Flowers, Decca, 1967.
Their Satanic Majesties Request, Decca, 1967.
Beggar's Banquet, Decca, 1968.
Let it Bleed, Decca, 1969.

Get Yer Ya Ya's Out, Decca, 1970.
Sticky Fingers, Rolling Stone, 1971.
Exile on Main Street, Rolling Stone, 1972.
Goat's Head Soup, Rolling Stone, 1973.
It's Only Rock and Roll, Rolling Stone, 1974.
Black and Blue, Rolling Stone, 1976.
Some Girls, Rolling Stone, 1978.
Emotional Rescue, Rolling Stone, 1980.
Tattoo You, Rolling Stone, 1981.
Undercover, Rolling Stone, 1983.
Dirty Work, Rolling Stone, 1986.
Steel Wheels, Rolling Stone, 1989.
Flashback, Rolling Stone, 1991.
Voodoo Lounge, Virgin, 1994.
Stripped, Virgin, 1995.
Bridges to Babylon, Virgin, 1997.

Sources

Economist, October 25, 1997.
Entertainment Weekly, March 6, 1992.
Guitar Player, September, 1993; October, 1993.
New Republic, December 24, 1984.
Playboy, October , 1989.
Rolling Stone, November 24, 1983.

—Mary Alice Adams

Roxette

Pop group

Initially bogged down with comparisons to 1970s pop giants Abba, the members of Roxette became international superstars with the release of their second album *Look Sharp!* in 1988. Like fellow Swedes Abba, Roxette did produce a number of worldwide number one hits, but showed their own knack for composing infectiously catchy pop songs. Continuing with several albums that were almost as commercially successful, Roxette was warmly treated by most critics, who found guilty pleasure in the band's well-crafted tunes. After the somewhat disappointing album *Crash! Boom! Bang!* in 1994, Roxette retreated from the studio with a number of compilations, remixes, and re-releases, but announced that an album of fresh material would be offered to the world by the end of 1998.

Although rounded out by a number of studio musicians, for all intents and purposes Roxette is the duo of guitarist/vocalist Per Gessle and platinum-haired lead vocalist Marie Fredriksson, who met in Halmstad, Sweden in the mid-1970s, both of them struggling musicians. Fredriksson's primary influence came from jazz artists as diverse as the mournful chanteuse Billie Holiday and the improvisational outfit Henry Cow, while Gessle was thoroughly caught up in the style of American and British New Wave and power pop groups like Blondie and the Romantics. "With new wave, it was okay if you hit the wrong note," Gessle told *Musician*'s Mark Rowland in 1991. "I think that was the attitude that made you start playing guitar, because you're not really influenced by your school or parents."

Gessle and Fredriksson both made names for themselves with two markedly different recording careers, with Gessle writing wry lyrics for a pop band, and Fredriksson creating three solo albums of somber female vocals. However, by the mid-1980s the two friends decided to take advantage of their seeming incompatibility and formed Roxette in hopes of creating catchy, flashy pop music. "I don't think Roxette would ever have happened if Marie's and my records had been sort of the same," Gessle reflected to Rowland. "Marie had never had that type of song to sing before. And for me it was equally – opposite." In 1986, Roxette cut their debut album for EMI Sweden, an outing of twelve tracks recorded in their native tongue, entitled *Pearls of Passion*. The record yielded a number of hits in Roxette's homeland, including "Svarta glas" ("Black Glasses") but was not released to the rest of the world.

After a successful domestic tour in 1987, Gessle and Fredriksson decided to broaden their appeal by switching over to English, the language spoken in the crucial American and British markets. The resulting album, *Look Sharp!* was released by EMI in 1988, but initially failed to catch on outside of Sweden until an American exchange student gave a copy to a radio station in Minneapolis, Minnesota. The song "The Look" almost instantly became a national radio favorite, paving the ground for the official release of the song to rocket to the top of the American pop charts.

Look Sharp! had finally found a place in the heart of American listeners, who embraced the energy of Fredriksson's delivery of "Listen to Your Heart" and "Dangerous." On the whole, even the most jaded music journalism welcomed Roxette's crackerjack ability to produce catchy tunes during a relative drought of pop music. Critics like *Musician*'s Jon Young made no great claims for Roxette as innovators, however. "Not surprisingly, Roxette's music tends to fall apart when examined closely," Young wrote in June of 1989. "The playing (or programming) never transcends anonymity, and for all the sound and fury, the songs are eerily passionless. Which of course misses the point entirely. Rather than presuming to offer meaning or substance, *Look Sharp!* merely wants to join the modern media din. But it is kinda fun." Such equivocated praise comprised the overall flavor of most of Roxette's subsequent reviews.

After a popular European tour, Roxette began work on their follow-up to *Look Sharp!* and along the way decided to re-record one of the stronger cuts from *Pearls of Passion*, "It Must Have Been Love." The duo was so

Band members include **Pelle Alsing**, (born June 6, 1960, in Stockholm, Sweden), drums; **Vicki Benckert**, (born October 17, 1960, in Stockholm, Sweden), guitar, accordion, backing vocals; **Marie Fredriksson**, (born May 30, 1958, in Ostra Ljungby, Sweden), vocals; married Micke Bolyos; children: Inez Josefin; Oscar Mikael; **Per Gessle**, (born January 12, 1959, in Halmstad, Sweden), guitar, vocals; married Asa Nordin, 1993; children: Gabriel Titus; **Anders Herrlin**, (born September 17, 1961, in Halmstad, Sweden), bass guitar; **Jonas Isacsson**, (born June 10, 1959, in Umea, Sweden), guitar; **Clarence Ofwerman**, (born November 22, 1957, in Stockholm, Sweden), keyboards; **Staffan Ofwerman**, (born September 8, 1962, in Stockholm, Sweden), keyboards, percussion.

Band formed in 1986, in Halmstad, Sweden, by Gessle and Fredriksson, signed to EMI Sweden; released debut album *Look Sharp!*, 1988; contributed "It Must Have Been Love" to the *Pretty Woman* soundtrack, 1990; released *Joyride*, 1991; given their own postage stamp by the Swedish government, 1991; sold over a million copies of *Crash! Boom! Bang!* sampler through Mc-Donald's fast food chain, 1994; released greatest hits album *Don't Bore Us, Get To The Chorus!* worldwide, except in the U.S., 1995.

Addresses: *Record company*— EMI, 810 Seventh Avenue, New York, NY 10019. *Fan club*—wysiwyg:/ /10/http://www.roxette.nl/

those earlier legends of icy-cool pop, and some critics began to point out the discrepancy upon the release of their new album. "Overall, what ultimately defines *Joyride* are the performances, and that marks the most important difference between Roxette and Abba," J.D. Considine wrote in *Rolling Stone*. "By emphasizing its sense of personality, Roxette delivers more than just well-constructed hooks; this music has heart, something that makes even the catchiest melody more appealing."

While Roxette did not seriously depart from their established style with *Joyride*, the album did reveal an influx of new idea sources such as hip-hop and classic rock. Gessle himself made it clear that a credo of easygoing pop still ruled his songwriting efforts. "[T]he trick is not to think too much about it," he told *Musician*. "Try the first thing that pops into your mind, if it makes sense. If it's work, skip it. But if you have lots of instrumentalists and soloists, it makes the whole album much more interesting." In the final instance, the public's acceptance of *Joyride*'s selection of pop songs and ballads exceeded that of *Look Sharp!*, with the title cut and the single "Fading Like A Flower" scoring heavily on sales charts.

Hot on the heels of *Joyride,* Roxette launched a 108 date world tour that spanned four continents, piecing together a collection of live cuts and outtakes entitled *Tourism: Songs from the Studios, Stages, Hotel rooms, and Other Strange Places* along the way. While the album's success in the U.S. was limited, it eventually sold over four million copies worldwide. This was perhaps the first indication of Roxette's falling out with American audiences, but throughout the globe their popularity was still immense. Having become the biggest Swedish stars since Abba, the members of Roxette were commemorated by their country's government when Gessle and Fredriksson's faces were cast upon a series of postage stamps.

Roxette enjoyed a several year hiatus after their world tour, inciting talk of the band's breakup. Roxette dispelled such rumors with the release of *Crash! Boom! Bang!* in 1994, an album recorded in a number of locations that included London, England and the Isle of Capri. For many critics, however, the record was not worth the wait, and largely faulted the higher number of tunes sung by Gessle. "As with the duo's previous work, *Crash! Boom! Bang!* hits its best notes when Fredriksson is at the mike," judged *People* magazine. "Her vocals on the ballads 'Run To You,' 'What's She Like,' and the title song are more subtle and graceful than her partner's grating, affected rasp." *Entertainment Weekly*'s Devon Jackson was in agreement,

pleased with the strength of the ballad that it was the intended centerpiece of their next album, but instead it was integrated into the soundtrack for the 1990 film *Pretty Woman* as well as becoming a number one single. Soon after Gessle found a forgotten note left on a table reading "Hello, you fool! I love you," which became the lyrical hookline for another song equally worthy as a title track. The scrap of whimsical dialogue was transformed into the song "Joyride," the first single of the 1991 album of the same name.

Since the release of *Look Sharp!*, Roxette had been unduly compared to the Swedish group Abba. Aside from their Scandinavian heritage and penchant for crafting international hits, Roxette had little resemblance to writing that "[i]f only Per Gessle had let the charged up Marie Fredriksson sing vocals on all 15 songs, *Crash* might've qualified as an *un*qualified guilty pleasure."

Although sales of *Crash! Boom! Bang!* were not disastrous, it was Roxette's weakest performance to date, especially in the American market. Despite having initially courted U.S. listeners, Roxette began in turn to shy away from America, skipping over the country during their 1994 tour. For the rest of the world, Roxette were still hot property, as illustrated by the demand for their 1995 compilation release *Don't Bore Us, Get To The Chorus!* With its title aptly summing up Roxette's pure-pop-or-nothing philosophy, *Don't Bore Us* was a greatest hits *cum* remix package that sold over four million copies, even though EMI decided not to release it in the U.S.

Over the next few years, Roxette kept a lower profile than ever, surfacing only for an occasional repackaging of previously released material, including a collection of hard to find B-sides and remixes, *Roxette Rarities,* and the 1997 reissue of *Pearls of Passion*, the original having become an expensive collector's item. Roxette took one step further away from the English speaking world with the 1996 release *Baladas En Espanol*, a collection of twelve of Roxette's choice ballads re-recorded in Spanish. Still superstars across Europe and South America, Gessle and Fredriksson announced that a new Roxette album would be completed by the end of 1998.

Selected discography

Pearls of Passion, EMI Sweden, 1986; re-released 1997.
Look Sharp!, EMI, 1988.
Joyride, EMI, 1991.
Tourism: Songs from the Studios, Stages, Hotel Rooms, and Other Strange Places, EMI, 1992.
Crash! Boom! Bang!, EMI, 1994.
Don't Bore Us, Get To The Chorus!, EMI, 1995.
Baladas En Espanol, EMI, 1996.

Sources

Periodicals

Billboard, January 13, 1990; May 4, 1991; June 27, 1992; October 31, 1992
Entertainment Weekly, October 7, 1994.
Musician, June 1989; July 1991.
People, October 10, 1994.
Rolling Stone, June 27, 1991.

Online

The Daily Roxette, http://www.visakopu.net/dailyroxette (July 20, 1998).

—*Shaun Frentner*

Mitch Ryder

Singer, songwriter

As front man for one of the most raucuous "blue-eyed soul" bands of the 1960s, Detroit's Mitch Ryder howled high-energy medleys of rock and blues standards. His hard-driving "Devil With a Blue Dress On/ Good Golly Miss Molly" has a firm place in the canon of infectious dance tunes. But commercial success was fleeting for Ryder. His later work, while hailed by critics, has been largely ignored in his native country, though he has retained a large following in Europe three decades after disappearing from the U.S. pop charts.

Ryder was born as William Levise Jr. on February 26, 1945, in the Detroit enclave of Hamtramck. His father was a big band radio singer. Ryder grew up in the all-white suburb of Warren but learned about rhythm-and-blues music while spending summers with his grandmother in Detroit. Black culture attracted him; he told Rolling Stone's Kurt Loder that "it seemed a lot more vibrant than goin' out to see Fabian."

By the time he was in high school, Ryder was performing under the name Billy Lee in a group called Tempest. At 17, he started singing in a feverish Detroit soul club, the Village, and recorded an R&B single ("That's the Way It's Gonna Be/Fool for You") for a local gospel label, Carrie. Soon he started playing gigs at black clubs as the lead singer for a vocal trio, the Peps, whose other two members were black. His vocals were so soulful that fans sometimes mistook him for a light-skinned black man. His interracial experience set him apart in the days when the Motown sound was just starting to break through the color bar on mainstream pop radio stations.

Tiring of the constant turnover in the Peps, Ryder, in 1964, formed his own band, Billy Lee & the Rivieras, which included drummer John Badanjek, bass player Jim McCallister, and guitarists Jim McCarty and Joe Kubert. Soon they attracted a fanatical following as the house band at the Walled Lake Casino, the hottest spot on the Michigan teen scene, where they opened for Motown acts. They recorded a version of the Contours hit "Do You Want to Dance?" for a local label, Hyland. Having played with white and black musicians for white and black audiences, Ryder had quickly shown a mastery of the R&B-driven rock music that was galvanizing young people worldwide.

When legendary record producer Bob Crewe saw Billy Lee and the Rivieras steal the show at a Dave Clark Five concert, he recognized their potential and immediately signed the five Detroit boys to a contract with his New Voice label. In New York for the contract signing, they picked the name Mitch Ryder out of the Manhattan phone book. Because there already was a rock group called the Rivieras, the group was renamed the Detroit Wheels.

Mitch Ryder and the Detroit Wheels released their first single, "I Need Help," in the fall of 1965. It went nowhere. In December they recorded a medley, covering two rock standards, Little Richard's "Jenny, Jenny" and Chuck Willis's "C.C. Rider." Called "Jenny Take a Ride," the single was an instant success, hitting number ten on the Billboard charts in January 1966. Two months later, the group's cover of the Righteous Brothers' "Little Latin Lupe Lu" peaked at number 17. Their biggest hit followed that fall. It was an infectious remake of an obscure Motown record by Shorty Long, "Devil With a Blue Dress On" and another Little Richard screamer, "Good Golly Miss Molly." The provocative, hyperkinetic song reached number four on the Billboard charts in October 1966. Becoming an all-time favorite of the Baby Boomer generation, it was listed as one of the 100 best singles of the 1963-1988 era by Rolling Stone magazine.

Ryder's best songs with the Wheels had the electricity of live performances. The medleys became the group's concert trademark. At a time when black groups were finally busting through with "crossover" hits, Ryder and the Wheels consistently crossed over in the other direction, with their recordings always faring well on the R&B charts. In all, Ryder's string of hits in 1966 and 1967 presaged a later era when racial barriers in music became meaningless.

Born William Levise Jr., February 26, 1945, in Hamtramck. MI; married twice.

Professional singer under stage name Billy Lee with the Tempest, c. 1961; recorded "That's the Way It's Gonna Be/"Fool for You," Carrie, c. 1963; singer with the Peps, 1963-64; singer with Billy Lee & the Rivieras, renamed Mitch Ryder & the Detroit Wheels, 1964-67; released New Voice singles "Jenny Take A Ride" 1965; "Devil With a Blue Dress On/Good Golly Miss Molly" 1966; "Sock It To Me - Baby" 1967; became solo performer, 1967; released *The Detroit-Memphis Experiment,* Dot, 1969; formed band Detroit, 1971, released album *Detroit;* worked as laborer, Denver, 1972-77; resumed music career with *How I Spent My Summer Vacation,* Seeds & Stems 1978; *Naked But Not Dead,* Seeds & Stems, 1980; released *Never Kick a Sleeping Dog,* Riva, 1983; released several albums for German label Lane in 1980s and 1990s.

Addresses: *Agent*—Entertainment Services International, 6400 Pleasant Park Dr., Chanhassen, MN 55317.

Ryder and the Wheels recorded two more hits in early 1967, but their formula was already sounding predictable. "Sock It To Me - Baby!" charted at number six despite being banned on some radio stations for its sexual innuendos. Ryder's most bizarre medley was a merging of the Marvelettes' Motown hit "Too Many Fish in the Sea" and an old ditty dating back to 1939, "Three Little Fishes." When that medley managed only 24 on the charts, Crewe convinced Ryder that the Wheels' magic had run its course.

The group split up, and at Crewe's behest Ryder became a solo act, singing Vegas-style ballads. It was an inexplicable transformation, taking one of the most soulful white singers and remaking him as a glitzy crooner backed by sticky-sweet strings. Only one of Ryder's solo efforts for Crewe, "What Now My Love," made the Billboard charts, peaking at number 30.

When his fling as a Las Vegas lounge singer ended, Ryder broke bitterly with Crewe. Despite his string of hits, Ryder reportedly made only $15,000 as a Crewe property. Ryder traveled to Memphis, recording a unique album called The Detroit-Memphis Experiment with guitarist Steve Cropper. The 1969 release featured blues legends like Booker T & the MGs. While it was a commercial flop, it was a critical success. Ryder's disgust with Crewe's handling was evident in liner notes where he complained of "being raped by the music machine" and noted pointedly that "Mitch Ryder is the sole creation of William Levise, Jr."

Next, Ryder reunited with drummer Badanjek and formed a group called Detroit. An eponymous album released in 1972 featured a pulsating recording of the standard "Rock'N Roll" which became a favorite of musician Lou Reed. But while Ryder was earning kudos within the ranks of fellow rock musicians, his commercial career was going downhill. His new group burned itself out in short time. "We used to take acid just to stay awake, man," Ryder told Loder. "We couldn't have made a second album if they had wanted us to." Bitter and depressed and battling drugs and alcohol and a throat ailment, Ryder moved to Denver and worked for five years as a laborer in a warehouse, writing songs at night.

In 1978, Ryder re-emerged with a new eight-piece backup band and an album appropriately titled *How I Spent My Summer Vacation* on his own label, Seeds and Stems. Loder called the album Ryder's "unacknowledged masterpiece ... stark and transfixing." Written with his second wife Kim, the album's key songs were graphic accounts of homosexual encounters that Loder notes "may have been a bit too astonishing" for the era. Two years later Ryder followed with *Naked But Not Dead* on the same label. These brooding, dark albums helped trigger a renewed interest in Ryder in Europe, where his popularity eclipsed anything he enjoyed in the United States.

In the 1980s and 1990s, Ryder continued to churn out albums, mostly for the German label Line, including *Live Talkies, Got Change For a Million, Smart Ass, In the China Shop, La Gash, Rite of Passage, Beautiful Toulang Sunset,* and *Red Blood, White Mink.* In 1983, John Mellencamp produced an American release for Ryder on his Riva label, *Never Kick a Sleeping Dog.* It featured a gritty cover of Prince's "When You Were Mine" and a sizzling duet with Marianne Faithful on "A Thrill's A Thrill." Both Mellencamp and Bruce Springsteen claimed Ryder as a major influence on their work. Springsteen used some of Ryder's hits in his show-closing "Detroit Medley" during concerts in the 1980s. But a real comeback in the United States still eluded Ryder.

Ryder's popularity abroad allowed him enough income from record sales to keep him in the business. Into his

50s he was still working hard at his craft, writing and producing songs and performing at casinos, fairs and bars in Michigan, the Midwest and Europe. Unlike other performers who gained fame in the 1960s, the so-called "Godfather of Motor City Rock'n'Roll" was still churning out fresh music in the 1990s, rather than relying solely on his heart-pounding blasts from the past.

Selected discography

with the Detroit Wheels

Take a Ride, New Voice, 1966.
Breakout...!!, New Voice, 1966.
Sock It to Me, New Voice, 1966.
Greatest Hits, Roulette, 1987.
Rev Up: The Best of Mitch Ryder and the Detroit Wheels, Rhino, 1990.
All Hits, Sundazed, 1997.

with Detroit

Detroit, Paramount, 1971, reissued, 1987.

Solo albums

What Now My Love?, Dyno Voice, 1967.
All the Heavy Hits, Crewe, 1967.
The Detroit-Memphis Experiment, Dot, 1969.
How I Spent My Summer Vacation, Seeds & Stems, 1970.
Naked But Not Dead, Seeds & Stems, 1980.
Got Change For a Million, Line, 1981.
Live Talkies, Line, 1982.
SmartAss, Line, 1982.
Never Kick a Sleeping Dog, Riva, 1983.
Red Blood and White Mink, Line, 1989.

Sources

Books

Clarke, Donald, editor, *The Penguin Encyclopedia of Popular Music,* Viking, 1989.
Erdewine, Michael, editor, *All Music Guide to Rock,* Miller Freeman Books, 1997.
Hitchcock, H. Wiley and Stanley Sadie, editors, *New Grove Dictionary of American Music,* Macmillan, 1986.
Larkin, Colin, editor, *The Guinness Encyclopedia of Popular Music,* Guinness, 1992.
Rees, Dafydd, and Luke Crampton, *Rock Movers & Shakers,* Banson, 1991.

Periodicals

People, August 13, 1985.
Rolling Stone, September 1, 1983; September 8, 1988; February 9, 1989.

Online

http://www.esientertainment.com/ryder.htm
http://www.members.aol.com/RyderRock/

—Michael Betzold

Dino Saluzzi

Bandoneon player

Master bandoneon player Dino Saluzzi plays jazz on a traditional tango instrument, composing atmospheric pieces of great beauty, complexity, joy, and passion. The bandoneon, closely associated with tango music, is an instrument with a tonal and octave range as broad and colorful as the guitar, and Saluzzi is perceived as the musician who freed the tango from its fixed structure, often drawing from his bandoneon the harmonic qualities of a cathedral pipe organ.

Created in Germany in the 1840s and used by Italian musicians and other European immigrants to South America to play songs in Spanish, Fernando Gonzalez of *The Herald* wrote the bandoneon is, "a bittersweet sounding button squeezebox ... a sort of portable, poor man's church organ. It has improbably become the quintessential instrument of tango in the (bordellos) of Buenos Aires in the early 1900s." It was of Saluzzi's mastery of the instrument that *DownBeat*'s Dan Ouellette wrote, "Saluzzi commands attentive listening with a collection of pieces that strike deep emotional chords ... (he) wends his way into a reflective and celebrative musical landscape informed by jazz, classical, nuevo tango and South American folk music influences."

Timoteo "Dino" Saluzzi was born in 1935 in Campo Santo, a small village in the northwest Salta district of Argentina. Life in Campo Santo revolved primarily around the local sugar cane refining factory. Despite the lack of records, radio, and even electricity in Saluzzi's home, there was always music. His father played the guitar, mandolin, and bandoneon, and taught Saluzzi how to play the latter instrument when he was seven years old. Saluzzi played folk music on the bandoneon until an uncle who had traveled in Europe taught him to expand his repertoire. By the age of fourteen, Saluzzi had mastered the instrument enough to play in his first band, the Trio Carnavel. He studied music in Buenos Aires and began to play professionally, becoming a member of the symphonic Orquesta Estable at Radio El Mundo, Argentina's first radio station.

While in Buenos Aires, Saluzzi met Astor Piazolla, the name most readily associated with traditional tango bandoneon music, at a time when the term "tango nuevo" was first coined. The two artists respected each other but Saluzzi's approach to the instrument differed in that his music was a fusion of jazz and bandoneon, while maestro Piazolla was firmly ensconced in traditional tango music. Saluzzi refrained from placing a label on his approach to the instrument, preferring to express the widest range of emotion on his instrument as possible. He quit his radio orchestra job in 1956, at the age of twenty-one, and returned to the district of Salta to develop compositions and to incorporate elements of folk music. His music, from the very beginning of his career, never fell into an easily classified form of Latin American music. Although he didn't set out to be unconventional, Saluzzi's compositions have always been vital, eclectic, and more all-encompassing than traditional tango music.

Saluzzi went on to collaborate with Gato Barbieri on the saxophonist's *Chapter One: Latin America* release in the early 1970s, and he undertook numerous South American tours with Mariano Mores, playing concerts in Bolivia, Peru, Colombia, and Venezuela. Saluzzi also worked as an arranger and soloist for Enrique Mario Francini's *Sinfonica de Tango*, which took him to Japan in 1977. Two years later, in 1979, he created his first quartet, Cuarteto Dino Saluzzi, which was well-received in Europe. Saluzzi also co-founded the experimental chamber ensemble Musica Creativa.

Saluzzi released the solo album *Kultrum* in 1983, an album of "storytelling" that was created spontaneously in the studio. The album was an imaginary and remarkably vivid return to the small towns and villages of his youth. In *Kultrum*, Saluzzi reworked elements of South American Indian music, tango, backwater folk tunes, and other musical influences from his childhood. From the early 1980s onward, Saluzzi collaborated with numerous American and European jazz musicians, including bassist Charlie Haden, trumpeter Palle Mikkelborg, and percussionist Pierre Favre for *Once Upon A Time...Far Away in the South*, released in 1986, and trumpeter Enrico Rava for *Volver* in 1988.

His second solo album, *Andina*, was released in 1988, and further displayed his unique compositions and musical ability. Saluzzi also played with Haden's Liberation Music Orchestra and with the Rava/Saluzzi Quintet, which toured extensively. Saluzzi has performed with scores of distinguished musicians over the years, most notably Louis Sclavis, Edward Vesala, Charlie Mariano, Al DiMeola, David Friedman, and Anthony Cox. With all these musicians, Saluzzi succeeds in blending his distinct sound into the mix to create a rich, fulfilling sound. In discussing the album *Rios*, a writer for *Vintage Guitar* magazine said, "(Saluzzi is teamed) with bassist Anthony Cox and marimba and vibraphonist David Friedman. The music is joyous and full of life, a celebratory dialogue between the deep, sad sound of the bandoneon and the happy, rippling tones of the vibraphone. The trio complements each other perfectly."

In 1991, Saluzzi realized a personal dream by recording *Mojotoro* in Argentina with his brothers Felix and Celso and his son Jos'e on drums. His son began his music studies at the age of six, and plays piano, drums, percussion, and the guitar. Mojotoro was astounding in that it drew upon the full range of South American music: tango, folk, candina music, candombe, and the milonga music of the la Pampa providence. After the release of *Mojotoro*, the Saluzzi family became a popular institution of the European touring circuit.

Saluzzi released *Cit'e de la Musique* in 1997, featuring his brothers, son, and American bassist Marc Johnson—who had played with John Abercrombie, Bill Evans, and Ralph Towner. Ouellette wrote, "It's the elder Saluzzi's intuitive genius for playing with impeccable integrity of emotion that recommends *Cit'e de la Musique*, which should be required listening for lite jazz cats aspiring to break through superficialities and play truly enrapturing music."

Saluzzi dedicated a new composition, "Gorri'on," on *Cit'e de la Musique* to French filmmaker Jean-Luc Godard. It was a solo tribute, and Richard Henderson of *Escape* magazine declared, "Saluzzi's new album could easily function as an alternative soundtrack to Godard's *Alphaville,* or to any film noir for that matter. The nine selections on *Cit'e de la Musique* are haunting, shadowy, and intimate..." Saluzzi's compositions move deliberately yet tentatively through the mournfulness and joy of life, capturing emotion in music and orchestrating the wonder of the human experience. Saluzzi plans to collaborate on an album with the classical chamber musicians Rosamunde Quartet and, toward that end, played with the group in a series of lauded concerts in the string quartet's hometown of Munich.

Selected discography

Kultrum, ECM, 1983.
(with others) *Once Upon a Time—Far Away in the South,* ECM, 1986.
Andina, ECM, 1988.
(with others) *Volver,* ECM, 1988.
Mojotoro, ECM, 1991.

(with others) *Rios,* Intuition, 1997.
Cit'e de la Musique, ECM, 1997.

Sources

Periodicals

Down Beat, November 1997.
Escape, October 1997.
The Herald, June 13, 1997.
Vintage Guitar Magazine, July 1997.

Online

Microsoft's Musiccentral.msn.com
www.ecmrecords.com

Additional material for this profile was provided by ECM Records/BMG Classics.

—*B. Kimberly Taylor*

Shai

R&B group

In the early 1990s, a trend of harmonized male R&B acts such as Color Me Badd and Boyz II Men ushered in Washington D.C.'s Shai. Taking their cue from a number of somber influences of the past, including church choirs, doo-wop singers, and barber shop quartets, Shai's debut album *If I Ever Fall In Love,* topped both pop and R&B charts. While the critical merits of Shai's work were debated, none could deny the inspired delivery of the group's vocals. Shai followed up their debut with a number of releases that retained the same stunning arrangements which sometimes overshadowed the group's own songwriting.

Shai banded together in 1990 on the campus of Howard University in Washington, D.C. when English major Carl "Groove" Martin and music student Darnell Van Rensalier were pledging the fraternity of Alpha Phi Alpha. Despite the twosome's differences in educational background, they were bound by a shared love for a cornucopia of musical tastes, including hip-hop, the classic 1970s funk of singer/guitarist George Clinton, and instrumental soundtracks. Martin and Van Rensalier began entering local talent shows as an a cappella duo but soon decided that a quartet would offer more range. They attracted zoology major Marc Gay and Van Rensalier's ex-roommate Garfield Bright into their project.

Gay stumbled upon the name "Shai" in the *Egyptian Book of the Dead* while looking for a nickname for a fellow fraternity brother. The foursome decided to take the name, which means "personification of destiny," as their own. Taking their new moniker to heart, the group quickly set out to make themselves stars. Martin had written the song "If I Ever Fall In Love" during a cross-country car trip, and believed the song was an inspired gift. This made the group work even harder to find it a public. "I swear, that song came to me," Martin beamed to *People* in April of 1993. "Here's verse one; here's the chorus; here's verse two ... I didn't think about it. I didn't write it down. I didn't do anything. I think God sent it, I really do."

With a borrowed 100 dollars, Shai created its first demo tape but was unable to spark the interest of any talent scouts during a promotional visit to New York City. Undaunted, the quartet chose to enter "If I Ever Fall In Love" in a listener's choice contest at Washington, D.C. radio station WPGC. Although Shai later admitted to supplying several of the requests for the song themselves, the station's disc jockey was bombarded by phone callers. Not only did the song win the contest, but it infiltrated the playlists of WPGC and at sister stations in Houston, Texas and Phoenix, Arizona. Having eluded the usual channels of building success, Shai was quickly courted by Gasoline Alley, a branch of MCA records, with whom the group signed an impressive seven-album contract.

Shai released "If I Ever Fall In Love" as a single in the fall of 1992, and it was as popular nationally as it was in the group's hometown. With a variety of material already in hand, the group was able to squeeze the recording of their debut album, also called *If I Ever Fall In Love,* into the 1992 calendar. Recorded in several weeks, the record offered a number of ballads and up-tempo numbers in addition to the title cut, and broke the top ten in both R&B and pop charts, finally going double platinum in the following year.

There was no critical mandate on *If I Ever Fall In Love*'s overall merits, but most writers were in accord as to the strength of Shai's sensual vocal talents. "The effect is an intense, intimate emotional atmosphere," Michael Eric Dyson wrote of the album in *Rolling Stone.* "Shai joins the spiritual yearnings of [vocal contemporaries] Take Six with the secular pull of [Philadelphia soul quartet] Boyz II Men. That tension between desire and fulfillment give's Shai's work a haunting luminescence – and makes for a riveting art."

Other critics found that while the group's singing was pleasant enough, the overall strength of their material was an impediment. "Shai ... sing serious, mournful harmonies that work best on ballads like the a cappella title song as well as 'Comforter' and 'Sexual,'" penned

For the Record . . .

Members include **Garfield Bright,** (born October 21, 1969, in Nashville, TN), vocals; **Marc Gay,** (Born January 21, 1969, in Miami, FL), vocals; **Carl Martin,** ("Groove", born August 29, 1970, in Lafayette, LA), vocals; **Darnell Van Rensalier,** (born May 17, 1970, in Patterson, NJ), vocals.

Band formed in Washington, D.C. by Martin and Van Rensalier, 1990; won a "make-it-or-break-it" radio contest with demo tape, making "If I Ever Fall In Love" a local smash, 1992; signed a seven record deal with Gasoline Alley and release debut album *If I Ever Fall In Love,* 1992; perform at President Bill Clinton's Inauguration, 1993; appeared at Hall of Fame show at the legendary Apollo Theater alongside 1970s singers Al Green and Teddy Pendergrass in July of 1993; released *Right Back At Cha,* 1993; released *Blackface,* 1995.

Addresses: *Record company*—Gasoline Alley/MCA, 1755 Broadway, Eighth Floor, New York, NY, 10019.

Village Voice critic Nelson George in May of 1993. "But Shai's dance music is unconvincing and overall this twelve cut collection is too mellow by far." To Shai's credit, the band did write all of their material, with chief tunesmith Martin also taking on production duties – something that many of their "neo-doo-wop" contemporaries, such as Color Me Badd, were unable to do. Nonetheless, both "Comforter" and "Baby I'm Yours" also ranked high on more than one chart.

Shai capitalized on their national popularity with a number of live performances, including a European tour. Early in 1993, the group was given an impressive invitation to perform at the Presidential Inauguration which Shai accepted. Perhaps equally notable was the group's performance in New York City at the Apollo Theater's Hall of Fame all-star concert in June of 1993. Wearing zoot suits in homage to R&B harmonizers of the past, the group delivered a version of "Java Jive," a standard of the vocal quartet the Ink Spots during the 1940s and 1950s. Along with the suddenness of playing such prestigious events, Shai was also bemused by its newfound status as teen heartthrobs. "Sometimes girls scream and run in the opposite direction," Bright confessed to *People,* "or else they'll freeze with their mouths hanging open."

Shai finished off their busy year with the release of a collection of remixes and live tracks entitled *Right Back At Cha,* after which the group took a break from the studio. When the group returned to make their second full length album *Blackface,* Shai spent a great deal more time to craft their new songs than they had with their debut. "We were rushed on delivering that album [*If I Ever Fall In Love*]," Bright admitted to J.R. Reynolds in *Billboard* in 1995. "Since then, we've really got a chance to get to know each other musically, which helped fine-tune our focus for *Blackface,* which took nine months to produce."

The band concentrated on making a more rhythm-based effort with their second album, as well as on giving it a more adult-oriented appeal. Unfortunately, like many young groups who self-consciously opt for a mature image, Shai suffered in popularity and *Blackface* was an overall disappointment. Still, the band continued to make music and maintained that the album and its title were a perfect banner for Shai's uplifting "personification of destiny." "The face behind any face is a blank, empty face that you can draw on to obtain peace and creativity," Garfield explained to Reynolds. "There's a potential for everyone to connect. Every creature made up of energy – it's a totally positive vibe. The trick is to connect with it."

Selected discography

If I Ever Fall In Love, Gasoline Alley/MCA, 1992.
Right Back At Cha, Gasoline Alley/MCA, 1993.
Blackface, Gasoline Alley/MCA, 1995.

Sources

Billboard, January 9, 1993; July 3, 1993; August 19, 1995.
People Weekly, April 5, 1993.
Rolling Stone, April 1, 1993.
Village Voice, May 11, 1993.

—*Shaun Frentner*

The Shamen

Techno/dance band

Although many stylistic changes were to ensue after their debut album *Drop,* released in 1987, the Scottish-born dance outfit the Shamen continued to be anchored by the themes of mind-expansion, mysticism, and ecological concern that ran through their early guitar-oriented work. After discovering the vibrant subculture of rave music, the Shamen quickly embraced the potential of new technologies and became a chart-topping international attraction by the end of the decade with their album *En-Tact*, a work that helped popularize techno in the mainstream. After the tragic death of member Will Sin in 1991, the band's future was uncertain, but despite a hot and cold relationship with critics and battles with their label, One Little Indian, the Shamen continued to create engaging dance music in step with the age of the internet.

The Shamen were formed in 1986 by Colin Angus, a young native of Aberdeen, Scotland who dropped out of college to dabble in making psychedelic music along the lines of earlier groups like Pink Floyd and the Thirteenth Floor Elevators. After a promising EP release, "Young 'Till Yesterday," Angus created the album *Drop* and a series of like minded singles. As *Melody Maker* in a review of "Knature of a Girl," a single from early 1988, "the Shamen take the best fancies of Sixties psychedelia without turning into a period piece." Angus also showed his lineage to that decade's flower-power political agenda with songs like the anti-war protest

"Happy Days," which was soon used in a commercial campaign by a beer company obviously blind to Angus's lyrical thrust.

By 1988, the Shamen were joined by synth-player Will Sin, born in Glasgow, Scotland, and the band's direction began to change radically. Angus and Sin, who had met working at a psychiatric ward, moved to London, England where they were seduced by the energy of the city's culture of underground dance parties, or raves. In the beat-driven electronic music of acid house, Angus saw the next step in his journey. "I could recognize the psychedelic aspects of the music immediately, but it was immediately danceable," he recalled to Bob Gourley of the online magazine *Chaos Control.* "And the reports I was hearing about the parties, the multi-media events very like what I imagine events were like in the [19]60's in terms of massive light shows with strobes and oils and lots of people enjoying the company of one another in a psychedelically enhanced atmosphere of love."

Stripped down to a duo, Angus and Sin began to remodel the Shamen in light of acid house, resulting in the EP "What's Going Down?" and their second album *In Gorbachev We Trust*, a record which fused high-energy rhythms with trenchant comments on global politcs. Perhaps more importantly, the group dived into dance culture, launching their own series of concerts/parties under the name of Synergy in 1989. The Shamen's live presentation began to blur the boundaries between rock gigs and warehouse parties, for as Will Sin explained in an online profile, "we [were] trying to create our own context for best presenting what we do." It was also around this time that the duo met "Evil" Eddie Richards, an ex-milk deliverer, DJ, and rapper who soon joined the Shamen under the name Mr. C.

After several months of consideration, the Shamen joined the roster at the One Little Indian label, a label known for its groundbreaking pop groups such as the Sugarcubes and No-man. In the spring of 1990, the Shamen made their label debut with the single "Pro>Gen," which was also the first recording made with Mr. C supplying vocals. Although upon its first release, "Pro>Gen" only skimmed the surface of the Top 40, but the Shamen had decidedly veered towards making chart-oriented singles. *En-Tact,* the Shamen's first bona fide techno album, was released in the fall of 1990, selling over 100,000 copies and garnering solid critical reviews.

The Shamen were duly pleased by the massive amount of people they could reach as a hit-making outfit, and that the positivity shared at their Synergy parties need not be confined. "I really did feel at that moment that

For the Record . . .

Members include **Jhelisa Anderson**, (formerly of Soul Family Sensation), joined in 1992, vocals; **Colin Angus**, (born in Aberdeen, Scotland, the only member from the original lineup), vocals, songwriting, and programming; **Edward Richards** (Mr. C born in London, England), joined in 1990, vocals and dancing; **Will Sin**, (born Glasgow, Scotland, died while recording a video in the Canary Islands, May 22, 1991) joined the group in 1988, synthesizers and programming; **Victoria Wilson-James**, (formerly of the group Soul II Soul), joined 1995, vocals.

Band formed in 1986 by Angus in Scotland; released debut album *Drop* on Moeshka Records, 1987; relocated to London, England in 1988, released follow-up album *In Gorbachev We Trust,* 1989; signed to One Little Indian the same year; released breakthrough dance album *En-Tact*, 1990; performed on the British television show *Top of the Pops* the same year; "Ebeneezer Goode," the group's fifteenth single, became their first Number One hit, 1992; fourth album *Boss Drum* released, 1992; headlined at the Freedom of the City concert to 12,000 fans in Glasgow, Scotland, 1993; released final original album for One Little Indian, *Axis Mutatis*, 1995; announced the album *UV* would be their last, 1998.

Addresses: *Home*—P.O. Box 102, London, E15 2HH, U.K.; *Email*—shamen@moksha.demon.co.uk; *internet address*—www.drci.co.uk/drci/shamen.

everyone was feeling exactly the same," Angus told Tony Marcus in an online interview, "that this was it, we could take control, we had the power. That's what the "move any mountain" lyric from "Pro>Gen" is all about. Large numbers of people all with the same vibe." However, just as the Shamen were reaching international success, tragedy struck. While making a video in the Canary Islands for a re-release of "Pro>Gen" during the spring of 1991, Will Sin met with a strong undercurrent and drowned at the age of 31. Angus was deeply saddened by this loss, but after a brief hiatus, decided to continue with Mr. C. In the meantime, "Move Any Mountain –Pro>Gen '91" became a hit worldwide.

When the Shamen returned in 1992 with the single "LSI," or "Love-Sex-Intelligence," they had been joined by

singer Jhelisa Anderson, an ex-member of the group Soul Family Sensation. Adopting an image of rubber-clad club goers, and pushing the finger-wriggling Mr. C's energy to the forefront, the Shamen annoyed some critics with their euphoric club-culture forays, such as *Melody Maker,* who ran a series of cartoons lampooning Mr. C. The album which followed, *Boss Drum,* boasted a several other Top 10 singles such as "Ebeneezer Goode," itself making its U.K debut at number three. *Boss Drum* also marked the band's full departure into high-tech shamanism—a merging of electronics with the ancient mystical traditions of tribal cultures. On the "Re: Evolution," track, New Age writer Terence McKenna made a guest vocal appearance to draw a "connection between plant psychedelics, human evolution, all-night dancing, and eco-consciousness," as Marcus appraised. Released as a single, the soothing ambiance of "Re: Evolution" found its way into the U.K. Top 20 with almost no airplay.

Largely due to problems with One Little Indian, much time passed before the Shamen were able to release an album of new material, although a slew of remix projects trickled into record stores. In the meantime, the Shamen began exploring technology in forms that sometimes exceeded music alone. In addition to creating a soundtrack for "The Ozone," a children's show on the BBC network, the Shamen unveiled Nemeton, one of the first band-oriented interactive websites, seeing the use of cyberspace as an extension of Shamen's project. "We've always seen ourselves as an 'information band,'" Angus told Marcus, "so it was a natural step to connect to the internet."

The Shamen's focus upon electronic age mysticism was never more pointed than on their fifth studio album, *Axis Mutatis*, released in 1995. A sound aquarium of trance-inducing, flowing synth work, *Axis Mutatis* was the last Shamen record issued by One Little Indian, who reportedly preferred the group's dance-pop sensibilities over eclectic experiments. The album's "S2 Translation," for example, used a sequence of DNA codes to generate its electronic bleeps and pulses. However, while the album's sales were fair, the band's new level of global concerns seemed heavy-handed to many critics. As Lee Graham Bridges wrote for *Consumable* online, "there are some bands that can pull off being so-called 'political bands,' that is, bands that can address political issues in their music. Whether the Shamen are capable of this I cannot say, but they didn't quite pull it off this time…The Shamen need to realize that they don't need to make a statement in addition to the music—the music is the statement." *Melody Maker*'s Andrew Mueller was fully in accord with such criticism, claiming that "*Axis Mutatis* bulges with concepts and ideas for the sake of being seen to bulge with concepts and ideas....The Shamen should lighten up a bit. Nothing dates so badly as self-conscious futurism."

Although it was their political concerns that grated the nerves of many reviewers, the Shamen were unshaken, and continued to spread their philosophies in their music and web page. Risking a loss of sales, the Shamen decided to offer the song "Destination Eschaton" online before it was available in stores. As Angus explained to Calum Thompson in *Fly* magazine that "the aim was to focus attention on Nemeton, our web site, and perhaps to provide a prescient glimpse of how a medium like the net could be used to market music direct from the artist without the need for a record company."

In 1997, *The Remix Collection* was unveiled, over an hour of the Shamen's strongest material revamped by some of the biggest names in techno, such as 808 State, Orbital, and Richie Hawtin. While not a "greatest hits" package in the strictest sense, the collection was a perfect introduction for newcomers, and reminded critics of the vital role the Shamen had played in forging new dance music. "Bad politics, dodgy costumes, and 'trip to the tub with a rubba-dub-dub' rapping aside, much of *Collection* is fabulous pop music, chart-techno perfected," posited Neil Kulkarni in *Melody Maker* "Pretty much an index of early Nineties pop and still startlingly wonderful to this day."

Although the group kicked off the following year with a new single, "U-Nations," as well as plans for a new album entitled *UV*, they announced that these releases would probably mark the end of the Shamen. However, it would be unlikely that its members end their activities within music or otherwise. While Mr. C continued at the helm of his own techno label Plink Plonk, Angus delved into making even more esoteric music, generated through geometric formulas and even with the input of the human brain's electronic impulses. "We'll just carry on promoting what we believe in, and promoting our philosophies,"

Mr. C told *Melody Maker*. "That's what the Shamen are all about—getting shamanic philosophies, environmental issues, and planetary issues across in the mainstream via the pop medium."

Selected discography

Drop, Communion, 1987.
Strange Day Dreams, Moksha-Matieriali Sonori, 1988. (Compilation of early material)
In Gorbachev We Trust, Moksha-Demon, 1989.
En-Tact, One Little Indian, 1990.
Progeny, One Little Indian, 1991. (Remixes of "Pro>Gen")
Boss Drum, One Little Indian, 1992.
On Air, Band of Joy, 1993. (Radio 1 sessions)
Different Drum, One Little Indian, 1993. (Remixes of *Boss Drum* tracks)
Axis Mutatis, One Little Indian, 1995.
The Remix Collection, One Little Indian, 1997.
UV, Moksha, 1998.

Sources

Periodicals

Fly, January 6, 1996.
Jockey Slut, September 1995.
Melody Maker, March 5, 1988; October 28, 1995; November 4, 1995; January 11, 1997.

Online

http://www.chaoscontrol.com/archives/shamen.html
http://www.nemeton.com
http://www.shamen.ee/articles
http://www.users.cybercity.dk/~ccc24608/question.htm
http://www.westnet.com/consumable/1996/01.18/revshame.html

—*Shaun Frentner*

Silver Apples

Electronic rock

Scholars of electronic music consider the Silver Apples architects of a genre back to which Nineties techno, Eighties new wave, and Seventies progressive rock can be retraced. Formed in the late 1960s, the New York City band released two experimental albums and then disappeared—but "their music," wrote Robert Coyne years later in the *Rough Guide to Rock,* "still sounds shocking and exciting." The creative genius of the Silver Apples was the one-name Simeon, who built a queer, rudimentary synthesizer apparatus that emitted much of the band's eerie sound; he vanished when the band broke up, along with his self-named instrument. Rehearing the original Silver Apples, wrote Coyne, "suggests that the potential of electronic rock 'n' roll have been partially squandered."

Simeon was originally from eastern Tennessee, but grew up in New Orleans. He exhibited a talent for drawing and painting as a child, but also played the trumpet from an early age. He even performed with an established band, but when the budding musician was hit by a car at the age of 12, he lost his trumpet in the collision and his family could not afford to replace it. As a young adult, he moved to New York City to pursue a career in the visual arts, and one summer worked as a dishwasher at a camp in New York State to earn money. There, he and his colleagues—many of whom were bluegrass musicians—spent their off-hours jamming together, and

Simeon's love of music was rekindled. Back in New York City, they became a soul-and rock outfit called Random Concept, with Simeon behind the mike.

After Random Concept, Simeon then became a member of the Overland Stage Electric Band, which was also the house band at a Greenwich Village hangout called Cafe Wha! The Overland was a blues band, but one night around 1967 Simeon used an oscillator to add spooky outer-space-like sounds to a live session. Afterward, the band's leader informed Simeon that if he did that again, he would be released from his duties, but Cafe Wha!'s prescient owner sided with Simeon because he liked the odd sound. The owner then fired the Overland band and hired Simeon and Overland member Dan Taylor as his new house band. Taylor was a drummer whose previous experience included playing with Jimi Hendrix. He and Simeon named themselves the Silver Apples.

They began writing music together, with lyrics penned by a poet named Stanley Warren, and found approving audiences within New York City's hotbed of the avant-garde, Greenwich Village. Encouraged by the audience reception of the blips and bleeps Simeon pulled from a variety of electronic devices, he built a large, unwieldy instrument and named it after himself. The "Simeon" consisted of three plywood boxes, several oscillators and 86 telegraph keys. They were color-coded, and by using his fingers, elbows and feet, a variety of sounds could be extracted. Warren's lyrics attempted to evoke a literary counterpart; "smoldering charades of smoky verity....," as sung by Simeon, was one example. As *Village Voice* writer Richard Gehr explained in a 1997 profile, back then, "Taylor beat out lopsided rhythms on tom-tom drums tuned to the oscillators as Simeon pressed buttons and twirled knobs, creating sounds somewhere between those of a synthesizer and an effects-laden electric guitar."

Another writer, Brian Turner, described the Silver Apples live experience in an essay on the band for the Gallery of Sound web site: "Amidst the futuristic melodies and psych pop came flurries of electronic freakouts, where Simeon continued to hold down the foundation of the song with Taylor while creating amazing blasts of gurgling analog synth and other bizarre tones creating by homemade contraptions." The time and the place was right for just such experimentation, and hipster New Yorkers made up the Silver Apples fan base. They also attracted interest from the record industry in the days when experimental rockers such as Frank Zappa, Kim Fowley, and Velvet Underground were selling vinyl. The Apples were signed by Kapp Records, perhaps against the better judgment of all involved parties, for Kapp was also home to an odd roster that included Eartha Kitt and Burt Bachrach.

The Silver Apples' self-titled debut was released in 1968. The first single was "Oscillations"; "Seagreen Serenades," a homage to marijuana bliss, followed. Though *Silver Apples* was marketed by Kapp in a rather haphazard fashion, it sold a respectable number of copies and remained on the *Billboard* Top 100 album charts for ten weeks. Coyne, writing in the *Rough Guide to Rock*, termed it "amazing," laden with "sci-fi warbling, whistling and whizzing, fruity bass pulses and chattering, back-to-front drums."

The following year the Apples released a second album on Kapp, *Contact*. It offered a more diverse range of songs, but still relied heavily on the electronic whizz-bang generated from Simeon and his instrument. There were a few hook-laden, near-pop tunes, but also some slightly menacing, decidedly un-Woodstockian sentiments. Warren's atrocious poetry had been jettisoned, and Simeon wrote the lyrics for *Contact*'s songs instead. His bluegrass experience surfaced in one track that featured a banjo. "Wailing, wandering leads featured heavily along with a high-pitched, theremin-type sound," wrote the *Rough Guide to Rock*'s Coyne about the record, and cited "A Pox on You" as "their most enduring song."

Endure it did—*Contact* was the last recorded effort of the band for nearly thirty years. Three decades after its release, critics still concurred about the legacy left behind by the Apples. The *Village Voice*'s Gehr wrote that both LPs "strike a delicate balance between hard technophilia and flower-power romanticism"; Gehr also noted that the music from the Silver Apples was the direct precursor to the arty German synthesizer band Kraftwerk, who achieved an international cult following with several releases in the 1970s and 1980s. English bands like New Order were greatly influenced by Kraftwerk, as were future techno artists like Carl Craig.

Ran Out of Town

In support of *Contact*, the Silver Apples embarked upon an extensive tour and took the stage of some legendary music venues, including the Fillmore in San Francisco and Max's Kansas City in New York but other shows were less than well received. In some cases, they were booked as openers for Southern rock bands and their decidedly arty music incited the threat of violence from some audiences. Simeon and Taylor did go back into the studio to make a third album, but then Kapp went under, and the tapes rotted away in storage, never to be released. They soon disbanded and disappeared.

Yet the hard-to-get Silver Apples albums had always been revered among European devotees of progressive rock, and in 1994 a German label, TRC, issued a double-CD version of first two albums. Soon, other bands known for their love of vintage electronic instrumentation, such as Stereolab, started to cover their songs. An English label released an entire tribute album, *Electronic Evocations: A Tribute to the Silver Apples,* in 1995. Sony Music, who sensed a profitable resurgence, hired a private investigation service to track down Simeon and Taylor, but came up empty. Simeon, however, had simply returned to painting as a vocation and was living in Maryland. He had held a number of jobs over the years, including television reporter and ice-cream truck driver. One day, he visited an art gallery in Brooklyn, New York, and met Xian Hawkins, a keyboard player from the band Mobius Strip, who recognized his name. "He asked me if I knew what was going on," Simeon told Neil Strauss in the *New York Times*.

Resurrection

Urged by Hawkins's words, Simeon found the tribute album in a record store, and the telephoned label to thank them—"They promised us the world if we would create some new music for them," he told Strauss. Simeon then tried to track down Taylor himself, but had no luck. The Simeon instrument had also vanished, after Simeon left it under a friend's house in Alabama in the mid-1980s. So he recruited Hawkins, and added another keyboardist, backup singers, and a new drummer, Joe Propatier, who had played in a number of indie-rock bands. He also began writing new material.

The first new Silver Apples song since 1969, "Fractal Flow," was released on Enraptured Records in 1997. They debuted as a live act again in January of 1997 at the Knitting Factory in New York and the reception was a warm one from critics and fans of electronic music of all ages. They embarked on an extensive tour, including Europe and Japan, later that year and recorded new material with legendary alternative rock producer Steve Albini in his Chicago studios. There were ten new songs, and three revamped versions of original Silver Apples material on *Beacon,* released in 1997 on the California jazz label Whirlybird. Another record, *Decatur,* was planned for 1998, and the Beastie Boys were reportedly interested in re-issuing the original LPs on their Grand Royal label. The German hardcore techno band, Atari Teenage Riot, was eager to collaborate with Simeon, who seemed to have emerged from the years of obscurity with a healthy perspective on his newfound cult-hero status. "I feel like a like a caged animal that's suddenly been released and he's running around the zoo terrorizing people," he told the *New York Times.*

Selected discography

Silver Apples, Kapp, 1968.
Contact, Kapp, 1969.
Beacon, Whirlybird, 1997.
Decatur, Whirlybird, 1998.

Sources

Periodicals

New York Times, January 23, 1997.
Village Voice, February 4, 1997, p. 61.

Online

http://www.silverapples.com
http://www.roughguides.com/rock
http://www.whirlybirdrecords.com

—Carol Brennan

Frank Sinatra

Singer

AP/World Photos. Reproduced by permission.

Legendary singer Frank (Francis Albert) Sinatra was arguably one of the greatest—and most acclaimed—vocalists in this century; he made 1,414 studio recordings and had at least one song on the music charts every year between 1945 and 1995. He was as much noted for his passionate approach to life as for his music, and his ironclad self-confidence combined with classic good looks, pitched him into the realm of celebrity early in his career. He married high-profile actresses and starred in films himself, and his glamorous lifestyle eventually epitomized the Hollywood of the 1950s and 1960s. Frank Sinatra became an icon due to his romantic ballads, smooth, heartfelt vocal style, timeless material, and abundance of style. His singles "My Way" and "New York, New York" were so popular they transcended music to become a part of a larger, cultural bond. *Time* magazine's Jay Cocks wrote, "Not only does his music define the time and temper of the American decades in which it was made, but his singing moves those songs out of time into something indistinct, everlasting. In Sinatra's music, there is no past tense. You could say he was the greatest, and that's right. But ... there's nothing you can call him that doesn't in some way sell him short. Except Sinatra."

Legendary jazz vocalist Cassandra Wilson told *Time* magazine's Christopher John Farley in 1998, "I wish Frank Sinatra influenced more singers today. He comes from a time when it about the phrasing of a piece, the emotional content of a piece. He descended from Billie Holiday and singers who placed more emphasis on the lyrical content of the song." Bono, lead singer for Ireland's rock group U2, told Farley, "Rock-n-roll people love Frank Sinatra because Frank Sinatra has got what we want—swagger and attitude."

Frank Sinatra was born in Hoboken, NJ, on December 12, 1915 to Anthony Martin ("Marty") a boxer, boiler and fireman and Natalie Della ("Dolly") Garaventi Sinatra a midwife and saloon owner. His mother allegedly oversaw an illegal abortion service. Dolly Sinatra was a powerful figure in the local community, and her temperament was closely matched to that of her son's: both were fiery, determined, and strong-willed, traits that would describe Frank Sinatra throughout his long life and career. Sinatra was a lackluster student in school, and he decided while in his teens that he wanted to be a singer. A friend of Sinatra's named Maria Brush Schrieber told Kitty Kelley author of *His Way: The Unauthorized Biography of Frank Sinatra,* "He loved hanging around musicians, so I suggested he get an orchestra together for our Wednesday night school dances. He'd just started singing (publicly) a little bit (at about age seventeen), and in exchange for hiring the musicians he'd get to sing a few numbers with the band."

Born Francis Albert Sinatra, December 12, 1915 in Hoboken, NJ; died May 17, 1998; father named Anthony Martin (a boxer, boilermaker, and fireman); mother named Natalie Della Garaventi (a midwife and bar owner); married Nancy Barbato on February 4, 1939 (divorced 1951); married actress Ava Gardner on November 7, 1951 (divorced 1957); married actress Mia Farrow on July 19, 1966 (divorced 1968); married dancer Barbara Jane Blakeley Marx on July 11, 1976; children (first marriage) Nancy Sandra and Franklin Wayne.

Worked as a copy boy and reporter covering college sports for the Jersey Observer during the early 1930s; professional singer 1936-1998; sang with the Hoboken Four in 1937; featured singer with Harry James' MusicMakers from 1939-1940, with the Tommy Dorsey Orchestra 1940-42, and with Benny Goodman's band in 1942; began solo career in 1942; star of *Lucky Strike Hit Parade* radio program from 1943-1945; actor in more than 60 films, including *From Here To Eternity, 1953; The Man With The Golden Arm,* 1955; and *The Detective,* 1968; producer of and actor in the film *The First Deadly Sin,* 1980.

Awards: *Billboard* magazine's Top Band Vocalist, 1941; *Down Beat* magazine's Top Band Vocalist, 1943; recipient of Special Academy Award, 1945; Academy Award for Best Supporting Actor for *From Here To Eternity,* 1953; *Down Beat* magazine's Most Popular Male Vocalist and Top Pop Records Personality, 1954; Grammy Award for Best Album, 1959, 1965, and 1966, for Best Male Vocalist, 1959, 1965, and 1966, and for Record of the Year, 1966; Emmy Award, 1965; George Foster Peabody Award, 1965; Jean Hersholt Humanitarian Award from Motion Picture Academy of Arts and Sciences, 1971; Screen Actors Guild Award, 1972; Presidential Medal of Freedom, 1985; Kennedy Center Honor, 1986; Lifetime Achievement Award from National Association for the Advancement of Colored People (NAACP), 1987.

Sinatra's first real group was called The Three Flashes, a singing and dancing trio which, due to the addition of another "Flash," later became The Hoboken Four. Sinatra

is quoted in *His Way* as saying, "I always liked to sing and I liked to be around bands and to have a part of the band glamour. I couldn't play an instrument and I didn't care about learning to play one.... While I wasn't the best singer in the world, they weren't the best bands in the country, either." After taking voice lessons, Sinatra's mother used her influence with the musician's union to get him a job singing at the Rustic Cabin for $15 a week, and his performances were broadcast over the radio. Trumpeter Harry James, after recently leaving the Benny Goodman band, was searching for a singer for his new band in June of 1939 when he first heard Sinatra over the radio. He was so taken with Sinatra's voice that he went to the Rustic Cabin and hired Sinatra to sing with his MusicMakers for $75 per month. One of the early Sinatra-James hits was portentously titled, "All or Nothing at All". Unfortunately, reviews of the young Sinatra's singing were not favorable, and the band was even thrown out of the club, Victor Hugo's, after one particularly underwhelming session. After just seven months of his two-year contract, Sinatra quit the MusicMakers to join Tommy Dorsey's orchestra.

Career Blossomed with Dorsey

Sinatra came into his own while working with Dorsey. He learned about phrasing, dynamics, and style from the way Dorsey played his horn, and he enjoyed his work because Dorsey felt a singer should always be given a perfect setting. Sinatra worked diligently at developing his own style, and often slurred the vocals just enough to drive the young girls in the audience wild. One tale has it that Sinatra's agent, George Evans, planted screaming teenage girls in the front rows at Sinatra's shows as a ploy to create a sensation. If that's the case, the ploy worked. The Dorsey-Sinatra single, "I'll Never Smile Again," went to number one on the charts, and by 1941 Sinatra had dethroned Bing Crosby in the *Downbeat* magazine poll for Top Band Vocalist. In January of 1942, Sinatra recorded four solo songs and was on the verge of leaving Dorsey's band. The two had grown very close and Dorsey was even godfather to Sinatra's daughter, so when Sinatra left the band in September of 1942, it marked the end of their friendship.

In December of 1942 Sinatra sang with Benny Goodman's band, widely considered the most popular band at the time, at New York City's Paramount, earning $1,250 a week. He also appeared in the movie "Higher and Higher". He was criticized for not serving in the armed forces during World War II at time when patriotism was running high. In *His Way,* he is quoted as saying, " I've planned my career. From the first minute I walked on stage I determined to get exactly where I am." In 1946 he signed a five-year contract with MGM for $260,000 annually to make movies at a time when he was at the top of the music polls and had sold more than ten million records. By 1949, Sinatra had dropped to number 49 in the top 50 in record sales, due to his emphasis on a movie career at the expense of his music career. At this juncture in his career, his films didn't take off as planned and his marriage to first wife Nancy Barbato was shaky.

Ava Gardner a Major Influence

In 1951 he divorced Nancy and married high-profile actress Ava Gardner. Their stormy marriage lasted for only five years, but Gardner was instrumental in securing his role in the film *From Here To Eternity*. Sinatra had desperately yearned for the role, and when he landed it he was overjoyed. He garnered an Oscar for Best Supporting Actor, and went on to appear in *The Man With The Golden Arm, Pal Joey, Some Came Running, A Hole in the Head, The Joker is Wild, The Manchurian Candidate,* and more than 52 other movies. Gardner also had a profound effect on his singing. Veteran music arranger Nelson Riddle told Kelley, "It was Ava who did that, who taught him how to sing a torch song. That's how he learned. She was the greatest love of his life and he lost her."

Sinatra's collaboration with Riddle began when he left the Columbia label in 1952 and signed with Capitol. He was teamed with Riddle and the two collaborated on such hits as "My One and Only Love," "A Foggy Day," "My Funny Valentine," and 1954's *Billboard* top single, the million-disc seller, "Young At Heart". After a ten-year hiatus, Sinatra had returned to the top of the charts. His string of million-sellers continued with "Love and Marriage," "Learnin" the Blues," "The Tender Trap," "All The Way," "Witchcraft," and "Hey, Jealous Lover." In 1956 he divorced Ava Gardner, and dated a succession of entertainment figures such as Liz Taylor, Lauren Bacall, Judy Garland, and Juliet Prowse. His personal life sometimes overshadowed his public persona: affiliations with reputed mobsters like Sam Giancana caused him much grief and truncated his invitations to president J.F. Kennedy's white house parties. Cocks wrote, "There was ... an Italian street-kid swagger that made such good cover for his black-and-blue soulfulness....that attitude was a dodge ... protecting his private preserve of deepest feeling and experience, saving it for where it was needed most: the songs."

Sinatra's 1965 album, *September of My Years,* won a Grammy Award, and in 1971 he announced his retirement at a farewell show at L.A.'s Music Center. His retirement was short-lived and he returned with a television special and a new album, Ol' Blue Eyes is Back, in 1973. Sinatra was regarded in the music world as the consummate professional. Quincy Jones produced Sinatra's 1984 release, L.A. Is My Lady, and described his experience with Sinatra for *Downbeat:* "He came in at 2 p.m., and in less than two hours we had rehearsed, had keys and routinesn on ten songs.... Frank is one take, that's it. If the band's not in shape, he leaves them behind ... he came in at 7[:00], and at 8:20, baby, we went home. None of that three month stuff." Sinatra was criticized for performing in Sun City, South Africa, in the early 1980s, yet he devoted a lot of energy to fighting racism and performing community services. He received numerous awards along these lines, including the Philadelphia Freedom Medal and the Presidential Medal of Freedom. When Sinatra released *Duets* in 1993, which featured some of the brightest stars in music singing with him, he further underscored the fact that his appeal and his music are universal.

Cocks wrote, "The proud champion of classic American pop fought a pitched battle against the engulfing tide of rock in the '60s. Became music's elder statesman in the '70s. Then the resurgent master of the '80s. And—at last, at the end of his days—the icon who could be forgiven anything for a song." He died of a heart attack on May 14, 1998 in Los Angeles, California. He is survived by his wife and three children.

Selected discography

Albums; released by Capitol

Song For Young Lovers, 1954
Swing Easy, 1954.
In The Wee Small Hours, 1955.
Songs For Swingin' Lovers, 1956.
Close To You, 1957.
A Swingin' Affair, 1957.
Where Are You', 1957.
A Jolly Christmas From Frank Sinatra, 1957.
Come Fly With Me, 1958.
Only the Lonely, 1958.
Come Dance With Me, 1959.
Look To Your Heart, 1959.
No One Cares, 1959.
Nice 'n' Easy, 1960.
Sinatra's Swingin' Session, 1961.
All The Way, 1961.
Come Swing With Me, 1961.
Point of No Return, 1962.
Sinatra Sings of Love and Things, 1962.
Point of No Return, 1962.

Frank Sinatra Sings Rodgers and Hart, 1963.
Tell Her You Love Her, 1963.
The Selected Johnny Mercer, 1963.
The Great Hits of Frank Sinatra, 1964.
The Selected Cole Porter, 1965.
Forever Frank, 1966.
The Movie Songs, 1967.
Duets, 1993.

Released by Reprise

Ring A Ding-Ding, 1961.
Sinatra Swings, 1961.
I Remember Tommy, 1961.
Sinatra and Strings, 1962.
Sinatra and Swingin' Brass, 1962.
All Alone, 1962.
Sinatra-Basie, 1963.
The Concert Sinatra, 1963.
Sinatra's Sinatra, 1963.
Frank Sinatra Sings Days of Wine and Roses, Moon River and Other Academy Award Winners, 1964.
Sinatra-Basie: It Might As Well Be Swing, 1964.
Softly, As I Leave You, 1964.
Sinatra '65, 1965.
September of My Years, 1965.
A Man and His Music, 1965.
My Kind of Broadway, 1965.
Moonlight Sinatra, 1966.
Strangers in the Night, 1966.
Sinatra-Basie: Sinatra at the Sands, 1966.
That's Life, 1966.
Francis Albert Sinatra & Antonio Carlos Jobim, 1967.
Frank Sinatra and Frank & Nancy, 1967.
Francis A. & Edward K., 1968.
Cycles, 1968.
My Way, 1969.
A Man Alone, 1969.
Watertown, 1970.
Sinatra & Company, 1971.
Ol' Blue Eyes Is Back, 1973.
Some Nice Things I've Missed, 1974.

The Main Event/Live From Madison Square Garden, 1974.
Trilogy (three record lp), 1980.
She Shot Me Down, 1981.
The Reprise Collection (4 CD set), 1992.
Sinatra and Sextet: Live in Paris (1962 recording), 1994.
Everything Happens to Me, 1996.

On Qwest:

L.A. Is My Lady (arranged by Quincy Jones), 1984.

On Columbia:

Frank Sinatra—The voice: The Columbia Years, 1943-1952, 1986.
Swing and Dance with Frank Sinatra, 1996.

Sources

Books

Ewen, David, *All the Years of American Popular Music,* Prentice-Hall, 1977.
Kelley, Kitty, *His Way: The Unauthorized Biography of Frank Sinatra,* Bantam, 1986.
Marsh, Dave and John Swenson, eds., *The Rolling Stone Record Guide,* Random House/Rolling Stone Press, 1979.
Simon, George T., *The Big Bands,* Schirmer Books, 1967.

Periodicals

Down Beat, March, 1985; April, 1985.
Rolling Stone, June 12, 1980; September 18, 1980.
Time, May 25, 1998.

Online

www.musicnet.com/franksinatra/discography

—B. Kimberly Taylor

Snow

Rap musician

In the predominantly urban-based, African-American world of rap, Caucasian newcomers have been characteristically met with suspicions of cultural appropriation, as was the case with comic-book flash in the pan Vanilla Ice, who fabricated his past to give him the street-wise credibility many "gangster" rappers wear on their sleeve. Irish-Canadian Snow had no need for such phony publicity, as his childhood was steeped in the harsh pressures of city life, as well as to the sounds of Jamaican inspired reggae. When his debut single "Informer" rocketed to the top of the sales charts in the Untied States and Canada, the singer was serving prison time for a knifing to which he pleaded innocent. Nevertheless, Snow was dogged by comparisons to Vanilla Ice from the onset and found himself with the burden of proving he was not a mere novelty. Unfortunately, after his debut album *12 Inches of Snow*, the rapper proved that his rugged life did not equal a musical career with several lackluster follow ups.

Born into a working-class Toronto housing project in 1970, Snow (Darrin Kenneth O'Brien) was beset with obstacles from his beginning. Raised by his struggling divorced mother Donna, Snow quickly found himself in the thick of the gang violence and crime that would color the lyrics of his future recordings. "I never had nothin' to do except drink and fight," Snow told Nicholas Jennings in *Maclean's* magazine. "Sometimes, I'd fantasize that I was Bruce Lee, or maybe one of the guys in Kiss. But mostly, I just hung out and got into trouble." After dropping out of the ninth grade, Snow began racking up a criminal record with the Canadian police.

Although Toronto's Allenbury projects facilitated Snow's involvement with violence and his near alcoholism, the environment also bore the seeds that would save him. Snow's neighborhood was largely populated by West Indian immigrants and descendants who retained their rich heritage of dance hall reggae music. Immersed in reggae, Snow demonstrated a nimble tongue able to churn out the tricky rhythms of that music's vocal style, a use of dialect called *patois*. With his friend and DJ Martin Prince, Snow began impromptu performances in local basement parties, upending the biases of those who first noticed only the rapper's skin color. "People would think he was a cop or something," Prince told Jennings. "But when he started rapping, people freaked out."

Before Snow was able to mature as a rap performer, however, his violent life would cause a temporary setback. In 1989, when Snow was only 19, he had been involved in a knife fight, an entanglement which, several years later, sent the rapper to the Metro Toronto East Detention Center on charges of attempted murder. Although it was eight months before Snow was acquitted of all charges, he kept himself busy with his music. Fueled by the experience of his incarceration, Snow penned the song "Informer" and shared it with his fellow inmates, winning their admiration. "That gave me courage," Snow told Jennings. "I knew that if I could rock that crowd, I could rock any crowd."

Before being sentenced to jail, Snow had been introduced by Prince to New York rapper MC Shan, who saw potential in the Canadian and arranged for a meeting with producers David Eng and Steve Salem. The duo quickly committed several tracks to record and test-marketed the track "Lonely Monday Morning" on the EastWest label. Satisfied with the results, Snow's new managers opted to release "Informer" as a single in 1993, when the singer himself was still serving time, but they could not have anticipated its wildfire popularity. Despite the fact that many listeners could not unscramble Snow's rocket-paced *patois* delivery, which was actually accompanied by subtitles in its video, the song sold at an alarming rate. "It's irresistible, it's incomprehensible, and it's a Number One hit," wrote Greg Sandow in *Entertainment Weekly*. "We're talking about 'Informer,' a happily propulsive little tune that has to be the most likely smash in years."

After "Informer" dominated the top position on sales charts in the United States and Canada for seven weeks— a record matched in Canada only by rocker

For the Record . . .

Born Darrin Kenneth O'Brien, 1970, in Toronto, Canada; son of a cab driver and Donna, a homemaker; two brothers and one sister; daughter Justuss, born April of 1996.

Began rapping in the dance hall reggae style at basement parties in the late 1980s in his predominately West Indian neighborhood; signed to Atlantic subsidiary EastWest and released debut single "Informer" and album *12 Inches of Snow,* 1993; began first live tour, 1993; released the disappointing follow-up album, *Murder Love,* 1995; sued by ex-partner DJ (Martin) Prince for alleged breach of an oral contract, 1997; released both *Justuss* and *Greatest Hits,* 1997.

Awards: Platinum certification for "Informer" and *12 Inches of Snow,* 1993.

Addresses: *Record company*—Elektra/Asylum, 75 Rockefeller Plaza, New York, NY, 10019.

Bryan Adams—Snow's debut album *12 Inches of Snow* was released. The record featured twelve new songs which explored rhythm and blues and traditional rap along with dance hall reggae, all of them composed by Snow. While the album's sales were on par with the single, much of the impetus came from the buzz of "Informer" alone. When Snow's follow-up single "Girl, I've Been Hurt," a slow tempo ballad, failed to generate the same interest as its predecessor, Snow was burdened with the pressure of proving he was more than a novelty act and comparisons with Vanilla Ice were flung from all quarters.

While Snow's stay in the limelight was relatively short-lived, his visibility did spark greater interest in his often overlooked genre of music, as well as Canadian artists in general. "The success of Snow has not started any stampede to sign white or black dance hall rappers," wrote Daniel Cauldeiron in *Billboard*, "but the media waves he's set off may yet draw attention to the nation's eager ragga, ruffneck, and yardie [all styles of reggae] wannabes." Besides Jamaican acts Shabba Ranks and Buju Banton, few proponents of dance hall reggae had made it into the mainstream, and unlike these two, none of Snows notoriety came from advocating of anti-gay violence.

After leaving EastWest for Elektra, Snow released *Murder Love* in 1995 and *Justuss* in 1997. As the gap in time between records suggests, Snow had become more meticulous in his production—*Justuss* was created in Jamaica and Toronto over a period of seven months with three different engineers. In addition, his vocal delivery had grown smoother, and despite his continuing friction with Canadian law, his lyrics took on positive political and social subjects. Spurred by his initial success and the birth of his daughter, Justuss, in April of 1996, after whom the album is named, Snow made it a point to shed his destructive life of violence and excessive drinking. "Having this success has really opened my mind to the possibilities in life and places which have changed the way I go through this life," Snow mused."

Sadly enough, Snow's growth as a person was not paralleled by new fertility as a songwriter. Aside from his new lyrical themes, Snow's second and third albums left both critics and listeners cold, and their songs generated only minor hits. To make matters worse, Snow was sued by his former friend Prince in 1997. Claiming that he had not been compensated for his role in *12 Inches of Snow.* Prince was awarded the sum of one and a half million dollars by a New York jury. Perhaps fearing that Snow might quickly loose any credibility, Elektra released a surprisingly premature greatest hits package that year, despite Snow's obvious dearth of actual hits. Nevertheless, as many careers have made clear, the 28 year old Snow may see yet another turn for the better.

Selected discography

12 Inches of Snow, Atlantic, 1993.
Murder Love, Elektra/Asylum, 1995.
Justuss, Elektra/Asylum, 1997.
Greatest Hits, Elektra/Asylum, 1997.

Sources

Periodicals

Billboard, August 21, 1993, June 28, 1997.
Entertainment Weekly, April 2, 1993.
Maclean's, May 3, 1993.
People Weekly, April 10, 1993.
Rolling Stone, September 16, 1993.

Online

http://imusic.com/showcase/urban/snow.html

—Shaun Frentner

Superdrag

Rock band

Hailing from Knoxville, Tennessee, Superdrag brought their apparent 1960s influences into their signature 1990s pop rock sound. Their style stood out among the popular grunge rock bands of the early to mid-1990s. As Randy Ridge wrote in Tennessee Monthly, "Superdrag's sound is a refreshing, forward-looking departure from the stale and recycled grunge rock riffs that have dominated modern radio.

The seeds of Superdrag were planted in 1991 from the remnants of other Knoxville bands. Singer/guitarist John Davis, drummer Don Coffey, Jr., and bassist Mike Smithers had previously started a band called Punchwagon. After recording a five-song demo and performing four or five shows, the group disbanded. Mike Smithers went on to form a band called 30 Amp Fuse (Davis and Coffey later performed on his group's debut album). Around the same time, bassist Tom Pappas and guitarist Brandon Fisher had also started a band called The Used, which self-released a cassette called *Shameless Self Promotion*. After its release, John Davis joined The Used as a drummer.

After The Used released another tape in 1993 called *Rock and Roll Party,* Davis left the band to go in his own musical direction. He began writing and recording his own music at home and named the project Superdrag. After he had songs ready, Davis decided he wanted to

perform live, so he recruited his roommate Brandon Fisher and former bandmate Don Coffey, Jr. Soon, Tom Pappas also joined the group. They made their debut at Knoxville's Mercury Theater, and Superdrag had officially blossomed. When the club closed down later that year, they were undaunted. They continued to play by throwing parties in their own house and performing there.

When all the members recorded the original version of the song "Whitey's Theme," the chemistry of the group began to come together. "We did a demo in my bedroom," John Davis said in the band's record company bio. "It just seemed to click. At the time, that really seemed to define our sound to a lot of people." While Superdrag was performing and recording, The Used also continued to perform around Knoxville. Both bands existed simultaneously for a year before The Used disbanded.

Although the members of Superdrag all had an early interest in music, they each left behind nonmusical paths to fully concentrate on the band. John Davis left the University of Tennessee where he was studying Liberal Arts. Brandon Fisher had already graduated from the University of Tennessee with a degree in English, and had plans to go to graduate school and eventually to teach college level literature. Don Coffey, Jr., whose father was an attorney, was working as an investigator in the Knoxville District Attorney's office.

In 1994, Superdrag self-released their first EP *Stereo 360 Sound.* They grabbed the attention of independent label Darla Records, which re-released five of the songs from the EP as singles. Superdrag got their first break with their debut single "Senorita," which was included on a CD that was packaged with an issue of *CMJ Magazine,* a national rock magazine that focused on up-and-coming bands. The group continued to release singles on both Darla Records and Arena Records, which gained notoriety among the music industry and press.

The cumulation of all this recognition resulted in a record contract with Elektra Records in 1995. Since they had already amassed attention as an "indie band," they received some criticism for signing to a major label. "We never had any illusion about being any puritan sort of indie band," John Davis told Jason Ferguson in *Magnet.* "I mean, we put out indie records, but we never saw ourselves as an 'indie band.' We just wanted the best distribution possible for our stuff, and obviously, WEA [Warner Elektra Atlantic Distribution] is a pretty good way to get your record out."

Before they released their Elektra debut, they put out an album on Darla Records called *The Fabulous 8-Track Sound of Superdrag.* It set the stage for their major label

For the Record . . .

Members include **Don Coffey, Jr.**, drums; **John Davis**, vocals/guitar; **Brandon Fisher**, guitar; **Tom Pappas**, bass.

Band formed in Knoxville, Tennessee, 1991; self-released EP *Stereo 360 Sound*, 1994; released singles on Darla Records, 1994; signed to Elektra Records, 1995; released *The Fabulous 8-Track Sound of Superdrag* on Darla Records, 1995; released *Regretfully Yours* on Elektra, 1995; released *Head Trip in Every Key*, 1998.

Addresses: *Record company*—Elektra Records, 75 Rockefeller Plaza, New York, NY 10019.

debut *Regretfully Yours,* which was produced by Tim O'Heir, who had also produced bands like Belly, Sebadoh, and Come. After the LP hit the streets, so did the band. They performed more than 250 shows during their worldwide tour with bands such as Better Than Ezra, Letters to Cleo, Archers of Loaf, and Polara. Their first single, "Sucked Out," quickly climbed the charts and the video spent 10 weeks as MTV's Buzz Bin choice. It was followed by another hit single called "Destination Ursa Major."

Tragedy briefly struck the band in 1996, when John Davis suffered a mental breakdown. The stress of the touring and pressure of success, along with drug use was reported as the cause. While on a double dose of LSD, Davis emptied his bank account and spent the money on alcohol, food, and flowers. He had planned to have a party and give away all of his possessions. After the incident, he began treatment for anxiety and depression.

"I think what I was trying to do was destroy my ego, because that's the thing I felt was holding me back," Davis explained to Jon Wiederhorn in *Rolling Stone.* Davis said his drug use had started to limit his ambition and diminish his self-confidence. Once he had his breakdown, he sought counseling, stopped using drugs, and returned to writing and recording with the band.

Superdrag rebounded from the setback and returned to the studio with producer Jerry Finn, who had previously produced Rancid, Green Day, and the Smoking Popes. In 1998, they released *Head Trip in Every Key.* Taking a departure from the fuzzy guitar sounds and jagged vocals they had become known for, they moved in a new and cleaner direction. "Because of the success of the last album, we had much more time on this one, much more access to other kinds of instrumentation," Davis said in the band's record company bio. "If you listen to the album as a whole, you'll hear a lot of nice little crescendos; you'll hear full separation. The whole album seems to come at you."

"These songs are a 180-degree turn from what we did before," Brandon Fisher told Wayne Bledsoe in the *Knoxville News-Sentinel.* The first single from the album, "Do the Vampire," initially received moderate success.

However, Superdrag recognized the significance of their achievement in garnering such rapid success as a young band from Knoxville, Tennessee. "Obviously, Knoxville has running water, and it's not a ghost town or anything, but in many ways it's like being from Mars," John Davis told Jon Wiederhorn in Rolling Stone. And no matter what twists and turns Superdrag's career takes, they don't plan to quit music if they lose their popularity. "I'm going to do this until I'm dead," Davis explained to Wiederhorn, "whether it's being pressed on commercial records or on my own four-track like I used to."

Selected discography

The Fabulous 8-Track Sound of Superdrag, Darla Records, 1995.
Regretfully Yours, Elektra Records, 1995.
Head Trip in Every Key, Elektra Records, 1998.

Sources

Periodicals

Guitar World, October 1996.
Knoxville News-Sentinel, August 17, 1997.
Magnet, April/May 1996.
Raygun, April 1996.
Rolling Stone, August 22, 1996.
Tennessee Monthly, September 1996.

Online

"Superdrag," http://www.elektra.com/alternative_club/superdrag/
"Superdrag Bio," http /www.superdrag.com

—Sonya Shelton

The Surfaris

Pop band

The story of the Surfaris is similar to scores of other bands of the 1950s and 1960s. Plagued by deceitful record company practices, elusive royalty payments, and of course the ever popular "too much, too soon" teenaged rock'n'roll effect, the Glendora, California quintet's saga is one that has been repeated many times. The Surfari's tale displays the saddening paradox of vital music being made by un-business savvy kids who, only in it for the fun, unknowingly fill the coffers of the record executives who profit the most from their naive golden geese.

The Surfaris, like many other Southern California bands of the early 1960s, were initially influenced by Dick Dale's 1961 single "Let's Go Trippin." Dale's sound, created with a loud trebly Fender Stratocaster through a wall of spring reverb was fast, with his pick moving in staccato bursts carrying the melody over a backing characterized by an incessant ride cymbal and snare hits on the twos and fours. A whooshing, gusty, almost ghostly sound was created suggesting the feeling of riding a wave. With the popularization of surfing in southern California in the 1950s, a new genre of music was born.

A junior high school talent show in 1961 was The Surfaris beginning. A guitar teacher and his pupil, Bob Berryhill, took the stage and played "Rebel Rouser" by Duane Eddy. Fellow contestants Pat Connolly, also a guitarist,

and bass player Jim Fuller, remembered Berryhill and one year later asked him to join them for a party gig they had hustled up. Drummer, Ron Wilson was also recruited for the show. After receiving ten dollars for their show—at a Catholic school—the name The Surfaris was chosen. One reason they chose the name Surfaris was quite obviously from its surfing connotation. Some, however, have argued that the other inspirations for the name came from the vocal group of the time, The Safaris, or from the fledgling Beach Boys' first national hit, "Surfin' Safari."

With the later addition of a 12 year old saxophone player named Jim Pash, The Surfaris were complete and were taken under the tutelage of local record producer Dale Smallin, at whose house they practiced. In November of 1962, Smallin, who had become the band's manager, booked the band for a one hour session at Paul Buff's Pal Recording Studio in nearby Cucamonga. The band knocked out two tracks, "Wipe Out" and "Surfer Joe," which would make up their first single. "Surfer Joe" the song they had initially planned on recording was written by drummer Ron Wilson who, oddly enough, had been inspired to write the song about a cool "beach blondie" surfer dude who gets drafted into the armed forces, by a dream he had. The legendary "Wipe Out," with its maniacal laughter and sped up marching band drumming, was written in the studio, as an afterthought, primarily because the band just needed a B-side for "Surfer Joe."

Smallin, seeing major potential in the group, started showing the master copies of the newly recorded singles around to local major and independent labels. Among others, Capitol, Liberty, Del-Fi, and Era all turned down the option to release the single. Undaunted, Smallin paid for a pressing of 2000 records which came out on his own DFS label and the band sold the records at shows or gave them away to friends. Smallin continued to shop the Surfaris around and finally hit paydirt with the tiny Princess record label owned by John Marascalco. Signing a contract for an advance of $200 against future royalties and for the publishing of both songs to go to Marascalco's Robin Hood Music, The Surfaris were on their way.

By early 1963, the record started gaining popularity in markets like Fresno and Santa Barbara, California. Spurned by these regional successes, Princess's next move was to lease the masters to the major label Dot Records for national distribution. Starting to gain national air play, the Surfaris and Princess then sold the masters to Dot who signed the band to an album contract. Richard Delvy, who had hooked the band up with Princess actually ended up signing the contract

For the Record . . .

Band members have included **Bob Berryhill**, (from 1962-66), guitar; **Pat Connolly**, (from 1962-65), bass; **Ken Forsi**, (from 1965-66), bass; **Jim Fuller**, (from 1962- 66), guitar; **Jack Oldham**, (from 1966-67), bass; **Jim Pash**. (1962-1967), saxophone, guitar; **Guy Watson**, (in 1966), guitar; and **Ron Wilson**, (died c.1990, played in band from 1962-67), drums.

Formed in Glendora, California, 1962; signed to Princess records, 1963; won national distribution with Dot records, 1963; disbanded, 1967; reformed sporadically with original members through the 1970s and 1980s.

Awards: BMI award 1963, number one song "Wipe Out;" Australian record of the year award for "Wipe Out," 1964.

with his band, The Challengers. This piece of shadiness led to another band actually being the ones playing on the album. When The Surfaris realized that it wasn't them playing (they had also recorded the songs), their manager confessed that the reason was they weren't music union members. Shadier still was the fact that the Surfari's versions of "Wipe Out" and "Surfer Joe" were still used on the album. Filing suit, the band was released from their contract with Dot.

After the Dot debacle, the Surfaris signed with Decca records and recorded their first real album, *The Surfaris Play*. They also re-recorded "Wipe Out" and "Surfer Joe," since Princess Records still held the rights to the original versions. Unable to tour because of high school commitments, the band played local dances and recorded. A new single, "Point Panic," did fairly well on the charts and by February of 1964 *Hit City '64* was released. By the end of 1964, the band had toured Hawaii, Australia, and New Zealand, won a BMI award for "Wipe Out" as 1963's number one song, won a settlement from Dot records, and fired their manager, Dale Smallin.

By 1965, The Beatles and the British Invasion had been around for about a year and popular musical tastes were

shifting. Another Decca LP, *Hit City '65* was released and the band headed out to tour Japan, where they were still quite popular, having hit the Japanese charts at number two with their song, "Karen." By this time, the band was being produced by Gary Usher, former Brian Wilson collaborator who unsuccessfully tried to foist a sort of Beach Boys sound on the band. Their late 1965 release *It Ain't Me Babe,* saw them trying very hard to keep with the times. It also saw the departure of founding members Jim Fuller and Bob Berryhill. Pat Conolly had left the band a year earlier prior to their tour of Japan. With only Jim Pash and Ron Wilson still around from the first line up, the band continued on until 1967 when Jim Pash became a born again Christian. In an odd twist, the band's last two singles were released on Dot, whom they signed with again after leaving Decca.

Since the breakup, The Surfaris have regrouped several times for Surf revival shows, appearing at the First Annual Surfers Stomp in 1973 with the likes of Dick Dale, Jan and Dean, and The Marketts. They also re-recorded "Wipe Out" in 1976 for a K-Tel compilation. Through the eighties the band split off into two different sets of Surfaris with Berryhill, Pash, and Fuller staying in Southern California and Ron Wilson fronting a Northern California bunch of Surfaris. While most of their catalog has gone out of print, several compilation albums are still available. "Wipe Out" is still a mainstay of oldies radio formats.

Selected discography

"Wipe Out," Dot, 1963.
The Surfaris Play, Decca, 1963.
Hit City '64, Decca, 1964.
Fun City USA, Decca, 1964.
Hit City '65, Decca, 1965.
It Ain't Me Babe, Decca, 1965.
Wipe Out! The Best of the Surfaris, Varese Sarabande, 1994.

Sources

Surfin' Guitars: Instrumental Surf Bands of the Sixties, Robert J. Dalley, 1988, Surf Publications, California, USA.

—*Nathan Shafer*

Usher

Singer, actor

If the critical reception of Usher's 1994 self-titled debut album wasn't embraced universally by critics, the enormous commercial success of *Usher* gives the record claims to an auspicious beginning, and the fact that the singer was a mere 16 years old at the time of its release only redoubles its impressiveness. After forming a bond with sought-after producer/rapper Sean "Puffy" Combs, who had overseen Usher's first album, the young artist teamed up with award-winning producers Antonio "L.A." Reid and Kenny "Babyface" Edmonds to create the follow-up album, *My Way*. Boasting several strong singles, including the chart-topping "You Make Me Wanna" and "Nice & Slow," *My Way* ensured Usher platinum-selling certification along with his high school diploma. Setting his sights upon a generous scope of talents, Usher had concentrated on honing his vocal skills and songwriting, and even began to dabble as an actor in several television series, including *Moesha,* opposite singer Brandy. "This is just the beginning," Usher assessed in an online interview. "I feel like I've accomplished so much already, but I still have my whole life ahead of me and much more to do."

AP/Wide World Photos. Reproduced by permission.

Just the Beginning

Usher was born Usher Raymond IV, on October 14, 1979, in the small town of Chattanooga, Tennessee. Although left without a father, Usher never lacked the positive influence of a nurturing, supportive extended family of cousins and uncles, in addition to the powerful devotion of his mother Vanessa, who would later assume the role of Usher's manager. After relocating to Atlanta, Georgia with Usher and his younger brother James, Vanessa Raymond introduced her son to the church choir which she directed, and as is the case with many other R&B vocalists, the gospel experience was to prove invaluable training. However, Usher claims that an encounter with the 1970 hit single "I Want You Back" by the Jackson 5 was perhaps his first impetus towards a passion for singing. "That was my beginning, even before I started singing in church," Usher told *Entertainment Weekly*. "I used to hum and sing with the radio, but I wasn't really serious about it. But when I heard that song, I was inspired."

Conscious of her son's budding talents, Vanessa Raymond sought to give Usher a high profile by entering him in a number of talent competitions. Within a year, Usher

had scored heavily on the nationally televised *Star Search* program, a victory which prompted a scout for the LaFace label to tap the young crooner for an audition with producer L.A. Reid. With little hesitation, Reid signed Usher onto the LaFace roster to begin recording a full-length album with co-producer Sean "Puffy" Combs and several other technicians. Although hardly a seasoned veteran, the young Combs was a much needed guide to the even younger Usher, and the two have subsequently toured together. By 1994, the fruit of Combs and Usher's studio sessions was released under the straightforward title *Usher*, to little critical fanfare. Still, while *Usher*'s 14 tracks ultimately proved to be at best a training ground for the singer's emerging style, the album produced a gold-selling single, '"Think of You," which curried the favor of international audiences.

Before embarking upon his second full-length release, Usher kept to the task of refining his performance range, and also found time to lend his talents to several small projects. Taking advantage of Usher's already evident following of younger audiences, the Coca Cola company chose his voice to deliver their jingle for the 1995 holiday season. In addition, Usher collaborated with a number of vocalists to create the ad hoc outfit Black Men United, who harmonized on a track made expressly for the soundtrack for the film *Jason's Lyric*. To round out this busy schedule, which at that time still included schoolwork, Usher took his first steps in learning the craft of songwriting, hoping to add to his portfolio as a maturing entertainer. "I want to show people that I've grown a lot since my last album, and writing was a part of that process," Usher later told MTV *News* in the fall of 1997.

Turned to Songwriting

The first of Usher's efforts at tunesmithery could not have been any more encouraging. Co-written with Jermaine Dupri, an affiliate of the So So Def label, Usher's 1997 single "You Make Me Wanna" rocketed up the *Billboard* magazine sales charts, peaking at the number one position, where it remained for eleven consecutive weeks. In the wake of such massive popularity, the release of Usher's second album was to be a highly anticipated event for a growing base of fans, and as its eventual triple platinum-selling status would testify, *My Way* was up to the challenge. Benefiting from the talents of several of the recording industry's most lucrative producers, including L.A. Reid and Babyface, Usher's second album was a more diverse affair than his debut outing. "I wanted enough of everything so there's always a song you want to hear," Usher posited. Out of *My Way*'s nine tracks, six were penned by Usher along with Dupri, with whom Usher developed a lucid working relationship. "This time around I wanted people to know Usher," the singer explained on his homepage, "so Jermaine and I just hung out a lot so he got to see my life." Channeling both the tender and euphoric sides of Usher's life into recorded cuts, Usher and his collaborators came up with a number of upbeat dance songs as well as soulful ballads, the latter receiving the special touch of Babyface (who had produced award-winning ballads for the group Boyz II Men, as well as for his own career as a vocalist).

Despite a solid vote of endorsement from millions of listeners, Usher's relationship with some critical quarters did not improve. The *Rolling Stone* review for *My Way* was mixed at best. While *Rolling Stone* could not deny the infectiousness of "You Make Me Wanna," the album's opener, they found little else to recommend the album, writing that "Usher's voice lacks the force and nuance to make up for the thin, synthetic quality of the backing tracks. And you know there's a problem with the songwriting when you see the word *hook* plastered over the choruses in the lyric booklet." Nevertheless, audiences at large saw no problem with the catchiness of cuts like "Come Back" or the bass-centered "Just Like Me," nor with ballads such as "Nice & Slow," which was subsequently released as *My Way*'s second platinum-selling single.

Singer/Actor

As the stature of Usher's profile increased, so did the demand for his multiple talents. Proving again that he was more than simply a studio session musician, Usher fully roused an audience at the legendary Apollo theater in Harlem, New York in a much touted performance. "When you come to Apollo, you gotta sing, you gotta dance, you gotta give it up to the audience," Usher confided to MTV *News*. "They want to see that, and to get the response I got, when the song came on I came sliding out, all the audience bumrushed the stage. It's like, 'Damn! I think I'm a superstar.'" Such bravado made Usher a perfect candidate to round out the bill on cohort Sean "Puffy" Comb's own fall tour, as well as for later live dates supporting full-fledged stars Mary J. Blige and Janet Jackson. Nor did Usher's confidence stop at performing music, as his debut as an actor on the television series *Moesha* bore witness. After landing

the supporting role of Jeremy, opposite the title role played by teenage singing sensation Brandy Norwood, Usher coolly told *Jet* magazine that despite any formal training, "I'm a natural. I have a talent to take words off paper and relate to it."

At the turn of 1998, Usher's career seemed to be on an unstoppable upward trajectory, and not solely on the basis of consistently solid record sales. Finally given strong acknowledgment from critics, Usher was nominated for a Grammy Award for Best Male R&B Vocal Performance, and walked away with a statuette in the same category at the Soul Train Awards a month later. In addition, Usher's inaugural efforts as an actor resulted in a brief stint on the daytime soap opera *The Bold and the Beautiful*, as well as in an invitation to the big screen as an actor in a science fiction film. Pegged by *Essence* magazine to be one of a new "hot generation" of stars marked by youth and unshakable positiveness, Usher continues to sharpen his skills and widen his sights. "I guess I am an usher in a way," he quipped to *Jet* magazine. "I'm ushering in something very new, very fresh. Hopefully, it'll have longevity. That's my goal. I don't want to be stereotyped as just a hip hop artist or an R&B artist. I want to cover it all."

Selected discography

Usher, LaFace, 1994.
My Way, LaFace, 1997.

Sources

Periodicals

Ebony, January 1998.
Entertainment Weekly, April 3, 1998.
Jet, March 9, 1998.
Rolling Stone, December 25, 1997.
Time, February 23, 1998.

Online

www.aristarec.com/aristaweb/Usher/info.html
http://www.mtv.com/news/gallery/u/usher
http://www.spods.dcs.kcl.ac.uk/~richii/usher.html

—Sean Frentner

Richie Valens

Singer

Ritchie Valens died very young, yet his legacy remains a cornerstone of the history of rock and roll. Valens was a natural singer and performer, in touch with his audience and unaffected by fame. The songs and records that he left behind are classic rock and roll. As singer/songwriter Don McLean immortalized those times in the epic song "American Pie," he symbolized Valens's passing as "the day the music died."

Richard Steve Valenzuela was born on May 13, 1941, in Los Angeles, California, the son of Joseph Steve Valenzuela and Concepción (Connie) Reyes Valenzuela of San Fernando, California. Both of the Valenzuelas worked at a local munitions factory to support their family which consisted of young Valens and his older half-brother, Robert Morales—Connie's son from a former marriage. The family lived "from hand to mouth," with no money to spare. Joseph Valenzuela is remembered as a gruff and stern man who carried life-long scars from a mining accident.

Despite a rough exterior, Valens's father was nonetheless attentive and supportive of his only son. When Valens's parents divorced, his father took young Ritche son to Pacoima and raised him. Despite the upheaval, however, in the family's living arrangements, Valens maintained a close relationship with both his mother and his maternal relatives.

At Haddon Elementary School in Pacoima, Valens was a child who blended in with his average looks, average intelligence, and quiet disposition. His special talent and enthusiasm for playing the guitar did not become evident until he reached junior high school. Nonetheless, his father and other family members noted Valens interest in music when he was still a small child. It is rumored that on more than one occasion he built makeshift guitars from scavenged items such as cigar boxes, tin cans, and the like. Joseph Valenzuela eventually presented his son with a real guitar and encouraged the boy to play, especially at parties and get-togethers, although Valens himself was completely reticent at first. In time, Valens grew increasingly comfortable with performing; he always enjoyed the music, and he spent hours practicing whenever he had the chance. At first Valens envisioned himself as a "singing cowboy" and emulated the style of those heroes. It was not until later that Valens developed a personal style in his music.

While Valens was still at Haddon Elementary School his father's health was declining. He assed away in 1951, most likely from diabetes or a stroke. Young Valens was only eleven years old at that time. It is believed that he lived with an uncle in Santa Monica shortly afterwards and that he lived with an uncle in Norfolk, California for a time and attended Norfolk Elementary. Eventually Valens, along with his mother, his brother and two younger half-sisters, Connie Jr. and Irma, eventually settled into his late father's residence in Pacoima. Valens, who always spoke English with his father, picked up Spanish from his mother's family. Valens also learned new guitar chords and musical styles from other family members who also played the guitar, including one uncle in particular, John Lozano.

In September of 1954, the 13-year-old Valens enrolled at Pacoima Junior High School. By then he was very involved in his music. He enjoyed playing his guitar so much that he brought it to school with him regularly. Valens and his guitar were permanent fixtures on the Pacoima Junior High School grounds during recess periods, when he played and sang to the amusement of his schoolmates. Soon Valens was entertaining at school programs. His musical style evolved dramatically during those intermediate years. He encouraged his friends to sing along and contribute to the music, and helping him develop his "of the people"style. He also learned to establish a rapport with his audience and he acquired a penchant for improvising melodies and words. His record producers would note later that when Valens played a song it was different every time. His songs were like games, where everyone listening could take a turn, making up verses and singing. Valen sensitivity to his audience would be among his greatest assets during his brief career in which he established his own personal style of rhythm and blues.

In junior high, like in elementary school, Valens was an average student and non-descript academically. Industrial arts class, however, was his favorite class. He was skillful and artistic with his hands and he was known to have an excellent sense of form. Valens especially liked to bring his guitars to school, to work on them in the woodshop—restoring, repairing, and refinishing the old instruments that he collected, with painstaking attention.

Valens, but for his music and his beloved guitars, went relatively unnoticed in junior high school—although some Hispanic students called him "falso" because of his pale skin tones which belied his Mexican heritage. Overall, Valens was neither interested in matters of ethnicity and race, nor was he involved romantically with any particular girl; he blended with all who came to hear his music.

A few months before Valens finished junior high, early in 1957, a terrible and unusual tragedy befell Pacoima Junior High School. Two planes collided directly over the school. Three students were killed along with the entire crew of both planes. Ninety others were injured. Valens, who was attending his grandfather's funeral during the incident, was emotionally overwhelmed, and reportedly developed a fear of airplanes ... perhaps rightfully so because a shocking plane crash would ultimately claim young Valens's own life just two years and three days later. Valens' biographer, Beverly Mendheim, quoted a conversation related by Valens' uncle, Eliodoro Reyes. In talking with Valens sometime after the crash, Reyes

admonished his young nephew never to board an airplane, and Valens replied deliberately, "I'll never get on one of those."

As Valens's days at Pacoima Junior High School drew to a close, his career picked up speed and surged forward. Valens was in the habit of performing frequently for dance parties, car clubs, and at the American Legion Hall. Some of the parties were benefit programs sponsored by Valens' mother to help make ends meet. Valens by then had a new brother, Mario, still an infant. Other dances were sponsored and promoted by the Silhouettes, a band formed by William Jones and Gilbert Roach. Originally a quintet, the Silhouettes featured a piano, drums, vibes, saxophone, and Valens on guitar. In time, the band grew to include trumpets, additional saxophones, and a clarinet. The Silhouettes' repertoire consisted almost exclusively of rock and roll sounds but the group also performed music with a Latin flavor for weddings around town.

Early in 1958 a promoter named Doug Macchia taped a session of Valens along with the Silhouettes performing at a dance party. Soon after, Valens was approached by Bob (Keene) Keane, a record producer and owner of the new Del-Fi label. Keane, who saw Macchia's tape, was interested in the yet unknown Valens. He arranged for Valens to audition in May, about the time of Valens' 17th birthday. By the end of that summer, Keane released "Come On, Let's Go," an original Valens composition and Valens's first commercial recording. The entire chronology of Valens's rapid rise to stardom spans five hectic months following the release of his first hit single, after which Valens's career ended abruptly on February 3, 1959 in Clear Lake, Iowa.

Billboard cited Valens' first release, "Come On, Let's Go," as "pick of the week" for September 1, 1958. During that same month Valens made an 11-city tour of the East Coast. He appeared on Dick Clark's "American Bandstand" on October 6, at which point "Come On, Let's Go" reached number 42 on the charts. Valens, his east coast tour completed, returned to Southern California where he spent the rest of October, into November, performing in various locations including Disneyland, El Monte, and Long Beach. While in California, Valens went to Hollywood to film "Go Johnny Go" with Alan "Mr. Rock 'n' Roll" Freed and Chuck Berry. Valens appeared briefly in the film and sang "Ooh, My Head."

Keane, encouraged by the success of "Come On, Let's Go," released a double-sided Valens single, "Donna/La Bamba," which was cited in the *Billboard* Spotlight on November 17, 1958. During the Christmas holiday that year Valens performed again with Alan Freed in a

Christmas Jubilee along with Chuck Berry, the Everlys, Bo Diddly, Frankie Avalon, Eddie Cochran, and others. Meanwhile, his new single "Donna/La Bamba," appeared on the charts by the end of the year. Valens performed continually during the end of 1958; the exact dates and locations of the performances are uncertain. It is believed that he appeared in Baltimore, Maryland, Washington, D.C., Chicago, Illinois, Buffalo, New York, Toronto, Canada, and possibly in Honolulu, Hawaii with Buddy Holly. During that time Valens purchased a new house for himself and his family in Pacoima. "Donna" soared to second place on the *Billboard* chart by January of 1959.

On January 11, 1959, Valens made a television appearance on a rock-and-roll variety show, "The Music Shop." Valens then signed to a long-term contract to perform in a series of tours sponsored by General Artist Corporation (GAC). The first GAC tour was scheduled throughout the midwest during the winter months of 1959 along with Buddy Holly and the Crickets, J.P. "Big Bopper" Richardson, and a number of back-up artists including bassist Waylon Jennings and guitarist Tommy Allsup. Valens made two last stops, in West Covina and in Long Beach, before departing California for Chicago for the scheduled departure of the first GAC tour. The hectic tour was plagued by problems with the chartered buses. The performers were so cold during much of the trip that one drummer was hospitalized with frostbite. From Chicago the tour bus left for Milwaukee, Wisconsin, then on to Kenosha, and Eau Clair in Wisconsin. Next the performers traveled to Montevido and St. Paul in Minnesota, then on to Davenport and Fort Dodge in Iowa, and back to Duluth, Minnesota. By the evening of February 2, the tour was performing in Clear Lake, Iowa, after stopping in Appleton and Green Bay, Wisconsin.

It was the stop in Clear Lake that ultimately led to disaster when Buddy Holly, weary and exhausted from the slow, cold bus rides decided to charter a plane to the next tour stop in Moorhead, Minnesota. Holly arranged for a small Beechcraft Bonanza to take himself, Allsup, and Jennings to Fargo, North Dakota—from there the three planned to take ground transportation to Moorhead. By 1:00 a.m., when the plane was ready to leave Clear Lake, Jennings had conceded his seat on the plane to singer J.P. Richardson, a very large man who was extremely distraught and uncomfortable on the long bus rides. Allsup wanted very much to take the plane, but at Valens's persistence, Allsup gambled his seat on the plane over a coin toss. Valens was never characterized as impetuous, yet despite his avowed fear of flying he was gratified to win the toss. The night was too cold and foggy and the pilot was not instrument certified. The plane crashed over a corn field outside of Mason City, Iowa. The three passengers and the pilot were killed on impact. Ritchie Valens was only 17. His career as a rock and roll star was over less than one year after it started. A memorial service was held at his gravesite on the day that would have been his 18th birthday, May 13, 1959. The headstone on Valens's grave was inscribed, "Come On, Let's Go." Valens and his music were later remembered in a 1987 Hollywood Movie, *La Bamba*.

Selected discography

Singles

"Come On, Let's Go"/"Framed," Del-Fi, September 13, 1958.
"Come On, Let's Go"/"Dooby Dooby Wah," Pye-Int., 1958.
"Donna"/La Bamba," Del-Fi, November 17, 1958.

Albums

Ritchie Valens, (includes "Come On, Let's Go, Donna, Ooh, My Head, and La Bamba), Del-Fi, February 24, 1959
Ritchie Valens In Concert At Pacoima Junior High, Del-Fi, December 31, 1960.
Ritchie Valens' Greatest Hits, Del-Fi, April 20, 1963.
The History of Ritchie Valens, Rhino, July 1981.

Sources

Books

Goldrosen, John and John Beecher, *Remembering Buddy,* Penguin Books, New York, 1987.
Jennings, Waylon, *Waylon: an Autobiography,* Warner Books, 1996.
Mendheim, Beverly, *Ritchie Valens: The First Latino Rocker,* Bilingual Press, Tempe, AZ, 1987.
Shaw, Arnold, *The Rockin' 50s,* Da Capo Press, 1974.

Periodicals

Entertainment Weekly, February 3, 1995.

Online

"ROCKHOUSE Music Mail Express," May 23, 1998, http://www.musicmailexpress.com/mme.cgi/index.
Simon, Tom, "Ritchie Valens Page," http://www.crl.com/~tsimon/valens.htm. November 3, 1996.

—*Gloria Cooksey*

Velocity Girl

Rock band

Velocity Girl could very well stand as the poster children for the "indie," or independent rock group of the 1990s. Their blend of kooky, ironic songwriting and punk-evolved noise, delivered by a quintet of devoted record collectors fully devoid of rock-star bravura, epitomizes the style of pop music beloved to champions of small labels. After cutting their teeth on a number of singles, the band made the move to the influential Sub Pop label to release their debut album *Copacetic* in 1993. *Copacetic* quickly became the Sub Pop's biggest seller ever (surpassed only by Nirvana's mega-selling *Bleach*). The band's output since has varied in both reception and musical style, but throughout Velocity Girl has continued to expand the terrain of the catchy, three-minute pop song.

Formed around the University of Maryland in 1989, Velocity Girl, who took their name from an early B-side by the group Primal Scream, was originally comprised of vocalist Bridget Cross, bass player Kelly Riles, vocalist and guitar player Archie Moore, guitarist Brian Nelson, and drummer Jim Spellman. Cross soon departed from the group to join the eclectic outfit Unrest, but the remaining members quickly coaxed their friend Sarah Shannon to take her place and relocated to Washington, D.C. Shannon, a professionally trained singer, demonstrated a frail yet pleasant voice that would grow in range as Velocity Girl progressed.

Like most denizens of indie rock, Velocity Girl launched their recording career in 1991 with an onslaught of singles released only in a seven inch record format, often on highly collectible colored vinyl. With their seven inch single "My Forgotten Favorite," released on Slumberland Records, Velocity Girl had produced an instant classic of noise-pop that provoked favorable comparisons to the heavenly, washed-out guitar sound of British titans My Bloody Valentine. Before too long, the early releases of the band, themselves avid record buyers, became sought-after commodities that fetched stiff prices in specialty shops. "It's kind of flattering in a way to see that people would consider our records to be worth that much, but it's also very embarrassing and sad to see them on walls," guitarist Moore mused in an online interview. To remedy the situation, Slumberland later issued a six-track compact disc which compiled the band's rare first offerings. Nevertheless, Velocity Girl remained true to their roots in spite of subsequent major distribution, and continued to release occasional gems in the seven inch format.

The band had planned on stating the course of being independent heroes, but when the Sub Pop label tapped the group to produce their debut album, Velocity Girl not only accepted the offer but signed a five-record contract. Sub Pop, with whom Velocity Girl had already recorded a one-off split single alongside the Virginia outfit Tsunami, had a reputation for signing purveyors of the more abrasive school of "grunge" guitar rock, and the choice of adopting Velocity Girl into their ranks signified a step in a new direction for the Seattle label. In addition, the explosive mainstream success of Sub Pop's act Nirvana in 1991 gave the label a considerable amount of clout and visibility to offer their new addition. Heralded by the single "Crazy Town," the album *Copacetic* hit record stores in 1993 to a generally positive reception. Highlighted by tracks such as the sarcastic "Pop Loser" and "Crazy Town," the Bob Weston-produced *Copacetic* testified that while Velocity Girl was informed by the abstract, distorted sounds of guitar based bands like My Bloody Valentine or Ride, they were equally indebted to the less expansive legacy of tightly crafted bubblegum pop.

After playing a series of live dates with Tsunami and releasing a charming vinyl-only remake of the techno-pop favorite "Your Silent Face" by the band New Order, Velocity Girl created the second of their albums for Sub Pop in 1994. Entitled *Simpatico!*, the record offers even more in the way of catchy melodies and less of the wall of pure sound that marked the band's earlier releases. Producer Bob Weston was replaced by John Porter, who had worked with the seminal British band The Smiths, and the group found a more focused, crafted sound.

Members include **Archie Moore**, lead guitar, bass, vocals; **Brian Nelson**, guitar; **Kelly Riles**, bass, guitar; **Sarah Shannon**, vocals; **Jim Spellman**, drums. **Bridget Cross** originally supplied vocals, but left the group before any recorded output.

Velocity Girl formed in 1989 at the University of Maryland; released the classic single "My Forgotten Favorite" for Slumberland, 1991; signed five album contract with influential Sub Pop label and released debut album *Copacetic*, 1993; *Simpatico!*, 1994; announced plans of breaking up after their third album, *Gilded Stars and Zealous Hearts*, 1996.

Addresses: *Record company*—Sub Pop, PO Box 20645, Seattle WA 98120

Many fans and critics lauded their creation. "As on *Copacetic*, the textures are heaped on, but the musical lines are less runny, the riffs are sharpened, the hooks grab tighter, and the vocals skate out front," wrote critic Kim Ahearn in *Rolling Stone* magazine. "Velocity Girl have hit their stride with *Simpatico!* If this band continues to clarify and expand its sound, it may just redefine what it means to be indie." If this redefinition did not take hold overnight, Velocity Girl certainly passed muster in mainstream critical publications, such as *Stereo Review,* who gave the album's opening track "Sorry Again" a nod for best single of 1994.

However, in spite of the strength of the record, as well as singer Shannon's much improved voice, some die-hards felt that the smoother direction of the band meant compromising the unpolished, raw nature of independent music. Whether fueled by a bias against sugary melodies or by noise-rock purism, such responses had been foreseen by the band, as voiced by Moore in an online interview. "We're not afraid, but we're anticipating that a lot of indie-type people are going to think that it's a sell out kind of record or whatever. In complete honesty, it's the sort of record we've always wanted to make and if our other records didn't sound like that it's because we didn't know how to make them sound like that."

If *Simpatico!* represented a balance of sonic distortion and hummable refrains, Velocity Girl's third album, *Gilded Stars and Zealous Hearts*, began to fumble towards less inspired slickness. While the tendency towards pop had been one of the band's chief distinctions, on prior releases it had been tempered by experimental dabblings which were sorely needed on *Gilded Stars*. Additionally, the indie-based backlash towards excessive production values may have begun to hit home on the outfit's third album. Whereas *Copacetic* and *Simpatico!* had been created in studio-bursts of ten and twenty days, respectively, *Gilded Stars'* production time was spread across seven weeks under the direction of high-profile engineer Clif Norrell and the spontaneity of earlier records gave way to an over-polished quality. Although the album was not a disaster by any standards and was not without appeal, it was given a lukewarm reception from indie and mainstream critics alike, such as *Entertainment Weekly's* Michele Romero, who could find only "a few sprightly, memorable melodies featuring happy, strumming guitars behind boy-girl harmonies."

Ironically, while many reviewers and listeners found *Gilded Stars* a disappointment in terms of songwriting, Velocity Girl themselves thought the album stood as a sign of achievement in tunes and musicianship. "The playing for all the members has risen to a great degree," bassist Riles averred in an online interview. "Everyone's more confident on their instruments, there's more stuff we can do, and we can do it more purposefully." The disappointing results of the record may in fact have stemmed from a growing disinterest within the band itself. Key songwriter Moore had been diverting his attention towards his side project, the Heartworms, who released the album *Space Escapade* in 1995, and singer Shannon became preoccupied with her forthcoming marriage. In 1996, Velocity Girl announced that it would break up, but a final word has not been offered. At any rate, given the typical convoluted family tree of the indie band in general, it is a safe bet that the members of Velocity Girl will continue in a similar vein through other incarnations.

Selected discography

Velocity Girl EP, Slumberland, 1993.
Copacetic, Sub Pop, 1993.
Simpatico!, Sub Pop, 1994.
Gilded Stars and Zealous Hearts, Sub Pop, 1996.

Sources

Periodicals

Audio, June 1996.
Entertainment Weekly, March 22, 1996.

Interview, June 1994.
Rolling Stone, July 14, 1994.
Stereo Review, July 1994.

Online

http://www.subpop.com/bands/velocitygirl

—*Shaun Frentner*

Vienna Choir Boys

Concert choir

AP/Wide World Photos. Reproduced by permission.

The most famous youth choir in the world, the Vienna Choir Boys, celebrated its 500th year in existence in 1998. A holdover from the days of the Hapsburg dynasty in Europe, the Choir was once simply another jewel in the crown of a luxurious monarchy also known as the Holy Roman Empire. Yet with the emergence of Austria as a Republic after the end of World War I, the Vienna Choir Boys was similarly modernized. They began taking their characteristic sound, often described as "floating" and "angelic," to concert halls around the world. They serve as a national symbol for Austria, and are a beloved tourist attraction in Vienna proper.

The Vienna Choir Boys, known in German as *Die Wiener Saengerknaeben,* was for much of its history known as the Court Choir Boys. It served a function at the court of the Hapsburgs, hereditary rulers of an Austro-Hungarian Empire that once stretched across much of Europe. The Emperor Maximilian I founded the Choir in 1498 by issuing a command for 12 boys to be summoned to the Court and trained as singers. Like their modern-day counterparts, they were probably 10 to 14 years in age and possessed a good ear for music and an excellent voice in the soprano or alto range. The Choir would sing at church services and for banquets at the palace. The introduction of such a custom was probably partly the result of Maximilian I's 1477 marriage to Mary of Burgundy, since boys' choirs had been the fashion in the courts of her land. It may have also been evidence of a series of reforms introduced by Maximilian I in religious music.

Since then, the Vienna Choir Boys as an institution has achieved legendary status for its rigorous training in pursuit of perfection. There is a demanding audition and if a boy becomes one of the handful accepted yearly, a preparation course begins at age seven or eight at its official boarding school. At age nine, candidates must pass a musical aptitude test, then train further for another year, "during which time they must prove that they not only are able to sing but can also socialize and get along with their comrades," conductor Peter Marschik told the *Detroit Free Press* in 1984. The home of the Choir is Vienna's Augartenpalais, the former Imperial Palace that was once home to the Hapsburg royal family. Built in 1600s, it houses the boarding school for past, present, and future Choir members. Once a boy's voice has changed with puberty, they must exit the Choir, but can remain at school to finish their education up to the high school diploma level.

Vienna Choir Boys have gained renown not just for their singing talent but also for an ability to stoically endure a rather tough schedule for a youngster: the academic classes are demanding, including a great deal of foreign-language instruction, drama and stage movement, and they must rehearse two hours a day afterward; families are seen only on the weekends. However, the Augartenpalais, the school's home since the close of World War II, also boasts a skating rink and a swimming pool for the boys' use, and they spend the summer months in an adjunct school located in the Tyrolian Alps.

Several famous names in classical music history have been associated with the Vienna Choir Boys. Composer Joseph Haydn sang with them as a child, but technically belonged to the choir of a famous Vienna church, the Cathedral of St. Stephan. Franz Schubert was also a member, but was reputed to be more interested in composing music than completing his schoolwork. Many famous European conductors of the past two centuries have also been members. Other renowned names, such as Ludwig van Beethoven and Wolfgang Amadeus Mozart, have written works especially for the Choir, which also performs with the famed Vienna State Opera.

The Court Choir Boys changed its name in 1918 with end the of Austro-Hungarian Empire in the waning days of World War I. With the dissolution of the monarchy, the boys were at first all sent back to their parents. But the onetime rector of the imperial chapel, Monsignor Josef Schnitt, re-formed the Choir in the early 1920s and gave it its current name. The priest financed it with his own money, and devised the idea of putting the boys in little sailor uniforms, which was standard dress for upper-class children of the era. Decades later, the bestowing of this official costume to a new member is an illustrious ritual event.

In more modern times the training school for the Choir is funded by record sales and concert tours. There are actually four separate choirs of 25 boys each, so that some may perform in Vienna while others travel. One of Vienna's most popular tourist attractions is the weekly Solemn Mass sung at the Hofburg Chapel at the Augartenpalais, and one choir stays at home to carry on a custom that has remained unchanged since 1498. Only in 1978 was the Choir banned, in a much publicized flap, from performing on Christmas Day. A parent whose son had been dismissed from the Choir allegedly caused a stir by calling this violation of Austrian child labor laws to the attention of the authorities.

Entry into the Choir gives the boys immense opportunity for travel, since concert tours are regularly booked at some of the world's best known performance halls. They first sang in the Western Hemisphere in 1932, under Monsignor Schnitt's guidance, and are required to travel in groups when on the road, they are never allowed to venture out alone. Sometimes a choir member's voice will change while on tour, at which point he is discharged from his duties. Though he remains at the school, there is some difficulty in making this transition: "They're touring. They're singing. They're special in Austria. Then suddenly they have to go back to being average boys," the Choir's tour director told a *Chicago Sun-Times* reporter in 1968. "That's why we only let them give their first names to interviewers and don't let them think they're stars."

The Vienna Choir Boys are esteemed for their stage presence, which seems to confound anyone with the slightest acquaintance with boys of that age. After reviewing a 1980 performance, *Detroit Free Press* music critic John Guinn wrote that they "sang with an enthusiasm and polish that was quite disarming.... Best of all, they never pushed their voices, never resorted to the kind of yelling and hooting that characterizes so many boys' choirs." Guinn concluded by bemusing that "boys born in this wild century could so successfully carry on a tradition dating back nearly 500 years says something." Yet it seemed that as the choir neared its 500th anniversary, popular tastes in classical music had changed. *New York Times* writer Alex Ross, reviewing a 1992 Carnegie Hall performance, noted that they performed scenes from operettas in costume with English dialogue, and wondered if "at times they merely exploited the audience's hunger for cuteness and precociousness."

A new artistic director of the Vienna Choir Boys, Agnes Grossmann, came aboard in 1997 and launched a series of reforms. She and other management instituted shorter concert tours, a less demanding schoolday schedule, a new repertoire featuring works by modern composers, and, most famously, a decree that beginning in 1998 girls would be allowed in the primary school for musical education, they would not, however, be allowed into the Choir itself. Grossmann also oversaw the formation of an independent choir for Vienna concerts alone, whose singers could attend the school simply as day boarders.

Sources

Chicago Sun-Times, February 25, 1968.
Christian Science Monitor, June 4, 1974, p. 5C.
Detroit Free Press, January 22, 1980, p. 10A; December 9, 1984.
Detroit News, December 13, 1978.
New York Times, December 15, 1983; January 16, 1992; December 19, 1992.

—*Carol Brennan*

The Zombies

Rock band

As one of the first British invasion bands to storm the American charts in 1964, the Zombies distinguished themselves from their more raucous peers with a handful of jazzy, minor chord singles that have become classic pop songs. In fact, the Zombies were not only far more popular in the United States than their homeland, they had their biggest hit record several years after they disbanded.

Five schoolmates at the St. Albans Grammar School in Hertfordshire began playing together in the early 60s for fun. Upon graduation, they all had career paths chosen; singer Colin Blunstone was an insurance broker, drummer Hugh Grundy a banker, pianist Rod Argent and guitarist Paul Atkinson were going to the university, and bassist Chris White was enrolled in teacher's college. In 1964, just before going their separate ways, the band adopted the name "The Zombies" and entered a band contest sponsored by *The London Evening Post*.

The Zombies won and their prize included a recording contract with Decca Records. One of the band's hastily written originals "She's Not There" was chosen as their first single. Fame came quickly for the Zombies. A top twenty hit in Britain, "She's Not There", with its distinctive vocal harmonies and Argent's electric piano solo, rose to number two and sold a million copies in America in the wake of the Beatles' success there.

The band members explained the origin of their unorthodox name to *Melody Maker* soon after their first record became a hit. "We chose it from desperation", explained Chris White; "My first reaction was horror," Colin Blunstone broke in, "We did have alternatives like Chatterley and the Gamekeepers but we were desperate."

The Zombies would not have another major hit in England, but in 1965 "Tell Her No" became their second American top ten hit. The group played around the world to enthusiastic audiences from 1965-67, but soon became frustrated by their record company's craving only for songs in the mold of their big hits. In a 1971 *Melody Maker* profile, Blunstone reminisced about the Zombies breakup; "As tactfully as possible, he intimated that the group wasn't making the money they hoped to make, and he in particular was feeling entirely disenchanted with the music, business, and the whole scene. [The band] all talked about it, and decided that they should have a break." The Zombies decided to retire after recording an album on which the band members had complete control. Recording sessions held at Abbey Road Studios in London during the summer of 1967 produced the band's swan song, "Odessey and Oracle."

Though it is now considered a high water mark of 60s pop, "Odessey and Oracle" did not attract much attention upon its release in Britain, and would have possibly been forgotten if former Blood, Sweat, and Tears member and Columbia A & R man Al Kooper hadn't heard it during a trip abroad. Kooper adamantly insisted upon an American release; when Columbia finally relented, Kooper wrote in the sleeve notes, "While in London recently I acquired forty British LPS. Once home, I began to listen to all forty. This record stuck out like a rose in a garden of weeds."

The album seemed destined to fade into obscurity in the United States until "Time of the Season" began picking up airplay in various cities a year after it was released. The record eventually sold over two million copies. The band members turned down offers to reform and tour America in 1969. Undaunted, unscrupulous booking agents sent several bands called "The Zombies" on tour, which featured no original band members.

Some of the former Zombies continued their musical careers. Keyboardist Rod Argent and bassist Chris White formed a new band called Argent in 1972. Argent immediately had an international hit single with "Hold Your Head Up". Other artists had hits covering Argent material also, notably "Liar" by the Three Dog Night and "God Gave Rock n' Roll To You" by Kiss. Colin Blunstone had a successful solo career recording for Epic Records through the 70s, beginning with a version

Members include **Rod Argent**, electric piano and organ; **Paul Atkinson**, guitar; **Colin Blunstone**, (born June 24, 1945, Hatfield, Hertfordshire, England), vocals; **Hugh Grundy**, drums; **Chris White**, bass.

Formed c. 1963, St. Albans Grammar School, Hertfordshire, England; won recording contract with Decca Records; recorded for Decca Records c. 1964-66; recorded for CBS Records, c. 1967. Disbanded 1967. Reunited November 25, 1997 at the Jazz Cafe in London, England.

Awards: R.I.A.A. Gold Record Awards for million sales, "She's Not There", 1964; "Time of the Season", 1969.

---

of "She's Not There" backed by an orchestra and released under the pseudonym Neil McArthur.

Over the years since their breakup, The Zombies were remembered fondly enough for a *Melody Maker* writer to publicly wish for the band to reunite in a 1973 article entitled "Three Likely Reunions ... and Three We'd Like To See." After praising both Argent's and Blunstone's current music, writer Roy Hollingworth reasoned that "what Blunstone lacks now is some sense of identification, and what Argent lacks is an attractive frontman of sorts. Argent and Blunstone have worked together in the studio. It would be fine to see them go the whole way, so to speak."

Another bogus group calling itself "The Zombies" with no connection to the original band surfaced in 1988. According to *Variety,* "the band introduced its bassist Ronald Hugh Grundy as original Zombies drummer Hugh Grundy. The group explained Grundy's switch of instruments as an attempt to position 'the original Zombie' more prominently. ...The actual Grundy reacted with 'shocked amazement.'"

On November 25, 1997, the real Zombies did reunite to play their two biggest hits, "She's Not There" and "Time of the Season", at a party.in London to celebrate the release of the *Zombie Heaven* box set. Writer Dawn Eden recalled on The Zombies' Fan Web Page, "the five of them walked down the staircase from the balcony and

the stage, and the whole room was thrilled.... Hugh Grundy went into that familiar 'She's Not There' intro and the crowd voiced its approval.... After they finished a wonderful 'Time of the Season' (yes, they really did only two songs), they left the stage to huge applause. The applause continued for about six minutes." Despite the brevity of their career, The Zombies are one of the most esteemed British Invasion combos. In addition to several hit records, their discography contains many more hidden treasures.

Selected discography

The Zombies, Parrot, 1965.
Odessey & Oracle, Date/CBS, 1967, reissued Rhino, 1987.
Live On The BBC 1965-1967, Rhino, 1985.
Greatest Hits (rec. 1964-67), DCC, 1990.
Zombie Heaven, Ace, 1997.

Solo projects

(by Colin Blunstone), *Some Years: It's The Time of Colin Blunstone* (rec. 70s), Epic, 1993.
(with Rod Argent), Argent, "Hold Your Head High", Epic, 1972.
(with Rod Argent), *Argent Anthology* (rec. 70s), Epic.

Sources

Books

Joynson, Vernon, *Tapestry of Delights: The Comprehensive Guide to British Music of the Beat, R & B, Psychedelic, and Progressive Eras 1963-1976,* Borderline Productions, 1995.
Schaffner, Nicholas, *The British Invasion,* McGraw-Hill, 1983.

Periodicals

Cash Box, October 31, 1964.
Melody Maker, September 5, 1964; November 20, 1971; April 14, 1973.
Rolling Stone, February 1, 1969; December 13, 1969; May 28, 1970; March 2, 1972; April 1, 1982; September 8, 1988.
Variety, October 29, 1969; August 24, 1988.

Online

http://members.aol.com/bocad/zom.htm.

—*Jim Powers*

Cumulative Indexes

Cumulative Subject Index

Volume numbers appear in **bold**.

Ma, Yo-Yo **2**
Rostropovich, Mstislav **17**

Children's Music
Bartels, Joanie **13**
Cappelli, Frank **14**
Chapin, Tom **11**
Chenille Sisters, The **16**
Harley, Bill **7**
Lehrer, Tom **7**
Nagler, Eric **8**
Penner, Fred **10**
Raffi **8**
Rosenshontz **9**
Sharon, Lois & Bram **6**

Christian Music
Anointed **21**
Ashton, Susan **17**
Audio Adrenaline **22**
Champion, Eric **21**
Chapman, Steven Curtis **15**
dc Talk **18**
Duncan, Bryan **19**
Eskelin, Ian **19**
English, Michael **23**
4Him **23**
Grant, Amy **7**
Jars of Clay **20**
King's X **7**
Paris, Twila **16**
Patti, Sandi **7**
Petra **3**
Point of Grace **21**
Smith, Michael W. **11**
Stryper **2**
Waters, Ethel **11**

Clarinet
Adams, John **8**
Bechet, Sidney **17**
Braxton, Anthony **12**
Byron, Don **22**
Dorsey, Jimmy
  See Dorsey Brothers, The
English, Michael **23**
Fountain, Pete **7**
Goodman, Benny **4**
Herman, Woody **12**
Shaw, Artie **8**

Classical
Anderson, Marian **8**
Arrau, Claudio **1**
Baker, Janet **14**
Bernstein, Leonard **2**
Blegen, Judith **23**
Boyd, Liona **7**
Bream, Julian **9**
Brendel, Alfred **23**
Britten, Benjamin **15**
Bronfman, Yefim **6**
Caballe, Montserrat **23**

Canadian Brass, The **4**
Carter, Ron **14**
Casals, Pablo **9**
Chang, Sarah **7**
Clayderman, Richard **1**
Cliburn, Van **13**
Copland, Aaron **2**
Davis, Anthony **17**
Davis, Chip **4**
Fiedler, Arthur **6**
Galway, James **3**
Gingold, Josef **6**
Gould, Glenn **9**
Gould, Morton **16**
Hampson, Thomas **12**
Harrell, Lynn **3**
Hayes, Roland **13**
Hendricks, Barbara **10**
Heppner, Ben **23**
Herrmann, Bernard **14**
Hinderas, Natalie **12**
Horne, Marilyn **9**
Horowitz, Vladimir **1**
Jarrett, Keith **1**
Kennedy, Nigel **8**
Kissin, Evgeny **6**
Kronos Quartet **5**
Kunzel, Erich **17**
Lemper, Ute **14**
Levine, James **8**
Liberace **9**
Ma, Yo-Yo **2**
Marsalis, Wynton **6**
Masur, Kurt **11**
McNair, Sylvia **15**
McPartland, Marian **15**
Mehta, Zubin **11**
Menuhin, Yehudi **11**
Midori **7**
Mutter, Anne-Sophie **23**
Nyman, Michael **15**
Ott, David **2**
Parkening, Christopher **7**
Perahia, Murray **10**
Perlman, Itzhak **2**
Phillips, Harvey **3**
Rampal, Jean-Pierre **6**
Rostropovich, Mstislav **17**
Rota, Nino **13**
Rubinstein, Arthur **11**
Salerno-Sonnenberg, Nadja **3**
Salonen, Esa-Pekka **16**
Schickele, Peter **5**
Schuman, William **10**
Segovia, Andres **6**
Shankar, Ravi **9**
Solti, Georg **13**
Stern, Isaac **7**
Sutherland, Joan **13**
Takemitsu, Toru **6**
Toscanini, Arturo **14**
Upshaw, Dawn **9**
Vienna Choir Boys **23**
von Karajan, Herbert **1**

Weill, Kurt **12**
Wilson, Ransom **5**
Yamashita, Kazuhito **4**
York, Andrew **15**
Zukerman, Pinchas **4**

Composers
Adams, John **8**
Allen, Geri **10**
Alpert, Herb **11**
Anderson,, Wessell **23**
Anka, Paul **2**
Atkins, Chet **5**
Bacharach, Burt **20**
  Earlier sketch in CM **1**
Badalamenti, Angelo **17**
Beiderbecke, Bix **16**
Benson, George **9**
Berlin, Irving **8**
Bernstein, Leonard **2**
Blackman, Cindy **15**
Bley, Carla **8**
Bley, Paul **14**
Braxton, Anthony **12**
Brickman, Jim **22**
Britten, Benjamin **15**
Brubeck, Dave **8**
Burrell, Kenny **11**
Byrne, David **8**
  Also see Talking Heads
Byron, Don **22**
Cage, John **8**
Cale, John **9**
Casals, Pablo **9**
Clarke, Stanley **3**
Coleman, Ornette **5**
Cooder, Ry **2**
Cooney, Rory **6**
Copeland, Stewart **14**
  Also see Police, The **20**
Copland, Aaron **2**
Crouch, Andraé **9**
Curtis, King **17**
Davis, Anthony **17**
Davis, Chip **4**
Davis, Miles **1**
de Grassi, Alex **6**
Dorsey, Thomas A. **11**
Elfman, Danny **9**
Ellington, Duke **2**
Eno, Brian **8**
Enya **6**
Esquivel, Juan **17**
Evans, Bill **17**
Evans, Gil **17**
Fahey, John **17**
Foster, David **13**
Frisell, Bill **15**
Frith, Fred **19**
Galás, Diamanda **16**
Gillespie, Dizzy **6**
Glass, Philip **1**
Golson, Benny **21**
Gould, Glenn **9**

Fun Lovin' Criminals **20**
Gang of Four **8**
Hammer, M.C. **5**
Harry, Deborah **4**
  Also see Blondie
Ice-T **7**
Idol, Billy **3**
Jackson, Janet **16**
 Earlier sketch in CM **3**
Jackson, Michael **17**
 Earlier sketch in CM **1**
  Also see Jacksons, The
James, Rick **2**
Jones, Grace **9**
Madonna **16**
 Earlier sketch in CM **4**
Massive Attack **17**
Moby **17**
M People **15**
New Order **11**
Orbital **20**
Peniston, CeCe **15**
Pet Shop Boys **5**
Pizzicato Five **18**
Portishead **22**
Prince **14**
 Earlier sketch in CM **1**
Queen Latifah **6**
Rodgers, Nile **8**
Salt-N-Pepa **6**
Shadow, DJ **19**
Shamen, The **23**
Simmons, Russell **7**
Soul II Soul **17**
Sugar Ray **22**
Summer, Donna **12**
Technotronic **5**
TLC **15**
Tricky **18**
2 Unlimited **18**
Vasquez, Junior **16**
Village People, The **7**
Was (Not Was) **6**
Waters, Crystal **15**
Young M.C. **4**

Contemporary Instrumental/New Age
 Ackerman, Will **3**
 Arkenstone, David **20**
 Clinton, George **7**
 Collins, Bootsy **8**
 Davis, Chip **4**
 de Grassi, Alex **6**
 Enigma **14**
 Enya **6**
 Esquivel, Juan **17**
 Hedges, Michael **3**
 Isham, Mark **14**
 Jarre, Jean-Michel **2**
 Kitaro **1**
 Kronos Quartet **5**
 Legg, Adrian **17**
 Story, Liz **2**

Summers, Andy **3**
 Also see Police, The
Tangerine Dream **12**
Tesh, John **20**
Winston, George **9**
Winter, Paul **10**
Yanni **11**

Cornet
 Armstrong, Louis **4**
 Beiderbecke, Bix **16**
 Cherry, Don **10**
 Handy, W. C. **7**
 Oliver, King **15**
 Vaché, Jr., Warren **22**

Country
 Acuff, Roy **2**
 Akins, Rhett **22**
 Alabama **21**
  Earlier sketch in CM **1**
 Anderson, John **5**
 Arnold, Eddy **10**
 Asleep at the Wheel **5**
 Atkins, Chet **5**
 Auldridge, Mike **4**
 Autry, Gene **12**
 Bellamy Brothers, The **13**
 Berg, Matraca **16**
 Berry, John **17**
 Black, Clint **5**
 BlackHawk **21**
 Blue Rodeo **18**
 Bogguss, Suzy **11**
 Bonamy, James **21**
 Boone, Pat **13**
 Boy Howdy **21**
 Brandt, Paul **22**
 Brannon, Kippi **20**
 Brooks & Dunn **12**
 Brooks, Garth **8**
 Brown, Junior **15**
 Brown, Marty **14**
 Brown, Tony **14**
 Buffett, Jimmy **4**
 Byrds, The **8**
 Cale, J. J. **16**
 Campbell, Glen **2**
 Carpenter, Mary-Chapin **6**
 Carter, Carlene **8**
 Carter Family, The **3**
 Cash, Johnny **17**
  Earlier sketch in CM **1**
 Cash, June Carter **6**
 Cash, Rosanne **2**
 Chesney, Kenny **20**
 Chesnutt, Mark **13**
 Clark, Guy **17**
 Clark, Roy **1**
 Clark, Terri **19**
 Clements, Vassar **18**
 Cline, Patsy **5**
 Coe, David Allan **4**
 Collie, Mark **15**

Confederate Railroad **23**
Cooder, Ry **2**
Cowboy Junkies, The **4**
Crowe, J. D. **5**
Crowell, Rodney **8**
Cyrus, Billy Ray **11**
Daniels, Charlie **6**
Davis, Linda **21**
Davis, Skeeter **15**
Dean, Billy **19**
DeMent, Iris **13**
Denver, John **22**
 Earlier entry in CM **1**
Desert Rose Band, The **4**
Diamond Rio **11**
Dickens, Little Jimmy **7**
Diffie, Joe **10**
Dylan, Bob **21**
 Earlier sketch in CM **3**
Earle, Steve **16**
Flatt, Lester **3**
Flores, Rosie **16**
Ford, Tennessee Ernie **3**
Foster, Radney **16**
Frizzell, Lefty **10**
Gayle, Crystal **1**
Germano, Lisa **18**
Gill, Vince **7**
Gilley, Mickey **7**
Gilmore, Jimmie Dale **11**
Gordy, Jr., Emory **17**
Greenwood, Lee **12**
Griffith, Nanci **3**
Haggard, Merle **2**
Hall, Tom T. **4**
Harris, Emmylou **4**
Hartford, John **1**
Hay, George D. **3**
Herndon, Ty **20**
Hiatt, John **8**
Highway 101 **4**
Hill, Faith **18**
Hinojosa, Tish **13**
Howard, Harlan **15**
Jackson, Alan **7**
Jennings, Waylon **4**
Jones, George **4**
Judd, Wynonna
 See Wynonna
 See Judds, The
Ricochet **23**
Judds, The **2**
Keith, Toby **17**
Kentucky Headhunters, The **5**
Kershaw, Sammy **15**
Ketchum, Hal **14**
Kristofferson, Kris **4**
Lamb, Barbara **19**
Lang, K. D. **4**
Lawrence, Tracy **11**
LeDoux, Chris **12**
Lee, Brenda **5**
Little Feat **4**
Little Texas **14**
Louvin Brothers, The **12**

Rota, Nino **13**
Sager, Carole Bayer **5**
Sakamoto, Ryuichi **18**
Schickele, Peter **5**
Shankar, Ravi **9**
Taj Mahal **6**
Waits, Tom **12**
  Earlier sketch in CM **1**
Weill, Kurt **12**
Williams, John **9**
Williams, Paul **5**
Willner, Hal **10**
Young, Neil **15**
  Earlier sketch in CM **2**

Flugelhorn
Mangione, Chuck **23**
Sandoval, Arturo **15**

Flute
Anderson, Ian
  See Jethro Tull
Galway, James **3**
Lateef, Yusef **16**
Mann, Herbie **16**
Najee **21**
Rampal, Jean-Pierre **6**
Ulmer, James Blood **13**
Wilson, Ransom **5**

Folk/Traditional
Altan **18**
America **16**
Anonymous 4 **23**
Arnaz, Desi **8**
Baez, Joan **1**
Belafonte, Harry **8**
Black, Mary **15**
Blades, Ruben **2**
Bloom, Luka **14**
Blue Rodeo **18**
Brady, Paul **8**
Bragg, Billy **7**
Bromberg, David **18**
Buckley, Tim **14**
Bulgarian State Female Vocal Choir, The
  10
Byrds, The **8**
Campbell,, Sarah Elizabeth **23**
Carter Family, The **3**
Chandra, Sheila **16**
Chapin, Harry **6**
Chapman, Tracy **20**
  Earlier sketch in CM **4**
Chenille Sisters, The **16**
Cherry, Don **10**
Chieftains, The **7**
Childs, Toni **2**
Clannad **23**
Clegg, Johnny **8**
Cockburn, Bruce **8**
Cohen, Leonard **3**
Collins, Judy **4**
Colvin, Shawn **11**

Cotten, Elizabeth **16**
Crosby, David **3**
  Also see Byrds, The
Cruz, Celia **22**
  Earlier entry in CM **10**
de Lucia, Paco **1**
DeMent, Iris **13**
Donovan **9**
Dr. John **7**
Drake, Nick **17**
Dylan, Bob **3**
Elliot, Cass **5**
Enya **6**
Estefan, Gloria **15**
  Earlier sketch in CM **2**
Fahey, John **17**
Fairport Convention **22**
Feliciano, José **10**
Galway, James **3**
Germano, Lisa **18**
Gibson, Bob **23**
Gilmore, Jimmie Dale **11**
Gipsy Kings, The **8**
Gorka, John **18**
Griffith, Nanci **3**
Grisman, David **17**
Guthrie, Arlo **6**
Guthrie, Woody **2**
Hakmoun, Hassan **15**
Hardin, Tim **18**
Harding, John Wesley **6**
Hartford, John **1**
Havens, Richie **11**
Henry, Joe **18**
Hinojosa, Tish **13**
Ian and Sylvia **18**
Iglesias, Julio **20**
  Earlier sketch in CM **2**
Incredible String Band **23**
Indigo Girls **20**
  Earlier sketch in CM **3**
Ives, Burl **12**
Khan, Nusrat Fateh Ali **13**
Kingston Trio, The **9**
Klezmatics, The **18**
Kottke, Leo **13**
Kuti, Fela **7**
Ladysmith Black Mambazo **1**
Larkin, Patty **9**
Lavin, Christine **6**
Leadbelly **6**
Lightfoot, Gordon **3**
Los Lobos **2**
Makeba, Miriam **8**
Mamas and the Papas **21**
Masekela, Hugh **7**
McLean, Don **7**
Melanie **12**
Mitchell, Joni **17**
  Earlier sketch in CM **2**
Moffatt, Katy **18**
Morrison, Van **3**
Morrissey, Bill **12**
Nascimento, Milton **6**

N'Dour, Youssou **6**
Near, Holly **1**
Ochs, Phil **7**
O'Connor, Sinead **3**
Odetta **7**
Parsons, Gram **7**
  Also see Byrds, The
Paxton, Tom **5**
Pentangle **18**
Peter, Paul & Mary **4**
Pogues, The **6**
Prine, John **7**
Proclaimers, The **13**
Redpath, Jean **1**
Ritchie, Jean, **4**
Roches, The **18**
Rodgers, Jimmie **3**
Sainte-Marie, Buffy **11**
Santana, Carlos **1**
Seeger, Pete **4**
  Also see Weavers, The
Selena **16**
Shankar, Ravi **9**
Simon, Paul **16**
  Earlier sketch in CM **1**
Snow, Pheobe **4**
Steeleye Span **19**
Story, The **13**
Sweet Honey in the Rock **1**
Taj Mahal **6**
Thompson, Richard **7**
Tikaram, Tanita **9**
Toure, Ali Farka **18**
Van Ronk, Dave **12**
Van Zandt, Townes **13**
Vega, Suzanne **3**
Wainwright III, Loudon **11**
Walker, Jerry Jeff **13**
Watson, Doc **2**
Weavers, The **8**
Whitman, Slim **19**

French Horn
Ohanian, David
  See Canadian Brass, The

Funk
Avery, Teodross **23**
Bambaataa, Afrika **13**
Brand New Heavies, The **14**
Brown, James **2**
Burdon, Eric **14**
  Also see War
  Also see Animals
Clinton, George **7**
Collins, Bootsy **8**
Fishbone **7**
Front 242 **19**
Gang of Four **8**
Jackson, Janet **16**
  Earlier sketch in CM **3**
Khan, Chaka **19**
  Earlier sketch in CM **9**
Jamiroquai **21**

Guthrie, Woody **2**
Horton, Walter **19**
Lewis, Huey **9**
Little Walter **14**
McClinton, Delbert **14**
Musselwhite, Charlie **13**
Reed, Jimmy **15**
Thielemans, Toots **13**
Waters, Muddy **4**
Wells, Junior **17**
Williamson, Sonny Boy **9**
Wilson, Kim
  See Fabulous Thunderbirds, The
Wonder, Stevie **17**
  Earlier sketch in CM **2**
Young, Neil **15**
  Earlier sketch in CM **2**

Heavy Metal
AC/DC **4**
Aerosmith **22**
  Earlier sketch in CM **1**
Alice in Chains **10**
Anthrax **11**
Black Sabbath **9**
Blue Oyster Cult **16**
Cinderella **16**
Circle Jerks **17**
Danzig **7**
Deep Purple **11**
Def Leppard **3**
Dokken **16**
Faith No More **7**
Fishbone **7**
Ford, Lita **9**
Guns n' Roses **2**
Iron Maiden **10**
Judas Priest **10**
King's X **7**
Led Zeppelin **1**
L7 **12**
Megadeth **9**
Melvins **21**
Metallica **7**
Mötley Crüe **1**
Motörhead **10**
Nugent, Ted **2**
Osbourne, Ozzy **3**
Pantera **13**
Petra **3**
Queensryche **8**
Reid, Vernon **2**
  Also see Living Colour
Reznor, Trent **13**
Roth, David Lee **1**
  Also see Van Halen
Sepultura **12**
Skinny Puppy **17**
Slayer **10**
Soundgarden **6**
Spinal Tap **8**
Stryper **2**
Suicidal Tendencies **15**
Tool **21**

Warrant **17**
Whitesnake **5**
White Zombie **17**

Humor
Borge, Victor **19**
Coasters, The **5**
Demento, Dr. **23**
Jones, Spike **5**
Lehrer, Tom **7**
Pearl, Minnie **3**
Russell, Mark **6**
Sandler, Adam **19**
Schickele, Peter **5**
Shaffer, Paul **13**
Spinal Tap **8**
Stevens, Ray **7**
Yankovic, "Weird Al" **7**

Inventors
Fender, Leo **10**
Harris, Eddie **15**
Paul, Les **2**
Scholz, Tom
  See Boston
Teagarden, Jack **10**
Theremin, Leon **19**

Jazz
Adderly, Cannonball **15**
Allen, Geri **10**
Allison, Mose **17**
Anderson, Ray **7**
Anderson, Wessell **23**
Armstrong, Louis **4**
Art Ensemble of Chicago, The **23**
Avery, Teodross **23**
Bailey, Mildred **13**
Bailey, Pearl **5**
Baker, Anita **9**
Baker, Chet **13**
Baker, Ginger **16**
  Also see Cream
Barbieri, Gato **22**
Basie, Count **2**
Bechet, Sidney **17**
Beiderbecke, Bix **16**
Belle, Regina **6**
Bennett, Tony **16**
  Earlier sketch in CM **2**
Benson, George **9**
Berigan, Bunny **2**
Blackman, Cindy **15**
Blakey, Art **11**
Blanchard, Terence **13**
Bley, Carla **8**
Bley, Paul **14**
Blood, Sweat and Tears **7**
Brand New Heavies, The **14**
Braxton, Anthony **12**
Bridgewater, Dee Dee **18**
Brown, Lawrence **23**
Brown, Ray **21**
Brown, Ruth **13**

Brubeck, Dave **8**
Burrell, Kenny **11**
Burton, Gary **10**
Calloway, Cab **6**
Canadian Brass, The **4**
Carter, Benny **3**
  Also see McKinney's Cotton Pickers
Carter, Betty **6**
Carter, James **18**
Carter, Regina **22**
Carter, Ron **14**
Chambers, Paul **18**
Charles, Ray **1**
Cherry, Don **10**
Christian, Charlie **11**
Clarke, Stanley **3**
Clements, Vassar **18**
Clooney, Rosemary **9**
Cole, Holly **18**
Cole, Nat King **3**
Coleman, Ornette **5**
Coltrane, John **4**
Connick, Harry, Jr. **4**
Corea, Chick **6**
Davis, Anthony **17**
Davis, Miles **1**
DeJohnette, Jack **7**
Di Meola, Al **12**
Dirty Dozen **23**
Eckstine, Billy **1**
Eldridge, Roy **9**
  Also see McKinney's Cotton Pickers
Ellington, Duke **2**
Ellis, Herb **18**
Evans, Bill **17**
Evans, Gil **17**
Ferguson, Maynard **7**
Ferrell, Rachelle **17**
Fitzgerald, Ella **1**
Flanagan, Tommy **16**
Fleck, Bela **8**
  Also see New Grass Revival, The
Fountain, Pete **7**
Frisell, Bill **15**
Galway, James **3**
Getz, Stan **12**
Gillespie, Dizzy **6**
Goodman, Benny **4**
Gordon, Dexter **10**
Grappelli, Stephane **10**
Green, Benny **17**
Green, Grant **14**
Guaraldi, Vince **3**
Hackett, Bobby **21**
Haden, Charlie **12**
Hampton, Lionel **6**
Hancock, Herbie **8**
Hardcastle, Paul **20**
Hargrove, Roy **15**
Harris, Eddie **15**
Harris, Teddy **22**
Hawkins, Coleman **11**
Hawkins, Erskine **19**
Hedges, Michael **3**

Piano

Allen, Geri **10**
Allison, Mose **17**
Amos, Tori **12**
Arrau, Claudio **1**
Bacharach, Burt **20**
  Earlier sketch in CM **1**
Ball, Marcia **15**
Basie, Count **2**
Berlin, Irving **8**
Blake, Eubie **19**
Bley, Carla **8**
Bley, Paul **14**
Borge, Victor **19**
Brendel, Alfred **23**
Brickman, Jim **22**
Britten, Benjamin **15**
Bronfman, Yefim **6**
Brubeck, Dave **8**
Bush, Kate **4**
Charles, Ray **1**
Clayderman, Richard **1**
Cleveland, James **1**
Cliburn, Van **13**
Cole, Nat King **3**
Collins, Judy **4**
Collins, Phil **20**
  Earlier sketch in CM **2**
  Also see Genesis
Connick, Harry, Jr. **4**
Crouch, Andraé **9**
DeJohnette, Jack **7**
Domino, Fats **2**
Dr. John **7**
Dupree, Champion Jack **12**
Ellington, Duke **2**
Esquivel, Juan **17**
Evans, Bill **17**
Evans, Gil **17**
Feinstein, Michael **6**
Ferrell, Rachelle **17**
Flack, Roberta **5**
Flanagan, Tommy **16**
Frey, Glenn **3**
Galás, Diamanda **16**
Glass, Philip **1**
Gould, Glenn **9**
Green, Benny **17**
Grusin, Dave **7**
Guaraldi, Vince **3**
Hamlisch, Marvin **1**
Hancock, Herbie **8**
Harris, Teddy **22**
Helfgott, David **19**
Henderson, Fletcher **16**
Hinderas, Natalie **12**
Hines, Earl "Fatha" **12**
Horn, Shirley **7**
Hornsby, Bruce **3**
Horowitz, Vladimir **1**
Ibrahim, Abdulla **23**
Jackson, Joe **22**
  Earlier entry in CM **4**
Jarrett, Keith **1**

Joel, Billy **12**
  Earlier sketch in CM **2**
John, Elton **20**
  Earlier sketch in CM **3**
Johnson, James P. **16**
Jones, Hank **15**
Joplin, Scott **10**
Kenton, Stan **21**
Kissin, Evgeny **6**
Levine, James **8**
Lewis, Jerry Lee **2**
Lewis, Ramsey **14**
Liberace **9**
Little Richard **1**
Manilow, Barry **2**
Marsalis, Ellis **13**
Matthews, Eric **22**
McDonald, Michael
  See Doobie Brothers, The
McPartland, Marian **15**
McRae, Carmen **9**
McVie, Christine
  See Fleetwood Mac
Milsap, Ronnie **2**
Mingus, Charles **9**
Monk, Thelonious **6**
Morton, Jelly Roll **7**
Newman, Randy **4**
Nero, Peter **19**
Palmieri, Eddie **15**
Perahia, Murray **10**
Peterson, Oscar **11**
Post, Mike **21**
Powell, Bud **15**
Pratt, Awadagin **19**
Previn, André **15**
Professor Longhair **6**
Puente, Tito **14**
Pullen, Don **16**
Rich, Charlie **3**
Roberts, Marcus **6**
Rubinstein, Arthur **11**
Russell, Mark **6**
Schickele, Peter **5**
Sedaka, Neil **4**
Shaffer, Paul **13**
Solal, Martial **4**
Solti, Georg **13**
Spann, Otis **18**
Story, Liz **2**
Strayhorn, Billy **13**
Sunnyland Slim **16**
Sykes, Roosevelt **20**
Tatum, Art **17**
Taylor, Billy **13**
Taylor, Cecil **9**
Tyner, McCoy **7**
Vangelis **21**
Waits, Tom **12**
  Earlier sketch in **1**
Waller, Fats **7**
Weston, Randy **15**
Wilson, Cassandra **12**
Winston, George **9**

Winwood, Steve **2**
  Also see Spencer Davis Group
  Also see Traffic
Wonder, Stevie **17**
  Earlier sketch in CM **2**
Wright, Rick
  See Pink Floyd
Young, La Monte **16**

Piccolo

Galway, James **3**

Pop

A-ha **22**
Abba **12**
Abdul, Paula **3**
Adam Ant **13**
Adams, Bryan **20**
  Earlier sketch in CM **2**
Adams, Oleta **17**
Air Supply **22**
All-4-One **17**
Alpert, Herb **11**
America **16**
Amos, Tori **12**
Andrews Sisters, The **9**
Arden, Jann **21**
Arena, Tina **21**
Armatrading, Joan **4**
Arnold, Eddy **10**
Artifacts **23**
Astley, Rick **5**
Atkins, Chet **5**
Avalon, Frankie **5**
Bacharach, Burt **20**
  Earlier sketch in CM **1**
Backstreet Boys **21**
Bailey, Pearl **5**
Baker, Arthur **23**
Bananarama **22**
Bangles **22**
Basia **5**
Beach Boys, The **1**
Beatles, The **2**
Beaver Brown Band, The **3**
Bee Gees, The **3**
Belly **16**
Bennett, Tony **16**
  Earlier sketch in CM **2**
Benson, George **9**
Benton, Brook **7**
B-52's, The **4**
Better Than Ezra **19**
Blige, Mary J. **15**
Blondie **14**
Blood, Sweat and Tears **7**
Blue Rodeo **18**
BoDeans, The **20**
  Earlier sketch in CM **3**
Bolton, Michael **4**
Boo Radleys, The **21**
Boone, Pat **13**
Boston **11**

Jackson, Joe **22**
  Earlier entry in CM **4**
Jackson, Michael **17**
  Earlier sketch in CM **1**
  Also see Jacksons, The
Jacksons, The **7**
Jam, Jimmy, and Terry Lewis **11**
James **12**
James, Harry **11**
James, Rick **2**
Jarreau, Al **1**
Jayhawks, The **15**
Jefferson Airplane **5**
Jesus Jones **23**
Jodeci **13**
Joel, Billy **12**
  Earlier sketch in CM **2**
Johansen, David **7**
John, Elton **20**
  Earlier sketch in CM **3**
Johnston, Freedy **20**
Jolson, Al **10**
Jones, Quincy **20**
  Earlier sketch in CM **2**
Jones, Rickie Lee **4**
Jones, Tom **11**
Joplin, Janis **3**
Kaye, Carol **22**
Khan, Chaka **19**
  Earlier sketch in CM **9**
King, Ben E. **7**
King, Carole **6**
Kiss **5**
Kitt, Eartha **9**
Knight, Gladys **1**
Knopfler, Mark **3**
  Also see Dire Straits
Kool & the Gang **13**
Kraftwerk **9**
Kristofferson, Kris **4**
LaBelle, Patti **8**
Lauper, Cyndi **11**
Lee, Brenda **5**
Leiber and Stoller **14**
Lemper, Ute **14**
Lennon, John **9**
  Also see Beatles, The
Lennon, Julian **2**
Lennox, Annie **18**
Lightning Seeds **21**
Lewis, Huey **9**
Liberace **9**
Lightfoot, Gordon **3**
Lisa, Lisa **23**
Loeb, Lisa **19**
Loggins, Kenny **20**
  Earlier sketch in CM **3**
Lovett, Lyle **5**
Lowe, Nick **6**
Lush **13**
Lynne, Jeff **5**
MacColl, Kirsty **12**
Madonna **16**
  Earlier sketch in CM **4**

Mamas and the Papas **21**
Mancini, Henry **20**
  Earlier sketch in CM **1**
Manhattan Transfer, The **8**
Manilow, Barry **2**
Marley, Bob **3**
Marley, Ziggy **3**
Marsalis, Branford **10**
Martin, Dean **1**
Martin, George **6**
Marx, Richard **21**
  Earlier sketch in CM **3**
Mathis, Johnny **2**
Mazzy Star **17**
McCartney, Paul **4**
  Also see Beatles, The
McFerrin, Bobby **3**
McLachlan, Sarah **12**
McLean, Don **7**
McLennan, Grant **21**
Medley, Bill **3**
Melanie **12**
Michael, George **9**
Midler, Bette **8**
Mighty Mighty Bosstones **20**
Mike & the Mechanics **17**
Miller, Mitch **11**
Miller, Roger **4**
Milli Vanilli **4**
Mills Brothers, The **14**
Minnelli, Liza **19**
Mitchell, Joni **17**
  Earlier sketch in CM **2**
Money, Eddie **16**
Monkees, The **7**
Montand, Yves **12**
Moore, Chante **21**
Morrison, Jim **3**
Morrison, Van **3**
Morissette, Alanis **19**
Morrissey **10**
Mouskouri, Nana **12**
Moyet, Alison **12**
Murray, Anne **4**
Myles, Alannah **4**
Neville, Aaron **5**
  Also see Neville Brothers, The
Neville Brothers, The **4**
New Kids on the Block **3**
Newman, Randy **4**
Newton, Wayne **2**
Newton-John, Olivia **8**
Nicks, Stevie **2**
Nilsson **10**
Nitty Gritty Dirt Band **6**
No Doubt **20**
Nyro, Laura **12**
Oak Ridge Boys, The **7**
Ocasek, Ric **5**
Ocean, Billy **4**
O'Connor, Sinead **3**
Odds **20**
Oldfield, Mike **18**
Orchestral Manoeuvres in the Dark **21**

Orlando, Tony **15**
Osborne, Joan **19**
Osmond, Donny **3**
Page, Jimmy **4**
  Also see Led Zeppelin
  Also see Yardbirds, The
Page, Patti **11**
Parks, Van Dyke **17**
Parsons, Alan **12**
Parton, Dolly **2**
Pendergrass, Teddy **3**
Peniston, CeCe **15**
Penn, Michael **4**
Pet Shop Boys **5**
Peter, Paul & Mary **4**
Phillips, Sam **12**
Piaf, Edith **8**
Pizzicato Five **18**
Plant, Robert **2**
  Also see Led Zeppelin
Pointer Sisters, The **9**
Porter, Cole **10**
Prefab Sprout **15**
Presley, Elvis **1**
Priest, Maxi **20**
Prince **14**
  Earlier sketch in CM **1**
Proclaimers, The **13**
Prodigy **22**
Psychedelic Furs **23**
Pulp **18**
Queen **6**
Rabbitt, Eddie **5**
Raitt, Bonnie **3**
Rea, Chris **12**
Redding, Otis **5**
Reddy, Helen **9**
Reeves, Martha **4**
R.E.M. **5**
Republica **20**
Richard, Cliff **14**
Richie, Lionel **2**
Riley, Teddy **14**
Robbins, Marty **9**
Robinson, Smokey **1**
Rogers, Kenny **1**
Rolling Stones **3**
Ronstadt, Linda **2**
Ross, Diana **1**
Roth, David Lee **1**
  Also see Van Halen
Roxette **23**
RuPaul **20**
Ruffin, David **6**
Sade **2**
Sager, Carole Bayer **5**
Sainte-Marie, Buffy **11**
Sanborn, David **1**
Seal **14**
Seals, Dan **9**
Seals & Crofts **3**
Secada, Jon **13**
Sedaka, Neil **4**
Selena **16**
Shaffer, Paul **13**

Vandross, Luther **2**
Vasquez, Junior **16**
Vig, Butch **17**
Walden, Narada Michael **14**
Was, Don **21**
Watt, Mike **22**
Wexler, Jerry **15**
Whelan, Bill **20**
Willner, Hal **10**
Wilson, Brian
  See Beach Boys, The
Winbush, Angela **15**
Woods-Wright, Tomica **22**

Promoters
Clark, Dick **2**
Geldof, Bob **9**
Graham, Bill **10**
Hay, George D. **3**
Simmons, Russell **7**

Ragtime
Johnson, James P. **16**
Joplin, Scott **10**

Rap
Anthony, Marc **19**
Arrested Development **14**
Austin, Dallas **16**
Bambaataa, Afrika **13**
Basehead **11**
Beastie Boys, The **8**
Biz Markie **10**
Black Sheep **15**
Bone Thugs-N-Harmony **18**
Busta Rhymes **18**
Campbell, Luther **10**
Cherry, Neneh **4**
Combs, Sean "Puffy" **16**
Common **23**
Coolio **19**
Cypress Hill **11**
Das EFX **14**
De La Soul **7**
Digable Planets **15**
Digital Underground **9**
DJ Jazzy Jeff and the Fresh Prince **5**
Dr. Dre **15**
  Also see N.W.A.
Eazy-E **13**
  Also see N.W.A.
EPMD **10**
Eric B. and Rakim **9**
Franti, Michael **16**
Fugees, The **17**
Gang Starr **13**
Geto Boys, The **11**
Grandmaster Flash **14**
Gravediggaz **23**
Hammer, M.C. **5**
Heavy D **10**
House of Pain **14**
Ice Cube **10**
Ice-T **7**
Insane Clown Posse **22**

Jackson, Millie **14**
Kane, Big Daddy **7**
Kid 'n Play **5**
Knight, Suge **15**
Kool Moe Dee **9**
Kris Kross **11**
KRS-One **8**
L.L. Cool J. **5**
Last Poets **21**
MC Breed **17**
MC Lyte **8**
MC 900 Ft. Jesus **16**
MC Serch **10**
Master P **22**
Nas **19**
Naughty by Nature **11**
N.W.A. **6**
Notorious B.I.G. **20**
Pharcyde, The **17**
P.M. Dawn **11**
Public Enemy **4**
Queen Latifah **6**
Rage Against the Machine **18**
Riley, Teddy **14**
Rubin, Rick **9**
Run-D.M.C. **4**
Salt-N-Pepa **6**
Scott-Heron, Gil **13**
Shaggy **19**
Shanté **10**
Shocklee, Hank **15**
Simmons, Russell **7**
Sir Mix-A-Lot **14**
Snoop Doggy Dogg **17**
Snow **23**
Spearhead **19**
Special Ed **16**
Sure!, Al B. **13**
TLC **15**
Tone-Lōc **3**
Too $hort **16**
Tribe Called Quest, A **8**
Tricky **18**
2Pac **17**
Usher **23**
US3 **18**
Vanilla Ice **6**
Wu-Tang Clan **19**
Young M.C. **4**
Yo Yo **9**

Record Company Executives
Ackerman, Will **3**
Alpert, Herb **11**
Brown, Tony **14**
Busby, Jheryl **9**
Combs, Sean "Puffy" **16**
Davis, Chip **4**
Davis, Clive **14**
Ertegun, Ahmet **10**
Foster, David **13**
Gabriel, Peter **16**
  Earlier sketch in CM **2**
  Also see Genesis

Geffen, David **8**
Gordy, Berry, Jr. **6**
Hammond, John **6**
Harley, Bill **7**
Harrell, Andre **16**
Jam, Jimmy, and Terry Lewis **11**
Knight, Suge **15**
Koppelman, Charles **14**
Krasnow, Bob **15**
LiPuma, Tommy **18**
Madonna **16**
  Earlier sketch in CM **4**
Marley, Rita **10**
Martin, George **6**
Mayfield, Curtis **8**
Mercer, Johnny **13**
Miller, Mitch **11**
Mingus, Charles **9**
Near, Holly **1**
Ostin, Mo **17**
Penner, Fred **10**
Phillips, Sam **5**
Reznor, Trent **13**
Rhone, Sylvia **13**
Robinson, Smokey **1**
Rubin, Rick **9**
Simmons, Russell **7**
Spector, Phil **4**
Teller, Al **15**
Too $hort **16**
Wexler, Jerry **15**
Woods-Wright, Tomica **22**

Reggae
Bad Brains **16**
Big Mountain **23**
Black Uhuru **12**
Burning Spear **15**
Cliff, Jimmy **8**
Dube, Lucky **17**
Inner Circle **15**
Israel Vibration **21**
Marley, Bob **3**
Marley, Rita **10**
Marley, Ziggy **3**
Mystic Revealers **16**
Skatalites, The **18**
Sly and Robbie **13**
Steel Pulse **14**
Third World **13**
Tosh, Peter **3**
UB40 **4**
Wailer, Bunny **11**

Rhythm and Blues/Soul
Aaliyah **21**
Abdul, Paula **3**
Adams, Oleta **17**
Alexander, Arthur **14**
All-4-One **17**
Austin, Dallas **16**
Ballard, Hank **17**
Baker, Anita **9**
Ball, Marcia **15**

Cetera, Peter
  See Chicago
Chandra, Sheila **16**
Chapin, Harry **6**
Chapman, Steven Curtis **15**
Chapman, Tracy **4**
Chaquico,, Craig **23**
Charles, Ray **1**
Chenier, C. J. **15**
Childs, Toni **2**
Chilton, Alex **10**
Clapton, Eric **11**
  Earlier sketch in CM **1**
    Also see Cream
    Also see Yardbirds, The
Clark, Guy **17**
Clements, Vassar **18**
Cleveland, James **1**
Clinton, George **7**
Cochrane,, Tom **23**
Cockburn, Bruce **8**
Cohen, Leonard **3**
Cole, Lloyd **9**
Cole, Nat King **3**
Collins, Albert **4**
Collins, Judy **4**
Collins, Phil **2**
  Also see Genesis
Cooder, Ry **2**
Cooke, Sam **1**
  Also see Soul Stirrers, The
Collie, Mark **15**
Cooper, Alice **8**
Cope, Julian **16**
Corgan, Billy
  See Smashing Pumpkins
Costello, Elvis **12**
  Earlier sketch in CM **2**
Cotten, Elizabeth **16**
Crenshaw, Marshall **5**
Croce, Jim **3**
Crofts, Dash
  See Seals & Crofts
Cropper, Steve **12**
Crosby, David **3**
  Also see Byrds, The
Crow, Sheryl **18**
Crowe, J. D. **5**
Crowell, Rodney **8**
Daniels, Charlie **6**
Davies, Ray **5**
  Also see Kinks, the
de Burgh, Chris **22**
DeBarge, El **14**
DeMent, Iris **13**
Denver, John **22**
  Earlier sketch in CM **1**
Des'ree **15**
Diamond, Neil **1**
Diddley, Bo **3**
Difford, Chris
  See Squeeze
DiFranco, Ani **17**
Dion **4**

Dixon, Willie **10**
Doc Pomus **14**
Domino, Fats **2**
Donelly, Tanya
  See Belly
  Also see Throwing Muses
Donovan **9**
Dorsey, Thomas A. **11**
Doucet, Michael **8**
Dozier, Lamont
  See Holland-Dozier-Holland
Drake, Nick **17**
Dube, Lucky **17**
Duffy, Billy
  See Cult, The
Dulli, Greg **17**
  See Afghan Whigs, The
Dylan, Bob **21**
        Earlier entry in CM **3**
Earle, Steve **16**
Edge, The
  See U2
Edmonds, Kenneth "Babyface" **12**
Eitzel, Mark
  See American Music Club
Elfman, Danny **9**
Ellington, Duke **2**
Emerson, Keith
  See Emerson, Lake & Palmer/Powell
Emmanuel, Tommy **21**
English,, Michael **23**
Enigma **14**
Erickson, Roky **16**
Ertegun, Ahmet **10**
Escovedo, Alejandro **18**
Estefan, Gloria **15**
  Earlier sketch in CM **2**
Etheridge, Melissa **16**
  Earlier entry in CM **4**
Everly, Don
  See Everly Brothers, The
Everly, Phil
  See Everly Brothers, The
Fagen, Don
  See Steely Dan
Faithfull, Marianne **14**
Ferry, Bryan **1**
Flack, Roberta **5**
Flatt, Lester **3**
Fogelberg, Dan **4**
Fogerty, John **2**
  Also see Creedence Clearwater
Revival
Fordham, Julia **15**
Foster, David **13**
Frampton, Peter **3**
Franti, Michael **16**
Frey, Glenn **3**
  Also see Eagles, The
Fripp, Robert **9**
Frizzell, Lefty **10**
Gabriel, Peter **16**
  Earlier sketch in CM **2**
  Also see Genesis

Garcia, Jerry **4**
  Also see Grateful Dead, The
Gaye, Marvin **4**
Geldof, Bob **9**
George, Lowell
  See Little Feat
Gershwin, George and Ira **11**
Gibb, Barry
  See Bee Gees, The
Gibb, Maurice
  See Bee Gees, The
Gibb, Robin
  See Bee Gees, The
Gibbons, Billy
  See ZZ Top
Gibson, Debbie **1**
Gibson,, Bob **23**
Gift, Roland **3**
Gill, Vince **7**
Gilley, Mickey **7**
Gilmour, David
  See Pink Floyd
Gold, Julie **22**
Goodman, Benny **4**
Gordy, Berry, Jr. **6**
Gorka, John **18**
Grant, Amy **7**
Green, Al **9**
Greenwood, Lee **12**
Griffith, Nanci **3**
Guthrie, Arlo **6**
Guthrie, Woodie **2**
Guy, Buddy **4**
Haggard, Merle **2**
Hall, Daryl
  See Hall & Oates
Hall, Tom T. **4**
Hamlisch, Marvin **1**
Hammer, M.C. **5**
Hammerstein, Oscar
  See Rodgers, Richard
Hardin, Tim **18**
Harding, John Wesley **6**
Harley, Bill **7**
Harper, Ben **17**
Harris, Emmylou **4**
Harrison, George **2**
  Also see Beatles, The
Harry, Deborah **4**
  Also see Blondie
Hart, Lorenz
  See Rodgers, Richard
Hartford, John **1**
Hatfield, Juliana **12**
  Also see Lemonheads, The
Hawkins, Screamin' Jay **8**
Hayes, Isaac **10**
Healey, Jeff **4**
Hedges, Michael **3**
Hendrix, Jimi **2**
Henley, Don **3**
  Also see Eagles, The
Henry, Joe **18**
Hersh, Kristin
  See Throwing Muses

Cumulative Musicians Index

Volume numbers appear in **bold**.

A-ha **22**
Aaliyah **21**
Abba **12**
Abbott, Jacqueline
  See Beautiful South
Abbott, Jude
  See Chumbawamba
Abbruzzese, Dave
Abdul, Paula **3**
Abong, Fred
  See Belly
Abrahams, Mick
  See Jethro Tull
Abrams, Bryan
  See Color Me Badd
Abrantes, Fernando
  See Kraftwerk
AC/DC **4**
Ace of Base **22**
Ackerman, Will **3**
Acland, Christopher
  See Lush
Acuff, Roy **2**
Acuna, Alejandro
  See Weather Report
Adam Ant **13**
Adamendes, Elaine
  See Throwing Muses
Adams, Bryan **20**
  Earlier sketch in CM **2**
Adams, Clifford
  See Kool & the Gang
Adams, Craig
  See Cult, The
Adams, Donn
  See NRBQ
Adams, John **8**
Adams, Mark
  See Specials, The
Adams, Oleta **17**
Adams, Terry
  See NRBQ
Adams, Victoria
  See Spice Girls
Adams, Yolanda **23**
Adcock, Eddie
  See Country Gentleman, The
Adderly, Cannonball **15**
Adderly, Julian
  See Adderly, Cannonball
Adé, King Sunny **18**
Adler, Steven
  See Guns n' Roses

Aerosmith **22**
  Earlier sketch in CM **3**
Afghan Whigs **17**
Afonso, Marie
  See Zap Mama
AFX
  See Aphex Twin
Air Supply **22**
Ajile
  See Arrested Development
Akingbola, Sola
  See Jamiroquai
Akins, Rhett **22**
Alabama **21**
  Earlier sketch in CM **1**
Alarm **22**
Albarn, Damon
  See Blur
Albert, Nate
  See Mighty Mighty Bosstones
Alberti, Dorona
  See KMFDM
Albini, Steve **15**
Albuquerque, Michael de
  See Electric Light Orchestra
Alexakis, Art
  See Everclear
Alexander, Arthur **14**
Alexander, Tim
  See Asleep at the Wheel
Alexander, Tim "Herb"
  See Primus
Ali
  See Tribe Called Quest, A
Alice in Chains **10**
Alien Sex Fiend **23**
Alkema, Jan Willem
  See Compulsion
Allcock, Martin
  See Fairport Convention
  Also see Jethro Tull
Allen, April
  See C + C Music Factory
Allen, Chad
  See Guess Who
Allen, Dave
  See Gang of Four
Allen, Debbie **8**
Allen, Duane
  See Oak Ridge Boys, The
Allen, Geri **10**
Allen, Johnny Ray
  See Subdudes, The

Allen, Papa Dee
  See War
Allen, Peter **11**
Allen, Red
  See Osborne Brothers, The
Allen, Rick
  See Def Leppard
Allen, Ross
  See Mekons, The
All-4-One **17**
Allison, Luther **21**
Allison, Mose **17**
Allman, Duane
  See Allman Brothers, The
Allman, Gregg
  See Allman Brothers, The
Allman Brothers, The **6**
Allsup, Michael Rand
  See Three Dog Night
Alpert, Herb **11**
Alphonso, Roland
  See Skatalites, The
Alsing, Pelle
  See Roxette
Alston, Andy
  See Del Amitri
Alston, Shirley
  See Shirelles, The
Altan **18**
Alvin, Dave **17**
  Also see X
Am, Svet
  See KMFDM
Amato, Dave
  See REO Speedwagon
Amedee, Steve
  See Subdudes, The
Ament, Jeff
  See Pearl Jam
America **16**
American Music Club **15**
Amos, Tori **12**
Anastasio, Trey
  See Phish
Anderson, Al
  See NRBQ
Anderson, Andy
  See Cure, The
Anderson, Brett
  See Suede
Anderson, Cleave
  See Blue Rodeo
Anderson, Emma
  See Lush

Balch, Bob
　　See Fu Manchu
Balch, Michael
　　See Front Line Assembly
Baldursson, Sigtryggur
　　See Sugarcubes, The
Baldwin, Donny
　　See Starship
Baliardo, Diego
　　See Gipsy Kings, The
Baliardo, Paco
　　See Gipsy Kings, The
Baliardo, Tonino
　　See Gipsy Kings, The
Balin, Marty
　　See Jefferson Airplane
Ball, Marcia 15
Ballard, Florence
　　See Supremes, The
Ballard, Hank 17
Balsley, Phil
　　See Statler Brothers, The
Baltes, Peter
　　See Dokken
Balzano, Vinnie
　　See Less Than Jake
Bambaataa, Afrika 13
Bamonte, Perry
　　See Cure, The
Bananarama 22
Bancroft, Cyke
　　See Bevis Frond
Band, The 9
Bangles 22
Banks, Nick
　　See Pulp
Banks, Peter
　　See Yes
Banks, Tony
　　See Genesis
Baptiste, David Russell
　　See Meters, The
Barbarossa, Dave
　　See Republica
Barbata, John
　　See Jefferson Starship
Barber, Keith
　　See Soul Stirrers, The
Barbero, Lori
　　See Babes in Toyland
Barbieri, Gato 22
Bardens, Peter
　　See Camel
Barenaked Ladies 18
Bargeld, Blixa
　　See Einstürzende Neubauten
Bargeron, Dave
　　See Blood, Sweat and Tears
Barham, Meriel
　　See Lush
Barile, Jo
　　See Ventures, The
Barker, Paul
　　See Ministry

Barker, Travis Landon
　　See Aquabats
Barlow, Barriemore
　　See Jethro Tull
Barlow, Lou 20
　　Also see Dinosaur Jr.
Barlow, Tommy
　　See Aztec Camera
Barnes, Danny
　　See Bad Livers, The
Barnes, Micah
　　See Nylons, The
Barnes, Roosevelt "Booba" 23
Barnwell, Duncan
　　See Simple Minds
Barnwell, Ysaye Maria
　　See Sweet Honey in the Rock
Barr, Ralph
　　See Nitty Gritty Dirt Band, The
Barre, Martin
　　See Jethro Tull
Barrere, Paul
　　See Little Feat
Barrett, Dicky
　　See Mighty Mighty Bosstones
Barrett, (Roger) Syd
　　See Pink Floyd
Barron, Christopher
　　See Spin Doctors
Barrow, Geoff
　　See Portishead
Bartels, Joanie 13
Bartholomew, Simon
　　See Brand New Heavies, The
Bartoli, Cecilia 12
Barton, Lou Ann
　　See Fabulous Thunderbirds, The
Bartos, Karl
　　See Kraftwerk
Basehead 11
Basher, Mick
　　See X
Basia 5
Basie, Count 2
Bass, Colin
　　See Camel
Bass, Colin
　　See Chumbawamba
Batchelor, Kevin
　　See Big Mountain
　　See Steel Pulse
Batel, Beate
　　See Einstürzende Neubauten
Batiste, Lionel
　　See Dirty Dozen
Battin, Skip
　　See Byrds, The
Battle, Kathleen 6
Bauer, Judah
　　See Jon Spencer Blues Explosion
Baumann, Peter
　　See Tangerine Dream
Bautista, Roland
　　See Earth, Wind and Fire

Baxter, Jeff
　　See Doobie Brothers, The
Bayer Sager, Carole
　　See Sager, Carole Bayer
Baylor, Helen 20
Baynton-Power, David
　　See James
Bazilian, Eric
　　See Hooters
Beach Boys, The 1
Beale, Michael
　　See Earth, Wind and Fire
Beard, Frank
　　See ZZ Top
Beasley, Paul
　　See Mighty Clouds of Joy, The
Beastie Boys, The 8
Beat Farmers 23
Beatles, The 2
Beauford, Carter
　　See Dave Matthews Band
Beautiful South 19
Beaver Brown Band, The 3
Bechet, Sidney 17
Beck, Jeff 4
　　Also see Yardbirds, The
Beck, William
　　See Ohio Players
Beck 18
Becker, Walter
　　See Steely Dan
Beckford, Theophilus
　　See Skatalites, The
Beckley, Gerry
　　See America
Bee Gees, The 3
Beers, Garry Gary
　　See INXS
Behler, Chuck
　　See Megadeth
Beiderbecke, Bix 16
Belafonte, Harry 8
Belew, Adrian 5
　　Also see King Crimson
Belfield, Dennis
　　See Three Dog Night
Bell, Andy
　　See Erasure
Bell, Brian
　　See Weezer
Bell, Derek
　　See Chieftains, The
Bell, Eric
　　See Thin Lizzy
Bell, Jayn
　　See Sounds ofBlackness
Bell, Joshua 21
Bell, Melissa
　　See Soul II Soul
Bell, Ronald
　　See Kool & the Gang
Bell, Taj
　　See Charm Farm
Belladonna, Joey
　　See Anthrax

Bon Jovi, Jon
  See Bon Jovi
Bonamy, James **21**
Bonebrake, D. J.
  See X
Bone Thugs-N-Harmony **18**
Bonham, John
  See Led Zeppelin
Bonnecaze, Cary
  See Better Than Ezra
Bonner, Leroy "Sugarfoot"
  See Ohio Players
Bono
  See U2
Bonsall, Joe
  See Oak Ridge Boys, The
Boo Radleys, The **21**
Books
  See Das EFX
Boone, Pat **13**
Booth, Tim
  See James
Boquist, Dave
  See Son Volt
Boquist, Jim
  See Son Volt
Bordin, Mike
  See Faith No More
Borg, Bobby
  See Warrant
Borge, Victor **19**
Borowiak, Tony
  See All-4-One
Bostaph, Paul
  See Slayer
Boston **11**
Bostrom, Derrick
  See Meat Puppets, The
Bottum, Roddy
  See Faith No More
Bouchard, Albert
  See Blue Oyster Cult
Bouchard, Joe
  See Blue Oyster Cult
Bouchikhi, Chico
  See Gipsy Kings, The
Bowen, Jimmy
  See Country Gentlemen, The
Bowens, Sir Harry
  See Was (Not Was)
Bowie, David **23**
  Earlier sketch in CM **1**
Bowie, Lester
  See Art Ensemble of Chicago, The
Bowman, Steve
  See Counting Crows
Box, Mick
  See Uriah Heep
Boy Howdy **21**
Boyd, Brandon
  See Incubus
Boyd, Eadie
  See Del Rubio Triplets
Boyd, Elena
  See Del Rubio Triplets

Boyd, Liona **7**
Boyd, Milly
  See Del Rubio Triplets
Boyz II Men **15**
Bozulich, Carla
  See Geraldine Fibbers
Brad **21**
Bradbury, John
  See Specials, The
Bradshaw, Tim
  See Dog's Eye View
Bradstreet, Rick
  See Bluegrass Patriots
Brady, Paul **8**
Bragg, Billy **7**
Bramah, Martin
  See Fall, The
Brand New Heavies, The **14**
Brandt, Paul **22**
Brandy **19**
Branigan, Laura **2**
Brannon, Kippi **20**
Brantley, Junior
  See Roomful of Blues
Braxton, Anthony **12**
Braxton, Toni **17**
B-Real
  See Cypress Hill
Bream, Julian **9**
Breeders **19**
Brendel, Alfred **23**
Brennan, Ciaran
  See Clannad
Brennan, Enya
  See Clannad
Brennan, Maire
  See Clannad
Brennan, Paul
  See Odds
Brennan, Pol
  See Clannad
Brenner, Simon
  See Talk Talk
Brevette, Lloyd
  See Skatalites, The
Brickell, Edie **3**
Brickman, Jim **22**
Bridgewater, Dee Dee **18**
Briggs, James Randall
  See Aquabats
Briggs, Vic
  See Animals
Bright, Garfield
  See Shai
Bright, Ronnie
  See Coasters, The
Brightman, Sarah **20**
Briley, Alex
  See Village People, The
Brindley, Paul
  See Sundays, The
Britten, Benjamin **15**
Brittingham, Eric
  See Cinderella

Brix
  See Fall, The
Brockenborough, Dennis
  See Mighty Mighty Bosstones
Brockie, Dave
  See Gwar
Brokop, Lisa **22**
Bromberg, David **18**
Bronfman, Yefim **6**
Brooke, Jonatha
  See Story, The
Brookes, Jon
  See Charlatans, The
Brooks, Baba
  See Skatalites, The
Brooks, Garth **8**
Brooks, Leon Eric "Kix"
  See Brooks & Dunn
Brooks & Dunn **12**
Broonzy, Big Bill **13**
Brotherdale, Steve
  See Joy Division
  Also see Smithereens, The
Broudie, Ian
  See Lightning Seeds
Brown, Bobby **4**
Brown, Clarence "Gatemouth" **11**
Brown, Donny
  See Verve Pipe, The
Brown, Duncan
  See Stereolab
Brown, George
  See Kool & the Gang
Brown, Harold
  See War
Brown, Heidi
  See Treadmill Trackstar
Brown, Ian
  See Stone Roses, The
Brown, James **16**
  Earlier sketch in CM **2**
Brown, Jimmy
  See UB40
Brown, Junior **15**
Brown, Lawrence **23**
Brown, Marty **14**
Brown, Melanie
  See Spice Girls
Brown, Mick
  See Dokken
Brown, Norman
  See Mills Brothers, The
Brown, Rahem
  See Artifacts
Brown, Ray **21**
Brown, Ruth **13**
Brown, Selwyn "Bumbo"
  See Steel Pulse
Brown, Steven
  See Tuxedomoon
Brown, Tim
  See Boo Radleys, The
Brown, Tony **14**
Browne, Jackson **3**
  Also see Nitty Gritty Dirt Band, The

Cameron, G. C.
  See Spinners, The
Cameron, Matt
  See Soundgarden
Campbell, Ali
  See UB40
Campbell, Glen **2**
Campbell, Kerry
  See War
Campbell, Luther **10**
Campbell, Martyn
  See Lightning Seeds
Campbell, Phil
  See Motörhead
Campbell, Robin
  See UB40
Campbell, Sarah Elizabeth **23**
Campbell, Tevin **13**
CanadianBrass, The **4**
Cantrell, Jerry
  See Alice in Chains
Canty, Brendan
  See Fugazi
Capaldi, Jim
  See Traffic
Cappelli, Frank **14**
Captain Beefheart **10**
Cardigans **19**
Cardwell, Joi **22**
Carey, Danny
  See Tool
Carey, Mariah **20**
  Earlier sketch in CM **6**
Carlisle, Belinda **8**
Carlisle, Bob **22**
Carlos, Bun E.
  See Cheap Trick
Carlos, Don
  See Black Uhuru
Carlson, Paulette
  See Highway 101
Carnes, Kim **4**
Carpenter, Bob
  See Nitty Gritty Dirt Band, The
Carpenter, Karen
  See Carpenters, The
Carpenter, Mary-Chapin **6**
Carpenter, Richard
  See Carpenters, The
Carpenter, Stephen
  See Deftones
Carpenters, The **13**
Carr, Ben
  See Mighty Mighty Bosstones
Carr, Eric
  See Kiss
Carr, James **23**
Carr, Martin
  See Boo Radleys, The
Carr, Teddy
  See Ricochet
Carrack, Paul
  See Mike & the Mechanics
  Also see Squeeze

Carreras, José **8**
Carrigan, Andy
  See Mekons, The
Carroll, Earl "Speedo"
  See Coasters, The
Carruthers, John
  See Siouxsie and the Banshees
Cars, The **20**
Carter, Anita
  See Carter Family, The
Carter, A. P.
  See Carter Family, The
Carter, Benny **3**
  Also see McKinney's Cotton Pickers
Carter, Betty **6**
Carter, Carlene **8**
Carter, Helen
  See Carter Family, The
Carter, James **18**
Carter, Janette
  See Carter Family, The
Carter, Jimmy
  See Five Blind Boys of Alabama
Carter, Joe
  See Carter Family, The
Carter, June **6**
  Also see Carter Family, The
Carter, Maybell
  See Carter Family, The
Carter, Nell **7**
Carter, Nick
  See Backstreet Boys
Carter, Regina **22**
Carter, Ron **14**
Carter, Sara
  See Carter Family, The
Carter Family, The **3**
Carthy, Martin
  See Steeleye Span
Caruso, Enrico **10**
Casady, Jack
  See Jefferson Airplane
Casale, Bob
  See Devo
Casale, Gerald V.
  See Devo
Casals, Pablo **9**
Case, Peter **13**
Cash, Johnny **17**
  Earlier sketch in CM **1**
Cash, Rosanne **2**
Cassidy, Ed
  See Spirit
Cates, Ronny
  See Petra
Catherall, Joanne
  See Human League, The
Catherine Wheel **18**
Caustic Window
  See Aphex Twin
Cauty, Jimmy
  See Orb, The
Cavalera, Igor
  See Sepultura

Cavalera, Max
  See Sepultura
Cave, Nick **10**
Cavoukian, Raffi
  See Raffi
Cease, Jeff
  See Black Crowes, The
Cervenka, Exene
  See X
Cetera, Peter
  See Chicago
Chamberlin, Jimmy
  See Smashing Pumpkins
Chambers, Martin
  See Pretenders, The
Chambers, Paul **18**
Chambers, Terry
  See XTC
Champion, Eric **21**
Chance, Slim
  See Cramps, The
Chancellor, Justin
  See Tool
Chandler, Chas
  See Animals
Chandra, Sheila **16**
Chaney, Jimmy
  See Jimmie's Chicken Shack
Chang, Sarah **7**
Channing, Carol **6**
Chapin, Harry **6**
Chapin, Tom **11**
Chapman, Steven Curtis **15**
Chapman, Tony
  See Rolling Stones, The
Chapman, Tracy **20**
  Earlier sketch in CM **4**
Chaquico, Craig **23**
  Also see Jefferson Starship
Charlatans, The **13**
Charles, Ray **1**
Charles, Yolanda
  See Aztec Camera
Charm Farm **20**
Chea, Alvin "Vinnie"
  See Take 6
Cheap Trick **12**
Checker, Chubby **7**
Che Colovita, Lemon
  See Jimmie's Chicken Shack
Cheeks, Julius
  See Soul Stirrers, The
Chemical Brothers **20**
Cheng, Chi
  See Deftones
Chenier, C. J. **15**
Chenier, Clifton **6**
Chenille Sisters, The **16**
Cher **1**
Cherone, Gary
  See Extreme
Cherry, Don **10**
Cherry, Neneh **4**
Chesney, Kenny **20**

Colwell, David
  See Bad Company
Combs, Sean "Puffy" **16**
Comess, Aaron
  See Spin Doctors
Commodores, The **23**
Common **23**
Como, Perry **14**
Compulsion **23**
Confederate Railroad **23**
Congo Norvell **22**
Conneff, Kevin
  See Chieftains, The
Connelly, Chris
  See KMFDM
Connick, Harry, Jr. **4**
Connolly, Pat
  See Surfaris, The
Connors, Marc
  See Nylons, The
Conti, Neil
  See Prefab Sprout
Conway, Billy
  See Morphine
Conway, Gerry
  See Pentangle
Cooder, Ry **2**
Cook, Greg
  See Ricochet
Cook, Jeffrey Alan
  See Alabama
Cook, Paul
  See Sex Pistols, The
Cook, Stuart
  See Creedence Clearwater Revival
Cook, Wayne
  See Steppenwolf
Cooke, Sam **1**
  Also see Soul Stirrers, The
Cool, Tre
  See Green Day
Coolio **19**
Cooney, Rory **6**
Cooper, Alice **8**
Cooper, Jason
  See Cure, The
Cooper, Martin
  See Orchestral Manoeuvres in the Dark
Cooper, Michael
  See Third World
Cooper, Paul
  See Nylons, The
Cooper, Ralph
  See Air Supply
Coore, Stephen
  See Third World
Cope, Julian **16**
Copeland, Stewart **14**
  Also see Police, The
Copland, Aaron **2**
Copley, Al
  See Roomful of Blues
Corea, Chick **6**

Corella, Doug
  See Verve Pipe, The
Corgan, Billy
  See Smashing Pumpkins
Corina, Sarah
  See Mekons, The
Cornelius, Robert
  See Poi Dog Pondering
Cornell, Chris
  See Soundgarden
Cornick, Glenn
  See Jethro Tull
Corrigan, Brianna
  See Beautiful South
Cosper, Kina
  See Brownstone
Costello, Elvis **12**
  Earlier sketch in CM **2**
Coté, Billy
  See Madder Rose
Cotoia, Robert
  See Beaver Brown Band, The
Cotrubas, Ileana **1**
Cotten, Elizabeth **16**
Cotton, Caré
  See Sounds of Blackness
Cougar, John(ny)
  See Mellencamp, John
Counting Crows **18**
Country Gentlemen, The **7**
Coury, Fred
  See Cinderella
Coutts, Duncan
  See Our Lady Peace
Coverdale, David
  See Whitesnake **5**
Cowan, John
  See New Grass Revival, The
Cowboy Junkies, The **4**
Cox, Andy
  See English Beat, The
  Also see Fine Young Cannibals
Cox, Terry
  See Pentangle
Coxon, Graham
  See Blur
Coyne, Mark
  See Flaming Lips
Coyne, Wayne
  See Flaming Lips
Cracker **12**
Craig, Albert
  See Israel Vibration
Craig, Carl **19**
Crain, S. R.
  See Soul Stirrers, The
Cramps, The **16**
Cranberries, The **14**
Crash Test Dummies **14**
Crawford, Dave Max
  See Poi Dog Pondering
Crawford, Da'dra
  See Anointed
Crawford, Ed
  See fIREHOSE

Crawford, Michael **4**
Crawford, Steve
  See Anointed
Cray, Robert **8**
Creach, Papa John
  See Jefferson Starship
Cream **9**
Creedence Clearwater Revival **16**
Creegan, Andrew
  See Barenaked Ladies
Creegan, Jim
  See Barenaked Ladies
Crenshaw, Marshall **5**
Cretu, Michael
  See Enigma
Criss, Peter
  See Kiss
Croce, Jim **3**
Crofts, Dash
  See Seals & Crofts
Cronin, Kevin
  See REO Speedwagon
Cropper, Steve **12**
Crosby, Bing **6**
Crosby, David **3**
  Also see Byrds, The
Cross, Bridget
  See Velocity Girl
Cross, David
  See King Crimson
Cross, Mike
  See Sponge
Cross, Tim
  See Sponge
Crouch, Andraé **9**
Crover, Dale
  See Melvins
Crow, Sheryl **18**
Crowded House **12**
Crowe, J. D. **5**
Crowell, Rodney **8**
Crowley, Martin
  See Bevis Frond
Cruikshank, Gregory
  See Tuxedomoon
Cruz, Celia **22**
  Earlier sketch in CM **10**
Cuddy, Jim
  See Blue Rodeo
Cugat, Xavier **23**
Cult, The **16**
Cumming, Graham
  See Bevis Frond
Cummings, Burton
  See Guess Who
Cummings, Danny
  See Dire Straits
Cummings, David
  See Del Amitri
Cunningham, Abe
  See Deftones
Cunningham, Ruth
  See Anonymous 4
Cuomo, Rivers
  See Weezer

Ellington, Duke **2**
Elliot, Cass **5**
Elliot, Joe
  See Def Leppard
Elliott, Cass
  See Mamas and the Papas
Elliott, Dennis
  See Foreigner
Elliott, Doug
  See Odds
Ellis, Bobby
  See Skatalites, The
Ellis, Herb **18**
Ellis, Terry
  See En Vogue
Elmore, Greg
  See Quicksilver Messenger Service
ELO
  See Electric Light Orchestra
Ely, John
  See Asleep at the Wheel
Ely, Vince
  See Cure, The
  See Psychedelic Furs
Emerson, Bill
  See Country Gentlemen, The
Emerson, Keith
  See Emerson, Lake & Palmer/Powell
Emerson, Lake & Palmer/Powell **5**
Emery, Jill
  See Hole
Emmanuel, Tommy **21**
English, Michael **23**
English, Richard
  See Flaming Lips
English Beat, The **9**
Enigma **14**
Eno, Brian **8**
Enos, Bob
  See Roomful of Blues
Enright, Pat
  See Nashville Bluegrass Band
Entwistle, John
  See Who, The
En Vogue **10**
Enya **6**
EPMD **10**
Erasure **11**
Eric B.
  See Eric B. and Rakim
Eric B. and Rakim **9**
Erickson, Roky **16**
Erlandson, Eric
  See Hole
Errico, Greg
  See Quicksilver Messenger Service
Erskine, Peter
  See Weather Report
Ertegun, Ahmet **10**
Esch, En
  See KMFDM
Escovedo, Alejandro **18**
Eshe, Montsho
  See Arrested Development

Eskelin, Ian **19**
Esler-Smith, Frank
  See Air Supply
Esquivel, Juan **17**
Estefan, Gloria **15**
  Earlier sketch in CM **2**
Estrada, Roy
  See Little Feat
Etheridge, Melissa **16**
  Earlier sketch in CM **4**
Eurythmics **6**
Evan, John
  See Jethro Tull
Evans, Bill **17**
Evans, Dick
  See U2
Evans, Gil **17**
Evans, Mark
  See AC/DC
Evans, Shane
  See Collective Soul
Evans, Tom
  See Badfinger
Everclear **18**
Everlast
  See House of Pain
Everly Brothers, The **2**
Everly, Don
  See Everly Brothers, The
Everly, Phil
  See Everly Brothers, The
Everman, Jason
  See Soundgarden
Everything But The Girl **15**
Evora, Cesaria **19**
Ewen, Alvin
  See Steel Pulse
Exkano, Paul
  See Five Blind Boys of Alabama
Exposé **4**
Extreme **10**
Ezell, Ralph
  See Shenandoah
Fabian **5**
Fabulous Thunderbirds, The **1**
Faces, The **22**
Fadden, Jimmie
  See Nitty Gritty Dirt Band, The
Fagan, Don
  See Steely Dan
Fahey, John **17**
Fahey, Siobhan
  See Bananarama
Fairport Convention **22**
Faithfull, Marianne **14**
Faith No More **7**
Fakir, Abdul "Duke"
  See Four Tops, The
Falconer, Earl
  See UB40
Fall, The **12**
Fallon, David
  See Chieftains, The
Fink, Jr., Rat
  See Alien Sex Fiend

Fisher, Brandon
  See Superdrag
Forbes, Graham
  See Incredible String Band
Forsi, Ken
  See Surfaris, The
4Him **23**
Foxwell Baker, Iain Richard
  See Jesus Jones
Fredriksson, Marie
  See Roxette
Freiberg, David
  See Quicksilver Messenger Service
Freshwater, John
  See Alien Sex Fiend
Fuller, Jim
  See Surfaris, The
Fuqua, Charlie
  See Ink Spots
Fältskog, Agnetha
  See Abba
Fambrough, Henry
  See Spinners, The
Farley, J. J.
  See Soul Stirrers, The
Farndon, Pete
  See Pretenders, The
Farrar, Jay
  See Son Volt
Farrar, John
  See Shadows, The
Farrell, Perry
  See Jane's Addiction
Farris, Dionne
  See Arrested Development
Farris, Tim
  See Israel Vibration
Farriss, Andrew
  See INXS
Farriss, Jon
  See INXS
Farriss, Tim
  See INXS
Fatboy Slim **22**
Fay, Johnny
  See Tragically Hip, The
Fay, Martin
  See Chieftains, The
Fearnley, James
  See Pogues, The
Fehlmann, Thomas
  See Orb, The
Feinstein, Michael **6**
Fela
  See Kuti, Fela
Felber, Dean
  See Hootie and the Blowfish
Felder, Don
  See Eagles, The
Feldman, Eric Drew
  See Pere Ubu
Feliciano, José **10**
Fender, Freddy
  See Texas Tornados, The

Fugazi **13**
Fugees, The **17**
Fulber, Rhys
  See Front Line Assembly
Fuller, Blind Boy **20**
Fulson, Lowell **20**
Fu Manchu **22**
Fun Lovin' Criminals **20**
Furr, John
  See Treadmill Trackstar
Furuholmen, Magne
  See A-ha
Futter, Brian
  See Catherine Wheel
Gabay, Yuval
  See Soul Coughing
Gabriel, Peter **16**
  Earlier sketch in CM **2**
  Also see Genesis
Gadler, Frank
Gagliardi, Ed
  See Foreigner
Gahan, Dave
  See Depeche Mode
Gaines, Steve
  See Lynyrd Skynyrd
Gaines, Timothy
  See Stryper
Galea, Darren
  See Jamiroquai
Galás, Diamanda **16**
Gale, Melvyn
  See Electric Light Orchestra
Gallagher, Liam
  See Oasis
Gallagher, Noel
  See Oasis
Gallup, Simon
  See Cure, The
Galore, Lady
  See Lords of Acid
Galway, James **3**
Gambill, Roger
  See Kingston Trio, The
Gamble, Cheryl "Coko"
  See SWV
Gane, Tim
  See Stereolab
Gang of Four **8**
Gang Starr **13**
Gannon, Craig
  See Aztec Camera
Gano, Gordon
  See Violent Femmes
Garcia, Dean
  See Curve
Garcia, Jerry **4**
  Also see Grateful Dead, The
Garcia, Leddie
  See Poi Dog Pondering
Gardner, Carl
  See Coasters, The
Gardner, Suzi
  See L7

Garfunkel, Art **4**
Garland, Judy **6**
Garrett, Peter
  See Midnight Oil
Garrett, Scott
  See Cult, The
Garvey, Steve
  See Buzzcocks, The
Gaskill, Jerry
  See King's X
Gatton, Danny **16**
Gaudreau, Jimmy
  See Country Gentlemen, The
Gaugh, "Bud" Floyd, IV
  See Sublime
Gavurin, David
  See Sundays, The
Gay, Marc
  See Shai
Gaye, Marvin **4**
Gaynor, Mel
  See Simple Minds
Gayol, Rafael "Danny"
  See BoDeans
Gayle, Crystal **1**
Geary, Paul
  See Extreme
Gee, Rosco
  See Traffic
Geffen, David **8**
Geldof, Bob **9**
Genensky, Marsha
  See Anonymous 4
Genesis **4**
Gentling, Matt
  See Archers of Loaf
Gentry, Teddy Wayne
  See Alabama
George, Lowell
  See Little Feat
George, Rocky
  See Suicidal Tendencies
Georges, Bernard
  See Throwing Muses
Georgiev, Ivan
  See Tuxedomoon
Geraldine Fibbers **21**
Germano, Lisa **18**
Gerrard, Lisa
  See Dead Can Dance
Gershwin, George and Ira **11**
Gessle, Per
  See Roxette
GetoBoys, The **11**
Getz, Stan **12**
Giammalvo, Chris
  See Madder Rose
Gianni, Angelo
  See Treadmill Trackstar
Gibb, Barry
  See Bee Gees, The
Gibb, Maurice
  See Bee Gees, The

Gibb, Robin
  See Bee Gees, The
Gibbins, Mike
  See Badfinger
Gibbons, Beth
  See Portishead
Gibbons, Billy
  See ZZ Top
Gibbons, Ian
  See Kinks, The
Giblin, John
  See Simple Minds
Gibson, Debbie **1**
Gibson, Wilf
  See Electric Light Orchestra
Gibson, Bob **23**
Gifford, Katharine
  See Stereolab
Gifford, Peter
  See Midnight Oil
Gift, Roland **3**
  Also see Fine Young Cannibals
Gilbert, Gillian
  See New Order
Gilbert, Nicole Nicci
  See Brownstone
Gilbert, Ronnie
  See Weavers, The
Gilbert, Simon
  See Suede
Giles, Michael
  See King Crimson
Gilkyson, Tony
  See X
Gill, Andy
  See Gang of Four
Gill, Janis
  See Sweethearts of the Rodeo
Gill, Johnny **20**
Gill, Pete
  See Motörhead
Gill, Vince **7**
Gillan, Ian
  See Deep Purple
Gillespie, Bobby
  See Primal Scream
Gillespie, Dizzy **6**
Gilley, Mickey **7**
Gillian, Ian
  See Black Sabbath
Gillies, Ben
  See Silverchair
Gillingham, Charles
  See Counting Crows
Gilmore, Jimmie Dale **11**
Gilmour, David
  See Pink Floyd
Gin Blossoms **18**
Gingold, Josef **6**
Ginn, Greg
  See Black Flag
Gioia
  See Exposé

Grover, Charlie
  See Sponge
Grundy, Hugh
  See Zombies, The
Grusin, Dave **7**
Guaraldi, Vince **3**
Guard, Dave
  See Kingston Trio, The
Gudmundsdottir, Björk
  See Björk
  Also see Sugarcubes, The
Guerin, John
  See Byrds, The
Guess Who **23**
Guest, Christopher
  See Spinal Tap
Guided By Voices **18**
Gunn, Trey
  See King Crimson
Guns n' Roses **2**
Gunther, Cornell
  See Coasters, The
Gunther, Ric
  See Bevis Frond
Guru
  See Gang Starr
Guss, Randy
  See Toad the Wet Sprocket
Gustafson, Steve
  See 10,000 Maniacs
Gut, Grudrun
  See Einstürzende Neubauten
Guthrie, Arlo **6**
Guthrie, Robin
  See Cocteau Twins, The
Guthrie, Woody **2**
Guy, Billy
  See Coasters, The
Guy, Buddy **4**
Guyett, Jim
  See Quicksilver Messenger Service
Gwar **13**
Hacke, Alexander
  See Einstürzende Neubauten
Hackett, Bobby **21**
Hackett, Steve
  See Genesis
Haden, Charlie **12**
Hadjopulos, Sue
  See Simple Minds
Hagar, Regan
  See Brad
Hagar, Sammy **21**
  Also see Van Halen
Haggard, Merle **2**
Hakim, Omar
  See Weather Report
Hakmoun, Hassan **15**
Hale, Simon
  See Incognito
Haley, Bill **6**
Haley, Mark
  See Kinks, The
Halford, Rob
  See Judas Priest

Hall, Bruce
  See REO Speedwagon
Hall, Daryl
  See Hall & Oates
Hall, John S.
  See King Missile
Hall, Lance
  See Inner Circle
Hall, Randall
  See Lynyrd Skynyrd
Hall, Terry
  See Specials, The
Hall, Tom T. **4**
Hall, Tony
  See Neville Brothers, The
Hall & Oates **6**
Halliday, Toni
  See Curve
Halliwell, Geri
  See Spice Girls
Ham, Pete
  See Badfinger
Hamer, Harry
  See Chumbawamba
Hamilton, Arnold
  See Gravediggaz
Hamilton, Frank
  See Weavers, The
Hamilton, Katie
  See Treadmill Trackstar
Hamilton, Milton
  See Third World
Hamilton, Page
  See Helmet
Hamilton, Tom
  See Aerosmith
Hamilton, Tom
  See Aerosmith
Hamlisch, Marvin **1**
Hammer, Jan **21**
  Also see Mahavishnu Orchestra
Hammer, M.C. **5**
Hammerstein, Oscar
  See Rodgers, Richard
Hammett, Kirk
  See Metallica
Hammon, Ron
  See War
Hammond, John **6**
Hammond-Hammond, Jeffrey
  See Jethro Tull
Hampson, Sharon
  See Sharon, Lois & Bram
Hampson, Thomas **12**
Hampton, Lionel **6**
Hancock, Herbie **8**
Handy, W. C. **7**
Hanley, Kay
  See Letters to Cleo
Hanley, Steve
  See Fall, The
Hanna, Jeff
  See Nitty Gritty Dirt Band, The
Hanneman, Jeff
  See Slayer

Hannibal, Chauncey "Black"
  See Blackstreet
Hannon, Frank
  See Tesla
Hannan, Patrick
  See Sundays, The
Hansen, Mary
  See Stereolab
Hanson **20**
Hanson, Isaac
  See Hanson
Hanson, Paul
  See Gravediggaz
Hanson, Taylor
  See Hanson
Hanson, Zachary
  See Hanson
Hardcastle, Paul **20**
Hardin, Eddie
  See Spencer Davis Group
Hardin, Tim **18**
Harding, John Wesley **6**
Hardson, Tre "Slimkid"
  See Pharcyde, The
Hargrove, Kornell
  See Poi Dog Pondering
Hargrove, Roy **15**
Harket, Morten
  See A-ha
Harley, Bill **7**
Harms, Jesse
  See REO Speedwagon
Harper, Ben **17**
Harper, Raymond
  See Skatalites, The
Harrell, Andre **16**
Harrell, Lynn **3**
Harrington, Carrie
  See Sounds of Blackness
Harrington, David
  See Kronos Quartet
Harris, Addie "Micki"
  See Shirelles, The
Harris, Damon Otis
  See Temptations, The
Harris, Eddie **15**
Harris, Emmylou **4**
Harris, Evelyn
  See Sweet Honey in the Rock
Harris, Gerard
  See Kool & the Gang
Harris, James
  See Echobelly
Harris, Jet
  See Shadows, The
Harris, Joey
  See Beat Farmers
Harris, Kevin
  See Dirty Dozen
Harris, Lee
  See Talk Talk
Harris, Mark
  See 4Him
Harris, Mary
  See Spearhead

Hidalgo, David
  See Los Lobos
Higgins, Jimmy
  See Altan
Higgins, Terence
  See Dirty Dozen
Highway 101 **4**
Hijbert, Fritz
  See Kraftwerk
Hill, Brendan
  See Blues Traveler
Hill, Dusty
  See ZZ Top
Hill, Faith **18**
Hill, Ian
  See Judas Priest
Hill, Lauryn "L"
  See Fugees, The
Hill, Scott
  See Fu Manchu
Hill, Stuart
  See Shudder to Think
Hillage, Steve
  See Orb, The
Hillier, Steve
  See Dubstar
Hillman, Bones
  See Midnight Oil
Hillman, Chris
  See Byrds, The
  Also see Desert Rose Band, The
Hinderas, Natalie **12**
Hinds, David
  See Steel Pulse
Hines, Earl "Fatha" **12**
Hines, Gary
  See Sounds of Blackness
Hinojosa, Tish **13**
Hirst, Rob
  See Midnight Oil
Hirt, Al **5**
Hitchcock, Robyn **9**
Hitchcock, Russell
  See Air Supply
Hitt, Bryan
  See REO Speedwagon
Hodo, David
  See Village People, The
Hoenig, Michael
  See Tangerine Dream
Hoffman, Guy
  See BoDeans, The
  Also see Violent Femmes
Hoffman, Kristian
  See Congo Norvell
Hoffs, Susanna
  See Bangles
Hogan, Mike
  See Cranberries, The
Hogan, Noel
  See Cranberries, The
Hoke, Jim
  See NRBQ
Hole **14**
Holiday, Billie **6**

Holland, Brian
  See Holland-Dozier-Holland
Holland, Bryan "Dexter"
  See Offspring
Holland, Dave
  See Judas Priest
Holland, Eddie
  See Holland-Dozier-Holland
Holland, Julian "Jools"
  See Squeeze
Holland-Dozier-Holland **5**
Hollis, Mark
  See Talk Talk
Hollister, Dave
  See Blackstreet
Holly, Buddy **1**
Holmes, Malcolm
  See Orchestral Manoeuvres in the Dark
Holmstrom, Peter
  See Dandy Warhols, The
Holt, David Lee
  See Mavericks, The
Honeyman, Susie
  See Mekons, The
Honeyman-Scott, James
  See Pretenders, The
Hood, David
  See Traffic
Hook, Peter
  See Joy Division
  Also see New Order
Hooker, John Lee **1**
Hoon, Shannon
  See Blind Melon
Hooper, Nellee
  See Soul II Soul
  Also see Massive Attack
Hooters **20**
Hootie and the Blowfish **18**
Hope, Gavin
  See Nylons, The
Hopkins, Doug
  See Gin Blossoms
Hopkins, Lightnin' **13**
Hopkins, Nicky
  See Quicksilver Messenger Service
Hopwood, Keith
  See Herman's Hermits
Horn, Shirley **7**
Horn, Trevor
  See Yes
Horne, Lena **11**
Horne, Marilyn **9**
Horner, Jessica
  See Less Than Jake
Hornsby, Bruce **3**
Horovitz, Adam
  See Beastie Boys, The
Horowitz, Vladimir **1**
Horton, Jeff
  See Northern Lights
Horton, Walter **19**
Hossack, Michael
  See Doobie Brothers, The

House, Son **11**
House of Pain **14**
Houston, Cissy **6**
Houston, Whitney **8**
Howard, Harlan **15**
Howe, Brian
  See Bad Company
Howe, Steve
  See Yes
Howell, Porter
  See Little Texas
Howlett, Liam
  See Prodigy
Howlin' Wolf **6**
H.R.
  See Bad Brains
Hubbard, Greg "Hobie"
  See Sawyer Brown
Hubbard, Preston
  See Fabulous Thunderbirds, The
  Also see Roomful of Blues
Huber, Connie
  See Chenille Sisters, The
Hudson, Earl
  See Bad Brains
Hudson, Garth
  See Band, The
Huffman, Doug
  See Boston
Hughes, Bruce
  See Cracker
Hughes, Glenn
  See Black Sabbath
Hughes, Glenn
  See Village People, The
Hughes, Leon
  See Coasters, The
Human League, The **17**
Humes, Helen **19**
Humperdinck, Engelbert **19**
Humphreys, Paul
  See Orchestral Manoeuvres in the Dark
Hunt, Darryl
  See Pogues, The
Hunter, Alberta **7**
Hunter, Mark
  See James
Hunter, Shepherd "Ben"
  See Soundgarden
Hurley, George
  See fIREHOSE
Hurst, Ron
  See Steppenwolf
Hutchence, Michael
  See INXS
Hutchings, Ashley
  See Fairport Convention
  Also see Steeleye Span
Huth, Todd
  See Primus
Hyatt, Aitch
  See Specials, The
Hyde, Michael
  See Big Mountain

Jasper, Chris
  See Isley Brothers, The
Jaworski, Al
  See Jesus Jones
Jay, Miles
  See Village People, The
Jayhawks, The **15**
Jayson, Mackie
  See Bad Brains
Jazzie B
  See Soul II Soul
Jean, Wyclef **22**
  Also see Fugees, The
Jeanrenaud, Joan Dutcher
  See Kronos Quartet
Jeczalik, Jonathan
  See Art of Noise
Jefferson, Blind Lemon **18**
Jefferson Airplane **5**
Jefferson Starship
  See Jefferson Airplane
Jenifer, Darryl
  See Bad Brains
Jenkins, Barry
  See Animals
Jennings, Greg
  See Restless Heart
Jennings, Waylon **4**
Jensen, Ingrid **22**
Jerry, Jah
  See Skatalites, The
Jessee, Darren
  See Ben Folds Five
Jessie, Young
  See Coasters, The
Jesus and Mary Chain, The **10**
Jesus Jones **23**
Jesus Lizard **19**
Jethro Tull **8**
Jett, Joan **3**
Jimenez, Flaco
  See Texas Tornados, The
Jimmie's Chicken Shack **22**
Joannou, Chris
  See Silverchair
Jobim, Antonio Carlos **19**
Jobson, Edwin
  See Jethro Tull
Jodeci **13**
Joel, Billy **12**
  Earlier sketch in CM **2**
Johansen, David
  See New York Dolls
Johansen, David **7**
Johanson, Jai Johanny
  See Allman Brothers, The
Johansson, Glenn
  See Echobelly
Johansson, Lars-Olof
  See Cardigans
John, Elton **20**
  Earlier sketch in CM **3**
Johns, Daniel
  See Silverchair

Johnson, Alphonso
  See Weather Report
Johnson, Bob
  See Steeleye Span
Johnson, Brian
  See AC/DC
Johnson, Courtney
  See New Grass Revival, The
Johnson, Danny
  See Steppenwolf
Johnson, Daryl
  See Neville Brothers, The
Johnson, Eric
  See Archers of Loaf
Johnson, Eric **19**
Johnson, Gene
  See Diamond Rio
Johnson, Gerry
  See Steel Pulse
Johnson, James P. **16**
Johnson, Jerry
  See Big Mountain
Johnson, Lonnie **17**
Johnson, Matt
  See The The
Johnson, Mike
  See Dinosaur Jr.
Johnson, Ralph
  See Earth, Wind and Fire
Johnson, Robert **6**
Johnson, Scott
  See Gin Blossoms
Johnson, Shirley Childres
  See Sweet Honey in the Rock
Johnson, Tamara "Taj"
  See SWV
Johnston, Bruce
  See Beach Boys, The
Johnston, Freedy **20**
Johnston, Howie
  See Ventures, The
Johnston, Tom
  See Doobie Brothers, The
JoJo
  See Jodeci
Jolly, Bill
  See Butthole Surfers
Jolson, Al **10**
Jon Spencer Blues Explosion **18**
Jones, Adam
  See Tool
Jones, Benny
  See Dirty Dozen
Jones, Booker T. **8**
Jones, Brian
  See Rolling Stones, The
Jones, Busta
  See Gang of Four
Jones, Claude
  See McKinney's Cotton Pickers
Jones, Darryl
  See Rolling Stones, The
Jones, Davy
  See Monkees, The

Jones, Denise
  See Point of Grace
Jones, Elvin **9**
Jones, Geoffrey
  See Sounds of Blackness
Jones, George **4**
Jones, Grace **9**
Jones, Hank **15**
Jones, Jamie
  See All-4-One
Jones, Jim
  See Pere Ubu
Jones, John Paul
  See Led Zeppelin
Jones, Kendall
  See Fishbone
Jones, Kenny
  See Faces, The
Jones, Kenny
  See Who, The
Jones, Marshall
  See Ohio Players
Jones, Maxine
  See En Vogue
Jones, Michael
  See Kronos Quartet
Jones, Mic
  See Big Audio Dynamite
  Also see Clash, The
Jones, Mick
  See Foreigner
Jones, Orville
  See Ink Spots
Jones, Philly Joe **16**
Jones, Quincy **20**
  Earlier sketch in CM **2**
Jones, Rickie Lee **4**
Jones, Robert "Kuumba"
  See Ohio Players
Jones, Ronald
  See Flaming Lips
Jones, Sandra "Puma"
  See Black Uhuru
Jones, Simon
  See Verve, The
Jones, Spike **5**
Jones, Stacy
  See Veruca Salt
Jones, Stacy
  See Letters to Cleo
Jones, Steve
  See Sex Pistols, The
Jones, Terry
  See Point of Grace
Jones, Thad **19**
Jones, Tom **11**
Jones, Will "Dub"
  See Coasters, The
Joplin, Janis **3**
Joplin, Scott **10**
Jordan, Lonnie
  See War
Jordan, Louis **11**
Jordan, Stanley **1**

King, Jon
  See Gang of Four
King, Kerry
  See Slayer
King, Philip
  See Lush
King Ad-Rock
  See Beastie Boys, The
King Crimson 17
King Missile 22
King, Jr., William
  See Commodores, The
Kingston Trio, The 9
King's X 7
Kinks, The 15
Kinney, Sean
  See Alice in Chains
Kirk, Rahsaan Roland 6
Kirk, Richard H.
  See Cabaret Voltaire
Kirke, Simon
  See Bad Company
Kirkland, Mike
  See Prong
Kirkwood, Cris
  See Meat Puppets, The
Kirkwood, Curt
  See Meat Puppets, The
Kirtley, Peter
  See Pentangle
Kirwan, Danny
  See Fleetwood Mac
Kiss 5
Kisser, Andreas
  See Sepultura
Kissin, Evgeny 6
Kitaro 1
Kitsos, Nick
  See BoDeans
Kitt, Eartha 9
Klein, Jon
  See Siouxsie and the Banshees
Klezmatics, The 18
Klibrun, Duncan
  See Psychedelic Furs
Klugh, Earl 10
Kmatsu, Bravo
  See Pizzicato Five
KMFDM 18
Knight, Gladys 1
Knight, Jon
  See New Kids on the Block
Knight, Jordan
  See New Kids on the Block
Knight, Larry
  See Spirit
Knight, Peter
  See Steeleye Span
Knight, Suge 15
Knopfler, David
  See Dire Straits
Knopfler, Mark 3
  See Dire Straits

Know, Dr.
  See Bad Brains
Knowledge
  See Digable Planets
Knox, Nick
  See Cramps, The
Knox, Richard
  See Dirty Dozen
Knudsen, Keith
  See Doobie Brothers, The
Konietzko, Sascha
  See KMFDM
Konishi, Yasuharu
  See Pizzicato Five
Konto, Skip
  See Three Dog Night
Kool & the Gang 13
Kool Moe Dee 9
Kooper, Al
  See Blood, Sweat and Tears
Koppelman, Charles 14
Koppes, Peter
  See Church, The
Korn 20
Kottke, Leo 13
Kotzen, Richie
  See Poison
Kowalczyk, Ed
  See Live
Kraftwerk 9
Krakauer, David
  See Klezmatics, The
Kramer, Joey
  See Aerosmith
Kramer, Wayne
  See MC5, The
Krasnow, Bob 15
Krause, Bernie
  See Weavers, The
Krauss, Alison 10
Krauss, Scott
  See Pere Ubu
Kravitz, Lenny 5
Krayzie Bone
  See Bone Thugs-N-Harmony
Krazy Drayz
  See Das EFX
Kretz, Eric
  See Stone Temple Pilots
Kreutzman, Bill
  See Grateful Dead, The
Krieger, Robert
  See Doors, The
Kriesel, Greg
  See Offspring
Kris Kross 11
Kristofferson, Kris 4
Krizan, Anthony
  See Spin Doctors
Kronos Quartet 5
Kropp, Mike
  See Northern Lights
KRS-One 8
Krupa, Gene 13

Krusen, Dave
  See Pearl Jam
Kulak, Eddie
  See Aztec Camera
Kulick, Bruce
  See Kiss
Kunkel, Bruce
  See Nitty Gritty Dirt Band, The
Kunzel, Erich 17
Kurdziel, Eddie
  See Redd Kross
Kuti, Fela 7
LaBar, Jeff
  See Cinderella
LaBelle, Patti 8
LaBrie, James
  See Dream Theater
LaPread, Ronald
  See Commodores, The
Lack, Steve
  See Veruca Salt
Lacy, Steve 23
Lady Miss Kier
  See Deee-lite
Ladybug
  See Digable Planets
Ladysmith Black Mambazo 1
Lafalce, Mark
  See Mekons, The
Lagerburg, Bengt
  See Cardigans, The
Laine, Cleo 10
Laine, Denny
  See Moody Blues, The
Laird, Rick
  See Mahavishnu Orchestra
Lake, Greg
  See Emerson, Lake & Palmer/Powell
  Also see King Crimson
LaLonde, Larry "Ler"
  See Primus
Lally, Joe
  See Fugazi
Lamb, Michael
  See Confederate Railroad
Lamble, Martin
  See Fairport Convention
Lamm, Robert
  See Chicago
Landreth, Sonny 16
Lane, Jani
  See Warrant
Lane, Jay
  See Primus
Lane, Ronnie
  See Faces, The
lang, k. d. 4
Langan, Gary
  See Art of Noise
Langford, Jon
  See Mekons, The
Langley, John
  See Mekons, The

Little Texas **14**
Little Walter **14**
Littrell, Brian
　See Backstreet Boys
Live **14**
Living Colour **7**
Llanas, Sam
　See BoDeans
Llanas, Sammy
　See BoDeans, The
L.L. Cool J. **5**
Lloyd, Charles **22**
Lloyd, Richard
　See Television
Lloyd Webber, Andrew **6**
Locke, John
　See Spirit
Locking, Brian
　See Shadows, The
Lockwood, Robert, Jr. **10**
Lodge, John
　See Moody Blues, The
Loeb, Lisa **23**
Loewe, Frederick
　See Lerner and Loewe
Loggins, Kenny **20**
　Earlier sketch in CM **3**
Lombardo, Dave
　See Slayer
London, Frank
　See Klezmatics, The
Lopes, Lisa "Left Eye"
　See TLC
Lopez, Israel "Cachao" **14**
Lord, Jon
　See Deep Purple
Lords of Acid **20**
Loria, Steve
　See Spirit
Lorson, Mary
　See Madder Rose
Los Lobos **2**
Los Reyes
　See Gipsy Kings, The
Loughnane, Lee
　See Chicago
Louison, Steve
　See Massive Attack
Louris, Gary
　See Jayhawks, The
Louvin Brothers, The **12**
Louvin, Charlie
　See Louvin Brothers, The
Louvin, Ira
　See Louvin Brothers, The
Lovano, Joe **13**
Love and Rockets **15**
Love, Courtney
　See Hole
Love, Gerry
　See Teenage Fanclub
Love, Laura **20**
Love, Mike
　See Beach Boys, The

Love, Rollie
　See Beat Farmers
Loveless, Patty **21**
　Earlier sketch in CM **5**
Lovering, David
　See Cracker
　Also see Pixies, The
Love Spit Love **21**
Lovett, Lyle **5**
Lowe, Chris
　See Pet Shop Boys
Lowe, Nick **6**
Lowell, Charlie
　See Jars of Clay
Lowery, David
　See Cracker
Lozano, Conrad
　See Los Lobos
L7 **12**
Lucas, Trevor
　See Fairport Convention
Luccketta, Troy
　See Tesla
Lucia, Paco de
　See de Lucia, Paco
Luciano, Felipe
　See Last Poets
Luke
　See Campbell, Luther
Lukin, Matt
　See Mudhoney
Luna **18**
Lupo, Pat
　See Beaver Brown Band, The
LuPone, Patti **8**
Lush **13**
Luttell, Terry
　See REO Speedwagon
Lydon, John **9**
　Also see Sex Pistols, The
Lyfe, DJ
　See Incubus
Lynch, Dermot
　See Dog's Eye View
Lynch, George
　See Dokken
Lyngstad, Anni-Frid
　See Abba
Lynn, Lonnie Rashid
　See Common
Lynn, Loretta **2**
Lynne, Jeff **5**
　Also see Electric Light Orchestra
Lynne, Shelby **5**
Lynott, Phil
　See Thin Lizzy
Lynyrd Skynyrd **9**
Lyons, Leanne "Lelee"
　See SWV
Ma, Yo-Yo **2**
MacColl, Kirsty **12**
MacDonald, Eddie
　See Alarm
Macfarlane, Lora
　See Sleater-Kinney

MacGowan, Shane
MacIsaac, Ashley **21**
MacKaye, Ian
　See Fugazi
Mack Daddy
　See Kris Kross
Mackey, Steve
　See Pulp
MacNeil, Michael
　See Simple Minds
MacPherson, Jim
　See Breeders
Madan, Sonya Aurora
　See Echobelly
Madder Rose **17**
Madonna **16**
　Earlier sketch in CM **4**
Mael, Ron
　See Sparks
Mael, Russell
　See Sparks
Magehee, Marty
　See 4Him
Maghostut, Malachi Favors
　See Art Ensemble of Chicago, The
Maginnis, Tom
　See Buffalo Tom
Magnie, John
　See Subdudes, The
Magoogan, Wesley
　See English Beat, The
Maher, John
　See Buzzcocks, The
Mahoney, Tim
　See 311
Malda, Raine
　See Our Lady Peace
Maimone, Tony
　See Pere Ubu
Makeba, Miriam **8**
Malcolm, Hugh
　See Skatalites, The
Malcolm, Joy
　See Incognito
Male, Johnny
　See Republica
Malins, Mike
　See Goo Goo Dolls, The
Malkmus, Stephen
　See Pavement
Malley, Matt
　See Counting Crows
Mallinder, Stephen
　See Cabaret Voltaire
Malo, Raul
　See Mavericks, The
Malone, Tom
　See Blood, Sweat and Tears
Malone, Tommy
　See Subdudes, The
Mamas and the Papas **21**
Mancini, Henry **20**
　Earlier sketch in CM **1**
Mandrell, Barbara **4**

McCready, Mike
  See Pearl Jam
McCready, Mindy **22**
McCulloch, Andrew
  See King Crimson
McCulloch, Ian **23**
McCullough, Danny
  See Animals
McD, Jimmy
  See Jimmie's Chicken Shack
McDaniel, Chris
  See Confederate Railroad
McDaniels, Darryl "D"
  See Run-D.M.C.
McDermott, Brian
  See Del Amitri
McDonald, Barbara Kooyman
  See Timbuk 3
McDonald, Ian
  See Foreigner
  Also see King Crimson
McDonald, Jeff
  See Redd Kross
McDonald, Michael
  See Doobie Brothers, The
McDonald, Pat
  See Timbuk 3
McDonald, Steven
  See Redd Kross
McDorman, Joe
  See Statler Brothers, The
McDougall, Don
  See Guess Who
McDowell, Hugh
  See Electric Light Orchestra
McDowell, Mississippi Fred **16**
McEntire, Reba **11**
MC Eric
  See Technotronic
McEuen, John
  See Nitty Gritty Dirt Band, The
McFarlane, Elaine
  See Mamas and the Papas
McFee, John
  See Doobie Brothers, The
McFerrin, Bobby **3**
MC5, The **9**
McGee, Brian
  See Simple Minds
McGee, Jerry
  See Ventures, The
McGeoch, John
  See Siouxsie and theBanshees
McGinley, Raymond
  See Teenage Fanclub
McGinniss, Will
  See Audio Adrenaline
McGrath, Mark
  See Sugar Ray
McGraw, Tim **17**
McGuigan, Paul
  See Oasis
McGuinn, Jim
  See McGuinn, Roger

McGuinn, Roger
  See Byrds, The
M.C. Hammer
  See Hammer, M.C.
McGuire, Mike
  See Shenandoah
McIntosh, Robbie
  See Pretenders, The
McIntyre, Joe
  See New Kids on the Block
McJohn, Goldy
  See Steppenwolf
McKagan, Duff
  See Guns n' Roses
McKay, Al
  See Earth, Wind and Fire
McKay, John
  See Siouxsie and the Banshees
McKean, Michael
  See Spinal Tap
McKee , Julius
  See Dirty Dozen
McKee, Maria **11**
McKeehan, Toby
  See dc Talk
McKenna, Greg
  See Letters to Cleo
McKenzie, Christina "Licorice"
  See Incredible String Band
McKenzie, Derrick
  See Jamiroquai
McKenzie, Scott
  See Mamas and the Papas
McKernan, Ron "Pigpen"
  See Grateful Dead, The
McKinney, William
  See McKinney's Cotton Pickers
McKinney's Cotton Pickers **16**
McKnight, Brian **22**
McKnight, Claude V. III
  See Take 6
McLachlan, Sarah **12**
McLagan, Ian
  See Faces, The
McLaren, Malcolm **23**
McLaughlin, John **12**
    Also see Mahavishnu Orchestra
McLean, A. J.
  See Backstreet Boys
McLean, Don **7**
McLennan, Grant **21**
McLeod, Rory
  See Roomful of Blues
MC Lyte **8**
McLoughlin, Jon
  See Del Amitri
McMeel, Mickey
  See Three Dog Night
McMurtry, James **10**
McNabb, Travis
  See Better Than Ezra
McNair, Sylvia **15**
McNeilly, Mac
  See Jesus Lizard

MC 900 Ft. Jesus **16**
McPartland, Marian **15**
McQuillar, Shawn
  See Kool & the Gang
McRae, Carmen **9**
M.C. Ren
  See N.W.A.
McReynolds, Jesse
  See McReynolds, Jim and Jesse
McReynolds, Jim
  See McReynolds, Jim and Jesse
McReynolds, Jim and Jesse **12**
MC Serch **10**
McShane, Ronnie
  See Chieftains, The
McShee, Jacqui
  See Pentangle
McTell, Blind Willie **17**
McVie, Christine
  See Fleetwood Mac
McVie, John
  See Fleetwood Mac
McWhinney, James
  See Big Mountain
McWhinney, Joaquin
  See Big Mountain
Mdletshe, Geophrey
  See Ladysmith Black Mambazo
Meat Loaf **12**
Meat Puppets, The **13**
Medley, Bill **3**
Medlock, James
  See Soul Stirrers, The
Meehan, Tony
  See Shadows, The
Megadeth **9**
Mehta, Zubin **11**
Meine, Klaus
  See Scorpions, The
Meisner, Randy
  See Eagles, The
Mekons, The **15**
Melanie **12**
Melax, Einar
  See Sugarcubes, The
Mellencamp, John **20**
  Earlier sketch in CM **2**
Melvins **21**
Mendel, Nate
  See Foo Fighters
Mengede, Peter
  See Helmet
Menken, Alan **10**
Menuhin, Yehudi **11**
Menza, Nick
  See Megadeth
Mercer, Johnny **13**
Merchant, Natalie
  See 10,000 Maniacs
Mercier, Peadar
  See Chieftains, The
Mercury, Freddie
  See Queen
Mertens, Paul
  See Poi Dog Pondering

Morrison, Claude
  See Nylons, The
Morrison, Jim **3**
  Also see Doors, The
Morrison, Sterling
  See Velvet Underground, The
Morrison, Van **3**
Morrissett, Paul
  See Klezmatics, The
Morrissey **10**
  Also see Smiths, The
Morrissey, Bill **12**
Morrissey, Steven Patrick
  See Morrissey
Morton, Everett
  See English Beat, The
Morton, Jelly Roll **7**
Morvan, Fab
  See Milli Vanilli
Mosbaugh, Garth
  See Nylons, The
Mosely, Chuck
  See Faith No More
Moser, Scott "Cactus"
  See Highway 101
Mosher, Ken
  See Squirrel Nut Zippers
Mosley, Bob
  See Moby Grape
Mothersbaugh, Bob
  See Devo
Mothersbaugh, Mark
  See Devo
Mötley Crüe **1**
Motörhead **10**
Motta, Danny
  See Roomful of Blues
Mouzon, Alphonse
  See Weather Report
Moye, Famoudou Don
  See Art Ensemble of Chicago
Moyse, David
  See Air Supply
Mould, Bob **10**
Moulding, Colin
  See XTC
Mounfield, Gary
  See Stone Roses, The
Mouquet, Eric
  See Deep Forest
Mouskouri, Nana **12**
Moyet, Alison **12**
M People **15**
Mr. Dalvin
  See Jodeci
Mudhoney **16**
Mueller, Karl
  See Soul Asylum
Muir, Jamie
  See King Crimson
Muir, Mike
  See Suicidal Tendencies
Muldaur, Maria **18**
Mulholland, Dave
  See Aztec Camera

Mullen, Larry, Jr.
  See U2
Mullen, Mary
  See Congo Norvell
Mulligan, Gerry **16**
Murcia, Billy
  See New York Dolls
Murdock, Roger
  See King Missile
Murph
  See Dinosaur Jr.
Murphy, Brigid
  See Poi Dog Pondering
Murphy, Dan
  See Soul Asylum
Murphy, Michael
  See REO Speedwagon
Murphy, Peter **22**
Murphey, Michael Martin **9**
Murray, Anne **4**
Murray, Dave
  See Iron Maiden
Murray, Dee
  See Spencer Davis Group
Mushroom
  See Massive Attack
Musselwhite, Charlie **13**
Mustaine, Dave
  See Megadeth
  Also see Metallica
Mutter, Anne-Sophie
Mwelase, Jabulane
  See Ladysmith Black Mambazo
Mydland, Brent
  See Grateful Dead, The
Myers, Alan
  See Devo
Myles, Alannah **4**
Mystic Revealers **16**
Myung, John
  See Dream Theater
Nadirah
  See Arrested Development
Naftalin, Mark
  See Quicksilver Messenger Service
Nagler, Eric **8**
Najee **21**
Nakamura, Tetsuya "Tex"
  See War
Nakatami, Michie
  See Shonen Knife
Narcizo, David
  See Throwing Muses
Nascimento, Milton **6**
Nashville Bluegrass Band **14**
Nastanovich, Bob
  See Pavement
Naughty by Nature **11**
Navarro, David
  See Jane's Addiction
Nawasadio, Sylvie
  See Zap Mama
N'Dour, Youssou **6**
Ndegéocello, Me'Shell **18**

Ndugu
  See Weather Report
Near, Holly **1**
Neel, Johnny
  See Allman Brothers, The
Negron, Chuck
  See Three Dog Night
Neil, Chris
  See Less Than Jake
Neil, Vince
  See Mötley Crüe
Nelson, Brian
  See Velocity Girl
Nelson, David
  See Last Poets
Nelson, Errol
  See Black Uhuru
Nelson, Rick **2**
Nelson, Shara
  See Massive Attack
Nelson, Willie **11**
  Earlier sketch in CM **1**
Nesbitt, John
  See McKinney's Cotton Pickers
Nesmith, Mike
  See Monkees, The
Ness, Mike
  See Social Distortion
Neufville, Renee
  See Zhane
Neumann, Kurt
  See BoDeans
Nevarez, Alfred
  See All-4-One
Neville, Aaron **5**
  Also see Neville Brothers, The
Neville, Art
  See Meters, The
  Also see Neville Brothers, The
Neville, Charles
  See Neville Brothers, The
Neville, Cyril
  See Meters, The
  Also see Neville Brothers, The
Neville Brothers, The **4**
Nevin, Brian
  See Big Head Todd and the Monsters
New Grass Revival, The **4**
New Kids on the Block **3**
Newman, Randy **4**
Newmann, Kurt
  See BoDeans, The
New Order **11**
New Rhythm and Blues Quartet
  See NRBQ
Newson, Arlene
  See Poi Dog Pondering
Newton, Paul
  See Uriah Heep
Newton, Wayne **2**
Newton-Davis, Billy
  See Nylons, The
Newton-John, Olivia **8**
New York Dolls **20**

Nibbs, Lloyd
  See Skatalites, The
Nicholas, James Dean "J.D."
  See Commodores, The
Nicholls, Geoff
  See Black Sabbath
Nichols, Gates
  See Confederate Railroad
Nichols, Todd
  See Toad the Wet Sprocket
Nicks, Stevie **2**
  Also see Fleetwood Mac
Nico
  See Velvet Underground, The
Nicol, Simon
  See Fairport Convention
Nicolette
  See Massive Attack
Nielsen, Rick
  See Cheap Trick
Nilija, Robert
  See Last Poets
Nilsson **10**
Nilsson, Harry
  See Nilsson
Nirvana **8**
Nisbett, Steve "Grizzly"
  See Steel Pulse
Nitty Gritty Dirt Band, The **6**
Nobacon, Danbert
  See Chumbawamba
Nocentelli, Leo
  See Meters, The
No Doubt **20**
Nolan, Jerry
  See New York Dolls
Nomiya, Maki
  See Pizzicato Five
Noone, Peter
  See Herman's Hermits
Norica, Sugar Ray
  See Roomful of Blues
Norman, Jessye **7**
Norman, Jimmy
  See Coasters, The
Norris, Jean
  See Zhane
Northey, Craig
  See Odds
Norum, John
  See Dokken
Norvell, Sally
  See Congo Norvell
Norvo, Red **12**
Notorious B.I.G. **20**
Novoselic, Chris
  See Nirvana
Nowell, Bradley James
  See Sublime
NRBQ **12**
Nugent, Ted **2**
Nunn, Bobby
  See Coasters, The
N.W.A. **6**

Nutter, Alice
  See Chumbawamba
Nylons, The **18**
Nyman, Michael **15**
Nyolo, Sally
  See Zap Mama
Nyro, Laura **12**
Oakes, Richard
  See Suede
Oakey, Philip
  See Human League, The
Oakley, Berry
  See Allman Brothers, The
Oak Ridge Boys, The **7**
Oasis **16**
Oates, John
  See Hall & Oates
O'Brien, Kenneth
  See Snow
O'Brien, Derek
  See Social Distortion
O'Brien, Dwayne
  See Little Texas
O'Bryant, Alan
  See Nashville Bluegrass Band
Ocasek, Ric
  See Cars, The
Ocasek, Ric **5**
Ocean, Billy **4**
Oceans, Lucky
  See Asleep at the Wheel
Ochs, Phil **7**
O'Connell, Chris
  See Asleep at the Wheel
O'Connor, Billy
  See Blondie
O'Connor, Daniel
  See House of Pain
O'Connor, Mark **1**
O'Connor, Sinead **3**
O'Day, Anita **21**
Odds **20**
Odetta **7**
O'Donnell, Roger
  See Cure, The
Odmark, Matt
  See Jars of Clay
Ofwerman, Clarence
  See Roxette
Ofwerman, Staffan
  See Roxette
Ogletree, Mike
  See Simple Minds
Ogre, Nivek
  See Skinny Puppy
O'Hagan, Sean
  See Stereolab
Ohanian, David
  See Canadian Brass, The
O'Hare, Brendan
  See Teenage Fanclub
Ohio Players **16**
O'Jays, The **13**
Oje, Baba
  See Arrested Development

Olafsson, Bragi
  See Sugarcubes, The
Olander, Jimmy
  See Diamond Rio
Oldfield, Mike **18**
Oldham, Jack
  See Surfaris, The
Olds, Brent
  See Poi Dog Pondering
Oliver, Joe
  See Oliver, King
Oliver, King **15**
Olson, Jeff
  See Village People, The
Olson, Mark
  See Jayhawks, The
Olsson, Nigel
  See Spencer Davis Group
Onassis, Blackie
  See Urge Overkill
Ono, Yoko **11**
Orange, Walter "Clyde"
  See Commodores, The
Orb, The **18**
Orbison, Roy **2**
Orbital **20**
Orchestral Manoeuvres in the Dark **21**
O'Reagan, Tim
  See Jayhawks, The
Orff, Carl **21**
Orlando, Tony **15**
O'Riordan, Cait
  See Pogues, The
O'Riordan, Dolores
  See Cranberries, The
Örn, Einar
  See Sugarcubes, The
Örnolfsdottir, Margret
  See Sugarcubes, The
Orr, Benjamin
  See Cars, The
Orr, Casey
  See Gwar
Orrall, Frank
  See Poi Dog Pondering
Orzabal, Roland
  See Tears for Fears
Osborne, Bob
  See Osborne Brothers, The
Osborne, Buzz
  See Melvins
Osborne, Sonny
  See Osborne Brothers, The
Osborne Brothers, The **8**
Osbourne, Ozzy **3**
  Also see Black Sabbath
Osby, Greg **21**
Oskar, Lee
  See War
Oslin, K. T. **3**
Osman, Mat
  See Suede
Osmond, Donny **3**
Ostin, Mo **17**

Otis, Johnny **16**
Ott, David **2**
Our Lady Peace **22**
Outler, Jimmy
　See Soul Stirrers, The
Owen, Randy Yueull
　See Alabama
Owens, Buck **2**
Owens, Campbell
　See Aztec Camera
Owens, Ricky
　See Temptations, The
Oyewole, Abiodun
　See Last Poets
Page, Jimmy **4**
　Also see Led Zeppelin
　Also see Yardbirds, The
Page, Patti **11**
Page, Steven
　See Barenaked Ladies
Paice, Ian
　See Deep Purple
Palmer, Carl
　See Emerson, Lake & Palmer/Powell
Palmer, Clive
　See Incredible String Band
Palmer, David
　See Jethro Tull
Palmer, Jeff **20**
Palmer, Keeti
　See Prodigy
Palmer, Phil
　See Dire Straits
Palmer, Robert **2**
Palmer-Jones, Robert
　See King Crimson
Palmieri, Eddie **15**
Paluzzi, Jimmy
　See Sponge
Pamer, John
　See Tsunami
Pankow, James
　See Chicago
Panter, Horace
　See Specials, The
Pantera **13**
Papach, Leyna
　See Geraldine Fibbers
Pappas, Tom
　See Superdrag
Parazaider, Walter
　See Chicago
Paris, Twila **16**
Park, Cary
　See Boy Howdy
Park, Larry
　See Boy Howdy
Parkening, Christopher **7**
Parker, Charlie **5**
Parker, Graham **10**
Parker, Kris
　See KRS-One
Parker, Maceo **7**
Parker, Tom
　See Animals

Parkin, Chad
　See Aquabats
Parks, Van Dyke **17**
Parnell, Lee Roy **15**
Parsons, Alan **12**
Parsons, Dave
　See Bush
Parsons, Gene
　See Byrds, The
Parsons, Gram **7**
　Also see Byrds, The
Parsons, Ted
　See Prong
Parsons, Tony
　See Iron Maiden
Parton, Dolly **2**
Partridge, Andy
　See XTC
Pasemaster, Mase
　See De La Soul
Pash, Jim
　See Surfaris, The
Pasillas, Jose
　See Incubus
Pass, Joe **15**
Pastorius, Jaco
　See Weather Report
Paterson, Alex
　See Orb, The
Patinkin, Mandy **20**
　Earlier sketch CM **3**
Patti, Sandi **7**
Patton, Charley **11**
Patton, Mike
　See Faith No More
Paul, Alan
　See Manhattan Transfer, The
Paul, Les **2**
Paul, Vinnie
　See Pantera
Paul III, Henry
　See BlackHawk
Paulo, Jr.
　See Sepultura
Pavarotti, Luciano **20**
　Earlier sketch in CM **1**
Pavement **14**
Paxton, Tom **5**
Payne, Bill
　See Little Feat
Payne, Scherrie
　See Supremes, The
Payton, Denis
　See Dave Clark Five, The
Payton, Lawrence
　See Four Tops, The
Pearl, Minnie **3**
Pearl Jam **12**
Pearson, Dan
　See American Music Club
Peart, Neil
　See Rush
Pedersen, Herb
　See Desert Rose Band, The

Peduzzi, Larry
　See Roomful of Blues
Peek, Dan
　See America
Peeler, Ben
　See Mavericks, The
Pegg, Dave
　See Fairport Convention
　Also see Jethro Tull
Pegrum, Nigel
　See Steeleye Span
Pence, Jeff
　See Blessid Union of Souls
Pendergrass, Teddy **3**
Pengilly, Kirk
　See INXS
Peniston, CeCe **15**
Penn, Michael **4**
Penner, Fred **10**
Pentangle **18**
Pepper, Art **18**
Perahia, Murray **10**
Pere Ubu **17**
Peretz, Jesse
　See Lemonheads, The
Perez, Louie
　See Los Lobos
Perkins, Carl **9**
Perkins, John
　See XTC
Perkins, Percell
　See Five Blind Boys of Alabama
Perkins, Steve
　See Jane's Addiction
Perlman, Itzhak **2**
Perlman, Marc
　See Jayhawks, The
Pernice, Joe
　See Scud Mountain Boys
Perry, Brendan
　See Dead Can Dance
Perry, Doane
　See Jethro Tull
Perry, Joe
　See Aerosmith
Perry, Steve
　See Journey
Perry, Virgshawn
　See Artifacts
Persson, Nina
　See Cardigans
Peter, Paul & Mary **4**
Peters, Bernadette **7**
Peters, Dan
　See Mudhoney
Peters, Joey
　See Grant Lee Buffalo
Peters, Mike
　See Alarm
Petersen, Chris
　See Front Line Assembly
Peterson, Debbi
　See Bangles
Peterson, Garry
　See Guess Who

Prince, Prairie
  See Journey
Prine, John **7**
Prior, Maddy
  See Steeleye Span
Proclaimers, The **13**
Prodigy **22**
Professor Longhair **6**
Prong **23**
Propatier, Joe
  See Silver Apples
Propes, Duane
  See Little Texas
Prout, Brian
  See Diamond Rio
Psychedelic Furs **23**
Public Enemy **4**
Puente, Tito **14**
Pullen, Don **16**
Pulp **18**
Pulsford, Nigel
  See Bush
Pusey, Clifford "Moonie"
  See Steel Pulse
Pyle, Andy
  See Kinks, The
Pyle, Artemis
  See Lynyrd Skynyrd
Q-Tip
  See Tribe Called Quest, A
Quaife, Peter
  See Kinks, The
Queen **6**
Queen Ida **9**
Queen Latifah **6**
Queensryche **8**
Querfurth, Carl
  See Roomful of Blues
Quicksilver Messenger Service **23**
Rabbitt, Eddie **5**
Rabin, Trevor
  See Yes
Raffi **8**
Rage Against the Machine **18**
Raheem
  See GetoBoys, The
Rainey, Ma **22**
Rainey, Sid
  See Compulsion
Raitt, Bonnie **23**
  Earlier sketch in CM **3**
Rakim
  See Eric B. and Rakim
Raleigh, Don
  See Squirrel Nut Zippers
Ralphs, Mick
  See Bad Company
Ramone, C. J.
  See Ramones, The
Ramone, Dee Dee
  See Ramones, The
Ramone, Joey
  See Ramones, The
Ramone, Johnny
  See Ramones, The

Ramone, Marky
  See Ramones, The
Ramone, Ritchie
  See Ramones, The
Ramone, Tommy
  See Ramones, The
Ramones, The **9**
Rampal, Jean-Pierre **6**
Ramsay, Andy
  See Stereolab
Ranaldo, Lee
  See Sonic Youth
Randall, Bobby
  See Sawyer Brown
Raney, Jerry
  See Beat Farmers
Ranglin, Ernest
  See Skatalites, The
Ranken, Andrew
  See Pogues, The
Ranking Roger
  See English Beat, The
Rarebell, Herman
  See Scorpions, The
Raven, Paul
  See Prong
Ray, Amy
  See Indigo Girls
Raybon, Marty
  See Shenandoah
Raye, Collin **16**
Raymonde, Simon
  See Cocteau Twins, The
Rea, Chris **12**
Read, John
  See Specials, The
Reagon, Bernice Johnson
  See Sweet Honey in the Rock
Redding, Otis **5**
Redd Kross **20**
Reddy, Helen **9**
Red Hot Chili Peppers, The **7**
Redman, Don
  See McKinney's Cotton Pickers
Redman, Joshua **12**
Redpath, Jean **1**
Reece, Chris
  See Social Distortion
Reed, Jimmy **15**
Reed, Lou **16**
  Earlier sketch in CM **1**
  Also see Velvet Underground, The
Reese, Della **13**
Reeves, Dianne **16**
Reeves, Jim **10**
Reeves, Martha **4**
Reich, Steve **8**
Reid, Charlie
  See Proclaimers, The
Reid, Christopher
  See Kid 'n Play
Reid, Craig
  See Proclaimers, The
Reid, Delroy "Junior"
  See Black Uhuru

Reid, Don
  See Statler Brothers, The
Reid, Ellen Lorraine
  See Crash Test Dummies
Reid, Harold
  See Statler Brothers, The
Reid, Janet
  See Black Uhuru
Reid, Jim
  See Jesus and Mary Chain, The
Reid, Vernon **2**
  Also see Living Colour
Reid, William
  See Jesus and Mary Chain, The
Reifman, William
  See KMFDM
Reinhardt, Django **7**
Reitzell, Brian
  See Redd Kross
Relf, Keith
  See Yardbirds, The
R.E.M. **5**
Renbourn, John
  See Pentangle
Reno, Ronnie
  See Osborne Brothers, The
REO Speedwagon **23**
Replacements, The **7**
Republica **20**
Residents, The **14**
Restless Heart **12**
Revell, Adrian
  See Jamiroquai
Rex
  See Pantera
Reyes, Andre
  See Gipsy Kings, The
Reyes, Canut
  See Gipsy Kings, The
Reyes, Nicolas
  See Gipsy Kings, The
Reynolds, Nick
  See Kingston Trio, The
Reynolds, Robert
  See Mavericks, The
Reynolds, Sheldon
  See Earth, Wind and Fire
Reznor, Trent **13**
Rhodes, Nick
  See Duran Duran
Rhodes, Philip
  See Gin Blossoms
Rhodes, Todd
  See McKinney's Cotton Pickers
Rhone, Sylvia **13**
Rich, Buddy **13**
Rich, Charlie **3**
Richard, Cliff **14**
Richard, Zachary **9**
Richards, Edward
  See Shamen, The
Richards, Keith
  See Rolling Stones, The
Richards, Keith **11**
  Also see Rolling Stones, The

Rowlands, Bruce
  See Fairport Convention
Rowlands, Tom
  See Chemical Brothers
Rowntree, Dave
  See Blur
Roxette **23**
Rubin, Mark
  See Bad Livers, The
Rubin, Rick **9**
Rubinstein, Arthur **11**
Rucker, Darius
  See Hootie and the Blowfish
Rudd, Phillip
  See AC/DC
Rue, Caroline
  See Hole
Ruffin, David **6**
  Also see Temptations, The
Ruffy, Dave
  See Aztec Camera
Rundgren, Todd **11**
Run-D.M.C. **4**
RuPaul **20**
Rush **8**
Rush, Otis **12**
Rushlow, Tim
  See Little Texas
Russell, Alecia
  See Sounds of Blackness
Russell, Graham
  See Air Supply
Russell, John
  See Steppenwolf
Russell, Mark **6**
Russell, Mike
  See Shudder to Think
Rutherford, Mike
  See Genesis
  Also see Mike & the Mechanics
Rutsey, John
  See Rush
Ryan, David
  See Lemonheads, The
Ryan, Mark
  See Quicksilver Messenger Service
Ryan, Mick
  See Dave Clark Five, The
Ryder, Mitch **23**
  Earlier sketch in CM **11**
Ryland, Jack
  See Three Dog Night
Rzeznik, Johnny
  See Goo Goo Dolls, The
Sabo, Dave
  See Bon Jovi
Sade **2**
Sadier, Laetitia
  See Stereolab
Saffron,
  See Republica
Sager, Carole Bayer **5**
Sahm, Doug
  See Texas Tornados, The

Saloman, Nick
  See Bevis Frond
Saluzzi, Dino **23**
Sam, Watters
  See Color Me Badd
Sammy, Piazza
  See Quicksilver Messenger Service
Secrest, Wayne
  See Confederate Railroad
Shai **23**
Shamen, The **23**
Shannon, Sarah
  See Velocity Girl
Shaw, Adrian
  See Bevis Frond
Sherinian, Derek
  See Dream Theater
Shirley, Danny
  See Confederate Railroad
Shively, William
  See Big Mountain
Silver Apples **23**
Simpson, Rose
  See Incredible String Band
Sin, Will
  See Shamen, The
Sinatra, Frank **23**
  Earlier sketch in CM**1**
Snow **23**
Spellman, Jim
  See Velocity Girl
St. Hubbins, David
  See Spinal Tap
St. John, Mark
  See Kiss
St. Marie, Buffy
  See Sainte-Marie, Buffy
St. Nicholas, Nick
  See Steppenwolf
Sainte-Marie, Buffy **11**
Sakamoto, Ryuichi **19**
Salerno-Sonnenberg, Nadja **3**
Saliers, Emily
  See Indigo Girls
Salisbury, Peter
  See Verve, The
  Also see Pizzicato Five
Salmon, Michael
  See Prefab Sprout
Salonen, Esa-Pekka **16**
Salt-N-Pepa **6**
Sam and Dave **8**
Sambora, Richie
  See Bon Jovi
Sampson, Doug
  See Iron Maiden
Samuelson, Gar
  See Megadeth
Samwell-Smith, Paul
  See Yardbirds, The
Sanborn, David **1**
Sanchez, Michel
  See Deep Forest
Sanctuary, Gary
  See Aztec Camera

Sanders, Ric
  See Fairport Convention
Sanders, Steve
  See Oak Ridge Boys, The
Sandman, Mark
  See Morphine
Sandoval, Arturo **15**
Sandoval, Hope
  See Mazzy Star
Sands, Aaron
  See Jars of Clay
Sanford, Gary
  See Aztec Camera
Sangare, Oumou **22**
Sanger, David
  See Asleep at the Wheel
Santana, Carlos **20**
  Earlier sketch in CM 1
Santiago, Joey
  See Pixies, The
Saraceno, Blues
  See Poison
Sasaki, Mamiko
  See PulpSanders, Pharoah **16**
Satchell, Clarence "Satch"
  See Ohio Players
Satriani, Joe **4**
Savage, Rick
  See Def Leppard
Savage, Scott
  See Jars of Clay
Sawyer Brown **13**
Sawyer, Phil
  See Spencer Davis Group
Saxa
  See English Beat, The
Saxon, Stan
  See Dave Clark Five, The
Scaccia, Mike
  See Ministry
Scaggs, Boz **12**
Scanlon, Craig
  See Fall, The
Scarface
  See Geto Boys, The
Schelhaas, Jan
  See Camel
Schemel, Patty
  See Hole
Schenker, Michael
  See Scorpions, The
Schenker, Rudolf
  See Scorpions, The
Schenkman, Eric
  See Spin Doctors
Schermie, Joe
  See Three Dog Night
Scherpenzeel, Ton
  See Camel
Schickele, Peter **5**
Schlitt, John
  See Petra
Schloss, Zander
  See Circle Jerks, The

Simmons, Russell **7**
Simmons, Trinna
  See Spearhead
Simon, Carly **22**
  Earlier sketch in CM **4**
Simon, Paul **16**
  Earlier sketch in CM **1**
Simone, Nina **11**
Simonon, Paul
  See Clash, The
Simons, Ed
  See Chemical Brothers
Simins, Russell
  See Jon Spencer Blues Explosion
Simple Minds **21**
Simpson, Denis
  See Nylons, The
Simpson, Derrick "Duckie"
  See Black Uhuru
Simpson, Mel
  See US3
Simpson, Ray
  See Village People, The
Sims, David William
  See Jesus Lizard
Sims, Neil
  See Catherine Wheel
Sinatra, Frank **1**
Sinclair, David
  See Camel
Sinclair, Gord
  See Tragically Hip, The
Sinclair, Richard
  See Camel
Sinfield, Peter
  See King Crimson
Singer, Eric
  See Black Sabbath
Singh, Talvin
  See Massive Attack
Sioux, Siouxsie
  See Siouxsie and the Banshees
Siouxsie and the Banshees **8**
Sir Mix-A-Lot
Sir Rap-A-Lot
  See Geto Boys, The
Sirois, Joe
  See Mighty Mighty Bosstones
Siverton
  See Specials, The
Sixx, Nikki
  See Mötley Crüe
Sixx, Roger
  See Less Than Jake
Skaggs, Ricky **5**
  Also see Country Gentlemen, The
Skatalites, The **18**
Skeoch, Tommy
  See Tesla
Skillings, Muzz
  See Living Colour
Skinny Puppy **17**
Sklamberg, Lorin
  See Klezmatics, The

Skoob
  See Das EFX
Slash
  See Guns n' Roses
Slayer **10**
Sleater-Kinney **20**
Sledd, Dale
  See Osborne Brothers, The
Sledge, Percy **15**
Sledge, Robert
  See Ben Folds Five
Slick, Grace
  See Jefferson Airplane
Slijngaard, Ray
  See 2 Unlimited
Sloan, Eliot
  See Blessid Union of Souls
Slovak, Hillel
  See Red Hot Chili Peppers, The
Sly and Robbie **13**
Small, Heather
  See M People
Smalls, Derek
  See Spinal Tap
Smart, Terence
  See Butthole Surfers
Smashing Pumpkins **13**
Smear, Pat
  See Foo Fighters
Smith, Adrian
  See Iron Maiden
Smith, Bessie **3**
Smith, Brad
  See Blind Melon
Smith, Chad
  See Red Hot Chili Peppers, The
Smith, Charles
  See Kool & the Gang
Smith, Curt
  See Tears for Fears
Smith, Debbie
  See Curve
Smith, Debbie
  See Echobelly
Smith, Fran
  See Hooters
Smith, Fred
  See Blondie
Smith, Fred
  See MC5, The
Smith, Fred
  See Television
Smith, Garth
  See Buzzcocks, The
Smith, Joe
  See McKinney's Cotton Pickers
Smith, Kevin
  See dc Talk
Smith, Mark E.
  See Fall, The
Smith, Michael W. **11**
Smith, Mike
  See Dave Clark Five, The
Smith, Parrish
  See EPMD

Smith, Patti **17**
  Earlier sketch in CM **1**
Smith, Robert
  See Cure, The
    Also see Siouxsie and the Banshees
Smith, Robert
  See Spinners, The
Smith, Shawn
  See Brad
Smith, Smitty
  See Three Dog Night
Smith, Steve
  See Journey
Smith, Tweed
  See War
Smith, Wendy
  See Prefab Sprout
Smith, Willard
  See DJ Jazzy Jeff and the Fresh Prince
Smithereens, The **14**
Smiths, The **3**
Smyth, Joe
  See Sawyer Brown
Sneed, Floyd Chester
  See Three Dog Night
Snoop Doggy Dogg **17**
Snow, Don
  See Squeeze
Snow, Phoebe **4**
Soan, Ashley
  See Del Amitri
Sobule, Jill **20**
Solal, Martial **4**
Soloff, Lew
  See Blood, Sweat and Tears
Solti, Georg **13**
Sondheim, Stephen **8**
Sonefeld, Jim
  See Hootie and the Blowfish
Sonic Youth **9**
Sonnenberg, Nadja Salerno
  See Salerno-Sonnenberg, Nadja
Sonni, Jack
  See Dire Straits
Sonnier, Jo-El **10**
Son Volt **21**
Sorum, Matt
  See Cult, The
Sosa, Mercedes **3**
Soul Asylum **10**
Soul Coughing **21**
Soul Stirrers, The **11**
Soul II Soul **17**
Soundgarden **6**
Sounds of Blackness **13**
Sousa, John Philip **10**
Spampinato, Joey
  See NRBQ
Spampinato, Johnny
  See NRBQ
Spann, Otis **18**
Sparks **18**
Sparks, Donita
  See L7
Special Ed **16**

Stuart, Marty **9**
Stuart, Peter
  See Dog's Eye View
Stubbs, Levi
  See Four Tops, The
Styne, Jule **21**
Subdudes, The **18**
Sublime **19**
Such, Alec Jon
  See Bon Jovi
Suede **20**
Sugar Ray **22**
Sugarcubes, The **10**
Suicidal Tendencies **15**
Sulley, Suzanne
  See Human League, The
Sullivan, Jacqui
  See Bananarama
Summer, Donna **12**
Summer, Mark
  See Turtle Island String Quartet
Summers, Andy **3**
  Also see Police, The
Sumner, Bernard
  See Joy Division
  Also see New Order
Sundays, The **20**
Sun Ra **5**
Sunnyland Slim **16**
Super DJ Dmitry
  See Deee-lite
Supremes, The **6**
Sure!, Al B. **13**
Sutcliffe, Stu
  See Beatles, The
Sutherland, Joan **13**
Svenigsson, Magnus
  See Cardigans
Svensson, Peter
  See Cardigans
Svigals, Alicia
  See Klezmatics, The
Swarbrick, Dave
  See Fairport Convention
Sweat, Keith **13**
Sweet, Matthew **9**
Sweet, Michael
  See Stryper
Sweet, Robert
  See Stryper
Sweethearts of the Rodeo **12**
Sweet Honey in the Rock **1**
Swing, DeVante
  See Jodeci
SWV **14**
Sykes, John
  See Whitesnake
Sykes, Roosevelt **20**
Sylvain, Sylvain
  See New York Dolls
Tabac, Tony
  See Joy Division
Tabor, Ty
  See King's X

TAFKAP (The Artist Formerly Known as
  Prince)
  See Prince
Taggart, Jeremy
  See Our Lady Peace
Tait, Michael
  See dc Talk
Taj Mahal **6**
Tajima, Takao
  See Pizzicato Five
Takac, Robby
  See Goo Goo Dolls, The
Takanami
  See Pizzicato Five
Takemitsu, Toru **6**
Take 6 **6**
Talbot, John Michael **6**
Talcum, Joe Jack
  See Dead Milkmen
Talking Heads **1**
Tandy, Richard
  See Electric Light Orchestra
Tangerine Dream **12**
Taree, Aerle
  See Arrested Development
Tate, Geoff
  See Queensryche
Tatum, Art **17**
Taupin, Bernie **22**
Taylor, Andy
  See Duran Duran
Taylor, Billy **13**
Taylor, Cecil **9**
Taylor, Chad
  See Live
Taylor, Courtney
  See Dandy Warhols, The
Taylor, Dave
  See Pere Ubu
Taylor, Dick
  See Rolling Stones, The
Taylor, Earl
  See Country Gentlemen, The
Taylor, James **2**
Taylor, James "J.T."
  See Kool & the Gang
Taylor, John
  See Duran Duran
Taylor, Johnnie
  See Soul Stirrers, The
Taylor, Koko **10**
Taylor, Leroy
  See Soul Stirrers, The
Taylor, Melvin
  See Ventures, The
Taylor, Mick
  See Rolling Stones, The
Taylor, Philip "Philthy Animal"
  See Motörhead
Taylor, Roger
  See Duran Duran
Taylor, Roger Meadows
  See Queen
Taylor, Teresa
  See Butthole Surfers

Teagarden, Jack **10**
Tears for Fears **6**
Technotronic **5**
Teenage Fanclub **13**
Te Kanawa, Kiri **2**
Television **17**
Teller, Al **15**
Tempesta, John
  See White Zombie
Temple, Michelle
  See Pere Ubu
Temptations, The **3**
Tennant, Neil
  See Pet Shop Boys
10,000 Maniacs **3**
Terminator X
  See Public Enemy
Terrell, Jean
  See Supremes, The
Terry, Boyd
  See Aquabats
Tesh, John **20**
Tesla **15**
Texas Tornados, The **8**
Thacker, Rocky
  See Shenandoah
Thain, Gary
  See Uriah Heep
Thayil, Kim
  See Soundgarden
The The **15**
They Might Be Giants **7**
Thielemans, Toots **13**
Thin Lizzy **13**
Third World **13**
Thomas, Alex
  See Earth, Wind and Fire
Thomas, David
  See Pere Ubu
Thomas, David
  See Take 6
Thomas, David Clayton
  See Clayton-Thomas, David
Thomas, Dennis "D.T."
  See Kool & the Gang
Thomas, George "Fathead"
  See McKinney's Cotton Pickers
Thomas, Irma **16**
Thomas, Mickey
  See Jefferson Starship
Thomas, Olice
  See Five Blind Boys of Alabama
Thomas, Ray
  See Moody Blues, The
Thomas, Rozonda "Chilli"
  See TLC
Thompson, Chester
  See Weather Report
Thompson, Danny
  See Pentangle
Thompson, Dennis
  See MC5, The
Thompson, Les
  See Nitty Gritty Dirt Band, The

Unruh, N. U.
　　See Einstürzende Neubauten
Uosikkinen, David
　　See Hooters
Upshaw, Dawn **9**
Urge Overkill **17**
U2 **12**
　Earlier sketch in CM **2**
Usher **23**
Utley, Adrian
　　See Portishead
Vaché, Jr., Warren **22**
Vachon, Chris
　　See Roomful of Blues
Vai, Steve **5**
　　Also see Whitesnake
Valens, Ritchie **23**
Valenti, Dino
　　See Quicksilver Messenger Service
Valentine, Gary
　　See Blondie
Valentine, Hilton
　　See Animals
Valentine, Rae
　　See War
Valenzuela, Jesse
　　See Gin Blossoms
Valli, Frankie **10**
Valory, Ross
　　See Journey
van Dijk, Carol
　　See Bettie Serveert
Van Gelder, Nick
　　See Jamiroquai
Van Hook, Peter
　　See Mike & the Mechanics
Vandenburg, Adrian
　　See Whitesnake
Vander Ark, Brad
　　See Verve Pipe, The
Vander Ark, Brian
　　See Verve Pipe, The
Vandross, Luther **2**
Van Halen **8**
Van Halen, Alex
　　See Van Halen
Van Halen, Edward
　　See Van Halen
Vanilla Ice **6**
Van Rensalier, Darnell
　　See Shai
Van Ronk, Dave **12**
Van Shelton, Ricky **5**
Van Vliet, Don
　　See Captain Beefheart
Van Zandt, Townes **13**
Van Zant, Johnny
　　See Lynyrd Skynyrd
Van Zant, Ronnie
　　See Lynyrd Skynyrd
Vasquez, Junior **16**
Vaughan, Jimmie
　　See Fabulous Thunderbirds, The
Vaughan, Sarah **2**

Vaughan, Stevie Ray **1**
Vedder, Eddie
　　See Pearl Jam
Vega, Bobby
　　See Quicksilver Messenger Service
Vega, Suzanne **3**
Velocity Girl **23**
Velvet Underground, The **7**
Ventures, The **19**
Verlaine, Tom
　　See Television
Verta-Ray, Matt
　　See Madder Rose
Veruca Salt **20**
Verve, The **18**
Verve Pipe, The **20**
Vettese, Peter-John
　　See Jethro Tull
Vicious, Sid
　　See Sex Pistols, The
　　Also see Siouxsie and the Banshees
Vickrey, Dan
　　See Counting Crows
Victor, Tommy
　　See Prong
Vienna Boys Choir **23**
Vig, Butch **17**
Village People, The **7**
Vincent, Vinnie
　　See Kiss
Vincent, Gene **19**
Vinnie
　　See Naughty by Nature
Vinton, Bobby **12**
Violent Femmes **12**
Virtue, Michael
　　See UB40
Visser, Peter
　　See Bettie Serveert
Vito, Rick
　　See Fleetwood Mac
Vitous, Mirslav
　　See Weather Report
Voelz, Susan
　　See Poi Dog Pondering
Volz, Greg
　　See Petra
Von, Eerie
　　See Danzig
von Karajan, Herbert **1**
Vox, Bono
　　See U2
Vudi
　　See American Music Club
Waaktaar, Pal
　　See A-ha
Wade, Adam
　　See Shudder to Think
Wade, Chrissie
　　See Alien Sex Fiend
Wade, Nik
　　See Alien Sex Fiend
Wadenius, George
　　See Blood, Sweat and Tears

Wadephal, Ralf
　　See Tangerine Dream
Wagoner, Faidest
　　See Soul Stirrers, The
Wagoner, Porter **13**
Wahlberg, Donnie
　　See New Kids on the Block
Wailer, Bunny **11**
Wainwright III, Loudon **11**
Waits, Tom **12**
　Earlier sketch in CM **1**
Wakeling, David
　　See English Beat, The
Wakeman, Rick
　　See Yes
Walden, Narada Michael **14**
Walford, Britt
　　See Breeders
Walker, Clay **20**
Walker, Colin
　　See Electric Light Orchestra
Walker, Ebo
　　See New Grass Revival, The
Walker, Jerry Jeff **13**
Walker, T-Bone **5**
Wallace, Bill
　　See Guess Who
Wallace, Ian
　　See King Crimson
Wallace, Richard
　　See Mighty Clouds of Joy, The
Wallace, Sippie **6**
Waller, Charlie
　　See Country Gentlemen, The
Waller, Fats **7**
Wallflowers, The **20**
Wallinger, Karl **11**
Wallis, Larry
　　See Motörhead
Walls, Chris
　　See Dave Clark Five, The
Walls, Denise "Nee-C"
　　See Anointed
Walls, Greg
　　See Anthrax
Walsh, Joe **5**
　　Also see Eagles, The
Walters, Robert "Patch"
　　See Mystic Revealers
War **14**
Ward, Andy
　　See Bevis Frond
Ward, Andy
　　See Camel
Ward, Andy
　　See Chumbawamba
Ward, Bill
Ward, Michael
　　See Wallflowers, The
　　See Black Sabbath
Ware, Martyn
　　See Human League, The
Wareham, Dean
　　See Luna

Wilk, Brad
  See Rage Against the Machine
Wilkeson, Leon
  See Lynyrd Skynyrd
Wilkie, Chris
  See Dubstar
Wilkinson, Geoff
  See US3
Wilkinson, Keith
  See Squeeze
Williams, Andy **2**
Williams, Boris
  See Cure, The
Williams, Cliff
  See AC/DC
Williams, Dana
  See Diamond Rio
Williams, Deniece **1**
Williams, Don **4**
Williams, Eric
  See Blackstreet
Williams, Fred
  See C + C Music Factory
Williams, Hank, Jr. **1**
Williams, Hank, Sr. **4**
Williams, James "Diamond"
  See Ohio Players
Williams, Joe **11**
Williams, John **9**
Williams, Lamar
  See Allman Brothers, The
Williams, Lucinda **10**
Williams, Marion **15**
Williams, Milan
  See Commodores, The
Williams, Otis
  See Temptations, The
Williams, Paul **5**
  See Temptations, The
Williams, Phillard
  See Earth, Wind and Fire
Williams, Terry
  See Dire Straits
Williams, Vanessa **10**
Williams, Victoria **17**
Williams, Walter
  See O'Jays, The
Williams, Wilbert
  See Mighty Clouds of Joy, The
Williams, William Elliot
  See Artifacts
Williamson, Robin
  See Incredible String Band
Williamson, Sonny Boy **9**
Willie D.
  See Geto Boys, The
Willis, Clarence "Chet"
  See Ohio Players
Willis, Kelly **12**
Willis, Larry
  See Blood, Sweat and Tears
Willis, Pete
  See Def Leppard
Willis, Rick
  See Foreigner

Willis, Victor
  See Village People, The
Willner, Hal **10**
Wills, Bob **6**
Wills, Aaron (P-Nut)
  See 311
Wills, Rick
  See Bad Company
Willson-Piper, Marty
  See Church, The
Wilmot, Billy "Mystic"
  See Mystic Revealers
Wilson, Anne
  See Heart
Wilson, Brian
  See Beach Boys, The
Wilson, Carl
  See Beach Boys, The
Wilson, Carnie
  See Wilson Phillips
Wilson, Cassandra **12**
Wilson, Chris
  See Love Spit Love
Wilson, Cindy
  See B-52's, The
Wilson, Don
  See Ventures, The
Wilson, Dennis
  See Beach Boys, The
Wilson, Eric
  See Sublime
Wilson, Jackie **3**
Wilson, Kim
  See Fabulous Thunderbirds, The
Wilson, Mary
  See Supremes, The
Wilson, Nancy **14**
  See Heart
Wilson, Patrick
  See Weezer
Wilson, Ransom **5**
Wilson, Ricky
  See B-52's, The
Wilson, Robin
  See Gin Blossoms
Wilson, Ron
  See Surfaris, The
Wilson, Shanice
  See Shanice
Wilson, Wendy
  See Wilson Phillips
Wilson Phillips **5**
Wilson-James, Victoria
  See Shamen, The
Wilton, Michael
  See Queensryche
Wimpfheimer, Jimmy
  See Roomful of Blues
Winans, Carvin
  See Winans, The
Winans, Marvin
  See Winans, The
Winans, Michael
  See Winans, The

Winans, Ronald
  See Winans, The
Winans, The **12**
Winbush, Angela **15**
Winfield, Chuck
  See Blood, Sweat and Tears
Winston, George **9**
Winter, Johnny **5**
Winter, Kurt
  See Guess Who
Winter, Paul **10**
Winwood, Muff
  See Spencer Davis Group
Winwood, Steve **2**
  Also see Spencer Davis Group
  Also see Traffic
Wiseman, Bobby
  See Blue Rodeo
WishBone
  See Bone Thugs-N-Harmony
Withers, Pick
  See Dire Straits
Wolstencraft, Simon
  See Fall, The
Womack, Bobby **5**
Wonder, Stevie **17**
  Earlier sketch in CM **2**
Wood, Chris
  See Traffic
Wood, Danny
  See New Kids on the Block
Wood, Ron
  See Faces, The
  Also see Rolling Stones, The
Wood, Roy
  See Electric Light Orchestra
Woods, Gay
  See Steeleye Span
Woods, Terry
  See Pogues, The
Woodson, Ollie
  See Temptations, The
Woodward, Keren
  See Bananarama
Woody, Allen
  See Allman Brothers, The
Woolfolk, Andrew
  See Earth, Wind and Fire
Worrell, Bernie **11**
Wray, Link **17**
Wreede, Katrina
  See Turtle Island String Quartet
Wren, Alan
  See Stone Roses, The
Wretzky, D'Arcy
  See Smashing Pumpkins
Wright, Adrian
  See Human League, The
Wright, David "Blockhead"
  See English Beat, The
Wright, Heath
  See Ricochet
Wright, Hugh
  See Boy Howdy